'A systematic conversation between the *capabilities approach*, as developed by Martha Nussbaum and Amartya Sen, and the grand tradition of *sociological theory* of Marx, Weber, Parsons and Habermas has long been overdue and this is precisely what Spiros Gangas offers in his original and ambitious new book. By revisiting the main tenets of the capabilities approach in light of contemporary sociological debates on normativity and social crises, Gangas articulates interdisciplinary arguments that handle successfully insights from philosophy, critical theory, economics and sociology itself in both their conceptual and normative sophistication. The result not only does justice to these traditions but also carries them forward.'

– Daniel Chernilo, *Professor of Sociology, Universidad Adolfo Ibáñez, Chile, and Visiting Professor of Social and Political Thought, Loughborough University, UK*

Sociological Theory and the Capability Approach

Sociological Theory and the Capability Approach connects normative strands of sociological theory to the fusion of ethics and economics proposed by Amartya Sen's and Martha Nussbaum's Capability Approach (CA). Spanning classical (Hegel, Marx, Durkheim, Scheler, Weber) and contemporary debates (Parsons, Giddens, Luhmann) it identifies areas that bridge the current gap between sociology and CA. It thus builds on explanatory and normative concerns shared by both traditions.

Engaging readers from sociology and CA, Spiros Gangas suggests that the proposed dialogue should be layered along the main areas of value-theory, economy and society, extending this enquiry into the normative meaning attached to being human. To this end, the book reconstructs the notion of agency along the tracks of Nussbaum's central human capabilities, considering also alienation and the sociology of emotions. It concludes by addressing the CA through the lens of social institutions before it takes up the challenge of ideological fundamentalism and how it can be effectively confronted by CA.

This original book provides a fresh perspective on CA as it embeds it in the rich pool of sociological theory's accomplishments. As an exercise in theoretical and normative convergence, it will be required reading for academics and students in social theory, cultural theory, philosophy and human development studies.

Spiros Gangas is Associate Professor in the Department of Sociology at Deree – the American College of Greece. His principal areas of research are classical and contemporary sociological theory, value-theory, capability approach and film studies.

International Library of Sociology
Founded by Karl Mannheim

Editors: John Holmwood and Vineeta Sinha

Travel Connections
Tourism, Technology and Togetherness in a Mobile World
Jennie Germann Molz

Mobilising Modernity
The Nuclear Moment
Ian Welsh

Illness as a Work of Thought
A Foucauldian Perspective on Psychosomatics
Monica Greco

Social Class Language and Education
Denis Lawton

Housing Needs and Planning Policy
Problems of Housing Need & 'Overspill' in England & Wales
J Barry Cullingworth, J.B. Cullingworth

European Cosmopolitanism
Colonial Histories and Postcolonial Societies
Edited by Gurminder K. Bhambra and John Narayan

Sociological Knowledge and Collective Identity
S.N. Eisenstadt and Israeli Society
Stavit Sinai

Sociological Theory and the Capability Approach
Spiros Gangas

For more information about this series, please visit: www.routledge.com/International-Library-of-Sociology/book-series/SE0143

Sociological Theory and the Capability Approach

Spiros Gangas

LONDON AND NEW YORK

First published 2020 by Routledge

2 Park Square, Milton Park, Abingdon, Oxon, OX14 4RN
605 Third Avenue, New York, NY 10017

Routledge is an imprint of the Taylor & Francis Group, an informa business

First issued in paperback 2020

British Library Cataloguing-in-Publication Data
A catalogue record for this book is available from the British Library

Library of Congress Cataloging-in-Publication Data
Names: Gangas, Spyros, 1967- author.
Title: Sociological theory and the capability approach / Spiros Gangas.
Description: Abingdon, Oxon ; New York, NY : Routledge, 2020. |
Series: International library of sociology | Includes bibliographical references and index.
Identifiers: LCCN 2019028914 (print) | LCCN 2019028915 (ebook) |
ISBN 9781138488694 (hbk) | ISBN 9781351039666 (ebk)
Subjects: LCSH: Educational sociology. |
Capabilities approach (Social sciences)
Classification: LCC LC191 .G257 2020 (print) | LCC LC191 (ebook) |
DDC 306.43--dc23
LC record available at https://lccn.loc.gov/2019028914
LC ebook record available at https://lccn.loc.gov/2019028915

ISBN: 978-1-138-48869-4 (hbk)
ISBN: 978-0-367-72669-0 (pbk)

Typeset in Times New Roman
by Wearset Ltd, Boldon, Tyne and Wear

For Ioulia and Niki-Heraklia

Contents

Figures

Acknowledgements

I came across Amartya Sen's work as a postgraduate student when in 1992 I taught as a tutor a module in sociology at the University of Edinburgh. I then rediscovered Sen through the work of Kosmas Psychopedis during the late 1990s, whose work on value-theory and normativity exerted considerable influence on my subsequent research questions. These research questions were further illuminated and enriched by John Holmwood. He has always been a constant source of inspiration since my postgraduate years. We have started exchanging views on the Capability Approach (CA) in 2010 and he has generously offered comments (constructive and critical) on parts of the manuscript. I am thus grateful to his long-lasting contribution.

Previous sections of the book have been presented at various conferences at Cambridge (UK), Athens and Yokohama. I would thus like to thank, respectively, conference session organizers Leonidas K. Cheliotis, Nate Hinerman and Bruce Friesen for accepting my papers. In 2014, Masahito Takahashi was kind enough to invite me at the always very hospitable Kobe College to give a talk on CA. Ronald Anderson's work on the sociology of suffering proved a solid bridge to my understanding of CA. I am thus grateful to our valuable conversations in Athens and Yokohama. I am also indebted to my colleague and friend, Masahiro Hamashita, with whom I have held several discussions on issues of ethics in light of the many problems that afflict the contemporary world. His gentle, stoic and dispassionate perspective on various topics has always set the bar at heights difficult for me to reach.

For the purposes of writing this book I relied on two previously published journal articles. I thank Sage Publishers for the kind permission to reproduce the following:

Gangas, Spiros. 'From Alienation to Capability Deprivation: Reconstructing a Sociological Concept'. (The final, definitive version of this paper has been published in *Social Science Information* 53 (1): 54–75, 2014 by SAGE Publications Ltd, All rights reserved. © Spiros Gangas.)

Gangas, Spiros. 'From Agency to Capabilities: Sen and Sociological Theory'. (The final, definitive version of this paper has been published in *Current Sociology* 64(1): 22–40, 2016 by SAGE Publications Ltd, All rights reserved. © Spiros Gangas.)

While the published articles are self-sufficient, for the purpose of this book a revision was necessary in order to avoid cumbersome duplication and to enrich the topics with newly discovered material. For example, in Chapter 3 I have added a few pages on Daniel Bell's unpublished manuscript on natural law and utopia:

> Bell, Daniel. 1996b. 'The Re-birth of Utopia: The Path to Natural Law.' *Daniel Bell Personal Archive.* Collection no. 18559, Box 53, Folder 12. Harvard University Archives. Accessed on: 5 June 2018.

I would thus like to thank David Bell for giving me permission to quote from this unpublished manuscript, as well as Jordy Bell for helpful correspondence. The manuscript was made available to me courtesy of Harvard University Archives. I thus thank Megan Sniffin-Marinoff (University Archivist), Virginia Hunt (Associate University Archivist for Collection Development and Records Management Services) and Juliana Kuipers (Senior Collection Development Curator/Archivist) who responded swiftly to my request for permission.

I also thank the two anonymous reviewers who commented positively on my book proposal. Mihaela Ciobotea (Editorial Assistant at Routledge) has been extremely helpful in answering all my queries. I am indebted to Charlotte Parkins who was a superb copy editor; she proved instrumental in correcting my English and, generally, in improving the final shape of the book. I also thank Gerhard Boomgaarden (Commissioning Editor and Routledge Senior Publisher) for supporting the idea of a book in sociological theory and the CA and entrusting its publication in the Routledge International Library of Sociology Series. This is a major privilege for me since I still recall the educational impetus I derived from that series as an undergraduate, as a postgraduate student at the University of Edinburgh and as a professional in the field.

Writing up the book would not have been possible if Deree – the American College of Greece had not provided me with a sabbatical leave during Fall Semester 2018. The John S. Bailey Library staff at Deree were always extremely helpful, yet I need to single out Vicky Tseroni (Associate Dean of Libraries) and Angeliki Palaiologopoulou (Assistant to the Dean for Subscription Resources) who processed immediately all my pressing inter-library loan requests. I have also benefited from students in my sociological theory courses over the years of teaching at Deree who have enabled me through their sharp questions and comments to clarify my thinking.

Obviously, I need to stress that I am solely responsible for this book's limitations.

Finally, I wish to express my gratitude to my wife Ioulia Papazoglou. She has, in many ways, been a source of support during the arduous process of writing the book. My daughter Niki-Heraklia has been a constant reminder of why children prefigure the utopia of what CA is striving to accomplish. It is to both that I dedicate this book.

Abbreviations

AGIL	Adaptation, Goal-Attainment, Integration, Latent-Pattern Maintenance
BCM	Beyond the Capitalist Market
CA	Capability Approach
CCL	Central Capabilities List
EU	European Union
IMF	International Monetary Fund
ISIS	Islamic State of Iraq and Syria
LETS	Local Exchange Trade Systems
MM	Moralization of Market
OECD	The Organisation for Economic Co-operation and Development
RM	Regulated Market
SRM	Self-Regulated Market
TINA	There is no Alternative
UBI	Universal Basic Income

Introduction

Sociological theory and the Capability Approach (CA)

This book explores the possibility of sociological theory's normative broadening. To pursue this possibility, I enquire if normative strands in sociological theory can develop into a research programme aided by the theoretical and policy paradigm of the Capability Approach (henceforth CA).[1] Known also as 'Capabilities Approach' or 'Human Development Approach' the programme that I consider as sociological theory's best suited normative partner is rooted in the writings of Nobel laureate economist Amartya Sen and philosopher Martha Nussbaum.

The normative driving force in CA is articulated around a disarmingly direct and solid question: 'What is a person able to do and to be?' In formulating this question CA is animated first by the ethical and policy urgency of making unjust situations in society more just. Thus, by default, it possesses an inbuilt sociological reasoning simply because injustice occurs in real societies and cultural contexts. Second, this central question contains, at least implicitly, additional sociological qualifications about the ethical content and scope we attach to human agency. It asks: 'What sort of irreducible, but also interdependent, social settings need to be in place in order for people to have the freedom to choose the lifestyle they have reason to value?' As we shall see throughout *Sociological Theory and the Capability Approach*, CA brackets ultimate justifications of first principles of justice and instead endorses the urgent task of converting people's rights into a set of capabilities that would enable persons to function beyond a minimum threshold of human dignity. In essence, therefore, human dignity is the core value CA defends. Its representatives aspire though to refine it and operationalize its constitutive dimensions, hoping to render a capabilities-based theory of justice sufficiently flexible and thus relevant to culturally diverse contexts where people are vulnerable to various sufferings. These can stem from rigid or precarious social structures, nefarious functioning of organizations, from culturally embedded and oppressive values or from other identity constraints specific to a situation, category or group. Thus, CA entails an uncompromising concern with the problem of human suffering and its social causes.

The strong placement of CA in economics, philosophy and development studies indicates its promising scope of theoretical and empirical growth.

Indeed, to make CA digestible to wider audiences but without compromising its sophistication, Sen and Nussbaum have provided less technical and lay exegeses of its tenets and overall rationale.[2] Other scholars in dialogue with CA have helped to extend significantly the programme's reach.[3] Disseminating CA to audiences beyond economics – as was the case with Sen's extremely lucid *Development as Freedom* (1999) – did not go unnoticed by sociologists. Sporadic work on CA during the mid-2000s increased during the 2010s in what could be perceived as the discipline's renewed interest in normative issues (see, indicatively, Bonvin and Laruffa 2018; Bonvin, Laruffa and Rosenstein 2018; Borghi 2018; De Munck 2018; Déneulin and McGregor 2010; Feldman and Gellert 2006; Gangas 2014, 2016; Holmwood 2013; Hvinden and Halvorsen 2018; Kremakova 2013; Walby 2012; Zimmermann 2006, 2018).

Sociological Theory and the Capability Approach continues and extends this discussion on what is admittedly a relatively new normative environment in sociology. It is motivated by the conviction that the conflict between various reappraisals of the normative which address the 'human' as a problem of categories (e.g. Archer 2000), as a normative compass (Chernilo 2013) worthy of being reconstructed, or even as an index of sociological theory's disenchantment (e.g. Turner 2010) can be mitigated if attention tilts to CA. For example, Burawoy's (2005) call for 'public sociology' and his positive gesture towards CA (2005, 23n.9) functions as an index of sociology's replenishment of normative explanation in conjunction with rendering economics a value-laden domain of knowledge as CA also hopes to demonstrate. As much of the current discontent over sociology's normative efficacy focuses on the problematic relationship between sociology and economics, an overlapping problem shift in both disciplines through the lens of CA can build interdisciplinary dialogue anew.

A very brief overview of CA

According to a prominent scholar of CA this paradigm 'is a broad normative framework for the evaluation and assessment of individual well-being and social arrangements, the design of policies, and proposals about social change in society' (Robeyns 2005, 94). The central category of CA is, of course, 'capabilities'. Capabilities refer to the potential but also to the actual power of what a person is able to do and achieve in terms of valued choices. Sen tells us that a person's 'capability refers to the alternative functionings that are feasible for her to achieve. Capability is thus a kind of freedom: the substantive freedom to achieve alternative functioning combinations (or, less formally put, the freedom to achieve various lifestyles)' (Sen 1999, 75). 'Functionings' comprise, quite broadly, the 'various doings and beings' a 'person actually achieves' and indicate 'a person's well-being' (Sen 1985, 197–198). Thus, functionings consist of outcomes of the freedom to make use of and to be in control of one's capabilities. As Sen puts it: 'A functioning is an achievement, whereas a capability is the ability to achieve' (1987b, 36). If Sen insists on people's capabilities, this is because a valued capability enables a person to function in society, that is, to have the real opportunity to choose between alternative lifestyles. Hence, people's freedom to choose the lifestyles that they have reason to value is of paramount significance for the entire CA. Such functionings, which may vary from being able to work, rest or enjoy good health to 'achieving self-respect or being socially integrated' (Sen 1993, 31), constitute the set from which their combinations elicit the actual capabilities of persons to lead the lifestyles they have reason to value. Which functionings appear as more salient than others at a given point or context depends on the value-orientations of agents and of wider collectivities.

From this basic template of capabilities and functionings we may construe that the human being according to CA consists a far broader and normatively complex agent of action than usually assumed by utilitarian models. One example here is the CA understanding of wealth. Wealth is to be prized not in itself but only if it leads to certain good functionings. If acquiring wealth implies leading a stressful life then wealth as such cannot be considered a good thing as it would jeopardize a person's health. It would also not be considered good if its methods of accumulation entail capability deprivation for others, at least in an obvious and particularly intense and immediate way, as for example, when corporate expansionism activates immediately environmental, social, psychological and moral hazards for workers who need to access market opportunities (e.g. sweatshop labour). As Sen (1999, 28–29) emphasizes, slaves in the United States had a basket of commodities of favourable comparison to free-labourers, yet that economic adequacy was not tied to other functionings that required the freedom denied by the system of slavery. In fact, a careful consideration of the spectrum of functionings adduced reveal an 'individual' entangled with social arrangements that support and presumably enhance her placement in the life of the community. Therefore, inbuilt in CA is the provision – empirical as well as logically deduced – that the person's capability is incumbent upon the sociocultural setting and the institutions within which the self articulates her social existence.

Constructed as 'substantive freedoms', capabilities denote a person's available trajectory of choices and the actual social, political, legal, economic and moral space that actualizes these choices. For CA this is a space of public deliberation that keeps open the possibility of the expansion of choices beyond given constraints. The freedom aspect of capabilities is further distinguished to: a) *the process aspect of freedom*, which being procedural is concerned with how these freedoms become actual. For example, the freedom of political participation is one such instance of process freedom. Beyond their instrumental function as means, political freedoms 'have to be understood as constitutive parts of the *ends* of development in themselves' (Sen 1999, 291 [original emphasis]); b) the *opportunity aspect of freedom*, which bears on the degree to which people can actually achieve what they have reason to value. For example, it is important to give people the material security to raise a family without conceding education or career options and leave up to people themselves if they will choose this particular lifestyle. Both moments of freedom constitute the lifeblood of Sen's project.

The ethical hard core of CA was delineated and broadened in Nussbaum's version of a Central Capabilities List (henceforth, CCL). The list is obviously not conclusive and it has constituted a source of fruitful controversy with Sen who believes that a lexical order of capabilities risks appearing 'dogmatic' (Sen 2005, 159). For Nussbaum, however, the CCL is set up as a minimally binding template because each capability is held to be irreducible. (Issues of interrelationship between capabilities will be taken up in Chapters 3, 4 and 6.) The CCL includes the following capabilities:

1 Life (a life not open to the risk of premature and painful death; a life worth living; dignity).
2 Bodily Health (nourishment, reproduction, shelter; generally, enjoying good health).
3 Bodily Integrity (freedom of movement; security against all forms of physical and sexual violence).
4 Senses, Imagination and Thought (educational capacities and choices to pursue scientific, artistic literary and other projects).
5 Emotions (web of affective attachments to people and things; experience of love, care, gratitude, grief, justified anger).
6 Practical Reason (capability to choose; liberty of conscience; formation of a practical conception of the good).
7 Affiliation (web of affiliations including, but not limited to: a) cooperative interaction with others, recognition and sympathy for others; b) self-respect and provisions of nondiscrimination).
8 Other Species (social life in concert with and concern for animals, plants and natural habitat).
9 Play (ability to enjoy recreational activity, to laugh and to play).
10 Political and Material Control over One's Environment (*Political control*: Political participation in political choices that shape a governed society; rights of free speech and association; *Material control*: Ability to hold property, property rights, right to seek employment on an equal basis with others, dignified relation to working conditions, fellowship and mutual recognition with other workers). (These ten capabilities are adapted and abridged from Nussbaum 1992, 216–223; 2000, 78–80; 2006, 76–78; 2011, 33–34.)

Since the articulation of the CCL the growth of CA coincided with an ensued debate about the necessity of a specification of capabilities. The characteristics of the CCL have been regarded as selective, potentially too inelastic for practical purposes, and even too insensitive to the deliberative processes that would enable people across different contexts and circumstances to add or, should they freely desire it, to design anew a capabilities list. For Sen:

> to insist on a fixed forever list of capabilities would deny the possibility of progress in social understanding and also go against the productive role of

> public discussion, social agitation, and open debates. I have nothing against the listing of capabilities but must stand up against a grand mausoleum to one fixed and final list of capabilities.
>
> (2004, 80)

This qualified reluctance to strengthen the binding foundation of CA via a CCL accommodates, for Sen, an appreciation of the contingency of sociocultural reality, which can offset any normative mapping that is carved on stone. Public reasoning and collective agitation, as he contends, are part and parcel of how groups and communities express grievances and how people mobilize to waive barriers to what they perceive as institutional deprivations of their capabilities and freedoms.

By contrast, Nussbaum believes that the theoretical venture of CA should not be inhibited from Sen's humbler model of pragmatically accomplished outcomes. She insists that CA offers the only viable alternative to standard models of developmental growth 'in an era of urgent human problems and unjustifiable human inequalities' (Nussbaum 2011, xii). How can this confident assertion be sociologically incarnated is the task of this book.

Some limitations of sociological theory

Current sociological diagnoses indicate a rapidly saturating 'postsocial' society (Streeck 2016 but also, Bauman and Donskis 2016; Beck 2012; Offe 2015). Regardless of the explanatory sharpness of such pessimistic accounts, this emerging pattern of social crises denotes a solid symptom of a society that is strewn with social problems and an acute sense of paralysis in the domain of collectively coordinated praxis. However, for all their merits, such accounts can derail normative approaches in sociology and other disciplines because they tend, unwittingly perhaps, to indulge in a rhetoric of negation, denuding, so to speak, the 'social' of its sociality. Thus, the danger of missing opportunities for alliances among disciplines and social actors within and outside academia can exacerbate the already acute feelings of helplessness. Given that the heartland of the current crisis is often located in Europe (paradoxically, since Europe is often presented as the ideal region for integration and capability flourishings) it is rather surprising that sociological literature (e.g. Castells et al. 2018) keeps ignoring CA as a potential partner in the design and proposal of solutions, even if CA scholars have addressed the integration of CA to a specifically regional European Union (EU) agenda (De Leonardis, Negrelli and Salais 2012; Papadopoulos and Tsakloglou 2008; Salais and Villeneuve 2004). Having this acute sense of crisis in mind, the chapters about to unfold will hopefully persuade the reader that current challenges to democratic and pluralist integration in society urge us to reconsider how both sociology and CA may prove less resistant to synthesis than hitherto assumed by their practitioners. Since the dire and ongoing economic and political consequences of the 2007 financial meltdown along concomitant social dislocations across national, regional and global levels, sociology's exasperation at the normative vacuum hit code red (Castells et al., 2018; Habermas, 2012, 2015; Streeck, 2014, 2016; Walby 2017).[4]

Because these diagnoses challenge the validity and integrative capacity of current institutional arrangements, they revisit and construe the problem of justice as a normative project that is internal to the function of modernity's institutions. The validation of the moral core of such rational institutions is not limited to the role of cultural values but is also refracted across specific modes of social interaction.

This is the substantive reason behind my call to a normative enrichment. A call to an enrichment requires thus that we revisit one of sociology's central question: 'How do we live together?' This seemingly trivial question implies that people's choices are placed in a framework of values and norms. It is also an issue that coincides with the explanatory drive of sociology, namely the question of: 'How is society possible?' (A question pursued by Spencer, Durkheim, Simmel, Parsons and many others.) Opportunities, constraints, instrumental templates for efficiency in the pursuit of individual goals make each person the addressee of a collective imperative in the shape of a 'we'. Indeed, this collective configuration of a 'we' (our sense of belongingness to a group and a community) which we, in sociology, as observers as well as actors in everyday life, ascribe to the overarching concept 'Society', is premised on the ability of each agent to act in ways that enable her to shape social surroundings so that her aspirations and actions can be duly expressed and fulfilled. This way of conceiving the pattern of action for each person must initially subscribe to a notion of a common horizon of values. Out of this pool of normative coordinates, individuals make choices, drawing on social memberships across local, regional, national and global systems or networks of interaction. In forming horizons of choices, individuals by virtue of their social membership are brought to consider how their own choices bear on other agents. In effect, actors confront the normative challenge that the choices made possess collective legitimacy. The latter requirement is premised on the interdependence and living space of these different levels of human sociality, which elicit complex mechanisms that sanction human behaviour. (In other words, the issue that arises is if choices are pursued without generating each time a major conflict over the everyday life that agents consider as rightly theirs.)

Such claims on the collective grounds of agency reveal a standard motif in sociology, namely the problem of values and norms and how these underpin human action in society. Notwithstanding the professed interest in this problem, sociological theory has yet to yield a framework for action that can generate sufficient consensus about its core principles. Tacit agreement on normative issues is often readily available on the level of ideal culture. In the reality of sociological practice and theory-building, however, this idyllic picture is wanting. While on the level of an ideal discourse in the discipline most sociologists would openly consider action in terms of policy and justice as conjoined to the problem of human dignity – therefore, we presume, they would be reluctant to publicly accept as valid an explanatory model where people's decisions about how they should manage their lives *must* involve undue suffering, grinding deprivation, alienation, violence and unfreedom – nonetheless, the theoretical trajectories of the discipline have hardly attained a pragmatic degree of fruitful consensus that aligns with what is publicly embraced as a common academic concern.[5] As Nussbaum (1992, 203) trenchantly observes '[c]ontemporary assaults on "essentialism" and on nonrelative accounts of human functioning' have not only been on dramatic rise but, if carried to their logical conclusion, can seriously harm public policy. I shall argue, therefore, that sociology can and ought to learn from CA on this front, precisely because the latter has configured a conceptual tool that is explanatory, deliberative and relevant to people's lives (daily routines and projective aspirations).[6]

This rough sketch of a complicated debate in our discipline brings us into the heart of this book's purpose. For if people can flourish in terms of their richly textured potential (physical, cognitive, emotional, imaginative, moral) under the aegis of collectively forged norms and values, then sociology's systematic concern with *what* an individual can accomplish, what she can become so that she senses that her potential is not wasted or destroyed, along with the conditions under which these possibilities can materialize, forms a legitimate enough reason to embed sociological theorizing into a wider normative framework.

In the final remarks of an introductory book on capabilities Martha Nussbaum writes:

> The Capabilities Approach is offered as a contribution to national and international debate, not as a dogma that must be swallowed whole. It is laid out to be pondered, digested, compared with other approaches – and then, if it stands the test of argument, to be adopted and put to practice.'
>
> (2011, 187)

Sociological Theory and the Capability approach carries forward this dual task. First, it contributes to this discussion by expanding the platform of public debate on the problem of justice to include sociological theory beyond development economics and moral philosophy. A sociological approach to justice did not seem to inspire CA although the social did appear in the homage of CA to John Rawls' theory of justice or in some sporadically proposed synergies with Habermas' notion of the public sphere. Instead of coupling political theories of justice to sociological knowledge the theoretical addressee of CA was deprived of sociological bridges to the 'social' even if CA rendered the 'social' an integral part of its normative map. This remapping of the 'social' within CA can be fruitful if CA aspires to expand its programmatic principles and articulate a vision of the 'good society'. Second, in spite of the marked omission of sociology in core principles of CA, my book argues that CA survives the test of argument, mostly with success, and offers currently the most forceful, hopeful and persuasive defence of a normative paradigm in social science. One crucial reason for this superiority is that the nexus of commonly cherished values and a conceptual reworking of these among CA scholars is supported by spectacular consensus.[7]

To be sure, CA does not consider itself a normative citadel but rather an 'approach' that is grounded on deliberative inscriptions. Its major asset is its cultural, geographical and institutional flexibility and its capacity for diversification across sociocultural contexts is never stretched to a degree of transfiguring or distorting its overarching vision, the hard core, so to speak, of its ethical assumptions or its dedicated policy scope. Thus, to recall a trope from Imre Lakatos' epistemology, the ramifications and adaptive revisions of the logic and methodology of CA have had a progressive, rather than a stagnating, relation to empirical social reality and to the problems it aspired and is designed to solve.[8]

Plan of the book

This book is divided into three parts and seven chapters, each chapter addressing a core feature of sociological theory and its connection to CA. Yet all chapters argue that this potential for synthesis is not tension-free.

Chapter 1 charts in some detail the controversy over values and reassesses its relevance for contemporary debates on the ethical constitution of social order. For analytical purposes I schematize the argument along two tracks. First I look at the problem of value-relevance. Here values are accommodated in explanation but the very object of explanation (i.e. society) is constituted as an 'irrational' realm. No teleological value is acceded towards which historical societies converge. Second, and in the antipodes of this approach, I probe into the idea that renders value-laden questions endemic to sociology and social science in the additional qualification that construes society to be constituted as an object of explanation invested with value; *pace* the work of Durkheim, Scheler, Myrdal, Marcuse and Putnam I enquire into the validity of the idea that reality is constituted via values, hoping to situate CA beyond the 'fact/value' distinction.

Chapter 2 revisits the role economics have played in the shape and transformation of sociological theory. While sociologists have no recourse to a single paradigm for theorizing economy *and* society, normative conceptions of the market economy's emdeddedness in society abound. These deserve reexamination in light of CA's normative problem shift within economics. Starting with classical sociology I address the problem of value-integration in line with industrial society's economic configuration. Sen's work in particular is animated by a spirit of synthesis between Adam Smith and Karl Marx. The normative aspects of Smith, elided in most minimalist versions of classical economics, and the radical aspects of Marx are repeatedly drawn out by Sen. As we shall see, however, this moralization of market forces does not carry yet the idea of radical needs *qua* capabilities into a social form of economic cooperation beyond capitalism. I shall argue that although Sen's version of CA offers a promising renewal of the 'embeddedness' argument (Polanyi) its methodological approach over-relies on economics and thus lacks fine-tuning to sociology and in particular to theoretical models that address the problem of market embeddedness in society. This sort of direct engagement with the social reconstitution of the market must deploy a shape of social integration that is both functional and normative (e.g. Wilkinson and Pickett 2010). So although CA considers a reattachment to the 'social' to be inscribed to its core values, the 'social' is conceptualized either as a residual category in an approach that nonetheless advocates the 'end of value-free economics' (Putnam and Walsh 2012) or figures in the shape of a set of institutional protections for human development and freedom (Sen 1999), yet with no systematic sociological justification in place.

Part II is designed to rethink the problem of human agency through the lens of CA. Chapter 3 suggests that any new normative understanding of agency, like the one that Sen and Nussbaum offer, can gain from sociological theory's recourse to notions similar to capability, namely the agent's capacity for action. Sen's version of CA articulates the agent's capability to make valued choices as its normative/analytical bedrock. It offers powerful concepts that can enable sociologists to rebuild the category of agency. Seeing this affinity as an opportunity for reworking the normative dimensions of sociological theory, and drawing on sociology's accomplishments in this field, I argue that the normative components of Sen's notion of capabilities are not necessarily locked into an individualist approach to agency, typical of economic thought, but, rather, contain a social core that has been prefigured primarily by Parsons and to a lesser extent by Giddens. This discussion will also touch upon epistemological consequences of the category of agency and will contextualize the proposed reconstruction in light of current debates on the position of natural law in sociological theory.

Chapter 4 opens up the idea of agency to challenges posed by Marxism's core concept of alienation. Among sociology's normative narratives alienation figures as one of the most captivating, influential and contested. Anchored in Hegel and Marx the idea of alienation generated valuable theoretical and empirical tools for explanation; it also offered a normative critique of modernity's pathologies. However, the concept of alienation needs to be reconstructed because its multidimensionality yields mutually exclusive accounts. A fruitful model for a contemporary reconstruction and renewal is the idea of capability deprivation. This chapter, therefore, seeks to accomplish the dual task of showing what capability deprivation can replace in the standard accounts of alienation and what can be productively retained. This proposed recalibration of a normative notion of agency entertains the possibility of exploring anew the normative challenge of human essentialism.

Chapter 5 discusses Martha Nussbaum's work on political emotions, shame and anger. Moreover, it will chart the problem shift within CA from the normative reconstruction of economic agency to the reconstruction of justice in the emotional fortification of the self. Drawing on the rich pool of sociological writings on the sociology of emotions but primarily using Max Scheler's critique of *ressentiment* and Axel Honneth's theory of the struggle for recognition, Nussbaum's work on emotions will be contextualized and expanded in the direction of the effects of inequality and capability deprivation 'under the skin' (Wilkinson and Pickett 2010). At the same time Nussbaum's project on emotions will be reassessed as an opportunity to rethink the politics of emotions in terms of social dislocations of the self. In this respect linkages to Durkheim's sociology of emotions will take up further Nussbaum's idea of 'civic friendship'. Sociological aspects of Nussbaum's work on emotions usher considerations of the institutional spheres that nourish care, cooperation, affection and solidarity as opposed to those institutional deformations that choke positive moral sentiments.

If, as this book argues, CA can offer a promising and sustainable normative compass for rethinking the social, then it cannot cede from visualizing how the capable self's choices and freedoms are supported by social institutions. This is the task of Part III. Chapter 6 shows how the work on institutions and social systems in sociological theory (Durkheim, Parsons, Habermas, Luhmann, Honneth) yield opportunities but also challenges for the growth of CA towards the vision of a just society. I shall draw on those interpretations of CA that leave open the possibility of a Hegelian reconstruction of *Sittlichkeit*. I shall argue that institutional preconditions for constitutive and instrumental freedoms as they appear in CA are not entirely free of the sociological evolutionism of modernization theory; in fact, they bear resemblance to Parsons' analytical scheme of functional prerequisites (AGIL). It is therefore at this point that sociology's role can be pivotal in stretching CA to meet its own latent institutional prerequisites. Yet the culmination of the social inscription of agency on institutions must be grounded on a notion of reciprocity and thus this chapter concludes with an assessment of how much historical content can be accommodated into CA without jettisoning its sufficiently and purposely indeterminate zone of deliberative application.

A contemporary assessment of the horizon of human freedom and dignity in institutional arrangements that are designed to enable human flourishing along the lines of a CCL raises today serious concerns and justified hesitation. Chapter 7, therefore, addresses a current wave of fundamentalist ideologies that emanate from inchoate interdependencies between societies, networks and social systems (e.g. TINA ('there is no alternative') narratives). These narratives are not hyperboles of a discipline fascinated by a politics of despair. For all his intellectual sobriety, Sen, even before the Great Recession, adumbrated humanity's challenges in stark colours (Sen 1999, xi). Faced with a resurgence of nationalism and other partitionist defences of identity-politics that Sen (2006) also warned about, I reactivate critically the idea of the 'tyranny of values', a notion that stems from conservative social theory (Nicolai Hartmann, Carl Schmitt). This seemingly odd detour from the normative social theory I endorse and defend throughout this proposed synthesis is a heuristic move. It aims to turn value-fundamentalism on its head and use the threat of value-tyranny ('fundamentalism' for Parsons) not as an argument in favour of value-incommensurability or decisionist value-choice (an unwittingly inbuilt risk in CA value-pluralism), but, rather, via CA, as an index of how capability deprivations assume a fictional 'compensation' in terms of identity-fulfilment under conditions of institutional value-fundamentalisms. Sen's critique of economic, political and religious fundamentalism will be reassessed in light of current socioeconomic and political challenges in both the developing and the developed world.

Selected authors are discussed in what is a book that is not designed to offer a thorough interpretive exegesis of each thinker. Instead, I hope to convey a systematic thread that binds CA to patterns of normativity that I discern in Hegel's philosophy, Marx's critique of capitalism and notion of a human essence, the normative functionalism of Durkheim and Parsons, Weber's and Scheler's standpoints on values and Critical Theory. To anticipate the criticism that the inherent incompatibility between some of these theoretical paradigms in sociology (e.g. Marx versus Parsons, Weber versus Durkheim) inserts a methodological collage to CA, I need to stress that the criticism is valid only for those with a proclivity to compartmentalize theoretical standpoints and jettison conceptual couplings; the latter enable us to grasp conceptual tensions in our cherished models and encourage us to engage with bridge-building for broader theoretical projects with hitherto shirked partners.

Precisely because I liken CA to sociological theory and in spite of some inevitable eclecticism in the authors I choose to discuss, I rely on several extracts of a variety of length and semantic density. To write a book that invents an entirely new conceptual language is both beyond my intention and competence. Rather, I find it more helpful to install to CA sociological 'hooks' that reflect entire conceptual constellations from the founders of the discipline to contemporary legacies. Thus, the reader can automatically check if the way I read these conceptual building blocks is both accurate and pertinent for a fruitful but urgent dialogue between CA and sociological theory.

Notes

1 Throughout the book the abbreviation CA will stand both for the singular noun used by Amartya Sen (i.e. *the capability approach*) and for Nussbaum's plural use of the noun (i.e. *the capabilities approach*). Notwithstanding some substantive differences between Sen and Nussbaum over the scope of capabilities, CA forms a single and robust programme for human development. As the book's argument will unfold, the differences and similarities between Sen's and Nussbaum's versions will be rendered clear. I will treat though CA as a comprehensive vision and leave up to the reader to judge if the differences in the two versions should have been further highlighted.

2 If someone wishes to start with Sen's ideas the best, most cogent, and less technical work is *Development as Freedom* (1999). His *On Ethics and Economics* (1987a) is also a lucid programmatic text. Sen's *The Idea of Justice* (2009) crowns his normative programme. Nussbaum's *Women and Human Development* (2000) and *Frontiers of Justice* (2006) constitute major statements of CA. If though someone prefers a shorter but equally forceful overview of CA, along with the modifications Nussbaum proposes, *Creating Capabilities* (2011) is essential reading. In lucid article format, both Sen (1985, 2005) and Nussbaum (1992, 2005) offer the nub of CA.

3 The most systematic and elaborate monograph on CA remains, I think, the excellent study *Ethics of Global Development* (2008) by David A. Crocker. Alkire (2007) provides also a sharp analysis of Sen's ideas and recently Robeyns (2017) provides a reappraisal of CA. Others (Fukuda-Parr 2003; Robeyns 2005) provide very good and short overviews of CA. Edited volumes (Bruni, Comim and Pugno 2008; Comim, Qizilbash and Alkire 2008; Déneulin and Shahani 2009; Déneulin, Nebel and Sagovsky 2006; Kaufman 2006) expand CA into diverse areas of policy concern.

4 Nowhere in these critiques does CA figure as a viable alternative. Indicatively, in a book (Elliott and Turner 2012) that represents 'Society' through the idioms of 'structure', 'solidarity', 'creation' and concludes with a litany of sociological (or even journalistic) descriptions of the social as 'feral societies', 'entertainment societies' or 'catastrophic societies' (due to the accumulation of ecological and energy risks, to the growing dependence of agents, to the simulated universe of social media or to the spectacular withdrawal of solidarity from the public sphere), the problem-solving potential of sociology remains largely unaddressed. Even when India's problems of ethnic conflicts receive some attention the work of CA is not being picked up as a relevant torchlight for exiting the tunnel of essentialist identity divisions and the capability deprivations that often inflate them. (This happens in spite of the authors' passing reference (2012, 150) to Nussbaum on the issue of cosmopolitan ethics.) The issues raised by the authors are not to be disputed; indeed, they pose a serious challenge to our hitherto moral and normative categories – even within sociology – as they force us to reflect on the very possibility of the 'social'. What my book aims to accomplish is to explore what possibilities may lie ahead so that sociology avoids regress to eschatology and that its accomplishments do not suffer a normative neutralization that settles for the defeat of rational deliberation and normative institutions in the face of the flood of unrest, injustice, unsustainable lifestyles and 'casualization' of violence (either through the screen of mobile phones or through the transformation of streets, cafés, squares, churches and mosques of metropolitan centres, as well as rural wastelands across the globe, into battlegrounds of fundamentalist beliefs).

5 Equality, justice, the quality of social life in the era of globalization, the ideal of unity and diversity, solidarity and subjectivity, among others, are standard foci that bring sociologists together from all over the world at international congresses and conferences (e.g. International Sociological Association, European Sociological Association). Although normative paradigms differ, there are no voices that renounce sociology's legitimate concern over these issues. All aim at empowering humans and at integrating societies based on schemes that value diversity and, somewhere in the process, adduce a 'right' to capability-fulfilment. However, critiques of humanism, logocentrism and normativity abound among the discipline's voices. A similar symptom was diagnosed by Leo Strauss. For him the consensus among social scientists about the value of democracy was paradoxically accompanied by a historicist critique of the 'good' and a new positivism as its epistemological but tacit corollary with disastrous political implications evident in 1933 (Strauss 1957, 355). Things may not be as gloomy as in that era. Yet, the sense of crisis on multiple fronts urges a fusion of horizon on the basis of values that most, if not all, social scientists share. This injunction is not meant to neglect that founding ideals like freedom, democracy, justice and equality is a complex and ongoing process of 'contested knowledge' (Seidman 1994). The paradox though still remains: Is contested knowledge in search of justifying and founding what itself posits as unconditional (i.e. freedom, democracy, justice, equality) and thus uncontested? Or maybe, as Strauss contends, historicist (relativist or deconstructionist) paradigms open the gates to any '1933'?

6 Drawing on a personal testimony, this was Alain Touraine's injunction to sociologists in his closing speech of the XVII ISA World Congress at Gothenburg (11–17 July 2010). This is an urgent task so that sociological theory can reclaim 'sociological imagination' and unsettle, prudently, fixed judgments in our horizon of familiarity without though undermining totally the latter. For the judicious political and normative use of theory, precisely in the capacity for imagination it activates, see Nussbaum (2007, 952–954).

7 The 'cartwheel' view of CA (Robeyns 2016, 404) identifies some axiomatic core assumptions (e.g. capability, functionings) subject to consensus across the spectrum of CA. Robeyns accommodates in semi-autonomous format (as wedge-shaped sectors) other areas of disagreement and debate (as, for example, in the approach's

meta-theoretical commitments, its normative pool, its measurement metrics etc.). Thus, Robeyns provides a fruitful visualization of CA and indicates potential problem shifts of a progressive sort.

8 I will argue that Sen understands this development of explanatory adequacy in terms close to Lakatos' research programmes (something similar but without mentioning Lakatos appears in Robeyns, 2016). For example, Sen fuses Adam Smith's and Marx's arguments repeatedly and offers a refreshing alternative to liberal accounts which underplay material constraints and inequalities and to Marxian indictments on capitalism. His research programme is progressive to the extent that it answers questions both Adam Smith and Marx raised but, additionally, aims at renovating the solutions each offered in light of current challenges posed by social reality. Where it tends to show potentially degenerating symptoms, these can be traced in the persistent repulsion of sociological theory. If a theoretical synthesis between CA and sociological theory can be forged, then we can expect a progressive problem shift within sociology that can enact the normative and the empirical under a new concept of the capable agency. Here, I am far from applying a model of scientific growth in the natural sciences to the social sciences arbitrarily. Lakatos himself suggests that 'the methodology of research programmes may be applied not only to norm-impregnated historical knowledge but to any normative knowledge, including even ethics and aesthetics' (1978, 133n.4).

References

Alkire, Sabine. 2007. *Valuing Freedoms: Sen's Capabilities Approach and Poverty Reduction.* Oxford: Oxford University Press.

Archer, Margaret. 2000. *Being Human: The Problem of Agency.* Cambridge: Cambridge University Press.

Bauman, Zygmunt, and Leonidas Donskis. 2016. *Liquid Evil. Living with TINA.* Cambridge: Polity.

Beck, Ulrich. 2012. *Twenty Observations on a World of Turmoil.* Cambridge: Polity.

Bonvin, Jean-Michel, and Francesco Laruffa. 2018. 'Deliberative Democracy in the Real World, the Contribution of the Capability Approach.' *International Review of Sociology* 28 (2): 1–18.

Bonvin, Jean-Michel, Francesco Laruffa, and Emilie Rosenstein. 2018. 'Towards a Critical Sociology of Democracy: The Potential of the Capability Approach.' *Critical Sociology* 44 (6): 953–968.

Borghi, Vando. 2018. 'From Knowledge to Informational Basis: Capability, Capacity to Aspire and Research.' *Critical Sociology* 44 (6): 899–920.

Bruni, Luigino, Flavio Comim, and Maurizio Pugno, eds. 2008. *Capabilities and Happiness.* Oxford: Oxford University Press.

Burawoy, Michael. 2005. 'For Public Sociology.' *American Sociological Review* 70 (1): 4–28.

Castells, Manuel, Olivier Bouin, João Caraça, Gustavo Cardoso, John Thompson, and Michel Wieviorka, eds. 2018. *Europe's Crises.* Cambridge: Polity.

Chernilo, Daniel. 2013. *The Natural Law Foundations of Modern Social Theory: A Quest for Universalism.* Cambridge: Cambridge University Press.

Comim, Flavio, Mozaffar Qizilbash, and Sabina Alkire, eds. 2008. *The Capability Approach: Concepts, Measures and Applications.* Cambridge: Cambridge University Press.

Crocker, David. 2008. *Ethics of Global Development: Agency, Capability, and Deliberative Democracy.* Cambridge: Cambridge University Press.

De Leonardis, Ota, Serafino Negrelli, and Robert Salais, eds. 2012. *Democracy and Capabilities for Voice: Welfare, Work and Public Deliberation in Europe*. Brussels: P.I.E. Peter Lang.

De Munck, Jean. 2018. 'Human Rights and Capabilities: A Program for a Critical Sociology of Law.' *Critical Sociology* 44 (6): 921–935.

Déneulin, Séverine, and Allister McGregor. 2010. 'The Capability Approach and the Politics of a Social Conception of Wellbeing.' *European Journal of Social Theory* 13 (4): 501–519.

Déneulin, Séverine, Mathias Nebel, and Nicholas Sagovsky, eds. 2006. *Transforming Unjust Structures: The Capability Approach*. Dordrecht: Springer.

Déneulin, Séverine, and Lila Shahani, eds. 2009. *An Introduction to the Human Development and Capability Approach*. Abingdon: Earthscan from Routledge.

Elliot, Anthony, and Bryan Turner. 2012. *On Society*. Cambridge: Polity.

Feldman, Shelley, and Paul Gellert. 2006. 'The Seductive Quality of Central Human Capabilities: Sociological Insights into Nussbaum and Sen's Disagreement.' *Economy and Society* 35 (3): 423–452.

Fukuda-Parr, Sakiko. 2003. 'The Human Development Paradigm: Operationalizing Sen's Ideas on Capabilities.' *Feminist Economics* 9 (2–3): 301–317.

Gangas, Spiros. 2014. 'From Alienation to Capability Deprivation: Reconstructing a Sociological Concept.' *Social Science Information* 53 (1): 54–75.

Gangas, Spiros. 2016. 'From Agency to Capabilities: Sen and Sociological Theory.' *Current Sociology* 64 (1): 22–40.

Habermas, Jürgen. 2012. *The Crisis of the European Union: A Response*. Cambridge: Polity.

Habermas, Jürgen. 2015. *The Lure of Technocracy*. Cambridge: Polity.

Holmwood, John. 2013. 'Public Reasoning without Sociology: Amartya Sen's Theory of Justice.' *Sociology* 47 (6): 1171–1186.

Hvinden, Bjorn, and Rune Halvorsen. 2018. 'Mediating Agency and Structure in Sociology: What Role for Conversion Factors?' *Critical Sociology* 44 (6): 865–881.

Kaufman, Alexander, ed. 2006. *Capabilities Equality: Basic Issues and Problems*. New York: Routledge.

Kremakova, Milena. 2013. 'Too Soft for Economics, Too Rigid for Sociology, or Just Right? The Productive Ambiguities of Sen's Capability Approach.' *European Journal of Sociology* 54 (3): 393–419.

Lakatos, Imre. 1978. *The Methodology of Scientific Research Programmes*. Cambridge: Cambridge University Press.

Nussbaum, Martha. 1992. 'Human Functioning and Social Justice. In Defense of Aristotelian Essentialism.' *Political Theory* 20 (2): 202–246.

Nussbaum, Martha. 2000. *Women and Human Development: The Capabilities Approach*. Cambridge: Cambridge University Press.

Nussbaum, Martha. 2005. 'Women's Bodies: Violence, Security, Capabilities.' *Journal of Human Development* 6 (2): 167–183.

Nussbaum, Martha. 2006. *Frontiers of Justice: Disability, Nationality, Species Membership*. Cambridge, MA: The Belknap Press of Harvard University Press.

Nussbaum, Martha. 2007. 'On Moral Progress: A Response to Richard Rorty.' *The University of Chicago Law Review* 74 (3): 939–960.

Nussbaum, Martha. 2011. *Creating Capabilities*. Cambridge, MA: The Belknap Press of Harvard University Press.

Offe, Claus. 2015. *Europe Entrapped*. Cambridge: Polity.

Papadopoulos, Fotis, and Panos Tsakloglou. 2008. 'Social Exclusion in the EU: A Capability-based Approach.' In *The Capability Approach: Concepts, Measures and Applications*, edited by Flavio Comim, Mozaffar Qizilbash, and Sabina Alkire, 242–267. Cambridge: Cambridge University Press.

Putnam, Hilary, and Vivian Walsh, eds. 2012. *The End of Value-Free Economics*. London: Routledge.

Robeyns, Ingrid. 2005. 'The Capability Approach: A Theoretical Survey.' *Journal of Human Development* 6 (1): 93–114.

Robeyns, Ingrid. 2016. 'Capabilitarianism.' *Journal of Human Development and Capabilities* 17 (3): 397–414.

Robeyns, Ingrid. 2017. *Well-Being, Freedom and Social Justice: The Capability Approach Re-Examined*. Cambridge: Open Book Publishers.

Salais, Robert, and Robert Villeneuve, eds. 2004. *Europe and the Politics of Capabilities*. Cambridge: Cambridge University Press.

Seidman, Steven. 1994. *Contested Knowledge: Social Theory in the Postmodern Era*. Oxford: Blackwell.

Sen, Amartya. 1985. 'Well-Being, Agency and Freedom: The Dewey Lectures 1984.' *The Journal of Philosophy* 82 (4): 169–221.

Sen, Amartya. 1987a. *On Ethics and Economics*. Oxford: Basil Blackwell.

Sen, Amartya. 1987b. 'The Standard of Living: Lecture II, Lives and Capabilities.' In *The Standard of Living: The Tanner Lectures, Clare Hall, Cambridge 1985*, edited by Geoffrey Hawthorn, 20–38. Cambridge: Cambridge University Press.

Sen, Amartya. 1993. 'Capability and Well-Being.' In *The Quality of Life*, edited by Martha Nussbaum and Amartya Sen, 30–53. Oxford: Clarendon Press.

Sen, Amartya. 1999. *Development as Freedom*. Oxford: Oxford University Press.

Sen, Amartya. 2004. 'Dialogue. Capabilities, Lists, and Public Reason: Continuing the Conversation.' *Feminist Economics* 10 (3): 77–80.

Sen, Amartya. 2005. 'Human Rights and Capabilities.' *Journal of Human Development* 6 (2): 151–166.

Sen, Amartya. 2006. *Identity and Violence: The Illusion of Destiny*. London: Penguin.

Sen, Amartya. 2009. *The Idea of Justice*. Cambridge, MA: The Belknap Press of Harvard University Press.

Strauss, Leo. 1957. 'What is Political Philosophy?' *The Journal of Politics* 19 (3): 343–368.

Streeck, Wolfgang. 2014. *Buying Time. The Delayed Crisis of Democratic Capitalism*. London: Verso.

Streeck, Wolfgang. 2016. *How Will Capitalism End? Essays on a Failing System*. London: Verso.

Turner, Stephen. 2010. *Explaining the Normative*. Cambridge: Polity.

Walby, Sylvia. 2012. 'Sen and the Measurement of Justice and Capabilities: A Problem in Theory and Practice.' *Theory, Culture and Society* 29 (1): 99–118.

Walby, Sylvia. 2017. *Crisis*. Cambridge: Polity.

Wilkinson, Richard, and Kate Pickett. 2010. *The Spirit Level: Why Equality is Better for Everyone*. London: Penguin.

Zimmermann, Bénédicte. 2006. 'Pragmatism and the Capability Approach: Challenges in Social Theory and Empirical Research.' *European Journal of Social Theory* 9 (4): 467–484.

Zimmermann, Bénédicte. 2018. 'From Critical Theory to Critical Pragmatism: Capability and the Assessment of Freedom.' *Critical Sociology* 44 (6): 937–952.

Part I

Values, economy and society

1 Valuing values in sociology and the Capability Approach

Methodological preamble

Having sketched the major tenets of CA and precisely because this paradigm holds fast to its normative thrust, it is important, before we disentangle the suspension of the 'fact/value' dichotomy (Putnam 2002) endorsed by Sen and Nussbaum, to revisit the controversy over values and how it figures in the sociological positions that concern us here. The following account is by no means exhaustive. I only address the standpoints about values in sociological arguments that I believe capture better the strengths, the deficits and the potential of CA. The main focus of the ensuing discussion is the question if a priori principles of valuation are defensible in a multidimensional social reality. Is an a priori value discernible, and can it generate a value-oriented social theory and a new form of social ethics (like Hegel's *Sittlichkeit* or Durkheim's organic solidarity)? At the same time the question of rationality will be taken up as we need to assess CA by recourse to problems of value-relevance in research. Because the latter research requirement can be implicated in a tension with the 'interests' of society and its conflicting constituencies, the problem of value will buttress the epistemological justification of CA and its overarching ethical approach to human agency. This is more pressing, as the explanatory inadequacies generated by value-dogmatism and relativism still have an impact in moral philosophy and sociology. Thus, a return to the role of values in social theory deserves reexamination.

Before I discuss how CA is coupled to important traditions in sociology on the problem of values, it is appropriate early at this point to clear the ground from potential hazards of interpretation and hidden agendas. This methodological prescription I take from Gunnar Myrdal (1958). Although I do not share all of Myrdal's arguments about values I follow him in at least two assumptions:

1 First, that there is no disinterested approach to social scientific inquiry as Weber's methodological writings about value-relevance have shown. To select a slice of reality and pose questions in need of answers presupposes an interest in it. The latter is mixed with valuations about the worth (or the worthlessness) of social reality. What Myrdal, following Weber, adds is that

value-relevance stands or falls in terms of validity; in other words, if it is formulated in terms appropriate to the scientific community and to the subjects whose perspective and life is in question.

2 Second, because of the need for analytical distinctions in identifying a problem area and selecting relevant question, social science is inevitably entangled in some a priori assumptions, which qualify as valuations. For Myrdal there is no exit from an a priori assumption about the totality called reality that forms social science's subject-matter even if we approach it through diverse theoretical and policy lenses depending on criteria of value-relevance.

For all its merits Myrdal's account is, I think, incomplete. Two standpoints require qualification: The first issue has to do with selection itself. In selecting from social reality according to my value-relevant interests I presuppose some knowledge of what I omit from the delineated object. The latter is, of course, society in its complex and richly textured historical permutations. As Hegel has shown in the systematic transposition of philosophy to a social theory oriented to institutional shapes of freedom, value-relevant problem areas are not sliced off from a chaotic reality (since, totality includes also, for Hegel, its own negation, namely, 'nothingness') but from points of view, already placed within the object and its movement (i.e. humanity, its conceptual categories and the value of freedom implicated in the realization of human potential under and through institutional spheres of justice). This was the task of his, still in many ways unsurpassed, Hegel's *The Phenomenology of Spirit* ((1807) 1977). Somewhere, in our value-relevant selections, totality is accompanying our perceptions, interests and data-collections. This totality is not some sort of hubristic methodological or ontological presumption about Absolute Knowledge. Rather, and in Hegel's footsteps, it has more to do with the shared and internal criteria according to which human beings freely comprehend and fashion the world they inhabit. In other words, the cryptic a priori that Myrdal is forced to attach to social scientific explanation as a binding (value-relevant) elimination of irrelevant causal sequences, and as a requirement that can initiate the scientific observation itself, appears now in different light.

The second standpoint aims to highlight this a priori. Myrdal's judgment is important in recognizing the position of values in social science, especially if we consider that his theses address economics. However, something more is needed in explanation and I think it is Herbert Marcuse who supplies it. Marcuse likens social theory to two cardinal value-judgments:

1 The judgment that human life is worth living, or rather can be and ought to be made worth living. This judgment underlines all intellectual effort; it is the *a priori* of social theory, and its rejection (which is perfectly logical) rejects theory itself;
2 The judgment that, in a given society, specific possibilities exist for the amelioration of human life and specific ways and means of realizing these

> possibilities. Critical analysis has to demonstrate the objective validity of these judgments and the demonstration has to proceed on empirical grounds. The established society has available an ascertainable quantity and quality of intellectual and material resources. How can these resources be used for the optimal development and satisfaction of individual needs and faculties with a minimum of toil and misery? Social theory is historical theory, and history is the realm of chance in the realm of necessity. Therefore, among the various possible and actual modes of organizing and utilizing the available resources, which ones offer the greatest chance of an optimal development?
>
> (1964, 10)[1]

Marcuse tells us here that social theory even when functioning under the auspices of particular value-relevant prescriptions is nonetheless attached to some universally valid value-principle, which for Marcuse is condensed in the moral recognition of life's freedom and intrinsic worth (human dignity). Positivism or historicism cut off, arbitrarily, this chord to the universal values that social science is called to serve. As we shall discuss in Chapters 3 and 4 this natural law irreducibility of human dignity, although in need of contemporary reconstruction due to the historical conditions of social science itself, forms the 'unconditional' a priori judgment form which all science springs forth. With respect to the first a priori then, both sociological theory and CA are in concert. For example, in a report co-authored with Stiglitz and Fitoussi, Amartya Sen writes: 'Quality of life includes the full range of factors that make *life worth living*, including those that are not traded in markets and not captured by monetary measures' (Stiglitz, Sen and Fitoussi 2009, 216 [emphasis added]).[2]

With respect to the second of Marcuse's prerequisites, both social theory and CA fulfil it, albeit partially. If we consider Marcuse's Hegelian Marxism and Sen or Nussbaum's Kantian and liberal starting points, these two normative narratives intersect significantly and this overlap is predicated also on the Adam Smith–Karl Marx fusion that Sen's texts carefully deploy. For its part, sociology sought to explain capitalist modernity and to grasp the moment of its failure to deliver lives of plenitude for all its members; however, it acknowledged (including by Marxists) that the amelioration of human life has hardly reached similar heights in non-capitalist social formations. Thus, depending on the degree of deficits of capitalist markets and their ability to influence (and be influenced by) other institutional spheres of democratic societies, sociologists embraced a gamut of positions, which sought – at least explicitly – to forge workable solutions within shared and sharable democratic ideals, even if they opted for liberal or socialist configurations of how these ideals align with the force of markets. We can surmise that CA would recognize the potential of democratic societies (even those that are minimally democratic) but, unlike sociology, it would refrain from licensing the institutional spheres of modernity as reliable and universally valid matrices of freedom – even at those points where it accepts their validity – or from deciphering the intermediate spaces that couple ethical spaces of interaction and social memberships into a relatively coherent systemic whole. In other words, modernity as an 'unfinished' but binding project of intrinsically valuable modes of social membership geared to freedom and justice requires further reconstruction.

Weber, Scheler and the collective validity of values

In aiming to respond to the historical shift from tradition to modernity sociologists sought to explain how values hold societies together. At the same time, the historical nature of sociology's subject-matter raised all sorts of methodological concerns over the role of values in the sociologist's selection, description and explanation of a problem. Values and questions of normative validity and value-relevance became a cardinal issue dividing the discipline between mutually exclusive strands: some sociologists opted for value-free, disinterested research and others embraced a value-laden approach to explaining society. Classical sociology's controversy over values took shape under the umbrella of the complex and persistent debate over values in late-nineteenth century neo-Kantian philosophy. Thus, a newly founded sociology was set within irrevocable axiological and normative parameters.[3]

Following a long gestation of ideas, axiology (the then appropriate field of philosophy that dealt with the validity of values and value-judgments) oscillated, eventually, between a subjectivist and an objectivist theory of values. We can briefly note that subjectivists considered value-judgments to inhere in the subject's emotional and psychological needs as the latter were stirred by the perception and cognition of objects of 'value' (see, for example, Eaton 1930). It is thus the subject who confers value(s) to the world. Interests were also held to account for the attachment of value into objects and it was only a matter of time before the logical positivism of the Vienna Circle, since the mid-1920s, sought to purge analytical philosophy and logic from all 'metaphysical' assumptions including values and value-judgments. Not all logical positivists though felt eager to provide the ballast for logical rigour by tossing out values. Viktor Kraft, quite ingeniously, preserved the 'collective' as the realm that is most appropriate for seeking the validity of values. For Kraft values attain validity and thus become binding only under the aegis 'of an impersonal authority' ((1951) 1981, 144). As if in Durkheimian 'thought-style' Kraft claimed that:

> [t]he ground of their universal validity lies in their indispensability for civilization, in which the abilities specific to man are developed. In this way it is possible to establish the universal validity of the value of commerce and technology, of justice and morality, of education and instruction, of art and science (177).

The recognition on Kraft's part that the evaluative dimension must bear on the foundations of human civilization and the abilities best suited for human flourishing paves the way, unexpectedly perhaps, to considering this argument in light of how CA is situated in the complicated discussion over values.

A major figure in the value-controversy in sociology is of course Max Weber. Weber's complicated theory of values cannot be addressed in detail here but it will be taken up again shortly, once we complete the exposition of the objectivist value-theory. It suffices to recall that Weber's position entails a value-perspectivism with regard to the relevance of the problems that the sociologist is called to select. Value-relevance configures reality as a culturally conditioned object. Typified constructs, known as ideal-types, construct a phenomenon's essential features and operate as a methodological prerequisite for sociological interpretations of action. Their heuristic function (i.e. to abstract from reality logically interrelated features of a phenomenon and to enable the scientist to dwell in culturally specific, logically 'impure', historical understanding) is raised to a condition of possibility for social science in grasping subjective meanings in their richly textured cultural manifestations. Weber, thus, aligns himself with the epistemological position that imputes to reality infinite contingency. He concedes that social reality is indeed configured (and grasped by historical agents) on the basis of values, but these values are now 'founded' on ultimate and irrational decisions, even if they are routinely reproduced by the (individual and collective) actors in question. This methodological standpoint has its roots in Weber's ontology, which holds life (and, particularly, the rationalized differentiated modernity) to be marked by incommensurable value-spheres (religious, political, economic, aesthetic, erotic). For Weber, the ordinary consciousness caught up in 'routinized daily existence' cannot 'become aware, of this partly psychologically, partly pragmatically conditioned motley of irreconcilably antagonistic values' (Weber (1904) 1949, 18).[4] On how values are coordinated on the level of system integration is beyond the scope of Weber's argument; the dire political consequences of this subordination of values to a non-collective ground of validity are corroborated by the sympathy with which Weber's reactionary followers, like Carl Schmitt, or Marxist 'disciples', like Georg Lukács, enveloped his value-theory in order to extend it to a politics grounded in decisionism. This radicalization of value-pluralism against a normative explanation of values is accomplished, as we shall see later (Chapter 7), by Luhmann's systems theory. The fact remains that Weber's groundbreaking epistemology is thus, inevitably, coupled with the level of modernity's autonomous value-spheres and any effort on our part to address this problematic in a contemporary context of normativity must necessarily incorporate systemic and institutional dimensions of a differentiated process of value-formation in modernity's multiple spheres of social life.

Beyond the subjective theories of values which Kraft sought to weaken in a characteristically sociological mode, the objectivist approach to values held that values hold an 'eternal' status (this is the neo-Kantian and neo-Platonic strand from Lotze to Rickert and Scheler). In contrast to value-incommensurability (Weber), it was Max Scheler who sought to reinvigorate the possibility of conceiving the human being as the bearer of values. Scheler's philosophical anthropology radicalized the neo-Kantian postulate of the ideal validity of values. Scheler ((1916) 1973) sought to put values back onto solid foundations and thus inaugurated a phenomenological anthropology. He thus conceived the constitution of the person through the lens of a phenomenologically deduced hierarchical set of a priori values (those that Weber had relegated to the residual category of 'life' and Rickert had elevated to the ideal realm of timeless validity). These values (or value-modalities of man's openness to the world) cover the spectrum of values of pleasure, vitality, utility, justice, aesthetics to the value of the holy, which if translated in terms of forms of social togetherness culminate in an ecumenical cosmopolitan solidarity. It thus takes little imagination to convert Scheler's table into a phenomenological deduction of natural law. Scheler's value-hierarchy is of course too rigidly formulated for a contemporary moral philosophy or normative sociology to accept, which debunks a priori epistemologies. Yet it does offer a fruitful ground for reconstructing the human being in terms that entail a richly textured self, capable to relate to reality's contingencies in a value-relevant orientation. The difference with Weber's value-relevance is that for Scheler the value-modalities and the hierarchical logic upon which they are premised constitute, eventually, the human being. In providing a hierarchy of values, Scheler adumbrates the human being as a moral person, 'capable', so to speak, to realize herself in the world in terms of an entire range of a priori values.

I am fully aware here of the problem of associating value-hierarchies with a markedly non-hierarchical project like CA. Yet, such configurations of value(s) deserve reexamination. One reason is that they turn up unexpectedly when pragmatic and contingent problem-solving aims to eliminate them or at best to 'bracket' them. Let me thus consider here for a moment Parsons' view of the social system in terms of four functional imperatives. These fulfil different functions, which we cannot address in detail at the moment, but evidently, for Parsons, their interchanges are possible only as a 'cybernetic hierarchy'. We can recall Parsons' qualified explanation of the subsystems (L) and (I) as typically 'idealist' and of (A) and (G) as typically 'materialist' (Parsons 1966, 113). Scheler pursued a slightly different trail. His a priori hierarchy of values placed at its apex idealist values and, in the lower strata, materialist values. For Scheler the relation between each layer of value resorted to a logic of conditions. Scheler's scheme renders the higher value a condition for the lower, if by condition we mean here the mode by which lower values can be fulfilled. Thus a walk in the forest, for Scheler, would yield different degrees of emotive contentment if it has been preceded by the accomplishment of a higher value (e.g. philosophical meditation or artistic creation). No need though to pursue further Scheler complex phenomenological deductions. What I am interested in instead is the pattern shown in Figure 1.1. (It is based on the hierarchical priority Parsons imputes to L among the system of functional imperatives.)

If we use this analogy between Parsons and Scheler heuristically, rather than to extrapolate an unequivocal prioritization, then we can apply the four prerequisites to CA. I should state at the outset that I am not claiming that Nussbaum would

Figure 1.1 Scheler's value-hierarchy configured after Parsons' functional imperatives.

	Talcott Parsons (AGIL)	*Max Scheler (a priori value-hierarchy)*	
L	Latent-Pattern Maintenance	Values of the Holy	**L**
I	Societal Integration	Spiritual Values (Aesthetic – of Justice – Scientific)	**I**
G	Goal-Attainment	Vital Values	**G**
A	Adaptation	Utilitarian Values / Values of Sensibility	**A**

welcome the analogy of the CCL with Scheler's value-hierarchy. In all likelihood she would reject Scheler's axiological rigorism. Although Nussbaum welcomes other aspects of Scheler's thought (as we shall see in Chapter 5) she is silent about his value-theory. Thus we can only opine on the matter of Scheler's actual influence on the CCL. It should be clear that this is only my own contention and one that for champions of CA could appear heretical. But the reason for bringing those philosophical traditions together is quite simple. Scheler adumbrates a philosophical anthropology and following a Catholic predilection for natural law deduces phenomenologically the human person as a bearer of values. CA, as we shall see, makes a few gestures towards Roman Catholicism. It also has the human being in mind when it constructs a CCL. Now the tabulation between Parsons, Scheler and Nussbaum's CCL could appear as shown in Figure 1.2

In the set of the loose 'correspondences' between Scheler's typically Roman Catholic table of a priori non-formal (i.e. content-laden) values and the CCL, we notice a concentration of capabilities in the segments of the human person as a 'system' that relies on adaptive and goal-setting trajectories of action. If we recall Parsons' explanation of the subsystems (L) and (I) as typically 'idealist' and of (A) and (G) as typically 'materialist' then, judged within the limitations of this paradigmatic pattern, the CCL primes those factors that stress the

Figure 1.2 Martha Nussbaum's CCL and Max Scheler's value-hierarchy configured after Parsons' functional imperatives.

	Max Scheler (a priori value-hierarchy)	*Martha Nussbaum (The Central Capabilities List)*	
L	Values of the Holy	(C7) Affiliation	**L**
I	Spiritual Values (Aesthetic – of Justice – Scientific)	(C4) Senses, Imagination, Thought; (C7) Affiliation	**I**
G	Vital Values	(C1) Life; (C2) Bodily Health; (C3) Bodily Integrity; (C4) Senses, Imagination, Thought; (C5) Emotions; (C6) Practical Reason; (C8) Other Species; (C9) Play; (C10a) Control over political factors	**G**
A	Utilitarian Values/ Values of Sensibility	(C10b) Control of material factors(C1) Life; (C2) Bodily Health; (C3) Bodily Integrity; (C5) Emotions	**A**

corporeal, material, sensible and emotional repository of the human being, as well as its control over a material environment and its resources. Politically speaking the latter underscore the person's capability to actively participate in decision-making process pertinent to the public sphere. If, again, we resort to a cue offered by Scheler's sociology of knowledge, we can configure this analytical breakdown of capabilities after the pattern of relation between 'real' and 'ideal' factors. This pair of concepts that suffused German sociology from Weber to Scheler, is drawn upon systematically by Parsons too throughout his career (Parsons (1922) 1996, 21; (1973) 2006, 44–45). Yet, unlike Parsons' qualified idealism, the economic and political factors in Scheler function like 'sluices' that determine the magnitude of spiritual flow into history. Understood in this way, CA rightly primes these 'material' capabilities. For if life, bodily health, bodily integrity, emotions, practical reason, senses, thought, imagination, control over a material and political environment are not in place beyond an acceptably decent minimum and are, in contrast, in a state of precariousness and constant risk, then it may indeed be difficult to see how other capabilities, or the ones from which intellectual and artistic achievements can further fructify, can be realistically accomplished within a time-span relevant for the agents in question. Nussbaum makes an accommodation of thresholds and thus, although she rightly thinks that setting thresholds can be a complex exercise, the hierarchical intimation fashioned after Scheler figures as a legitimate possibility. She writes:

> Things now get complicated, for we want to describe two distinct thresholds: a threshold of capability to function, beneath which a life will be so impoverished that it will not be human at all, and a somewhat higher threshold, beneath which those characteristic functions are available in such a reduced way that although we may judge the form of life a human one, we will not think it a *good* life.'
>
> (Nussbaum 1992, 221 [original emphasis])

Here it is evident that the CCL is not a bundle of arbitrarily concocted capabilities. Although free of lexical orderings, the CCL – as its founder acknowledges – entails somewhere a hierarchical ordering. Again, we should not be taken by surprise here. Scheler is instructive once more when he suggests that a higher value is a foundation for a lower value. The main point is that if we accept a logic of thresholds – and I think we should – then the entire CCL turns into a sociological project with a functional–normative orientation. This would imply that control over the material and political resources functions as a condition for values like health, bodily integrity, play and interaction with other species to be felt at in line with a 'good life' – no matter how we define the latter at this stage. If valid, such an approach would entail a reversal of orthodox materialist accounts and instead would opt for making 'matter' (i.e. life) a value.

Scheler thus works out a proxy for the Kantian ethic of considering each person as an end and never entirely as a means. Thus, for Scheler, a minimal life of decent survival, nutrition and access to forms of pleasure of the body would certainly be important. If these capabilities, however, were severed from this person's actual opportunity set to realize herself as a being who is the bearer (and generator) not only of justice but also of intellectual faculties, or of a spiritual (religious) existence, or even of a utilitarian command of resources – although this latter point figures in a subordinate rank in Scheler's classification of values – then a person would fail significantly to experience herself as a fulfilled being-in-the-world.[5] As Scheler ((1916) 1973, 95) writes, life 'has these values in fact only insofar as *life* itself (in all its forms) *is* a bearer of values that take on certain heights in an objective scale'. Moreover, 'a *positive value of life* is the foundation of this value-series' (95 [original emphasis]). Salient here is Scheler's modality of non-divisibility of higher values (93). Although the acme of Scheler's scalar conception of values does not (nor need to) coincide with Nussbaum's, it nonetheless informs us about the ecumenical (universal) content of human togetherness. This is set up by Scheler in abstraction from divisive forms of togetherness, like the 'mass', *Gemeinschaft* and *Gesellshaft*, pointing towards what human beings feel as the 'holy' and all-encompassing world community. This vision of humanity, which, as Durkheim has shown, primes, under the value-system of modernity, the sacrality of the profane, is set up as the secular trustee of individual welfare. Thus the merely 'vital', as it were, values of the body, or of nutrition or of what is agreeable, are elevated to a material repertoire that all civic and professional morality should be concerned with. In spite of group and collective goals that contemporary society's ethical life pursues, interdependently via particular individual wills, the so-called 'lower' and 'profane' values are retained as a valuable and substantive index of society's moral progress. Thus, even for the elitist Scheler of the early phase of his thought, the higher values are jeopardized if the modality (i.e. value-relevance) of society is directed to lower values. This is precisely the point that Nussbaum finds palatable in Marx and Aristotle when she somehow accommodates a 'hierarchy' of values that occur in societies '*kata symbebekos*' (i.e. by accident and not by reason). Thus, Marx and Aristotle:

> agree in condemning societies that promote money and commodities to the status of ends in themselves, on the grounds that this confuses and *inverts values*, debasing humanity to the status of mere means, and alienates individuals from the truly human understanding of goods.
>
> (Nussbaum 1995, 119 [emphasis added])

'Fulfilment' for Scheler would thus be tantamount to a person being capable of relating to these 'higher' value-modalities of her personality and self after the basic values of nutrition and control over her bodily integrity are in place. It is thus intriguing, though hardly surprising, when Nussbaum concedes that the 'Roman Catholic doctrine squares quite well with the global and domestic demands of the Capabilities Approach' (2011, 93). Most likely it is Auguste Comte, and his 'religion of humanity', who figures as a source of inspiration here, given Nussbaum's generally favourable commentary on Comte (Nussbaum 2013).

But if we focus on the evaluative content of the CCL we may surmise that it is Scheler – the Catholic *fin de siècle* philosopher *par excellence*, himself heavily indebted to Comte – who appears as a likely partner to the CCL. As I shall discuss on several occasions, it is certainly plausible to suggest that the Roman Catholic cosmopolitan ethic – which became Scheler's moral banner during the late phase of his thought – aligns with the vision of CA for a qualified ethical cosmopolitanism that accommodates culturally diverse loyalties to the nation or to religion.

The objective theory of values is not exhausted by Scheler's a priori hierarchy. In its Hegelian version the objectivist standpoint replaces values with teleology and proceeds by demonstrating that reality, rather than being irrational, must be brought to reason (the conception of the 'good') as it is endowed with the potentiality for this elevation towards its immanent purpose to be possible. For Hegel, the concept of value (Deranty 2005) exceeds its economic determination and stretches to the Good's realization in modernity's shapes of social life (*Sittlichkeit*). It thus bears on an intersubjective approach to society and is designed within an extremely complex system to come full circle through the self-actualization of individual subjects.[6] Translated into sociology a portion of Hegel's transcendence of the fact/value distinction found support in Marx, Durkheim, Parsons and Critical Theory. For our purposes, the bridge between subjective and objective accounts of value is highlighted better by Durkheim. It was Durkheim who contended that the very validity, not only of values but of our very conceptual categories, must have its anchoring in collective sentiments that enable members of a community to articulate a solid sense of 'we'. The latter took shape in modernity as a nexus of cooperative relationships that draw their force from the values of moral individualism. It was the domain of collective functional needs ('necessity') that bolstered initially the cement of society that Durkheim associated with the configuration of 'mechanical solidarity'. In such types of institutional configurations where the collective validity of cognitive and moral categories draws on kin, religion and repressive law the agent's capability to fully realize her potential (the CCL) would depend on arbitrary circumstances given the non-reciprocal shape of constraints that prevail in the logic of 'mechanical solidarity'. Orderly arrangements retain their validity in inverse ratio to the mutually agreed will of agents to gain in autonomy. Where this will is released and expressed in the domestic or the public sphere it is usually met with particularistic approvals that draw on socially privileged types of ascribed identity (based on age, gender, race, ethnicity or religion); conversely, when this will asserts itself as free will it is met with repressive sanctions that the connotation 'mechanical' carries in Durkheim's conceptual system.[7]

The transition to modernity signalled for Durkheim a shift to a different ground of validity. This was still collective, but this time it drew its vitality from the principles of a democratic society and the moral code through the lens of which modern individuals associated (universally) with knowledge, tolerance and approbation of each other's particularistic horizons of choices based on diverse but institutionally inscribed binding social roles. Durkheim's belief on the moral progress of modernity was certainly not the norm among early sociologists. This is important to keep in mind because, as I shall suggest, CA has only partially articulated the institutional presuppositions of the 'good' and 'just' society that will galvanize institutional pathways to the CCL.

CA in the context of sociological value-theory

CA denies first the route of a value-free science and, second, it implies that objective reality is permeated by 'value' (human dignity), which in terms of theoretical adequacy CA can help to disclose. Both CA theory and policy are driven by the core principle of human dignity. This functions as the axiological a priori of CA. If removed, none of its contentions that follow can be meaningfully sustained. In other words, if human dignity (codified as the CCL) is founded merely on pragmatic grounds without transcendental justifications, or if it is severed in its entirety from a project that discerns in social reality rational spaces where it can flourish, then it concedes a significant asset of its diffusion-capacity. Unintentionally, CA must concede that the value-content implied in capability-empowerments finds no equivalent compensation in collective behavioural patterns and structural roles. This it claims to accomplish largely without recourse to a deeper scrutiny of structural causes in what are taken to be institutional deficits that hollow society's moral resources. Since CA – particularly Sen's supple notion of 'capability' – takes a qualified distance from transcendental accounts of justice and human dignity I will argue in favour of reconsidering such accounts, this time by reference to sociological justifications. Some patience will be required by the reader as a few further detours must be taken before I reattach CA to the problem of values.

As already suggested, the belief in modernity's grounding of values to institutional arrangements capable of yielding consensus and sufficient moral coordination among citizens, so that society functions according to the principles of human dignity and social justice, was shattered early on by Weber. Subsequently, it was taken to task most formidably by Niklas Luhmann. Luhmann will concern us later in the argument, yet a pause with respect to Weber is required not only for substantive reasons in this controversy over values, but also because, unintentionally maybe, CA – particularly Sen's version – seems to offer a normative and ethical reconstruction of a Weberian epistemology. In other words Sen's CA is designed to turn on its head the problem of contingency that troubled Weber so intensely. It hopes to redirect it, without jettisoning its ontological dimension, to serving ethical purposes and goals. Let us see if and how this happens.

In his critical essay on the economist Wilhelm Roscher, Weber provides a dense and difficult passage on the social scientific standpoint on reality. He writes:

> Thus far two possible theoretical goals of historical inquiry have been discussed. A choice in favor of *genetic* features as the theoretical goal and the

> deductive arrangement of these features under abstract, generally valid *formulae*, on the one hand. A choice in favor of the concretely *meaningful* features and the arrangement of these features in universal – but concrete – patterns, on the other. However, there appears to be a third possibility for the logical status of the historical development of cultural phenomena. Suppose one accepts the Hegelian theory of concepts and attempts to surmount the '*hiatus irrationalis*' between concept and reality by the use of 'general' concepts – concepts which, as metaphysical realities, comprehend and imply individual things and events as their instances of *realization*. Given this 'emanatist' conception of the nature and validity of the 'ultimate' concepts, the view of the relation between concept and reality as strictly *rational* is logically unobjectionable. On the one hand, reality can be deduced from the general concepts. On the other hand, reality is comprehended in a thoroughly perceptual fashion: with the *ascent* to the concepts, reality loses none of its perceptual content. The maximization of the content and the maximization of the extension of concepts are, therefore, not mutually unsatisfiable conditions. In fact, they are mutually inclusive. This is because the 'single case' is not only a member of the class, but also a part of the whole which the concept represents. It follows that the 'most general' concept, from which everything must be deducible, would be the concept which is richest in content.
>
> (Weber (1903–1906) 1975, 66–67 [original emphasis])

The first view charted by Weber tends to look at sociocultural reality by recourse to concepts, such as 'Volk' or 'Society' which, instead of functioning heuristically as means to select the relevant problem area for scientific scrutiny, are elevated to the status of holding an objective ontological status. This, for Weber, is an erroneous epistemological view and he imputes it to Roscher. We could even surmise that by analogy collective configurations, such as Durkheim's Society, could just as well be subsumed under Weber's criticism. They would be dismissed as ontological reifications. Weber's own view aligns with the second possibility of a social science that employs '*historical* concepts in order to bring into relief the *concrete* connections between *meaningful* aspects' (62 [original emphasis]) of sociocultural totalities. This can happen by devising ideal-types that reflect these meaningful constellations of conceptual purity without though raising any expectations for some 'idealist' match of their features in all their purity with reality. It is the operation of such typical categories that, according to Weber, puts order into the diversity of the historically coloured subject-matter of sociology. Essential here is Weber's reference to Emil Lask's idea of a *hiatus irrationalis*. Reality, for Lask, is approached by an act of abstraction. Our concepts select problem areas from reality's richness and thus qualify as cognitive slices of reality, which evidently are 'less' adequate than reality. The irrational dimension here is encapsulated in the idea that equipped with categories which are abstracted from reality the social scientist hopes to squeeze reality in schemata that refer only to parts of reality. This paradox can be resolved if the gulf between concepts and reality is seen as a transcendental condition for holding a perspective on reality. Some alleged full correspondence between concept and reality would in effect imply a perspectiveless historical science (see Oakes 1988, 49–53; Beiser 2008, 286–289).

Although Weber addresses a third possibility, eventually he did not regard it as methodologically legitimate. Hegel's dialectical architectonic that, as a logical system, 'contains' reality in its essential categories and includes also the movement from one to the other and the mediations that ensue until this reality becomes actual is, according to Weber, untenable. Concomitantly, reality's alignment with Reason and the quest for historically binding normative configurations that reflect the universality of freedom in its institutional arrangements prompted by the substantive value of justice are to be dismissed. As we have seen, Weber's epistemological and ontological perspective considers life as an inherently irrational spectacle of historically contingent forms of social action, only typically reconstructed by the sociologist's value-relevant perspective. Recognizing, and in fact incorporating, the normative value-objectivism of the Hegelian position in order to fatally undermine it, Weber anticipates the objectivist narrative of values. In this sceptical vein, Weber qualifies the 'Hegelian' position accordingly:

> Certainly, the dignity of the 'personality' lies in the fact that for it there exist values about which it organizes its life; – even if these values are in certain cases concentrated exclusively within the sphere of the person's 'individuality', then 'self-realization' in *those* interests for which it claims *validity* as *values*, is the idea with respect to which its whole existence is oriented. Only on the assumption of belief in the validity of values is the attempt to espouse value-judgments meaningful. However, to *judge* the *validity* of such values is a matter of *faith*. It may perhaps be a task for the speculative interpretation of life and the universe in quest of their meaning. But it certainly does not fall within the province of an empirical science in the sense in which it is to be practiced here.
>
> (Weber (1904) 1949, 55 [original emphasis])

The consequence of Weber's methodology, as is evident in this extract, is that despite the value-relevance of sociological topics, the assertion of the validity of values rests, ultimately, on irrational foundations. Faith, or commitment, are not assigned here the dialectical role they have in Hegel as dialectical adjuncts to reason. Rather, they function as an index of reality's unknowable status. Like the Kantian 'thing-in-itself' reality can be approximated strictly by recourse to regulative means. This is a motif that Weber shares with pragmatism, which in its turn is seen by many commentators as an appropriate mode of sustaining the normative project of freedom and justice in contemporary multicultural, systemically complex and highly contingent social settings and circumstances. Unwittingly maybe, CA shows signs of recourse to a Weberian approach to the social. It takes from Weber the recognition of reality's indeterminacy (and the many facets through which this can appear: cultural, historical, experiential, biographical) and reworks it so that, like Weber, it avoids rendering explanation (in the case of CA it is the explanation of justice) dependent on some 'complete', 'absolute' and 'perfect' normative idea or societal configuration (e.g. a utopian vision of a society free of conflicts, disparities or human flaws). Unlike Weber though, the detachment from a 'metaphysical' or 'transcendental' theory of justice of the good society and some sort of meta-value that can sustain it and suffuse it, is now tweaked, yet not in the direction of disabling normative and ethical ameliorations against social injustice (Weber's irrationality of reality thesis would concede this possibility even as a normative 'fiction' in the morally loaded Kantian sense). Rather, claims to validity of any putative collective configuration of justice are refracted through the deliberative perspective of participants in the democratic process, if capability actualization is to gain a legitimate purchase in the lives of those whose functionings are impeded by contingent social barriers. As we shall see, Sen insists on this view not because he espouses Weber's anti-rationalism but because, in anti-Weberian orientation, he seeks to conjoin rationality and freedom (Sen 2002a).

The reciprocity of rationality and freedom is based on the agents' 'reasoned scrutiny' of the choices they have reason to value in a given (contingent) social setting. Conversely, rationality relies on freedom. Accommodating the diversity of reasons to make informed choices is, according to Sen, an essential ingredient of a broad, but normatively rigorous, notion of rationality. This type of rationality operates beyond 'preselected mechanical axioms' or 'prespecified "appropriate" motivation' like maximization of self-interest. In an important passage Sen writes:

> Our motives are for us to choose – not, of course, without reason, but unregimented by the authoritarianism of some context-independent axioms or by the need to conform to some canonical specification of 'proper' objectives and values. The latter would have had the effect of arbitrarily narrowing permissible 'reasons for choice', and this certainly can be the source of a substantial 'unfreedom' in the form of an inability to use one's reason to decide about one's values and choices.
>
> (2002a, 5–6)

Sen's injunction is powerful enough to align with the autonomy he hopes to preserve for the historically and situationally specific standpoint of the agent who is called to decide on the 'things she has reason to value'. Agents have 'reasons to value' because they are free to act by recourse to what their social context – their 'habitus' (Bourdieu) – prescribes without a value-normative matrix being imposed on them by some external source (of course, the cultural external source has the status of a useful fiction simply because when I draw on my action-plan as a member of a community I also draw on borrowed resources from different cultural settings, 'as if' these constitute an externally validated source). Sen thus invokes the freedom to draw on motivational complexes, entangled with the organizational fabric of a social life, based also on some sort of cooperative nexus of interaction. Hence, freedom is given a space to be converted to pragmatically oriented action in line with real resources and trajectories, so that any sort of value-infringement stemming from 'external' or 'expert' agents is avoided. Sen, particularly in his critique of cultural relativism (Sen 2002a, 476–477), upholds the idea that 'authoritarian' value-impositions are also the property of a single culture. They do not always stem from external ideological invasions. Moreover, agents' motivations can extend and expand beyond their cultural horizons, however the latter may be defined.

This critique of cultural relativism incorporates the problem of values. It is rightly argued (Nussbaum and Sen 1989) that any notion of development must be assessed by reference to some values. These values are culturally patterned and form a major criterion for the validity of action that is held to be channelled towards development. What Nussbaum and Sen intend to argue is that cultures are not bound together by a single value; rather, a single culture (to be sure, an elusive notion itself) may promote diverse but also mutually exclusive values. A project about development is necessarily interlaced with a vision of societal change and, hence, its implementation affects some evaluative frame of reference of society. It is rightly recognized by the two thinkers that some sort of value-lag between accepted but unchangeable values and the objects valued can lead to 'object failure' (Nussbaum and Sen 1989, 300). As a result, activities or social relations contained in the value-orientation of a society fail to materialize.

An additional and maybe more fundamental type of value-change is 'value rejection' (300). Here, the collectively endorsed pattern of value-commitments is manifestly contested and rejected. The qualification Nussbaum and Sen introduce, and this belongs also to their robust critique of relativism, is that in the case of value-rejection what is of cardinal significance is the probability of the detachment of the stationary value-pattern as a result of reasoned internal critique. Because cultures are diverse collective entities and, as they demonstrate in the case of India, contain plural value-sets (302–306), the direction of society's transformation cannot be safely anchored in values of the past, in present values (these are deemed to be marked by 'object failures') or, of course, in future values. Since, as they hold, such value-orientations are unsafe, this pluralism of values is diverted into the pragmatic configuration of new value-patterns that stand the test of reasoned and public criticism. Appeal to public reasoning is of course a rigorous process of mutual testing of validity-claims in the sphere of the *demos*. Here the risk for CA is a lapse on grounding the validity of values on a social convention. As in Popper ((1934) 1980, 37), such an approach considers the emerging conventions to be products of reasoned debate and criticism, yet the purpose of the debate is held to reside not in a rational foundation but to be based on 'decision'.[8] Nussbaum and Sen come close to this position but they do make important qualifications. What generates the foundation of values is a process of societal self-evaluation that comes into fruition as the result of an 'internal' (by recourse to the particular cultural matrix), 'immersed' (incorporating the experiences and standpoints of people's experiences) and 'genuinely critical' (subjecting beliefs and practices into serious scrutiny) method of evaluation (Nussbaum and Sen 1989, 308). If these values figure as essential prerequisites this is because, for Nussbaum and Sen, all approaches to truth are 'value-laden'. They are launched from a particular perspective and this perspective is none other than 'human life' (312). The perspective of 'human life' invoked here functions as the bedrock of the ultimate moral validity of our standpoint on reality. As a methodological appeal to 'internal realism', as Nussbaum and Sen define this methodological desideratum, it serves the purpose of grounding criticism in immanent rather than external criteria (that may be the outcome of conceptual reification). Yet in this strategic move made by Nussbaum and Sen the immanent (internal) evaluation is only methodological. Why not normative too? Why isn't human life being considered an ultimate a priori value? This, as may be recalled, was Marcuse's transcendental normative condition. Instead, the epistemological wedlock of Aristotle and Putnam forged by CA generates the theoretical a priori that sees truth in 'pragmatic partnership' (310) with those whose experiences it aims to meaningfully connect. Following Putnam, Nussbaum and Sen accommodate truth in the shape of an 'internal realism' rather than a 'collapse into idealism and subjectivism' (312).[9]

Now two issues deserve further consideration here. One has to do with the last qualification. 'Idealism' is held clearly to be a vice, pragmatism a virtue. Regardless of the fact that a consistent pragmatist should have entertained the testing of the continuum of past, present and future valuations (because this is what generates the diversity of value-standpoints that renders internal critique possible) the problem of treating idealism as a priori antithetical to pragmatist internal realism begs the question of how idealism is understood. If, following Nussbaum and Sen, in their appellation of the self as a 'relational' entity, we consider the Aristotelian legacy they endorse, then this understanding of values could be seen as unmistakably Durkheimian and Hegelian. Nussbaum and Sen write:

> The effort to develop a position that is consistent over many issues frequently leads to the dropping of immoderate claims on a single issue. But his [Aristotle's, S.G.] method also relies upon the fact that the parties engaged in the procedure identify themselves as social beings (not as isolated units)-beings connected to one another by a network of relations, political, cognitive, emotional (and the political relation is best understood, he believes, as having emotional dimensions). Thus they conceive of the goal of the reflective process as the finding of a view according to which they can live together in a community – a shared and shareable view of value.
>
> (314)

In this brilliant extract Nussbaum and Sen, unwittingly maybe, endorse the essence of sociological idealism but in the shape of realism. Implicitly, they recognize that the dichotomy between the 'real' and the 'ideal' is a spurious one. If human beings do not act as feral selves or Crusoesque solitary entities then this must be inferred from the incontrovertible inductive fact that human beings live together (Durkheim (1893) 1960, 37–38). Human beings accomplish this togetherness via multiple, differentiated, but also complementary relations. This differentiated but shared way of life qualifies for Nussbaum and Sen as the outcome of an ongoing process of reflective argumentation (as broad as possible). This gives rise to a 'shared and shareable view of value'. Now, given their emphasis on Aristotle's primacy of emotions in the political fabrication of human sociality, it is worth recalling that the affective bonding among people joins them in groups and communities the members of which communicate their shared view of value.[10] This shared way of life is invested with value, exists as a value and is experienced as a value. Thus, the reality of people's mutual process of internal criticism about the replacement, partial rectification of the stationary value-pattern is theorized as a value! But the common sociality of the members of a community – this 'shared and shareable view of value' – is abstracted because the very conditions of internal critique are bracketed. This is the sort of pragmatist error that is reproduced by Nussbaum and Sen. It was this asymmetrical view of pragmatism that troubled Durkheim when he posited the foundational level of Society as the means of coordinating knowledge ((1895–1896) 1962, 267). Only if people in a community possess some sort of system and social integration, can 'shared' ways of life be thematized. This meta-level of sociality constitutes for Durkheim an object that is initially similar to the Kantian 'thing-in-itself'. Communities worship it but only in how it appears to them in the guises of God; namely, as a representation outside their own consciousness.

The Hegelian shift we propose takes this perspective further: As long as the 'thing-in-itself' is posited it is known. Now what counts as God has acquired, for Durkheim, additional moral determinations of secular validation, condensed under organic solidarity's elevation of human dignity as the supreme moral value. The internal critique's conditions of possibility powerfully adduced here by CA reside on both this modernist injunction about the value of the individual but also on what rightly Nussbaum and Sen presuppose when they refer to the possibility of 'internal critique'. The failure of a society to act by its own standards contains, however, its own negation. A negation that Durkheim's configuration of mechanical solidarity (the shape of a closed moral system grounded on repression and cultural homogeneity) already contains and is corroborated both empirically and normatively. Empirically because, as he demonstrates through the analysis of Australian tribes, tribal rituals are never merely local. They are composed of representations of 'inter-tribal associations', of divinities with influence and validity beyond the geographical contour of the tribe. Mythological entities extend, for Durkheim, beyond particularistic local barriers to an international sphere of the legitimacy of the tribal or the national communal life. It is this 'universalistic tendency' (Durkheim (1912) 1961, 474) that nourishes the sentiments in question for internal critique to be possible in a society that particularizes its cultural life in inverse direction of its immanent universal affectivity. Seen normatively, this inductive 'first fact' contains the logic of socialism that belongs to the very concept of 'society'. Discussing Saint-Simon, Durkheim approves the inductively undoubted fact that:

> in some shape or form internationalism is observed at all moments in history, for there has never been a people who lived in a state of hermetic isolation. Every society has always had something in common with the neighboring societies it most resembled.
>
> (Durkheim (1895–1896) 1962, 215)

The reference to internationalism and the cosmopolitan ethic that supports it will be reconsidered at the end of this book. For the time being, we can note that Durkheim's defence of affective moral sentiments of universal scope was not in itself a sufficient canopy; nor was the economic reconstruction of society under the moral standing of political vigilance a panacea. Durkheim's entire system presupposes communicative streams of mediations between the institutional spheres of organic solidarity. Thus it idealizes some form of internationalism based on solidary nation-state interdependence, reminiscent of the Kantian ideal of human autonomy's progression in history.

Of course, to return to the problem of cultural internal critique we need to grant that because agents in a culture are caught up into the empirical contingencies and historical circumstances of their lives they cannot fully recall the continuum of past, present and future valuations (although religion's compensation of suffering fulfils this function, as well as the secular ideal of autonomy in just societies that enables us to retrospectively disapprove past injustices *as if* human victims could have had the freedom to choose differently). Agents do, to be sure, recall – collectively and reflectively – a portion of this but the mechanism of collective recall is incumbent upon values. If deliberation presupposes the 'free' work of reflection and the real possibility of considering resourcefully the internal repository of diverse cultural valuations but also, as ingeniously Nussbaum and Sen point out, the cultural capability of considering alternative valuations from other cultures, then the entire enterprise of Nussbaum and Sen stops short of conceiving the pragmatist approach itself as part of an overarching idealist project. For one thing, as we have seen, the internal realism of a shared and relational way of life is experienced as an emotional effervescence. Social bonding has the capacity to elevate, and defer commitment to an object of valuation of a different order, only because human and social relations imply immersion between selves. This is not only a necessity but also an act of willful partial surrender of the self into a higher source of meaning and legitimacy. This higher notion called 'Society' is worthy of our respect because it is its collective continuity – the countless practices of making and remaking our relations – which 'others' synthesize along my agency my will, my desires and my action-plans. If this success of CA in bracketing the ideological anchoring of its practitioners in order to gain an entry into any sociocultural context is always premised on pragmatic contingency then one may wonder if the lessons learned from this process of capability-enhancement and the outcomes accomplished by CA can ever generate an institutional matrix that secures, sustains and develops further the goals of a CCL.

There is, I contend, a risk of categorial conservatism in the reluctance of CA to expand its pursuit of implementing values like freedom, justice and human dignity to a 'logic' of just and 'capable' institutions. Under the prerogative to dissociate itself from dichotomous discourses that separate facts from values, CA runs the risk of reproducing this very dichotomy. The logic that sees institutions only as provisional solutions to problems like income inequality, gender violence, famines and so on, must posit that the world of 'facts' is excessively contingent and that any institutional system cannot sustain an ethical shape (Hegel's *Sittlichkeit*, Marx's communist vision of associated producers, Durkheim's organic solidarity) that claims binding validity of its values, particularly if these coincide with those of CA. While it is undoubtedly the case that Sen and Nussbaum pursue and rigorously test CA in line with multiple institutions that seek to redesign their own normative map (e.g. Nussbaum 2006, 306–324) as well as to generate capabilities-based reforms of a general overlapping consensus (Nussbaum and Sen 1989, 320), the core principles of CA do not seem to contain a provision for a reconstruction of an institutional hub which would articulate just institutions. Consequently, the success of positing a nexus of 'ultimate' ends in the shape of the CCL comes to a halt as it stops short of some alleged institutional transcendentalism, an issue I shall take up in Chapter 6. This sociological reluctance across CA writings equates a transcendental theory of justice with 'perfectly just institutions' and surrenders, alongside its vision of a 'good society', a valuable tool that can suggest why and under what conditions capability deprivations and all sorts of sufferings may arise.

The recent opening of CA to pragmatism from voices within sociology that encourage it (Holmwood 2013, Zimmermann 2006, 2018) has much to offer in the face of reality's contingencies that can only be successfully funnelled into some normative accrual via public reasoning and situated agency. Relying mainly on John Dewey, these approaches, for all their differences, rightly bracket the substantive or even essentialist moments in CA. They liken Sen's substantive normative categories like freedom to an ongoing process of social interaction that requires subtle and pragmatically flexible operationalization. Given this turn in sociological literature on CA I shall only discuss the Dewey–Putnam heritage in CA and contend that other approaches to the value-constitution of social life provide necessary supplements to pragmatism.

A Durkheimian rejoinder

The distinguished philosopher Hilary Putnam, a champion of CA, regenerates the value-discourse and, following pragmatism, takes issue with the fact/value distinction. He argues (2002, 34–43) that 'thick' ethical concepts, like being 'cruel', can be used both descriptively and normatively and thus elide the demarcation between 'is' and 'ought'. To claim that a parent is cruel to her children is both a description and a normative criticism, without in need of adding a 'thin' normative qualification (like, 'she is a bad parent'). One may add that the normative thickness of the characterization 'cruel' in this example of parenthood draws, implicitly at least, in a form of social consequentialism (i.e. that cruelty is an act that damages the body, the psychological well-being of human personality and the sociality of the agent who suffers from it) and, moreover, that this sort of consequentialism acquires its force from an implicit teleological (ethical) assumption about (just) parenthood (e.g. Winfield 1998). Although this is not the place to advance this argument in detail, the upshot here is that a family or a caregiving niche cannot be described adequately, if cruelty and suffering for some of its members are ongoing practices, without some sort of normative weight being contained into the very notion of 'cruelty'. Because parenthood is an ongoing and complex process of socialization it cannot, of course, be compressed into the moments of cruelty. These may as well be exceptional, contingent (as arising from momentary anger, professional anxiety and thus of role-conflict strains) or routine in cases, for example, of caregivers' chronic substance addiction, or in terms of total coercion (physical, sexual, psychological, social) as in the infamous Fritzl case. The point is that no matter how many qualifications are introduced, the act of cruelty is normatively thick in its manifestation in experience and descriptive in terms of how this or that parent treats children. Even in the extreme case of 'cruel' decisions that mitigate a worst form of cruelty than the one actually inflicted, the tragedy and even incomprehensibility of being forced to choose from two 'cruel' options does not mitigate the fact that the suspension of cruelty (for all), requires cruelty for at least one person.[11]

Putnam's justifications extend to Sen and his version of CA. Putnam's qualified association of Sen with Weber's methodology (2002, 63) aims at distancing Sen from the risk of value-absolutism if by value-absolutism (or in a more modest way of putting it, of a value-laden methodology) we understand, *pace* Putnam, the following: that although the selection of the question we decide to address is value-relevant, the 'answer' we intend to provide should not be prescribed by the set of values we chose when we select a problem area for study. I don't think that Sen's work in economics is subject to this risk. Yet this way of construing the methodological challenge of bridging facts and values can be misleading. It can be taken to generate implications that shift Sen to the perspective of *hiatus irrationalis.* To divorce the question of values from reality imputes to Sen's project in the perspective that would empty reality from binding value-standpoints. This option Weber would endorse. The sympathetic critique against Sen's alleged 'methodological individualism' (Stewart and Déneulin 2002)[12] may have been effectively rebutted by Sen (2002b), yet both critique and rebuttal stop short of considering the mediations between the problem of a reality (which contains 'value') and a social science that judiciously pursues this specific disclosure of social reality in this axiological sense. Yet Sen's entanglement in the *hiatus irrationalis* does not aim to undermine value-objectivity but rather to take seriously value diffusion in society. Thus, the reformulation of the Weberian epistemological hiatus appears as 'the choice of evaluative space'

(Sen 1992, 20) from which, for instance, a problem like inequality will have to be addressed and studied. This is a second-order demarcation launched from within the first-order value-relevant distinction, which posits that inequality ought to be addressed, understood and confronted at those focal points where it is shown to obstruct people's agency, capabilities and functionings. (The latter criteria are by no means mutually reinforcing when studying inequality; taken together though they delineate the notion of a human person's freedom for self-realization from which the rest of distinctions emanate.) Instructive here is a short essay by Sen titled 'Description as Choice' (Sen 1982). Here Sen follows the value-problem in terms of the selection of an 'evaluative space'. Recognizing though that social science made a great effort to disentangle its entire epistemological integrity from the ballast it received by positivists, it now runs the risk of regress into a sort of prescriptive 'imperialism' (1982, 447). Chiding the work of a sociologist (i.e. Mollie Orshansky), whose work I confess I am at fault not to be familiar with, Sen takes issue with her claim that 'poverty is a value judgment' and 'like beauty, lies in the eye of the beholder' (Orshansky quoted in Sen 1982, 446). Sen's brief but caustic retort is that poverty is a descriptive judgment based obviously on selection. As such, it qualifies as a value for a given society the members of which select to describe it as a value-problem. In his words, 'poverty description will then *reflect* socially held value judgements rather than *be* value judgements themselves' (446 [original emphasis]). In the next paragraph, he tells us that to 'describe what prescriptions are made is a description, not a prescription' (446). It seems to me that Sen is correct to transfer the problem to the realm of social conventions but, as I have already argued, this is still a descriptive judgment because, as Sen admits, it only tells us what people hold to be a value. Thus, formally, it is of the same rank as the subjective theory of value endorsed by Orschansky. Who the 'beholder' is makes little difference in this case. If we follow, instead, as I do here, Durkheim, then the problem of value is transferred to the domain of collective validity. This approach, formally again, bears resemblance to the conventionalist understanding of value-judgments. The difference though is that not everything can qualify as a justified convention; in Durkheim, for instance, the status of value clearly entails a judgment about the value-constitution of the object (i.e. society and the extent to which it nourishes human dignity, or not.). Thus Durkheim abstracts towards what is only – epistemologically, not normatively though – implicit in Sen, namely the worth of the conventions for which poverty is selected as a problem: Or, in a qualified Weberian mode, the type of society for which alleviation of poverty would be 'relevant'. This realm of collective validity is obviated by CA in its entirety and it is ironic that logical positivists like Kraft had a keener eye for the social constitution of the value-problem. Of course, CA addresses this problem in its policy agenda; otherwise none of its (normative) selections (i.e. poverty, famine, gender, race, disability capability deprivations among others) would have been made and pursued. The tension I detect has to do with the policy – epistemology hiatus that, of course, Sen's partial orderings aim to justify. Instead of aiming at an 'all or nothing' requirement of perfect and complete orderings of preferences or value-rankings, the option of 'partial orderings' builds on the congruence and intersection of several distinct incomplete orderings or rankings.[13] This is indeed what informs CA policy. Yet to the extent that the policy outcome is not registered as a reentry into the (pragmatic) broadening of the type of social conventions (as a shared way of life), this hiatus raises justified complaints about the lack of an institutional approach to justice (and, I would add, to values)!

On this issue other sociologists formed an altogether different conception of the collective beyond, but also inclusive, of social conventions. In fact it was Durkheim's thought that sought to unfold the logic behind the equation of the Collective to Society and then to pursue linking Society, as an historical project, to the moral individualism that served as the ethical project of his sociology. In the triptych 'Collective–Society–Individual' Durkheim never divorced facts from values. In fact, like the striking ideas of Viktor Kraft, the collective figures as the ultimate realm of the validity of values. In other words, the object itself (human beings *living* in historical societies) is invested with value. It is the object's movement in history as the self-understanding of agents who gradually desire to see themselves as autonomous authors of their lives together that generates valued patterns of social interaction and hence the belief that reality contains value. Even if we assume that science abstains from ethical prescriptions, then we ought to reconsider the sense in which we qualify science with criteria of success and objectivity. Durkheim – in an impressive anticipation of Dewey's theory of values[14] but more in line maybe with Marcuse's sharp criticism of Dewey[15] – suggests that science:

> tells us simply what is necessary to life. But obviously, the *supposition, man wishes to live*, a very simple speculation, immediately transforms the laws science establishes into imperative rules of conduct. [...] Even on the ultimate question, whether we ought to wish to live, we believe science is not silent.
>
> (Durkheim (1893) 1960, 34–35 [original emphasis])

We can rightly assume that this is also Sen's vision of science. Sen's 1998 Nobel Prize on economics and his entanglement of ethics and economics confirm the normative scope of his understanding of science. The reservation expressed here has to do with the fact that, unlike Durkheim and partially in line with Dewey and Putnam, Sen brackets the internal possibility of science's axiological transformation following this ultimate value-judgment about man's desire to live (presumably, according to a lifestyle that reflects his control over the conditions of his life). In this sense he decouples the validity of scientific knowledge from its social conditions of possibility. The conditions of possibility of scientific knowledge require a degree of institutional coordination and legitimacy in the shared nexus of agents' lives, even if the latter are reproducing practically only lay 'scientific' explanations of reality. Durkheim writes that in:

> opposition to Kant, however, we shall show that the notion of duty does not exhaust the concept of morality. It is impossible for us to carry out an act simply because we are ordered to do so and without consideration of its content. For us to become the agents of an act it must interest our sensibility to a certain extent and appear to us as, in some way, desirable. [...] Something of the nature of duty is found in the desirability of morality. If it is true that the content of the act appeals to us, nevertheless its nature is such that it cannot be accomplished without effort and self-constraint. The *élan*, even the enthusiasm, with which we perform a moral act takes us outside ourselves and above our nature, and this is not achieved without difficulty and inner conflict. It is this *sui generis* desirability which is commonly called *good*.
>
> ((1924) 1974, 36 [original emphasis])

This remarkable passage from Durkheim bears on a number of significant sociological modifications on major epistemologies like Kant's and Hume's. The reference to 'desire' is crucial because it strikes at the heart of the idea of agency as an autonomous process of authorship of the self and the collective to which one belongs to.[16] The shift from Kantian moral rigorism to the content of morality enables Durkheim to adduce a normative content from the very movement of the real. For him, as we know, the movement of the real is logically and normatively tethered to the configurations of mechanical and organic solidarity. If there is 'effort' in bringing about morality and this practical engagement exalts us to experience our being under the auspices of a sacred realm, then this transcendence of the self is no other than the sociality to which the agent 'returns' as a co-author of her normative coordinates. In mechanical solidarity this co-authorship is blighted because it suffers from an undifferentiated shape of the collective experienced as a thoroughly 'external' force over the individual. In contrast, organic solidarity fosters a relation of the collective to the individual based on differentiation, intersection (interdependence) and communicative vitality among the human organs (ethical personhood) of morality's diffused differentiation into every tissue of the social fabric. Durkheim's solution to Hume's problem (namely, of the impossibility of deducing value-judgments from judgments of reality) is that both factual and value-judgments address reality. The difference lies in the fact that the reality to which value-judgments are directed is of a collective substance. If by morality we configure the nature of our sociality then the level of the 'good' must be sought in the collectively desired level of intersubjective institutions of mutuality and freedom. Thus, the 'principal social phenomena, religion, morality, law, economics and aesthetics, are nothing other than systems of values and hence of ideals' ((1924) 1974, 96). Sociology's task, for Durkheim, is to reconstruct the affective component of values through the 'negative' moment of desiring to, so to speak, transcend ourselves. We desire to do so not necessarily in terms of an ontology of labour (Hegel, Marx) which raises us to the status of becoming 'owners' of the world's materiality. Rather, the substructure, so to speak, beneath this materialist synthesis (division of labour) is the desire of being-oneself-in-the-other given human's capacity for reciprocal broadening but also (as an inbuilt deficit) of human incompleteness. In Durkheim's vision of human sociality this anthropological modicum is already theorized on the level of collective effervescence, which in itself stands for the 'ecstatic' (to move beyond oneself) positioning of the self in the world. This synthetic result of human connectivity may account for how Durkheim understands Kant's synthetic unification of empirical phenomena. Durkheim depicts it as the point where 'all the forces of the universe converge' creating a new synthesis which 'surpasses in richness, complexity and power of action all that went to form it' (97). Durkheim's equation of society's heightened consciousness with organic solidarity is justified on the grounds of a historically unfolded and consolidated mediation between the 'individual' and the 'collective'. In this mediation the 'human personality is a sacred thing; one dare not violate it nor infringe its bounds, while at the same time the greatest good in communion with others' (37). This approach to society and to ethics is, as I have argued elsewhere (Gangas 2007), of Hegelian roots and inspiration and it constitutes the normative focus with which CA, as I argue in this book, can be reconstructed sociologically.

'Valuing values' in CA[17]

Nussbaum confirms the commitment to the pragmatic approach to values founded on the open, democratic processes of deliberation in specific communities. She does not, however, jettison the valid claim made by agents when they invoke 'abstract values'. By 'abstract values' Nussbaum (1994) understands the set of universalistic values as these are inscribed in the 'abstract ethical language of rights, justice, equality, and personhood', the same abstract values that postmodern thought sought to demolish as useless fictions. At the other end, her pragmatic sympathies lead her to a position not far from Durkheim's views on judgments of value and judgments of reality. She, like him, holds that the dualism 'ideal and real' (Nussbaum 2013, 383–385) is simplistic and misleading because ideal sets of principles (like constitutions) operate in reality as founding pillars for coordinating countless trajectories of human action, aiming precisely to recognize, but also to mitigate, the real imperfections of people whose lives can never be fully elevated to the ideal normative blueprint of social life.

Because reference to binding values has been accompanied with suspicion, if not with hostility as in postmodern criticism, Nussbaum's argument about an overlapping consensus (American pragmatism, Kantian moral philosophy, Rawls' theory of justice, Habermas' communicative action, Sen's CA) rests on the 'rational justification of political values' (1994, 210), an assumption that is itself derivative of the possibility that such values must have accomplished a sufficient degree of consolidation in institutions and value-commitments of the modern democratic polity. Values, in other words, are only quasi-abstract. If, for example, we see human rights today as an important normative hook, especially for those who invoke them more desperately and ardently, as is the case of women's plights described in Nussbaum's article, then any such claim must be set as valid not simply through faith in the transcendent or, put in more secular terms, in their utopian projection of historical praxis but, rather, through a recall of their actuality in real societies and contexts.

Now Nussbaum provides us with a remarkable passage about how abstract values are felt by the agent. Invoking Kant's famous passage in the conclusion of *The Critique of Practical Reason* where he conjoins the infinity of the universe with the rational moral law of the human being as an end in itself (Kant (1788) 1997, 133), Nussbaum writes:

> speaking abstractly can be a way of expressing the special reverence and awe with which we regard certain ethical norms. We picture them as if they stood outside us, even though in a sense we are well aware that they stand within us, so that we can express our wish to be bound by them at all times, even we wish to do otherwise. [...] Kant here explicitly denies that the moral law is external. What he says is that he regards its presence in himself *with the same awe* with which he views the heavens.
>
> (1994, 212)

This Kantian formulation of the problem connects up to Durkheim's similar trope of society and the awe its collective representation incites in the individual consciousness. Like Kant, this moral constrain is not external, yet, paradoxically, it assumes the shape of externality, similar to the 'impact' the starry heavens assume in Kant's statement. The analogy between the externality of the moral law and the universe is reconstructed in Durkheim's ethical theory as the equation of society with God, and, consequently, with the authorship of the universe. But what Durkheim introduces with this seemingly eccentric equation is this: The mechanism for synthesis, indeed the very galaxy of individual forces and the way these mutually attract one another weaving the social fabric, is no other than Society clothed as the supra-individual force towards which we feel awe, reverence, fear and wonder. The exaltation of the moral law within me is the perspective of my life through the standpoint of universality; this universality matches, for Durkheim, the standpoint of a moralized world community that conforms to the regulative ideal of the authorship of social life from the perspective of autonomy. Kant's repeated religious semantics with respect to the force of morality are transposed by Durkheim to the realm of values that society, as a representation of collective labour, infuses to the daily realm of profane and secular life. While Nussbaum rightly underlines the impact of exaltation and awe in the moral law and its abstract values, the sociological semantics of locating the moral law into the higher authority of society is missing. This, I repeat, is the reason why Durkheim is so essential in recovering the force of normativity of CA. Durkheim writes that 'collective representations are the result of an immense cooperation, which stretches out not only into space but into time as well; to make them a multitude of minds have associated, united and combined their ideas and sentiments'; hence, as Durkheim adds in the same passage, the richer and more complex, nature of Society ((1912) 1961, 29). Thus, this abstraction of values and their ability to stir our emotions must come from a different reality, or from a different level of value coordination. Kant intuited of course the sociality of awe but this task was carried further by Hegel's project of transferring the awe-inspiring imprint of morality to the agent of synthesis of human freedom, the modern *Sittlichkeit*. This is an omission that CA needs, I think, to reconsider and, as is the case with Nussbaum, it points to the logical outcomes (but also the latent presuppositions) inbuilt in the moral compass of CA.

Durkheim's blend of Kant and Hegel equipped him with the epistemological and normative tools to uphold an abstraction and yet, simultaneously, to sublate it. For Society's richness of content and moral authority is not conceived as a reified realm. Rather, 'if society is something universal in relation to the individual, it is none the less an individuality itself, which has its own special physiognomy and its idiosyncracies; it is a particular subject and consequently particularizes whatever it thinks of' ((1912) 1961, 493). Justifying Kant's view of morality as the possibility of its extension to every will, Durkheim hopes to demystify it and, like pragmatism, dissolve the dualism, while at the same time taking it seriously as a moment of negation that is part and parcel of the willing effort (and the concomitant resistance with which it can be met) of the agent to fulfil himself in being-with-the-other. Nussbaum's Kantian defence of abstract values represents the inverse reflection of society's authority that capability deprivations tear apart. Because torn apart from this widest niche of collective meaning and congealed as contingent (and not universal in the Kantian sense) moral conditions, the invocation of the resolution of this conflict has to summon the 'Good' in the shape of abstract values. Elsewhere, Nussbaum (1999, 79–80) intimates this Kantian reverence in terms of the radical content of the value of human flourishing in unison with liberal principles. Again though a collective authority that has as its content the moral individualism she also endorses remains unaddressed.

Durkheim's final move here is, I think, Kantian although it prepares the road to Hegelian sociology. Durkheim writes that:

> [t]he kingdom of ends and impersonal truths can realize itself only by the cooperation of particular wills, and the reasons for which these participate in it are the same as those as those for which they cooperate. In a word, there is something impersonal in us because there is something social in all of us, and since all social life embraces at one both representations and practices, this impersonality naturally extends to ideas as well as to acts.
>
> (Durkheim (1912) 1961, 494–495)

Consequently, the task of sociology, which we shall take up further in Chapter 6, is to show how this value-relation of individuals to collectivity can be inscribed in the institutional arrangements of modernity, in spite of their deficiencies, dysfunctions and alienating moments. In this sense, Durkheim hopes to resolve, like

Hegel before him, the problem of morality and empirical life by explicating both the dignity of the human person as well as the moral dignity of the object (i.e. the movement of society's institutional configurations that enable the agent's particularity to become fulfilled through membership in rational 'we'-formations). This 'object' is the structure of the just and free society, over and above the failures of contingent historical formations of such social arrangements.

The solution to the problem of the fact/value dichotomy was, as we have seen with Marcuse's criticism of Dewey, part of the Marxist normative compass. We shall rekindle Marxism's compatibility issues with ethics in Chapter 4, particularly, since CA draws from Marx's inventory of implicit ethical values, mainly through the notion of abundance (Heller 1972), which partially informs the CCL. Sen's contribution to the theory of social justice provides a bridge between political liberalism and Marxian ethics, primarily because Sen prefers the discourse of values, updating thus value-theory's relevance to current issues regarding political and economic unfreedom. As I have argued elsewhere (Gangas 2010), CA has the advantage of restructuring economic categories and values from a normative perspective that emphasizes the institutional dimension of freedom.

The basic layer of values identified as freedom coupled with its negation in the form of 'capability deprivation' constitutes a 'recalcitrant fact' wherever and whenever economic configurations claim completeness, while still embedded in policies of social exclusion and capability deprivation. Although Sen is tactically right to refuse to uncouple incommensurability from the possibility of reasoned evaluation (travelling abroad and having a medical operation are incommensurable, he tells us, but there is no reason to doubt reasoned judgment about any of them) (Sen 2009, 240–241), both decisions have to be comprehended by recourse to the meta-value of a life that is worth living and the freedom (capability) of the agent to make that choice free of coercion and deprivation. Because this meta-value is often transferred to a sphere of commensurability with self-interest or with the commodity form of value, Sen's CA focuses on the institutional sphere of the free pursuit of individual interests. Studying the market as a value-laden component of society, yet one that appears either to function as independent of values or as a common denominator of all other values, is the project of Sen's 'ethics and economics' to which I now turn.

Notes

1 It should be noted that the a priori of life from which social theory begins and to which it returns is elucidated systematically in early Marcuse's brilliant reconstruction of Hegel's category of 'Life' (Marcuse (1932) 1987), which I shall take up again in Chapter 3.

2 We should add here – and this is crucial – that when Sen (1985, 180) rebuts the 'a priori requirement of the legitimacy of a moral principle' in moral justification he does not necessarily shy away from moral completeness (in the sense of binding value-judgments). Rather, he seems to suggest that morally binding acts do not seem to require a meta-moral justification in order for an absolute distinction between

moral and non-moral action (or principles) to be drawn. If the criterion of moral justification changes, then incompleteness or value-conflict may be bracketed and, thus, a way for thinking about broader moral rankings can reopen. (This is what lies, I think, behind the accommodation – but also 'negation' in the dialectical sense – of value-conflicts when capabilities and functionings become the relevant evaluative space, as opposed to utilities.) Differentiating values (as 'valuational priorities') into interdependent domains of 'instrumental freedoms', allows Sen to curb the one-dimensional conception, which opposes selfish to collective interest and, moreover, to tackle intermediate institutions, characterized by mixed practices of mediation between 'oneself and all' (Sen 1987, 20). Countering the premises of orthodox economic theories of 'development', Sen discloses the necessity of wider institutional arrangements couched in 'valuational priorities'. CA involves the very possibility of agents to *function* as *capable* of choosing objects of value (43). These values contribute substantially to the wider scope of justice revitalizing thus the main thrust in the natural law tradition along principles compatible with modern political institutions.

3 For the nineteenth-century intellectual climate that gave rise to the introduction of axiology (value-theory) in sociology, see Brecht (1959), Frondizi (1963) and Schnädelbach (1984). Still the most instructive and penetrating analysis on the merge of neo-Kantian epistemology and axiology among the classical founders of sociology seems to me to be Gillian Rose's *Hegel Contra Sociology* ((1981) 1995). The trail of value-theory into sociology up until late twentieth century is traced by Joas ((1997) 2000). We focus on neo-Kantianism because, as Beiser (2009) correctly argues, the problem of normativity and the fact–value relationship (the context of Putnam's defence of Sen) reached an unprecedented degree of sophistication in this episode in intellectual history with major protagonists Windelband, Lask and Rickert. For our purposes, replenishing the concept of value requires both a conception that takes off from real deprivations and sufferings, like CA, and one that does not lose sight of the epistemological battles over axiology from which it is doubtful if contemporary accommodations of normativity can be entirely disentangled.

4 We need to be constantly alert about the complexity of the controversy over values, particularly in Weber. Important here is Weber's defence of the 'value sphere' to which he imputes logical 'dignity'. Although he demarcates facts from values Weber, nonetheless, ascribes to value-commitments a major role in scientific inquiry, politics and agency. Bruun, having provided an exhaustive account of the value-problem in Weber, writes: 'Weber nowhere claims that 'value of values' can be *demonstrated* as valid; instead, he formulates it and supports it with the whole weight of his committed personality' ((2007) 2016, 75 [original emphasis]). This accommodation of the 'value of values' by sheer commitment operates, as will be shown later in this chapter, in stark contrast to Nussbaum's (1994) normative call to 'valuing values' and to the social validity of values as a universe of self-determining agents in just institutional arrangements.

5 It is of extreme significance to acknowledge that with respect to agency, capabilities can be indexed with a positive or negative value sign. Although there is no mention of Scheler (and his 'value-disvalue' modalities), Stewart and Déneulin (2002) place Sen's CA within the axiological agenda. They emphasize how agency is enveloped in structural environments that carry a positive or negative value-signification. For them:

> Sen asserts that development is a matter of expanding the capabilities that people have reason to value. These capabilities do not encompass the ability to do or be anything a human being can do or be since some capabilities have negative values (e.g., committing murder), while others may be trivial (riding a one-wheeled bicycle). Hence there is a need to differentiate between 'valuable' and non-valuable

> capabilities, and indeed, within the latter, between those that are positive but of lesser importance and those that actually have a negative value.
>
> (2002, 67)

It is probable that Scheler would concur. This request to differentiate values contains, implicitly at least, a prerogative to prioritize certain capabilities as opposed to others. This is the problem of value-hierarchy that Scheler attempted to found. The fact that Sen and Nussbaum (via the CCL) are forced to confront prioritization keeps the project of a rational normative hierarchy of values *qua* capabilities open and prescient.

6 The bulk of misinterpretations on Hegel's allegedly 'authoritarian' and oversocialized logic is fortunately behind us thanks to historical and scholarly work that has now demolished this myth. A Hegelian defence of value in terms of a coordination of 'different value systems' among interdependent societies, suggests that:

> the universal objective standard of value can only be the complete and comprehensive fulfilment of human personality, which is not, however, and cannot be, exclusively individual or subjective, because it can only be guaranteed through participation in a fully developed and comprehensive social structure,
>
> Harris (1987, 247–248)

7 These two terms that form (since Herbert Spencer) the bread and butter of systems theory carry, for Durkheim, a strong normative and critical load. This can be encapsulated in the idea that the 'mechanical' aspect is tied to notions of 'necessity', whereas the 'organic' dimension seems to carry denotations that make it compatible with the values of freedom and justice and the institutional matrix that supports it. The legacy here owes to Aristotle, Kant and Hegel (on the latter and Durkheim, see Gangas 2007). The two forms of social order (mechanical and organic solidarity), if these interpretations are plausible, as I believe they are, allow the possibility of a teleological argument, where the problem of how the agent acts in terms of his fulfilment and of choices made based on her will is largely heteronomous in the case of 'mechanical' solidarity (ends are assigned by an external to the agent cause, as if stemming from an abstractly transcendent entity). Solidarity in this case acquires a repressive or, even, a coercive force. In contrast, organic solidarity encapsulates a system of ends where the parts communicate freely, unblocked by external to their will constraints. This is now a system of institutional ends that partially coincides with modernity as Durkheim visualized it. Modernity's democratic morals suffuse society in its entirety, including, as we shall see in Chapter 2 the market. Organic solidarity is thus a system of autonomy (freedom) (Durkheim (1893) 1960, 130–131). On Durkheim's part, the dialectical mediation of one configuration by the other (i.e. the 'organic' spontaneity of agents in mechanical solidarity (which can be sublimated or repressed) and the 'mechanical' moments of constraints in organic solidarity (the binding and limiting function of the democratic constitution – the sociological shape of Rousseau's *volonté generale*)) betrays a function of these two types of 'social logic' beyond an ideal-typical function. (I shall take up briefly in Chapter 2 the Sen–Rousseau–Durkheim reconstruction).

8 The connection with Popper is not, I think, superficial nor does it aim to argue that Popper's approach to values informs Sen's vision. The problem with Popper and Sen in this case is that they both (paradoxically though for theories that ground epistemologies in openness and revisability of criteria of success) hesitate to posit a foundation from which scientific growth, political piecemeal revisions or comparative broadening are being launched and are tested themselves as successful standpoints beyond the value-judgments that are subject to broadening revisionary work. For example, in one of Sen's early pieces on values, we read that 'no value judgment is demonstrably basic' but instead can be hypothetically be considered as basic until surviving tests at

refutation. He adds that 'there is an obvious analogy with the practice in epistemology of accepting tentatively a factual hypothesis as 'true', until and unless some new observations refute that hypothesis' (Sen 1967, 53).

9 It needs to be recalled that Hegel contains also a melioristic ontology in texts like *The Phenomenology of Spirit*. But for Hegel, this happiness should obtain rational features, if it is to be coordinated – relationally as CA and pragmatists like Dewey propose – to others to whom they relate in determinate intersections of action-plans, behavioural patterns and institutional relations. Hegel's dialectics, at least in his social philosophy, is nothing other than the ladder of personal freedom in the series of logically interrelated institutional determinations of the self. Because this is a differentiated notion of freedom, it considers (rather than bluntly pushing them to the indeterminate realm of 'ifs') those spaces where negativity can be experienced as unhappiness or capability deprivation (impediment to self-actualization for Hegel) in the self's effort to own her sociality. This is not the place to engage in a systematic presentation of this claim. In his monumental commentary on Hegel's *Phenomenology* Harris has thoroughly demolished the mystification of Hegel in the hands of critics' mystification of criticism. In clarifying what Absolute Knowledge is, and aptly titling the relevant section 'The Republic of the Learned', Harris writes:

> Hegel's '*science* of experience' only becomes possible when the religious consciousness of the human community has become completely *rational*, i.e. when we can show that it is the objective expression of a logical consciousness of what human rationality (theoretical and practical) really *is*, and of what the natural boundaries and social conditions of its realization are. The social structure of the community – our universal shared consensus about how we ought to act, and how we are to treat one another, together with our consensus about 'values', i.e. about the goals which make life 'good' – all of this (and the institutions by which the consensus is maintained and where necessary enforced) is the substance of Reason.
> (1997b, 709 [original emphasis])

Pragmatists are also working within this universe of Reason because this is the universe conceptualized by us as members, ultimately, of a single universal community. Presumably, meliorism would not consider discarding as a result of life's and reality's 'ifs' the democratic consensus and the institutions that support it, those that is which give credence to pragmatism as a free, scientific and rational endeavour. The suspension of the fact/value dichotomy, as Putnam (2002) rightly discerns in Sen, must mean, if symmetry is to be maintained, that values need to be imputed to the subject-matter of what the pragmatic approach to knowledge (and communal life) must, by default, contain. This is no other than the freedom of the self and the freedom of rational, historically binding, social structures, in the absence of which the very pragmatist undertaking must always restart from a social ground zero. But this self, as Nussbaum and Sen concede, is a relational self, and thus capable of retaining her freedom to choose the lifestyles she has reason to value as a trajectory within the social institutions in relation to which capabilities are set up as abstractions by recourse to the values (as historically transcendental conditions of the possibility to be free) we know make life 'good' and in the absence of which capability would collapse into the very formalism that both Sen and Nussbaum struggle to overcome. This risk, however, is downplayed by Nussbaum (2001) when she primes an 'overlapping consensus' based – in line with Putnam, as she admits – on 'legitimate' interests without recourse to a deeper level of objectivity, accepting some incommensurability between different 'comprehensive doctrines' (887), similar to different versions of ultimate valuations couched on non-arbitrary criteria of value-relevance. It needs to be noted that Sen's arguments in favour of evaluative consequentialism require, albeit obliquely, a qualification about the specific historical circumstances (a global world of unprecedented systemic complexity) that render it an adequate approach to ethics. Sen thus recognizes that we:

> live in an interdependent world in which the realization of our respective freedoms interconnects in a variety of ways, and we cannot treat them each as an isolated island. The discipline of consequential evaluation forces us to take responsibility for our choices, since our actions influence other people's freedoms and lives as well as our own.
>
> (Sen 2000, 500)

There is a Weberian resonance here in terms of the ethics of responsibility and the realist requirements in a world governed by value-wars (see, for example, Weber (1904) 1949, 16).

10 Durkheim considers sociality as the proximity of individual selves and their social division of communal space and 'time' into regions and units to 'sympathetic values' (Durkheim (1912) 1961, 24). What is remarkable in Durkheim is the sociological intuition of the project of CA. Durkheim says that 'the development of the individual reproduces that of the species in abridged fashion' ((1893) 1960, 340). The abridgement invoked here is seen both as a moment of a fully lived life, that is a life *as if* desired to be lived universally, since it would partake of the capacities of the species. This is why Durkheim, after having identified the (causal) factors of division of labour, asserts that 'civilization can become an end, an object of desire, in short, an ideal' ((1893) 1960, 330). We would add that civilization can become a value. This, for Durkheim (340), is among the accomplishments of sociology: the reconciliation of 'mechanism' (i.e. causes) with value. The type of civilization that generalizes this reconciliation is organic solidarity. Its democratic, institutional structure (i.e. the form) and the ideals that support it has been gradually raised into its own content (i.e. the freedoms of its citizens to cooperate under complex (thus, invested with the germ of conflict) duties and processes in advanced division of labour).

11 This example is drawn from the case of a Greek mother who, as reported by Arendt ((1951) 1973, 452), was forced by the Nazis to select which of her three children should be executed. This type of moral dilemma cannot be countered effectively by Sen, when he advises 'relaxation of compulsiveness' and 'basicness' in how value-judgments are formed in order to resolve 'conflicts of values' (1967, 55). For Sen, 'basic' value-judgments are ones where 'no conceivable revisions of factual assumptions can make' a person 'revise the judgment' (50). Much of what this conflict of values is incumbent on has to do with the overarching context and framework within which the value-conflict is generated. Value-conflicts have profoundly different impact and degree of constraint, as suggested by Arendt's example. Putnam follows Sen in suggesting that no ultimate value-judgment can be seen as 'basic'. Putnam's verdict is that Sen claims that appeal to 'basic' value-judgments is ultimately an 'unverifiable' undertaking (Putnam 2002, 77). He bases his alignment with Sen on the latter's assumption that 'judgments on certain specific fields (e.g. the rightness of taking interests) must be basic in everyone's value system, does not seem to be particularly realistic' (Sen 1967, 53). Elsewhere, and on a similar to the Greek mother example, Sen (1985, 214–216) comments on moral dilemmas about killing someone to save others. In such cases, however, it is moral reasoning itself that is exploded (i.e. Arendt's version of 'radical evil') precisely because all options (and consequences) are available and equally terrible, given the coercive nature of the demand.

12 I tend to agree with the authors on the urgency of institutional amplification in Sen's programme. Yet there is a risk in the interpretation that imputes methodological individualism to Sen. Maybe the recourse to individualism (even if by this we mean the methodological approach that aligns with Weber) is animated by the heuristic

injunction to abstract from the justification of social settings, not because these are deemed innessential – as Sen (2002b) also emphatically admits – but because 'in the last instance' the problem of freedom can only be assessed practically (Kant) and by real flesh-and-blood persons (Marx). There is in Sen's CA – less so in Nussbaum's – a sort of 'cunning of Reason' at work. To construct an ethical and normative programme in line with individualism (even if the latter stems from utilitarianism) enables CA to 'imitate' the conceptual apparatus of what still appears in mainstream economics (and the political officials that still champion it) as a hegemonic discourse. It can thus operate as an immanent critique of substantive methodological individualism. Sen responds that the 'presence of individuals who think, choose, and act does not make an approach methodologically individualist; rather, the postulation that the individuals are separated and detached from each other would do that' (2002b, 81). Methodological individualism seems thus to be one side of a Janus-faced reality when the latter does not reproduce (and, consequently, does not confirm in everyday life) the content of Reason, which is no other than freedom. Thus in working from 'within' methodological individualism Sen, tactically at least, enables us to move beyond the illusion of a solitary and rational in his choices individual, detached from normative orientation, non-economic valuations, and without consideration of the capabilities that would enable such individuals (and the corresponding mappings of economists) to expand their practical choices in real settings. Citing Marx from the *Economic and Philosophical Manuscripts* on the abstraction 'Society' over and above individuals and the *Critique of the Gotha Program* and Marx's negation of the subsumption of the human being to the status of 'worker' only, Sen (2002b, 81) induces us to see individuals as holders of multiple identities, as intermeshed in multiple webs of affiliations. Methodological individualism is the obverse side of this abstraction. In the case of a reified notion of Society we deal with a unity from which the real, practical and free affirmation of a shared life is lacking and is only abstractly articulated. In the case of methodological individualism, persons are treated as singularities in the absence of any commitment to the relationships they surround them. In fact this abstraction does not give rise to a fictional Crusoean existence but to a community that 'reproduces' itself after the collective pattern of utilitarian ethics.

13 The unviability of artificially closed value-orderings does not suspend our ability to use freedom as a powerful tool in criticizing child labour, chattel slavery, chronic unemployment, debt bondage or servile marriage across societies. Sen invokes partiality here in a double way: first, by the demand that extreme poverty should be countered immediately without requiring a technical algorithm of the solution; second, even if the technical information was available, the required 'radical changes in ownership' would entail equally radical shifts on the level of political decisions (Sen 1987, 37). This invocation of partiality transforms the project of binding values into an open range of practice and policy-making and frees them from some unalloyed verity implied in absolute value-orderings. It is against this hastiness that a partial value-ranking ought to be defended (Sen 1995, 134). Sen does not reify incompleteness here. On the contrary, he supersedes it as he renders claims to absolute and complete orderings of values an impractical undertaking. To expect fully developed hierarchies of values, in order to start solving practical problems, is a demand that neither empirical life nor theory corroborate as an adequate practical and normative standpoint. The counter-factuality of the demand for completeness in values resides in the everyday capacity of agents to reflect, evaluate, shape, control and change their surroundings in committed ways, without recourse to complete value-orderings. Action freed from claims to absoluteness, however, does not imply decisionism. Rather, Sen takes seriously the rational recognition of agents in how they grasp the undesirable character of injustice and capability deprivation (would a rational being today recognize as desirable a premature death from undernourishment?). For Sen, admitting

'incompleteness does not make the use of a reasoned partial ordering "imperfect" in any sense' (2002a, 622). It is precisely the partiality of valuational priorities that allows us to reintegrate the concept of freedom in economics (see Sen 1984).

14 John Dewey's *Theory of Valuation* offers a standpoint on values that makes it directly relevant to our argument given pragmatism's influence on CA. The ongoing process of practical reflection on reality's contingency is underscored and the democratic mode of resolving and revising the scope and duration of the proposed and successful solutions is deemed essential for the process of value-formation. Dewey is right here, and I think that CA, by and large, would not deviate from Dewey's point that couples valuation to tensions of need-fulfilment encountered in reality. Dewey, in fact, connects this problem-solving capacity to the presence of evils we encounter in human experience (1939, 46–47). Based on this mismatch between desires, interests and possibilities Dewey intimates a latent theory of interlocking interests. This dialectical approach is not far from Hegel. We also know this from Dewey ((1897) 2010 himself (I thank John Holmwood for bringing this text to my attention) on Hegel's influence. Dewey writes: 'An interest represents not just a desire but a set of interrelated desires which have been found in experience to produce, because of their connection to one another, a definite order in the processes of continuing behavior' (1939, 54). Inserting the idea of the relational dimension of desire Dewey is forced to make further accommodations of human sociality into his theory of values. Dewey envisages a non-dualistic theory of valuation that will align 'the world of facts' and the 'world of values' (64). This, he tells us, is the practical challenge that 'sociology' or 'cultural anthropology' (63) will need to demonstrate and to found, so that further social scientific support is mustered towards 'behavior in which emotions and ideas, desires and appraisals, are integrated' (65). Ultimately, for Dewey, the capacity for valuation is likened to a species-being – to use Marx's phrasing – quality distinct from 'nonhuman behavior'. The integration of the knowledge of (non-human) reality with human traits and desires in the form of valued ends-in-view, constitutes, for Dewey, the goal of science, which, as he emphasizes, is 'itself *a* value' (66 [original emphasis]). Science is also 'the supreme means of the valid determination of all valuations in all aspects of human and social life' (66) The conflation of science with validity is an important step into the ground of the validity of values but, as I claim with reference to Durkheim, it is based on an abstraction from the set of other grounds of collective valuation that transfer validity to a still more foundational level. This level must be linked to the relational nexus of modern institutional arrangements that guarantee science's own free inquiry and dissemination of knowledge. I claim that Durkheim had anticipated the dualistic halt to which Dewey hits upon, in spite of the latter's commitment to non-dualism. For Durkheim, as indicated in the citations in the text, the desire to live can be compatible with the scientific knowledge that render this will-to-live (according to principles of autonomy and freedom) the content of scientifically validated knowledge. I think Sen is closer to this normative reading of value and desire that it may initially appear. He certainly primes the claim that 'I desire x because x is valuable for me' rather than 'x is valuable for me because I desire it' (Sen 1985, 190). He even leaves open the consideration of the sociality of value when he grants that someone else's desire may be seen as an indicator for value on the condition that 'I may value your desire fulfillment *as a consequence* of my valuing your success in getting what you yourself value' (190n. 14). Here we can glean the latent premise, that success in accessing what one values presupposes social arrangements where agents are free to choose the lifestyles they have reason to value. Thus, these social arrangements must somehow inscribe in their core values and processes the idea of moral individualism, i.e. the freedom and opportunity to desire 'objects' we value.

15 Marcuse's review of Dewey's essay on values culminates in an immanent critique that recognizes Dewey's meta-anthropological question on the 'reasonable' or

'unreasonable' status of desires and interests. Marcuse imputes a positivistic regress to Dewey when the overemphasis on concreteness and experience takes place at the cost of linking desires and conditions to what Dewey nonetheless recognizes, namely 'existing liabilities and potential resources' (Dewey 1939, 29). This appears to be a reformulation of the constraining/enabling features of an action situation. It points to the fact that although Dewey invites, as seen in the previous note, sociology as a scientific highlighter of the conditions under which desires and interests, as Marcuse critically notes (1941, 146), the delineation of the 'standards' of the 'reasonable' or 'unreasonable' desires and interests are wanting. Marcuse aims, of course, at a theory of valuation that is expected to demonstrate that if current valuations are historically consolidated and (ideologically) coded then, as Dewey also concedes, valuations prime 'the interest of a small group or special class in maintaining certain exclusive privileges and advantages, and that this maintenance has the effect of limiting both the range of the desires of others and their capacity to actualize them' (Dewey 1939, 59). Marcuse's critique of Dewey subsumes the latter's optimism about the revisable tests of valuations, when these are couched in authoritarian sources, to pragmatism's fascination with experience. Experience, Marcuse continues, corroborates fascist valuations about desires and interests built on cruelty and coercion. The freedom Dewey visualizes is in fact relegated to a 'utopian' niche vis-à-vis the subsumption of an ever-growing number of spheres of life to the code of instrumental rationality and of the materialist form of a dichotomous society of producers. By negating the exhaustion of utopia in any science of experience, Marcuse highlights the spurious division between 'is' and 'ought' affirmed by positivism, and, in spite of its formal defence of freedom, by Dewey's pragmatic epistemology of values. Experience thus becomes a weak criterion of the revision Dewey envisages if experience is marred by ubiquitous instances and solid facts of unfreedom. Regardless whether Marcuse's view of capitalist modernity can persuasively generate valid accounts of current institutions as spaces of complete unfreedom, he is, I think, right in claiming that in the prevailing material and intellectual condition of his debate with Dewey, 'the problem of values is, in the last analysis, identical with the problem of freedom' (1941, 147). When Marcuse addresses the 'valence' of values, as the 'realm which points beyond the respective factual situation' ((1929) 1980, 137), he is in effect positing the ideational hook, the 'scaffolding', so to speak, that Nussbaum too associates with a constitution of values 'as if they stood outside us' (1994, 212). To take recourse to an ideal realm of moral coordination is not in itself a fallacy any more than it is a fallacy of agents to project ends-in-view, while experience may not always provide all available means for the realization of these ends. Moreover, obstacles arising in experience may as well denote that the ends-in-view are at a given moment unattainable. We need to recall that, following Durkheim, the suggestion we are making is that the realm of valuations must somehow entail (as both Dewey and Marcuse recognize) a reference to (abstract) values by recourse to which empirical deficits, deprivation and all sorts of troubles that stall desires and interests may be curbed. In his essay on values, Durkheim emphatically dissociates the realm of ideal valuations from a 'cloud cuckoo land' ((1924) 1974, 94). For him ideals have also a 'material' or 'natural' dimension if they can indeed take effect in reality. Like Durkheim, Dewey also accommodates in his value-theory the 'desirable' social conditions and the causal connections that shape interests, not as an uncritical and fundamentalist certainty, but with a nuanced process of (self-) examination. He also rejects the idea of values descending 'from a moral Mount Sinai' (Dewey 1939, 32). Yet, he mistakenly, I think, equates pejoratively this realm with 'something at large or a priori' (32). Durkheim would endorse both the 'at large' authority of society (invoked anyway by Dewey) and the 'a priori' necessity of a value-standpoint on reality. Marcuse's objection is that a true science cannot treat the value of freedom on a par with all other valuations. Not only because science is essentially and constitutively tied to freedom (against prejudice, theocracy, political ideologies, technocratic colonization) in order to be exercised and diffused but because, as Marcuse concludes, 'freedom – and this is the profound result of Kant's analysis – is the only "fact" that "is" only in its creation; it cannot be verified except by being exercised' (1941, 148). If we return to Durkheim's views on pragmatism we see that despite unmistakable similarities he shares with pragmatists, the gist of his critique, like Marcuse, holds pragmatism in check because the latter 'cannot entail a hierarchy of values' (Durkheim (1955) 1983, 73), since, as we have already seen, Dewey primes science as the domain of freedom. Moreover, and unsurprisingly given Durkheim's equation of truth with collective validity (primed in history as organic solidarity), his objections raise the issue of truth's necessity and impersonality (73–75).

16 The famous Humean argument that 'ought' judgments cannot be extracted from 'factual' judgments is confronted in Hegelian lines as follows:

> Hume's standpoint is one of the Understanding: We *know* what a statement of 'fact' is, and what a 'desire' or an 'imperative' is; and we can see that they are logically independent. Hegel's response has been to show that in terms of our ordinary assumptions about what 'facts' are, we cannot have any proper knowledge; so we ought to reconsider our supposed certainty about facts. Then he showed that 'truth' is essentially an object of 'desire'; and now he is saying that an 'ought' statement that *is not* founded in 'what is' is 'without truth'. This is a claim that we must also reconsider our supposed knowledge of what 'ought' means, because only 'ought' statements that *are* derivable from 'what is' could possibly be 'desirable'. In other words, he is not saying that Hume is wrong or mistaken about the ordinary understanding of language, but rather that Hume's obvious rightness shows the inadequacy of that ordinary understanding.
>
> (Harris 1997a, 490–491 [original emphasis])

It is worth noting that the narrative of *The Phenomenology of Spirit* to which Harris refers here discloses itself from the 'we' perspective, i.e. from the perspective of the community of embodied (free) spirits. This, I think, is not an intimation too distant from Putnam's defence of Sen with respect to the validity of science and the transcendence of the fact/value dichotomy. Sen's (1966) preoccupation with Hume's law via Hare draws on the descriptive (content) features of universal value-judgments. By distinguishing 'basic' value-judgments (those that no factual assumption can engender revision for the holder of this value-judgment) from 'non-basic' value-judgments (those that allow such revisions in light of factual evidence), Sen (1967, 50) hopes to show that in the context of Hume's Law, action on the basis of purely 'basic' judgments would in all likelihood lack relevance to reality: their holder 'would answer every moral question that he can answer without knowing any of the facts [...]' (52).

17 A noteworthy attempt to rework the normative discourse of values, setting up our humanity as the 'value of values' is found in Korsgaard (2004, 85). For an extremely nuanced and complex discussion of values and the problem of valuation, see Nozick (1981).

References

Arendt, Hannah. (1951) 1973. *The Origins of Totalitarianism*. San Diego: Harcourt Brace Jovanovich.

Beiser, Frederick. 2008. 'Emil Lask and Kantianism.' *The Philosophical Forum* 39 (2): 283–295.

Beiser, Frederick. 2009. 'Normativity in Neo-Kantianism: Its Rise and Fall.' *International Journal of Philosophical Studies* 17 (1): 9–27.

Brecht, Arnold. 1959. *Political Theory: The Foundations of Twentieth-Century Political Thought*. Princeton: Princeton University Press.

Bruun, Hans. (2007) 2016. *Science, Values and Politics in Max Weber's Methodology*. Aldershot: Ashgate.

Deranty, Jean-Philippe. 2005. 'Hegel's Social Theory of Value.' *The Philosophical Forum* 36 (3): 307–331.

Dewey, John. 1939. *Theory of Valuation*. Chicago: The University of Chicago Press.

Dewey, John. (1897) 2010. 'Hegel's Philosophy of Spirit: 1897, University of Chicago.' Part II, Ch. 3. In *John Dewey's Philosophy of Spirit, with the 1897 Chicago Lecture on Hegel*. New York: Fordham University Press.

Durkheim, Émile. (1893) 1960. *The Division of Labor in Society*. New York: The Free Press.

Durkheim, Émile. (1912) 1961. *The Elementary Forms of Religious Life*. New York: Collier.

Durkheim, Émile. (1895–1896) 1962. *Socialism*. New York: Collier.

Durkheim, Émile. (1924) 1974. *Sociology and Philosophy*. New York: The Free Press.

Durkheim, Émile. (1955) 1983. *Pragmatism and Sociology*. Cambridge: Cambridge University Press.

Eaton, Howard. 1930. *The Austrian Philosophy of Values*. Norman: University of Oklahoma Press.

Frondizi, Risieri. 1963. *What is Value? An Introduction to Axiology*. Lasalle: Open Court.

Gangas, Spiros. 2007. 'Social Ethics and Logic: Rethinking Durkheim through Hegel.' *Journal of Classical Sociology* 7(3): 315–338.

Gangas, Spiros. 2010. 'Values, Crisis and Resistance: Prospects for Freedom Reconsidered.' In *Roots, Rites and Sites of Resistance: The Banality of Good*, edited by Leonidas Cheliotis, 12–35. Basingstoke: Palgrave Macmillan.

Harris, Errol. 1987. *Formal, Transcendental, and Dialectical Thinking: Logic and Reality*. Albany: State University of New York Press.

Harris, Henry. 1997a. *Hegel's Ladder. Volume I: The Pilgrimage of Reason*. Indianapolis: Hackett.

Harris, Henry. 1997b. *Hegel's Ladder. Volume II: The Odyssey of the Spirit*. Indianapolis: Hackett.

Hegel, Georg W. (1807) 1977. *Phenomenology of Spirit*. Oxford: Oxford University Press.

Heller, Agnes. 1972. 'Towards a Marxist Theory of Value.' *Kinesis* 5 (1): 7–76.

Holmwood, John. 2013. 'Public Reasoning without Sociology: Amartya Sen's Theory of Justice.' *Sociology* 47 (6): 1171–1186.

Joas, Hans. (1997) 2000. *The Genesis of Values*. Cambridge: Polity.

Kant, Immanuel. (1788) 1997. *Critique of Practical Reason*. Cambridge: Cambridge University Press.

Korsgaard, Christine. 2004. 'The Dependence of Value on Humanity'. In: *The Practice of Value* edited by R. Jay Wallace, 63–85. Oxford: Oxford University Press.

Kraft, Victor. (1951) 1981. *Foundations for a Scientific Analysis of Value*. Dordrecht: D. Reidel.

Marcuse, Herbert. 1941. 'Review: Dewey, John *Theory of Valuation*'. *Zeitschrift für Sozialforschung* 9 (1): 144–148.

Marcuse, Herbert. 1964. *One-Dimensional Man*. London: Sphere Books.

Marcuse, Herbert. (1929) 1980. 'The Sociological Method and the Problem of Truth.' In *Knowledge and Politics: The Sociology of Knowledge Dispute*, edited by Volker Meja and Nico Stehr, 129–139. London: Routledge.

Marcuse, Herbert. (1932) 1987. *Hegel's Ontology and the Theory of Historicity*. Cambridge, MA: The MIT Press.

Myrdal, Gunnar. 1958. *Value in Social Theory*. London: Routledge and Kegan Paul.

Nozick, Robert. 1981. *Philosophical Explanations*. Cambridge, MA: The Belknap Press of Harvard University Press.

Nussbaum, Martha. 1992. 'Human Functioning and Social Justice. In Defense of Aristotelian Essentialism.' *Political Theory* 20 (2): 202–246.

Nussbaum, Martha. 1994. 'Valuing Values: A Case for Reasoned Commitment.' *Yale Journal of Law and the Humanities* 6: 197–217.

Nussbaum, Martha. 1995. 'Aristotle on Human Nature and the Foundations of Ethics.' In *World, Mind and Ethics: Essays on the Ethical Philosophy of Bernard Williams*, edited by Jimmy Altham and Ross Harrison, 86–131. Cambridge: Cambridge University Press.

Nussbaum, Martha. 1999. *Sex and Social Justice*. New York: Oxford University Press.

Nussbaum, Martha. 2001. 'Political Objectivity'. *New Literary History* 32 (4): 883–906.

Nussbaum, Martha. 2006. *Frontiers of Justice: Disability, Nationality, Species Membership*. Cambridge, MA: The Belknap Press of Harvard University Press.

Nussbaum, Martha. 2011. *Creating Capabilities*. Cambridge, MA: The Belknap Press of Harvard University Press.

Nussbaum, Martha. 2013. *Political Emotions: Why Love Matters for Justice*. Cambridge, MA: The Belknap Press of Harvard University Press.

Nussbaum, Martha, and Amartya Sen. 1989. 'Internal Criticism and Indian Rationalist Traditions.' In *Relativism: Interpretation and Confrontation*, edited by Michael Krausz, 299–325. Notre Dame: University of Notre Dame Press.

Oakes, Guy.1988. *Weber and Rickert: Concept Formation in the Cultural Sciences*. Cambridge, MA: The MIT Press.

Parsons, Talcott. 1966. *Societies: Evolutionary and Comparative Perspectives*. Englewood Cliffs: Prentice-Hall.

Parsons, Talcott. (1922) 1996. 'The Theory of Human Behavior in Its Individual and Social Aspects.' *The American Sociologist* 27 (4): 13–23.

Parsons, Talcott. (1973) 2006. 'My Life and Work (In two parts): A Seminar with Talcott Parsons at Brown University.' *American Journal of Economics and Sociology* 65 (1): 1–58.

Popper, Karl. (1934) 1980. *The Logic of Scientific Discovery*. London: Hutchinson.

Putnam, Hilary. 2002. *The Collapse of the Fact/Value Dichotomy and Other Essays*. Cambridge, MA: Harvard University Press.

Rose, Gillian. (1981) 1995. *Hegel Contra Sociology*. London: Athlone.

Scheler, Max. (1916) 1973. *Formalism in Ethics and Non-Formal Ethics of Value*. Evanston: Northwestern University Press.

Schnädelbach, Herbert. 1984. *Philosophy in Germany 1831–1933*. Cambridge: Cambridge University Press.

Sen, Amartya. 1966. 'Hume's Law and Hare's Law.' *Philosophy* 41 (155): 75–79.

Sen, Amartya. 1967. 'The Nature and Classes of Prescriptive Judgments.' *Philosophical Quarterly* 17 (66): 46–62.

Sen, Amartya. 1982. 'Description as Choice.' Ch. 20 in *Choice, Welfare and Measurement*. Cambridge, MA: Harvard University Press.

Sen, Amartya. 1984. *Resources, Values and Development*. Cambridge, MA: Harvard University Press.

Sen, Amartya. 1985. 'Well-Being, Agency and Freedom: The Dewey Lectures 1984.' *The Journal of Philosophy* 82 (4): 169–221.

Sen, Amartya. 1987. *On Ethics and Economics*. Oxford: Basil Blackwell.
Sen, Amartya. 1992. *Inequality Reexamined.* Cambridge, MA: Harvard University Press.
Sen, Amartya. (1995) *Inequality Reexamined.* Cambridge, MA: Harvard University Press.
Sen, Amartya. 2000. 'Consequential Evaluation and Practical Reason.' *The Journal of Philosophy* 97 (9): 477–502.
Sen, Amartya. 2002a. *Rationality and Freedom.* Cambridge, MA: The Belknap Press of Harvard University Press.
Sen, Amartya. 2002b. 'Response to Commentaries.' *Studies in Comparative International Development* 37 (2): 78–86.
Sen, Amartya. 2009. *The Idea of Justice*. Cambridge, MA: The Belknap Press of Harvard University Press.
Stewart, Frances, and Séverine Déneulin. 2002. 'Amartya Sen's Contribution to Development Thinking.' *Studies in Comparative International Development* 37 (2): 61–70.
Stiglitz, Jospeh, Amartya Sen, and Jean-Paul Fitoussi. 2009. *Report by the Commission on the Measurement of Economic Performance and Social Progress.* Accessed 11 October 2018. http://ec.europa.eu/eurostat/documents/118025/118123/Fitoussi+Commission+report.
Weber, Max. (1904) 1949. *The Methodology of the Social Sciences.* New York: The Free Press.
Weber, Max. (1903–1906) 1975. *Roscher and Knies: The Logical Problems of Historical Economics.* New York: The Free Press.
Winfield, Richard Dien. 1998. *The Just Family.* New York: The State of New York University Press.
Zimmermann, Bénédicte. 2006. Pragmatism and the Capability Approach: Challenges in Social Theory and Empirical Research. *European Journal of Social Theory* 9 (4): 467–484.
Zimmermann, Bénédicte. 2018. 'From Critical Theory to Critical Pragmatism: Capability and the Assessment of Freedom.' *Critical Sociology* 44 (6): 937–952.

2 Economy and society

A CA-based synthesis?

Entering economic suffering

Amartya Sen's CA is animated by a passion to contribute to combating diverse deprivations in society. This is obvious from Sen's focus on famines and hunger up to the wider concern of CA with development ethics. Linking personal experience to ideas, a recurring episode of suffering supplies Sen's scientific prose with an evocative and moving autobiographical imagery. This is no other than the story of Kader Mia, a daily labourer, who had come to Dhaka to seek work and a bit of earning to feed his family. Although warned by his wife not to seek work in a Hindu area, particularly dangerous then due to communal riots between Hindus and Muslims, Kader Mia had no alternative but to take that risk. Chased by communal thugs he was eventually stabbed – witnessed by Sen who was ten at the time – and died later in the hospital (Sen 1999a, 8). Sen mentions this episode on a number of occasions and confesses that 'the terrible connection between economic poverty and comprehensive unfreedom (even the lack of freedom to live) was a profoundly shocking realization that hit my young mind with overpowering force' (Sen 2006, 173). Through this personal recollection Sen infuses his programme with one of the countless disturbing images of suffering gleaned from contexts of grinding poverty and unemployment.[1]

With this incident of suffering in mind, let us consider the following remark about economics:

> The dismal science, as Thomas Carlisle called it, however, is not doomed. It can be reborn when it takes stock of the new common anthropology and the intellectual and affective power of productive labor, and when it can in addition to capitalists and wage laborers account for the poor and the excluded who nonetheless always constitute the productive articulations of social being. For economics to function today it has to be formed around the common, the global, and social cooperation. Economics, in other words, must become a biopolitical science. Economic engineering, as Amartya Sen says, must turn to ethics.
>
> (Hardt and Negri 2004, 157)[2]

When these lines were written 3 years before the eruption of the late-2007 Great Recession, few could anticipate a disgruntled public's standpoint on the dismal state of economics and on the failure of its professionals to appreciate the systemic roots of the financial crisis. (We need not quote the countless editorials in major magazines and web sites of mainstream and alternative media that gasped with perplexity at the unintended financial implosion; we take this stock of information to be general knowledge, beyond dispute.) Economics, for Sen, may not be relegated to a 'dismal science' as Hardt and Negri contend. Yet, interestingly enough, Sen takes to task current economic orthodoxy invoking this particular phrase by Carlisle. In an essay titled 'The Economics of Happiness and Capability', Sen (2008) removes most of the blemish that accompanies economics due to its alleged incapacity to cope with famines, poverty, unemployment or systemic crises. For Sen, it is certainly not accurate to view economics as indifferent to happiness or human well-being. The traditions of welfarism and even of some strands of utilitarianism do indicate a concern with eudaimonistic ends. The problem is that the 'informational basis' of welfare economics started to shrink since logical positivism. Considering the impact of Arrow's 'impossibility theorem' (i.e. essentially, the idea that interpersonal comparison of utilities or options among actors is impossible, hence the 'impossibility' clause) and the consequent transference of utility rankings to an omniscient collective subject, Sen understands the solution to the crisis of economics to consist in specifying what the common denominator of interpersonal comparison can be. He writes:

> One route that some of us have tried to explore relates to Aristotle's pointer, in the Nicomachean Ethics, to the achievement of valuable functionings and to the ability to generate and enjoy such functionings. That ability to achieve combinations of functionings, which is often called 'capability', is really an expression of freedom, and can be interpreted as the freedom to attain different kinds of alternative lives (between which a person can choose).
>
> (Sen 2008, 23)

Though not prepared to dump economics *prior* to their ethical reenchantment, as Hardt and Negri intimate, Sen's programme is indeed driven forward by the demand for an ethically enriched economics. *The End of Value-Free Economics*, which is the title of a collection of essays (edited by Hilary Putnam and Vivian Walsh (2012)) and addresses this evaluative problem shift in economics, captures this normative reorientation with clarity and force. Continuing where Arrow's impossibility theorem concluded, namely that social choice becomes impossible if the informational base is narrow (Sen 1999a, 249–253), leads Sen to suggest that much of current economics orthodoxy treats aspects of human well-being and freedom as instrumental considerations, sidestepping their intrinsic moral significance. Economics thus risks occluding other broader considerations that bear on important values and enter the rationality of economic action. The advocated ethical enrichment of economics is premised on value-standpoints that clearly, as we discussed in Chapter 1, reject the 'fact/value' distinction (Anderson 1993; Putnam and Walsh 2012).

Sen also adds a marked but implicit sociological dimension to the problem of economics. Trying, as it were, to hit two birds with one stone, Sen hopes to broaden the informational basis in social choice while avoiding regress to some sort of complete ordering of preferences. Means to achieve this include taking into account 'social interaction' and the 'emergence of shared values and commitments' (Sen 1999a, 253). In fact, the much-aspired distinction between acceptable and unacceptable options in policy-making can be accommodated with broad but partial agreements even if social unanimity has not yet been secured. The overall picture of economy and society that emerges and includes this problem of informational broadening shall be the focus of the following sections. As the technical complexity of Sen's modification of welfare economics is beyond my competence, I shall only limit myself to discussing some generally known premises of Sen's ethical broadening of economics and rational action; simultaneously, I shall take up sociology's relevance and suggest that the approach that requests reembedding markets to society (Polanyi) merits reconsideration *pace* Sen's proposals. (For this injunction of CA to take recourse to Polanyi, see also Stewart 2010.)

Because of growing income and wealth inequality across a variety of factors (see Piketty (2013) 2017) the perception that market forces have had a politically sanctioned *carte blanche* to maximize and amass wealth and profit by recourse to contestable means since the 1980s has multiplied those voices of discontent across the political spectrum, which call for its moral recalibration. Thus, economic analysts depict the image of a runaway US finance capitalism where financial assets, derivatives and all sorts of profit-boosting instruments removed corporations from accountability, catapulted shareholder value to supremacy, squeezed further worker's wages and corroded capitalism's 'ethic' (Foroohar, 2016; Krippner 2011; Piketty (2013) 2017). Others recalled Minsky's neglected accuracy about capitalism's immanent predilection for a Ponzi-scheme phase of profit accumulation (see Wray 2016). Even though collective mobilization against the political and economic system that plunged most of nations into recession dissipated quickly, the dead-end of the neo-liberal phase of capitalism is still persistently underscored. If economists became less sanguine about their own conceptual and econometric toolkits, sociologists championed predictive success, albeit Pyrrhic in terms of any immediate impact.[3] It is within this jaundiced climate of the 'economy and society' interchange that a shift of focus to CA can be of help. Sen's work brings Adam Smith and Karl Marx into a fruitful dialogue, conducted under the possibility of a fusion of what are usually seen as only hermetically sealed horizons of laissez-faire economics and Marxism. As such, it provides an opportunity – at least for sociologists – to consider redrawing ideological boundaries that for many professionals in economics and sociology still seem hard to shuffle.

Economy and society (I): from embeddedness to vocabularies of motives

The relation between economy and society has been one fraught with strains (Barry 1970; Beckert (1997) 2002; Holmwood 2006), the chief of which pertains to the role of values in non-economic patterns of social life, as opposed to the utilitarian parameters within which the modern economy is held to operate. The motif of the underlying role of values in the vexing problem of conducting the, still terse, debate between economy and society, surfaces in conceptual categories across the ideological spectrum. In fact, Sen himself resorts to the phrase 'economy and society' (1999a, 162) when he addresses the interlocking of political, cultural and economic factors that need to be considered if economic catastrophes like famines are to be effectively confronted. On the matter of how the two disciplines understand the space for dialogue and shared problem areas, Holmwood (2013) suggests that, on the one hand CA advances arguments close to sociology's core issues, like inequality, yet on the other hand sociology, generally, misrepresents economics as a homogeneous bloc of orthodox assumptions regarding market efficiency. If this is the case then Amartya Sen's work provides an opportunity for bridging some of these unnecessary resilient disciplinary gaps.

Taking up the legacy of Marx's controversy with Hegel on the interdependence of the problem of justice to the problem of capitalist accumulation,[4] contemporary descriptions and explanations of the uncoupling of a free-market economy from a broader social system and from the shared normative assumptions that support it abound in sociology. From Marx to Durkheim's quest for a remoralized and just division of labour against the perils of anomie to Parsons' oversocialized model of society's integration, sociology fosters, as Beckert ((1997) 2002) has systematically discussed, a complex orientation to markets. This dual capacity of markets, at once dependent on wider networks (Granovetter 1985), yet remarkably resilient in the 'disembedded' logic of economic agents' behaviour, keeps active the troubling coupling of sociology to economics (see Calhoun and Derluguian, 2011). The perception of capitalism's resilience – in the shape of yet another, uncompleted, cycle of 'creative destruction' – is vivid and undeniable.

Apart from investigating empirically the market as a contested 'field' of symbolic struggles (Bourdieu, 2005), the market emerged as a sociological matrix the validity of which is undergoing some transformation subject to collective revalidations of functional classifications and symbolic frames. Thus, under the umbrella of the sociology of scientific knowledge, consolidated 'frames' of market efficiency or market externalities, for example, are placed within the flow of periodic renegotiations of collective resources. These validate which aspects of social interaction should enter an economic 'frame' (or more conventionally, a structured 'social fact') and what would continue to count as a real overflow of 'events' and 'possibilities' outside a given 'frame' (Callon 1998).[5] An emerging tendency is thus to theorize the 'problem of value' (Beckert 2009,

253–257) but no longer through the Parsonsian baseline of 'ultimate values'. This time, actors in the market situation determine the value of commodities, but in the absence of sufficiently particularized ultimate grounds, they can do so based on interactive networks within a specific market. This problem shift, however, seems to compress norms and all sorts of other cognitive and symbolic media in the practical map of actors to the law of value, precisely because a binding nexus of non-market values is held to matter only subjectively, without some overarching recall of ultimate values. These are held to be relevant chiefly from the standpoint of the market. (The motto 'honesty is the best policy but business is business' may have to do with values that are pertinent both to social integration and system integration, yet in common parlance it is uttered from the vantage point of the value-form which splits economic from moral values.) (For the gap between business ethics requirements and actual practices in firms, see Nussbaum 2005.)

We return thus to the tension identified by Marx as the problem of value. Because CA neglects the problem of the value form, it is sociologically more fruitful maybe to consider its proposed problem shift as a different vocabulary of motives. As C. Wright Mills had noted 'a motive tends to be one which is to the actor and to the other members of a situation an unquestioned answer to questions concerning social and lingual conduct' (1940, 907 [original emphasis removed]). Motives function as ultimate justifications and in the previous example about business and honesty the incommensurability of two motives (business profit motive versus honesty) embeds justification into incompatible milieux of action-patterns. These action-patterns are delimited by social frames and act as typical compressions of meaning. They thus derive their force and validity from 'situated actions' (910). The pragmatic approach adopted here by Mills precludes a lexical ordering of vocabularies, like for example, a vocabulary of human rights, a vocabulary of legal procedure or even a vocabulary of revolutionary praxis that would ease incommensurable justifications. He accommodates modification of vocabularies when situations change. Thus, in a cursory reference to the 'profit motive' of classical economics, Mills concedes that as an 'ideal-typical vocabulary' it is subject to modification, particularly when '*noneconomic* behavior and motives' (908n.15 (original emphasis)) have entered the business world. Seen through this lens, CA assists normative sociology in forming, in line with C. Wright Mills, new normative vocabularies that aim at bringing into common action-orientations actors from different social milieux. In fact, Nussbaum conceives the CCL precisely in such terms:

> The basic idea of the thick vague theory is that we tell stories of the general outline or structure of the life of a human being. We ask and answer the question, What is it to live as a being situated, so to speak, between the beasts and the gods, and with certain abilities that set us off from the rest of the world of nature and yet with certain limits that come from our membership in the world of nature?
>
> (Nussbaum 1990, 218)

Capabilities can indeed serve this function of a new vocabulary. Because agents resort to 'capabilities' (particularly when they feel or encounter barriers to choices they want, are capable of, and deem that they deserve to have) to offer justifications for choosing a pattern of action, moral motives are continuously likened to situational opportunities and exigencies. CA connects patterns of action to such lay justifications of actors when actors reflect on their trajectories in life and recall life chances and fulfilled or unfulfilled capabilities. It is thus not unexpected that Sen is attempting to bridge vocabularies of economic and ethical justification. The thesis 'development as freedom' is doing precisely this.

On different occasions, Nussbaum (2007, 959) and Sen (1993b, 203) report actual instances where the vocabulary of business and the vocabulary of freedom converge. However, too much focus on vocabularies only may turn efficacious, strategically at least, when normative vocabularies are turned circumstantial. As Boltanski and Chiapello ((1999) 2007) have painstakingly demonstrated the neutralization of normative claims on the part of workers and employees are not defused by some sort of knock-out assertion of power but, rather, become gradually 'displaced' in contingent circumstances. Thus, for them, 'critique always arrives behind displacement' (323 [original emphasis removed]). Recent work on CA has responded to such subtle discourse-shifts of neutralization (i.e. 'competencies', 'flexibility', 'adaptability') (see, for example, Zimmermann 2004; on the Darwinist twists to render adaptation the chief vocabulary versus 'quality of life' and capabilities, see Sen 2002, 484–500). In fact, the mediations between economy and society are aptly condensed by Boltanski and Thévenot when they suggest that a common method of reduction is at work. This reduction aims to unite the metaphysical levels of the individual and the collective. Hence, as they claim:

> sociological realism achieves reduction through the internalization of collective reality, a process that takes on the aspect of the unconscious. In economics, a comparable reduction is achieved by differentiation between goods and persons. The fact that the goods in question acquire value only if they are appropriated by persons masks the fact that they need to be qualified in terms of a common definition.
>
> ((1991) 2006, 30)

The following typology addresses this problem.

Economy and society (II): a heuristic typology

Given the tension between sociology and economics on recurring matters such as embeddedness, situated grammars of economic and non-economic motives and, ultimately, between values and the law of value, it is worth considering Sen's unequivocal statement about the necessity for markets:

> The central question is not – indeed it cannot be – whether or not to use the market economy. That shallow question is easy to answer. No economy in

> world history has ever achieved widespread prosperity, going beyond the high life of the elite, without making considerable use of markets and production conditions that depend on markets. It is not hard to conclude that it is impossible to achieve general economic prosperity without making extensive use of the opportunities of exchange and specialization that market relations offer. This does not deny at all the basic fact that the operation of the market economy can certainly be significantly defective under many circumstances, because of the need to deal with goods that are collectively consumed (such as public health facilities) and also (as has been much discussed recently) because of the importance of asymmetric – and more generally imperfect – information that different participants in the market economy may have.
>
> (Sen 2006, 137)

One may wonder though if this is the same Sen when he also argues that inequality and the problem of public goods, like the environment, imply that a 'solution to these problems will almost certainly call for institutions that take us beyond the capitalist market economy' (1999a, 267). A first answer is affirmative: Sen considers the market and the process of exchange of goods and services not only as co-existent with human society but additionally as a sphere of human freedom. Thus, one major obstacle that CA tries to remove is deprivations that inhibit people's freedom to enter the market and exit debt bondage, chattel slavery and domestic incarceration. This, in effect, is a modernist argument that we find in Marx – as Sen also recognizes (1999a, 7) – and Simmel ((1900) 1990).

However, if markets today were unproblematic containers of particularistic freedom, Sen would not be at pains to moralize them nor would he express discontent with organizations like the World Bank (1999a, xiii). By contrast, he is particularly neutral on International Monetary Fund (IMF) policies (185) for bail-out in countries that have defaulted, avoiding to consider the history and politics behind economic dependencies, something though he repeatedly emphasizes in the case of India. Because such ambiguities crop up in the thought of any complex and exciting thinker like Sen we shall have to somehow schematize the precise relation of the market to other social institutions in a typified format. This shall enable us to ascertain where Sen's proposal lies and how much intersecting space between these types can entertain a sociological reconstruction of a CA vision of 'economy and society'.[6] Once this broad stroke is in place, I shall revisit each cluster through the lens of CA.

We can thus heuristically classify the position with respect to economy and society around four main clusters:[7]

1 *The idea that the self-regulated market economy needs to be rendered 'free'*. In effect, whatever anomalies or crises appear since industrial capitalism's development, these are imputed to a market that is colonized or regulated by the state or by other institutions outside the economy, such as

customs, religion and other conventions. Versions of economic liberalism but most importantly neo-liberalism are the main exemplars of this view, although Luhmann's system's theory accommodates this request under the self-regulation and autopoiesis of the economy as a social system.[8] It is presupposed that economy's self-regulated logic suffocates from the intervention of other subsystems and thus needs to be rendered 'free'. (Cluster 1 will be condensed as SRM, which stands for a 'Self-Regulated Market'.)

2 *The idea that the free-market economy has historically been embedded in societal regulatory mechanisms.* The history of economy aside, this cluster incorporates also an 'ought' assumption, namely that the free-market economy should, if it is to act as a beneficiary to society, be subjected to mechanisms of regulation stemming from customs, religion or the state (as, for example, in dirigisme). (Cluster 2 will be referred to as RM, which stands for 'Regulated Market'.)

3 *The idea that any regulation of market forces qualifies chiefly as a moralization of the market.* This approach requires a reconfiguration of ideas (1) and (2): A moralization of the market is called for, assuming that the free-market (1) incorporates moral dimensions which need to be brought to the fore via (2) a regulation that is not only technical or mechanistic but 'organic' in the sense of processing the diffusion of collective values to the economy. (Cluster 3 will be referred as MM, which stands for a 'Moralization of the Market' (for this phrase, I drew on Stehr, Henning and Weiler, 2006).)

4 *Last, the idea that the free-market is inherently unstable marked by recurring moral anomie and alienation, which accentuate periodic systemic crises with often irreversible social damage, is raising demands for transcending capitalist markets altogether.* This model considers capitalist markets as inherently contradictory and permanently defective in generating the universality of moral contents that have been originally subscribed to the ideals of bourgeois democracies. In this fashion the free-market economy should be superseded by a different form of society with some centralized economic organization, presumably collective in authority, or, alternatively, governed by some sort of associative ownership of the means of production. The exemplary standpoint here is Marxism, in spite of its many variations. (Cluster 4 will be indexed as BCM, which stands for the thesis 'Beyond the Capitalist Market'.)

This sketchy template of standpoints is, of course, an abstraction and as such it operates with unavoidable simplification. It can be heuristically instructive though because it can represent the gradation of models that seek to explain the immensely complex question of the economy's relation to other social systems. Yet it would be hasty to treat it as merely an ideal-typical template. An alternative view would be to see these models as following a sequence of abstractions. If we represent the four models on the basis of Talcott Parsons' paradigmatic scheme of functional imperatives, then the template shown in Figure 2.1 could emerge.

Figure 2.1 Basic template of 'economy and society' models patterned after Parsons' functional imperatives.

	Talcott Parsons (AGIL)	*Economy and society models*	
L	Latent-Pattern Maintenance	Moralization of Market	L
I	Societal Integration	Beyond the Capitalist Market	I
G	Goal-Attainment	Self-Regulated Market	G
A	Adaptation	Regulated Market	A

Codified after Parsons' template of functional prerequisites the four models encapsulate moments of mediation between economy and society. Thus, the functional prerequisite of *Adaptation* corresponds to the perception of a market regulated by society (model RM). It assumes that economic systems operate in society in tight entanglement with other social arrangements. Economic activities like production and distribution of goods and services draw materially on a variety of resources (religious, political, kinship, symbolic in addition to the strictly 'material' components) in generating adaptive upgrading. The functional perquisite of *Goal-Attainment* raises the demand of market efficiency and thus seeks to detach it as an organizing principle from the economy's given and irreducible embededdness in society. It represents economic drives as if these are independent of societal modes of sanction and legitimation (model SRM). Thus, emphasis is given to the type of decision-making processes that will steer the economy's capacity for self-regulation. To counteract such self-steering reification of economic disembeddedness, the functional prerequisite of *Societal Integration* raises the problem of coordination in a society of cooperative agents who draw on influence and on deliberative processes for collective will-formation. I associate this function in Parsons with the BCM model that visualizes a society's economy unfettered from the capital–labour antagonism. Reaching its apogee in the vision of associated producers, this model intensifies the processes that will suspend class antagonisms; the 'difference' between producers and consumers (actually, the same agents) will be annulled. Finally, the way I use the function of *Latent Pattern-Maintenance* is taken to suggest that value-diffusion in the economy is tantamount to society's moral 'reclaim' of a self-regulated economy. It is thus captured best by the MM model.

Thus, the first model (i.e. SRM) in the sequence is chronologically subsequent to the middle two. It is a contemporary abstraction, which its advocates hold to be real and desirable. As already mentioned it coincides with the perception of market operation outside regulatory frameworks of social sanctions. Beginning with this abstraction from the chronologically prior RM model, I then proceed historically backwards, so to speak, arguing that market regulation and its fusion with other social arrangements consists in the configuration of the 'economy–society' under relatively undifferentiated systems: in societies, in other words, where system and social integration have not yet been decoupled. The third model (i.e. MM) in my sequence of exposition is one that generally reactivates the project of societal or cultural regeneration of market economies but leaves their overall 'logic' untouched. Thus, in response to 'crises' externalized to society by the mode of self-regulated markets, it attempts to rethink moral fusions with the economy so that its negative consequences are tempered; it also retains the economy's relative autonomy under conditions of advanced system differentiation and global division of labour. The MM model approaches 'regulation' in terms of an urgent moralization of market economies. Finally, the last model (i.e. BCM) seeks to accomplish the goals of fusion and moralization in terms that require a transition to non-capitalist economies. Thus, socialist and communist reconstructions of sorts (historical and also as thought-experiments) propose both 'fusion' with the rest of society's institutions and 'moralization', as this fusion would not be effected externally (as, for example, from a religious or even authoritarian state rule) but, rather it would be premised and grounded in the autonomous acts of agents willing to own their lives and the wealth their labour generates, upon which their capability-fulfilment rests.

Yet the abstraction of the historical dimension cannot in any sense be regarded as complete in this analytical scheme. To provide a further indication of historical constellations that approximate these types – as the very formulation of the typology itself is historically mediated and centred around capitalist modernity – we can momentarily intimate, following now a historical sequence, that: a) the *regulated market* model can cover a vast historical era that includes tribal, ancient and medieval economic systems. For all their cultural and historical diversity, such economies are generally regarded as precapitalist, marked by a low degree of economic differentiation from the rest of societal subsystems (religion, kinship, war etc.). I am inclined to include under this model fascist regulations of the free-market economy. Although fascism is historically subsequent to free-markets, 'logically' I regard it as a preceding stage as it seeks to turn the clock back as it were and, under the aegis of a romantic *Volk*, seeks to nationalize wealth. It qualifies thus as an attempt to recover a de-differentiated 'economy and society' rapport; b) the *self-regulated* model can in principle coincide with the 'great transformation' (Polanyi) of modern societies. It thus covers the market economy in its various permutations, all of which though preempt the goals of market efficiency and market justice. The apogee of this model is the historical advent of neo-liberalism (for a historical survey, see Harvey 2005, and for the recent drive to financialization, see Walby 2017). The disembedded economy becomes as it were 'embedded' in the operation of governments; c) the *moralization of market* model captures national projects of balancing market efficiency with ethical demands coupled to principles of social justice. Historical instances of it would include the New Deal in the United States and the capital–labour reconciliation that was forged in European social democracies and welfare-states from the postwar era to the 1970s; d) finally, the *beyond capitalist markets* model revolves around the long history in the unhappy tango of capitalism with socialist and communist ideals. Thus, in terms of a critique of capitalism, socialism's inception is born along with capitalism's discontents (see, for instance, Sombart 1909). As a blueprint of the 'just and free society' it is associated historically with the haughty 'experiments' in the former

Eastern bloc, China and Cuba but also with Robert Owen's utopian experimentations of the 'rational society'. If the model is to retain any contemporary relevance its validity must be detached from state and bureaucratic tyrannies. For this to happen, aspects of the Marxian project of emancipation that have been distorted (sometimes beyond recognition) by Soviet Marxism can be reassessed, first in light of robust core notions in Marx's writings and second, in terms of potential relevance to the much discussed economy's decoupling from ethics. Even if the BCM model is practically questionable as a vehicle for a radical politics of emancipation within the current phase of history's *interregnum*, it can nonetheless provide challenging possibilities for improvements in social justice. As Sen has shown with the 'Adam Smith–Karl Marx' synergy that his work invites, the intersection that Marx also accepted between capitalism and socialism cannot be seen solely as an unbridgeable hiatus. Given capitalism's crises (alienation, rising inequalities, wealth creation decoupled from merit) and the antinomy of holding to a project of human flourishing and freedom that has even fed capitalism's own rejuvenation (see Boltanski and Chiapello (1999) 2007), the interstice of mediation between capitalism and socialism seems welcoming for a project like CA. Let us explore now each cluster and begin adumbrating the salient areas where CA becomes normatively relevant within the 'economy and society' sociological discourse.

CA and the 'self-regulated market' (SRM) model

The SRM model has emerged as a deflationary reaction to critiques of the free-market economy. These critiques underline the self-regulated market's defects, most importantly its lack of regulation of economic activities. As Polanyi ((1944) 1957) famously argued, an allegedly self-regulated market dismantles and undermines the very foundations and fabric of society. Commodification in the form of profit, rent and interest of the social conditions of society's capability to reproduce itself, namely labour, land and money, was shown by Polanyi to unleash potentially irreparable damage to society, if not regulated. Against this thesis and under the auspices of the Austrian school of economics, Carl Menger, Friedrich A. Hayek and, under their guidance, Milton Friedman, subverted the claims that imputed deleterious societal outcomes of the operation of market forces. For them, regulation of markets implies a serious curtailment of the precariously conquered (vis-à-vis Fascism, Nazism, Stalinism and the precarious democracies in the then Third World) freedom of the individual and her choices.[9] A further liberalization of 'spontaneous' markets and a concomitant release of the market mechanism from society's supervisory tutelage intensified since the spectacular rise to prominence of 1980s neo-liberalism. Essential adjunct to this approach was the overemphasis on unintended consequences of action, an idea that Sen takes issue with, not simply because it is intuitively obvious (i.e. an agent or organization can never anticipate all outcomes of its actions and operative processes), but also because unintended outcomes are not by default unpredictable or unknowable. The task of replenishing economics with ethics is not to vitiate the insights of the Austrian School of economics and its justification of competitive markets. Rather, Sen requires a sufficiently broad opening of rational choice that makes values and public interest key variables in the emerging equation.

Regardless of the ideological leverage of self-regulated markets, what followed the demise of the era of reconciliation between capital and labour (New Deal, Keynesian welfare-state) has, demonstrably (Merkel 2014; Streeck 2016, 2014), disenfranchised the body politic, increased social inequality and subdued democracy to the logic of capital, as the top management's insistence to a 'faster decision making' that places a premium on a 'strong executive' (Merkel 2014, 123) signalled a marked decline in collective participation and deliberative democracy. In this sense, as Merkel argues, although 'embedded capitalism' (112) is compatible with democracy, current disembeddeed capitalism is not. My reading of Sen's CA does not discern the neo-liberal cocoon within which Sen's revision of economics seems, intentionally or not, to occupy. As I shall concern myself with some of these criticisms – mostly of Marxist origin – shortly, I need only to stress here that even if Sen provides an overly individualized vision of human capabilities at the expense of a materialist and structuralist focus on power asymmetries and hierarchies, this does not automatically suffice to place Sen in the camp of neo-liberalism. Such an interpretation, in order to qualify as valid, presupposes a sequence of abstractions. First, it ought to start from the elimination of the ethical dimension that Sen's value laden economics champion. Then it would need to continue by imputing an unconditional elevation of the individual as the sole agent of transformation and freedom sought by CA (missing thus the subtle dialectical consequences of Sen's model). Further, it should abstract from Sen's eclectic yet judicious recourse to Marx. Last, classifying Sen's CA into the neo-liberal paradigm would need to counter CA and any reconstruction of social structures aided by its normative vision at the moment – and this is crucial – where collective solutions and mobilizations against unjust structures, like those championed by Marxist orthodoxy, seem currently to wane, scattered to dispersed local areas of struggle, uncoordinated, and subject to the penetration of a fast-growing networked and flexible global division of social labour. For all his sympathies with aspects of libertarianism, Sen insists on avoiding the 'category mistake' that treats liberty and equality as mutually exclusive terms. Rather, '[l]iberty is among the possible *fields of application* of equality, and equality is among the possible *patterns* of distribution of liberty' (Sen 1992, 22–23 [original emphasis]).[10]

CA and the 'regulated market' (RM) model

Markets have always operated within society and in fusion with customs, religion, law, state, kinship and other institutional arrangements. This sociological fact is confirmed by the history of economies, anthropology and historical sociology. It suffices here to recall Marx's analysis in the *Grundrisse* of the 'forms which precede capitalist production' (Marx (1857–1858) 1973, 471–514).

Tribal, ancient and feudal economies were subsumed under social relations driven by kinship, war and master–slave hierarchies (see also Marx and Engels (1845) 1976: 32–35). Sen (1999a, 121) too likens 'precapitalist' constrains on the market (deriving from traditional values and habits) with constraints on competition. Others (e.g. Swedberg 1994, 273) proceeded with a different typology before reaching the contemporary discussion about the most developed and complex market of all, namely the capitalist market. This was a point when economists and sociologists agreed even if they adopted different methodologies and normative appraisals. Thus, comparative economic sociology made society the reference point in approaching the economy. Markets were seen as having a distinct relation to other social institutions, a relation though that varied significantly in history. Interpretive approaches on the 'economy–society' relation also vary considerably. For example, ideal-typical approaches encountered in Weber differ from dialectical–normative approaches in Durkheim and Marx. Yet a guiding thread in those three thinkers is that market and its profit-making activities have had a sustained as well as strained cohabitation with social norms and cultural values. I shall leave aside premodern types of markets and limit myself to some scattered remarks about capitalism.

Regardless whether modern markets succeeded in terms of whatever immanent criteria make them analytically autonomous, all parties in the 'economy–society' controversy recognize – at least as an empirical fact and not necessarily as a normative judgment – that market is a social structure, embedded in a wider social environment. The question that arises next is the concrete form of this embeddedness, as when, for example, another matter of contention is the degree of culture's impact on the economy (Di Maggio 1994). Second, a further vexing issue emerges: Is this embeddedness taking features of regulating economic 'functions' (or dysfunctions) that, in the last analysis, are held to jeopardize this very embeddeness? For instance, although Adam Smith accommodated legal, educational, infrastructural and moral conditions within the economy's proper function to the benefit of society, the latter accrued primarily 'as if' embededdness was itself 'invisible'. The upshot here is that while no serious economic sociology would be prepared to belittle the economy's functional and normative possibilities, the problematization of the economy's rapport with society is premised on the assumption that on the economy's side self-regulation qualifies as a demand that merits special claims of the economy to 'relative autonomy', compared to other social subsystems. This problem has led sociologists to recall 'institutional economics' (Hodgson 1994). Such shifts in economics challenge the hard core of neo-classical models of economic agency and the methodological individualism that aligns the analytical abstraction of the rational maximizer with a doctrine that treats social phenomena solely 'in terms of individuals – their properties, goals, and beliefs' (Elster 1982, 453).

For all their merits, embeddedness arguments carry the corrective middle-strand (against both an undersocialized, atomistic view of selfish agency and an oversocialized subsumption of economic action to collective values) only halfway. The normative content that the social trust upon which economic institutions rest could potentially energize, remains underspecified behind the social conventions, which 'embed' economy in society. For example, 'trust' can span a vast trajectory of social relations. From the trust that can sustain routine economic transactions, to the role of the local Mafia, it can stretch to 'local exchange trade systems' (LETS), to shared rituals that can latently contribute to strengthening economic efficiency (as among Japanese white-collar employees), and, even, to vast financial systems of trust, like stock markets and systems of transportation for commodities, services and people. This complex function of the 'fiduciary' requires normative clarification if a project of 'ethics and economics' is to distinguish between the nominal and the moral function of trust (see, for example, the Janus-faced value of the 'profit-motive' in Merton (1968) and Sen (1984)).

CA and the 'Moralization of Market' (MM) model

As a consequence of Polanyi's arguments, corrective calls for reembeddedness of markets in society take an upgraded twist. Now, beyond fused interchanges between markets and the rest of society, the market stands in need of moralization. As market risks for society became a focus of social struggles and economic reforms aiming at neutralizing the risk-factor (as in the discourse about 'externalities'), global capitalism's expansion left little room for feasible collective counterproposals, while, at the same time, global de-regulation brought to the fore serious moral hazards many of which accumulated in the Great Recession and its ongoing aftermath.

In social theory, a neo-Polanyian resurgence (Dale 2010; Fraser 2011) marks less partisan but equally alarmed discourses of market's unhappy relation to morality. This tension is encapsulated in Polanyi's idea of the 'double movement' where demands from market autonomy elicit societal protection and regulation of market forces. The second moment in the double movement acquires now a marked affinity to value-diffusion across market pores, so that the first movement (i.e. market expansion) be either curbed, thus minimizing externalities and social damages, or altered to such a degree that little of what we understand as a market economy physiognomy remains. In such renovation of the scholarly turf around 'ethics and economics' the relevance of CA did not go unnoticed (Beckert 2006, 109–110; Sayer 2006, 86, 94n.8). Yet, by and large, in economic sociology the full force of CA remains uncharted and little exploited, particularly as Sen's ethical replenishment of economics contains a Polanyian resonance. Viewing happiness and value solely in terms of commodities ignores, on Sen's account, a host of other non-commodified factors such as 'fresh air, absence of crime, social peace' (Sen 1999b, 27). If commodities become the sole determinant of a person's well-being then we risk a lapse into what Marx termed false-consciousness in the form of 'commodity fetishism' (19).

Sen has built CA with a view to broaden perceptions of the market that rely exclusively on utilitarianism. I thus see his proposal as a robust version of the MM model. This prerogative to moralize the market requires though an epistemological embeddedness too. In effect, this latter move calls for a major categorial shift that would address, for example, income inequality in terms of factors that convert incomes into capability sets and substantive freedoms (Sen 1993a).[11] While never rejecting the idea that a crucial factor of individual behaviour is self-interest, Sen questions with equal verve the latter as its sole determinant. The model of rational action that has become canonical for economic orthodoxy is challenged by Sen first on the grounds that actual behaviour may not conform to the ideal-typical construct; second, he takes issue with a narrowly defined concept of economic rationality on the part of the agent. Either as 'consistency of choice' or as 'maximization of self-interest', rationality acquires extremely thin features leading to significant explanatory and descriptive deviations from actual behaviour, not to mention to normative omissions. In fact, Sen expands rationality by making it dependent on a variety of interpretive templates that are 'external' to 'choice as such' (Sen 1987a, 14). Thus, in line with Parsons' refusal to demarcate rational action from wider normative orientations and motivations, Sen capsizes the narrow rationality thesis that imputes irrational motivations on those extrinsic factors if these are superimposed on the 'pure' utility maximization model.[12]

Through a similar lens the CA critique of preferences engages with the limited psychology of the rational agent whose preferences reveal and validate her freedom to act in the market. Such preferences are held to reveal a person's welfare. These are far too broad and can even include all sorts of nasty aspects (e.g. sadism), or very narrow motivational complexes (egocentricity), and can even be extremely difficult (actually, virtually impossible) to discard completely. Known as 'adaptive preferences' (Jon Elster) because they constitute a person's 'habitus' (Bourdieu), they are anchored in irrevocable processes of socialization and can further be rigidified in social fields of power and status. Moreover, desires and preferences are deemed unsatisfactory criteria for welfare approaches because preferences can be based on manipulation and deception. Nussbaum's (2000, 111–166) discussion of preferences and their susceptibility to false-consciousness goes largely undetected by standard approaches of welfarism. For this defect to be fixed, a CCL is required as an explicit substantive threshold for taking seriously people's desires and aims.

Starting from the methodologically individualist standpoint of self-interested behaviour, gets us, according to Sen, to intractably narrow and low in predictive power assumptions and models about real life situations. The culmination of this approach to human behaviour is utilitarianism, which, however, I shall not discuss.[13] The triptych 'self-centred welfare' (consumption), 'self-welfare goals' (maximization of one's own welfare) and 'self-goal choice' (Prisoner's Dilemma) (Sen 1987a, 80) stops short of inducing cooperative action and accommodating it in the matrix of economics. In fact, the ethical enrichment of economics takes the format of a latent sociology. To this effect Sen writes that: 'Behaviour is ultimately a social matter as well, and thinking in terms of what 'we' should do, or what should be 'our' strategy, may reflect a sense of identity involving recognition of other people's goals and the mutual interdependencies involved' (85). Although Sen recedes from ascribing to such 'interdependencies' some obvious 'intrinsic value' he nonetheless underscores their 'great *instrumental* importance' (85 [original emphasis]), which can contribute to enhancing the goals of a group to which one belongs.

Opulence is equally a limited criterion for determining a person or a community's standard of living. For although opulence may influence the standard of living (the latter a diversely defined concept by Sen's criteria too) it has to be considered as a single, rather than the cardinal factor. Sen does not hesitate to draw on both Adam Smith and Marx to illustrate this point and commend the latter's criticism of commodity fetishism mainly through the lens of providing a limited and erroneous criterion of the standard of living. Marx, as Sen (1987b, 16) contends, considers commodities as means rather than ends in themselves; the latter inversion mystifying entire population segments in an interaction pattern, prescribed solely by a command over commodities determined by class.[14]

It is no coincidence that to effect such tectonic shifts in economics, Sen is obliged to engage, as we showed in Chapter 1, in epistemological debates, many of which challenge the fact/value dichotomy in economics. Sen thus takes up a problem area carved by Kenneth Arrow (1977). In raising the issue of social responsibility and market efficiency, Arrow criticized the profit motive as an exclusive drive of economic efficiency. Beyond legal regulation, taxation and legal liability, Arrow pointed to ethical codes, which he considered not only as essential in themselves (as in medical ethics) but also as conditions – at least partial – of economic life at large (314). Interestingly enough, Arrow does not only rely on an 'externalist' ethical moderation of economic life via institutions. Rather, on this institutional lever, he adds the business firm's internal complexity. In effect, this means that the profit motive is not as diffuse as is usually taken to be. Plural affiliation and other normative commitments shared by a firm's constituencies 'dilute', as it were, the profit motive as a 'pure' goal orientation of an organization's function in society. This enables Arrow – and this appears in Sen too – to maintain ethical commitments in economic life without endorsing any sort of moral universalism that would pose the problem of market moralization in unrealistic terms. In a series of articles Sen (1985, 1993a, 1993b) accords to market economies a prominent place in society. Drawing on a variety of sources from ancient texts to early modernity's classical political economy, and obviously with a keen eye for contemporary controversies in economics, Sen recognizes three key facts: a) that market economies are extremely efficient mechanisms of generating a society's wealth and riches; b) market efficiency is Janus-faced, entailing also negative features: It can be set up as an arena of unscrupulous appetites for greed, unequal concentration and distribution of wealth, and thus sustain an image of 'independence' from its coupling to other institutions; and c) that critiques and correctives to market economies, rather that flowing from some pure deontology or from a castigation of negative labels against corporations and other economic agents, should, instead, be nuanced to a method of careful consequentialism.

It is thus obvious that Sen guards himself against the binaries of an unqualified criticism and a glorification of markets. An institution cannot be assessed,

Sen writes, if the deprivation of individuals who access it is not matched by 'the opportunity of being in another social arrangement with other types of institutions' (1985, 1). Thus, an assessment of markets – and we assume primarily of those in their most developed form that function today – needs to be supremely cautious in terms of viability of alternatives if an argument is to be extended to how markets enable of blight people's choices. Opting for a view and assessment of the market mechanism in terms of real outcomes raises, for Sen, the subsequent necessity of probing into consequences of market operation for wider and deeper structural arrangements. For instance, the ongoing controversy about market leverage of politics would be such an occasion. Moreover, the consequentialist approach would need to draw consequences under the umbrella of 'social values of well-being, freedom, and justice' (8). Thus, although Sen couples the evaluation of the market with an approach that assigns to it an entitlement value (i.e. sees it as a 'right'), he nonetheless, and rather emphatically, uncouples achievements – and what people have reason to value – from a 'foundational' or a priori anchoring of the market mechanism. He takes up (Sen 1999a) the challenge of embedding markets into a web of institutional prerequisites but the position to which he ultimately subscribes is that of stressing the difficulties of locking a market mechanism to a logic, be it functional or normative. For Sen, intractable problems ensue from any attempt to isolate 'empirical regularities' and from erecting 'an adequate moral criterion in terms of which the instrumentality of the market mechanism and its rivals can be judged' (1985, 19). Such attempts are fraught with difficulties if the market mechanism is abstracted from the consequences it generates (even if these are 'procedurally' correct and legitimate), many of which can be horrendous in the scope and intensity of the suffering caused.

Turning into the careful consequentialist approach to ethics that he cherishes, Sen (1993b) engages in a qualified critique of finance. He draws mainly on analyses of financial ethics from Kautilya, Aristotle and Adam Smith. It is certainly worth considering these sources that amplify Sen's erudite consideration on merits and demerits in finance. Yet, for the argument that concerns us here, the crux of the matter is that Sen cannot imagine economies outside the functions provided by finance. Any such projection seems to be plagued with many inefficiencies. Sen's normative critique of finance may turn out, however, to be more radical than he himself would be prepared to concede. The fiduciary responsibility of managers to shareholders, irrespective of potential or actual costs to third parties, is taken to task by Sen when he adduces Japanese corporations on the grounds that CEOs and workers occupy a less divisive organizational structure. The Japanese corporation's 'family structure' mitigates costs that may be transferred to workers in a firm, but it is not ultimately impervious to harms as it may transfer costs to other agents extraneous to the firm. The next move for Sen would be to undermine the framework of such in-group insulation when he takes to task defences of the financial sector including also insider-trading wrongdoings. Against arguments that reveal no immediate harm beyond those who trade money in such market cathedrals, Sen cites counterevidence about social losses that incur to the wider community when its financial sector is tarnished by such illegal practices. Sen is careful enough to disengage critiques of finance from righteous moral rhetoric. Moral inflation may not be irrelevant as an index of indignation on how economic dysfunctions impact people's lives but, on the whole, it clearly turns out to be inefficient because it usually substitutes moral crusades for empirical evidence and justified moral argumentation. The upshot here is that instead of moral fundamentalism, the 'fundamental' (in Sen's usage this may have to more with ultimate valuations) values that could potentially unite voices of scepticism against financial markets' systemic greediness may draw on the societal layers of the 'fiduciary'. If, in other words, society's overall foundations of trust are unduly pressured due to reckless behaviour on bankers' part and thus intensified the road to the post-2007 Great Recession, the ensuing social costs acquire an informal multiplier that may unduly defer costs to those agents (individual or collective) who rely the most on the very supervisory mechanisms Sen invokes (i.e. the state, collective values, the legal enforcement agencies). The argument here is Parsonsian, I think, and mobilizes (in its consequentialist dimension) both functional (i.e. a nation-state as a result of its financial sector collapse may enter odious and hard to bear bail-out programmes to avoid default) and normative (the damage to countless people's capabilities (unemployment) and functionings (postponement or suspension of projected family life)) considerations. Committed to non-dualism, Sen turns the debate over markets to the area of institutional interchanges. Thus, his thesis is epitomized in the principle that: 'Economic unfreedom can breed social unfreedom, just as social and political unfreedom can also foster economic unfreedom' (Sen 1999a, 8).

As a result, the picture that emerges is one of a sustained, moderate in its rhetoric, and informed in it justifications, moral supervision of market economies. Clearly, in recognizing the market's interdependence with other social institutions, Sen aims to broaden the baseline of the market's 'cognitive' map. This was after all the spirit behind his revision of Arrow's 'impossibility theorem'. Rather than reading the latter as a nihilist capitulation to impossible rankings of preferences, Sen sought to expand the baseline system of relevance by recourse to the evaluative space of capabilities. For example, instead of focusing only on the market's efficiency to generate various achievements Sen (1985) argues for a subsequent determination like the freedom to choose that could work backwards as an additional inscription to models of market efficiency. This proposal is augmented in *Development as Freedom* when instrumental freedoms, which aim to remodel growth as capability empowerment, instil to it normative criteria of policy success. While this strategy aligns with the flexibility orientation of CA, as I shall maintain in Chapter 6, it tends to reproduce those analytical prerequisites with which a general theory of society, morphologically similar to what Parsons sought to provide with the scheme of functional imperatives, in order to ease the tensions between economics and sociology (see Parsons and Smelser, 1956). These analytical prerequisites, as Holmwood (1996; 2006) has argued, are strewn with contradictions that Parsons sought unsuccessfully, yet under great theoretical duress to resolve. Yet, Parsons' system imperatives tend to reaffirm their axiomatic status if, as I shall claim in Chapter 6, they reappear in CA – and elsewhere – under a pragmatist agenda! In any case, the role of values in capitalism is for Sen indubitable. A triptych that he draws on includes 'institutions' (as in legal structures or contracts), 'behavioral ethics' and 'trust' (1999a, 262–263).[15] But in spite of the prerogative to moralize markets, Sen's work is faced with an intractable tension. He also writes:

> Despite its effectiveness, capitalist ethics is, in fact, deeply limited in some respects, dealing particularly with issues of economic inequality, environmental protection and the need for cooperation of different kinds that operate outside the market. But within its domain, capitalism works effectively through a system of ethics that provides the vision and the trust needed for successful use of the market mechanism and related institutions.
>
> (Sen 1999a, 263)

If, as we shall shortly argue, Sen stresses the conciliatory space between Adam Smith and Marx, what else could be expected on the level of mediations of capitalist markets with other social systems, if we exclude the socialist history of state-paternalism? With this problem in mind we can insist on the necessity of a theory of institutional spheres of justice. The request for such a theory is coupled in modernity's narratives with a recurring concern over the capitalist market's claims to independence. If the problems that trouble Sen are immanent in the market, beyond definitive taming, at what level of historical experience and normative adequacy is the vision of non-capitalist markets sensible? This ambiguity brings us to the last model.

CA and the 'beyond the capitalist market' (BCM) model

It must be evident that the failure of the moral regeneration of capitalism – as, for example, in the case for full employment – raised, as the Second World War was coming to an end, the issue of a democratic regulation of capitalism. This claim intensified following the traumatic history of authoritarian subsumptions of markets to national end under fascist statism (Kalecki 1943, 326–331; Polanyi (1944) 1957, 237–248). Sen's work, as our quote from Hardt and Negri illustrated, has not gone unnoticed by Marxist scholars. In some cases Sen's argument, particularly in *Development as Freedom*, has been met with reserved approbation. Sympathetic critics (Bagchi 2000; Harvey 2014) have noted the significance of Sen's humanist programme to remoralize the market and to empower the human being. Others, (e.g. Sayer 2012) accept CA in principle but require its attention to structural inequalities. Yet a problem that surfaces in the Marxist account of CA follows from Sen's reticence on the value-form and on capital's mode of reproducing inequality and dispossession. Contemporary corporate gigantism and the financialization of economy, coupled to the markets' sordid leverage on governments, is conspicuously underplayed by Sen. In addition, despite his deep knowledge of economic history, Sen is rather frugal with the problem of the colonial presuppositions of capital accumulation. His ethical programme is held to operate on the assumption that markets function according to the principles of the money-form and the contradictions (crises) that belong to the logic of capital. It is argued that CA restricts its scope to individually oriented freedom and fails to accommodate the morally dubious role of social structures and power relations and how these blight capacity fulfilment.

Sen's work is thus taken to appear as a neo-liberal appropriation of the market's 'soft' moralization. Thus, David Harvey (2014, 208–211), for example, recognizes Sen's progressive problem shift in economics that considers the freedom aspects of development, yet he reproaches the proposed model for not probing into the roots of the problem. Thus, capitalism's contradictions remain unaddressed. Harvey writes that systemic:

> oppositions get mentioned, but all of them, in Sen's universe are held to be manageable. That any of them might become absolute contradiction and the locus of crisis is ruled out by assumption or merely put down as bad management.
>
> (210)

The accumulation of crises due to the value-form is set up here as the modicum of radicalism that Sen's work should, according to Harvey, carry if it is to qualify as a wedge that can inspire struggles across the geopolitical space to counter global capitalism. For Harvey, Sen's entrapment to a moralization of markets approach precludes, ultimately, this option. Marxist critiques extend also to other directions. For instance, Sen is taken to task on a number of charges: because of political bias in favour of capitalist democracies (Navarro 2000); because the deliberative politics he proposes are abstracted from corporate and media power relations (Gellert and Feldman 2006; Sandbrook 2000); because his CA can be easily tweaked to fit a neo-liberal policy agenda (Dean 2000; Feldman 2010; Walby 2012); and because there is no space for accommodation of issues of struggle (Dean 2000).[16] Even when deviation from the neoclassical orthodoxy is recognized, Sen is taken to task for ignoring opulence. Thus, Cameron (2000), for example, thinks that capabilities should extend symmetrically, as it were, to considerations, following an extensive sociological literature from Simmel and Veblen to Marcuse, of how high-income categories undermine sustainability that charts the 'failure of opulence to enhance human capabilities and well-being' (1042). Sen, as things stand, figures more as a 'deviant reformist' than a 'revolutionary economist' (1037). In other cases (e.g. Prendergast 2005) Sen appears to present Marx's approval of the progressive aspects of capitalism in abstraction from capital's primitive accumulation and strictly through the formalism of right that Marx criticized. Last but not least, Sen is also held to lag behind rival institutional approaches to the market, like those of T.H Green and J.R. Commons (Prendergast 2011).

I shall deal with major defects but also valuable aspects of such criticisms at various points in the book (mostly in Chapter 4, which takes up the Marxian turn in CA). But to start clearing the ground against any impressions that Sen's CA figures as a disguised version of neo-liberal accounts of well-being, the TINA logic that sociologists diagnose as an ideological trope about neo-liberalism's historical triumph, is chosen by Sen as an index of deeply problematic diminutions of well-being. As he puts it, '[e]xtreme inequalities in matters of race, gender, and class often survive on the implicit understanding – to use a phrase that Margaret Thatcher made popular (in a different but somewhat related context – that "there is no alternative")' (Sen 1999a, 287). As most of the aforementioned critiques focus on globalization, it is worth pointing out that Sen hopes to rescue globalization from the dualist pincers of a pro- and anti-globalization approach. If one, for example, reads the short chapter on globalization in *Identity and Violence* (2006), it is immediately evident that Sen considers globalization as a diverse, historically rich human endeavour, that forges communicative, commercial, cultural, as well as moral bridges among societies. Having disentangled globalization from an axiologically one-dimensional approach (either as a linear realization of a market logic with beneficiaries across all corners of the planet or as a devastating process of capitalist exploitation), Sen considers the merits of those anti-globalization streams of protest, only to show that they adhere to a narrow perception of the market. They do so because they inflate its scope, subsume globalization under one of its dimensions (i.e. global market domination), and thus they neglect that they, too, as a global force of protest and coordination, belong also to the beneficiaries of globalization. Not only are 'omissions', like deprivations which cause enormous harm, being addressed by Sen, but 'commissions', too, like the systematic G8 arms trade and the trade barriers that pose additional hurdles on poorer nations; or with similar gravity of incurred deprivations, the patent laws that delay access to them by vulnerable populations (Sen 2006, 139–141), appear as impediments on markets expected to truly serve communities and their people. One issue with this catalogue of placing markets over people is the reluctance on Sen's part to trace them into the functional or ideological mechanism of 'power elites' and to delve on the scope of market transformation that can be rendered feasible on the global terrain. (The latter requirement though violates the rejection of perfect institutions that Sen's solutions try to disentangle from constituting a necessary and sufficient condition in solving serious social problems, like those that trouble, too, his radical critics.)

More moderate voices though follow CA and consider its applicability beyond the blind affirmation or negation of markets. Falling roughly under the RM/MM models of economy's relation to society, it is argued by advocates of this view that the flexibility of CA gives rise to greater compatibility between social rights and market efficiency. This happens because irreducible procedural prerequisites (e.g. legislation) of social rights, beyond their status as entitlements of 'equality of capability', operate as institutional filters that enable agents to convert their capabilities to economic and other functionings (see, for example,

Browne, Deakin and Wilkinson 2004). Thus, in this fashion, what is played up is the version of CA as a pragmatic toolkit (by no means normatively neutral, yet 'indifferent' on the substance of the self-regulated market). Hence, CA enters historical spaces of market and society, accommodating, from within so to speak, and without some a priori structural commitment as to the shape markets should eventually have, the fulfilment of social rights *qua* capabilities, '*without presupposing* any particular economic model or policy programme' (Browne, Deakin, and Wilkinson 2004, 212 [original emphasis]). This sort of situational and reflexive approach to CA is compatible with the growing recognition of contingency, contextuality, fluidity and pragmatic possibility for social reform, given the irreducible plurality of social contexts. Essentially, this perspective filters CA through a Weberian epistemological justification of contingency (see Chapter 1). Still though, it couples CA to the prospect of collective learning (as in corporate social responsibility) focusing on the gains for shared governance or for gender equality (entailing risks of public shaming should corporations keep ignoring). For these authors:

> [a] capability approach makes it possible to see that social rights, *in common with civil and political rights*, underpin market access and facilitate the extension of the division of labour and knowledge upon which, in the final analysis, a market order depends. This makes the concept of capability particularly useful for understanding the process of European construction, in which social rights and market integration have long been intertwined.
>
> (220 [original emphasis])

I chose this succinct conclusion to highlight the appeal and real potential of CA for bringing society and market closer to each another. The functionalist logic here is obviously tangential on specific historical accomplishments of European modernity coming from normative theories. The problem though remains if this embededdness of the market to society makes concessions to the reciprocity implied in such a relational nexus and thus misconstrues the market's impact on society (substantively or procedurally) as a limit-case of how far this mediation can be stretched. The current European crisis clearly indicates that mediations from the market side of things tend to be resourceful and stubborn in their capacity to curb social rights.

Against the bland positing of the value-form as the only authentic means of social transformation, CA can be seen as working primarily within the main outlines of humanist Marxism. This hypothesis may be plausible not only because Sen's alleged blindness to capitalism's contradictions seems to miss the mark but also because the reading of Marx adopted by Sen's Marxist critics is marked by the deflationary moment that Parsons (1969) conceptualized. Thus, as a consequence of this constant appeal to Marx's ultimate foundation (i.e. the value-form), Marxist orthodoxy downplays the vision of a socialist society configured around the social individual. When Marx, for example, comments on the 'great civilizing influence of capital' ((1857–1858) 1973, 409) and extolls the elevation of the individual to the level of a universal self-conception of agency rich in possibilities – formally at least – he incorporates these progressive moments of capital to the prospective vision of the social individual (for an excellent analysis of the social individual, see Gould 1978). But the social individual whose richness of potential comes to be expressed in bourgeois society and owes its manifestation in capital appears as a dichotomous embodiment of society and the individual. The abstraction consists in the fact that the irrelevance of the content of the worker's labour (for himself) comes to be converse to the riches (not only as commodities) he can enjoy and the capabilities to shape his talents and skills as a member of a multifaceted social relationship to nature and society. Given the fact that the abundance in riches Marx associates with the most advanced bourgeois society is accessed unequally (with result that considerable segments of society to be open to multiple moments of alienation), it makes sense to reconstruct CA along this fundamental (but historical) contradiction. Whereas Sen is held to ignore the structural causes of contemporary inequalities as these are aggravated by the value-form and lead to the paradox that 'despite an excess of wealth civil society is not rich enough' (Hegel (1821) 1967, §245), a different way of construing CA is to suggest that the focus on individual well-being and capability-enhancement is premised on one moment only of the process that Marx himself recognized during the formation of the social individual in bourgeois society.

In highlighting the ethical limitations of welfare economics and its empirically limited metrics with regards to information obtained for public decisions about ownership, Sen suggests that even 'if the necessary lump-sum transfers were identifiable and also economically feasible, issues of political feasibility can be, obviously, extremely important when dealing with such fundamental matters as radical changes in ownership' (1987c, 37). This economic prospect is deemed feasible but, as Sen suggests, stops short of the democratic political will that can put it into effect. Thus, on the one hand, as Bauman notes: 'Europe and the United States spend 17 billion dollars each year on animal food while, according to the experts, there is a 19-billion-dollar shortfall in the funding needed to save the world population from hunger' (2008, 249). Yet on the other hand, this equation – quite popular in any rhetoric of indignation – risks for Sen (1984, 292) to 'anthropomorphising nations' and treating them as individuals acting on criteria of 'per capita income'. Such reifications are voiced without consideration of the democratic process at work in each nation. Factoring the problem of informational limitation and of the complexity of moral judgments in reaching consensus, Sen (1984, 302) in one of the rare occasions of pessimism recedes into the incommensurable consequences of value-relevance within the *hiatus irrationalis*.

Sen's critique is launched from multiple blind spots in current economic orthodoxy. It is also a critique of economic categories, indeed of 'economic reason'. If the proposed shift to capabilities is explored in its deeper ramifications, at least in sociology, it can adumbrate a quite radical view of Sen that could surprise Marxist critics. Thankfully, I am not alone in holding this belief.

Recently, Tim Rogan (2017) placed Sen at the apex of a tradition of moral economists (Polanyi included) while in a short piece on the press, Sen is presented as 'the century's greatest critic of capitalism' (Rogan, 2018), precisely because his critique incorporates both the moral and the material dimension, and thus avoids the inertia of critique as a result of sterile binary camp wars.

Liberalism *and* socialism (I): the CA 'Adam Smith–Karl Marx' dialogue

Sen's work offers a refreshing possibility for fusing Adam Smith and Karl Marx into a single normative programme. Beyond the substantive merits of any such overlap, the fusion of the founder of political economy and a defender of competitive market with the capitalist market's most sophisticated critic entails value-added symbolism. For one thing it implies that positions held to be mutually exclusive can learn from one another if both are willing to explore common presuppositions. Reconsidering Adam Smith, Sen (1999a, 270) shows that the core of his thought about markets cannot be disentangled from ethical considerations. Smith's ethics seem to revolve around the idea of a person as an agent of sympathy and of his ideational potential to act as an 'impartial spectator'. (I shall take up some of these arguments about sympathy in Chapter 5.)

Working with Smith's moral intimations enables Sen to deduce sociality from what has been transfigured by later economists as an exclusively individual framework of rational, self-interested action. Sen thus highlights the contours of a social self, that is, a self who acts outside the much-invoked Gospel of *homo economicus*. This richer concept of the self is explicated as follows:

> Smith's conception of the rational person places this person firmly in the company of others-right in the middle of a society to which he belongs. The person's evaluation as well as actions invoke the presence of others, and the individual is not dissociated from the "public".
>
> (Sen 1999a, 271)

Not only is the individual embedded in society, he also acts 'in the presence of others'. This performative nuance in Sen suffices to make us recall that in Goffman's, for instance, 'presentation of self in everyday life', impression management requires that recognition is induced by the audience. Sen's oft-quoted example from Smith with respect to the procurement of the 'necessaries' which refer to commodities that secure not merely survival but the dignity to appear in public, shows that to 'present oneself in public' inserts into the economic process intersubjective criteria (not to be subject to shame) that require the 'capability to function' (Sen 1999a, 73) beyond what is required by a commodity bundle when the latter is usually abstracted from public expectations about what counts as dignity.

We observe that with this provision in place the idea of self-interested agency expands beyond recognition, if taken to operate strictly within the SRM model.

In his judicious reading of Adam Smith, Sen (1987a, 25n. 27) rightly discerns the sociohistorical setting within which the idea of self-interest is articulated. Beyond the fact that Smith conceived it as an antidote to various bureaucratic impediments, it is of interest to entertain the idea that self-interest should emerge under conditions of advanced division of labour as a collective value. Maybe in such a context of mutual sympathy and support for the poor (26–27), Smith's invocation of 'public spirit' is of equal sociological and normative importance. For Smith's public spirit is energized at those points when 'system' action has to be acted upon with a principle of 'moderation' instead of force (see Smith (1759) 1984, 233). Clearly, Adam Smith conceives here the public spirit in terms that function as an activation of collective forces when the spirit of the 'system' (narrowly defined self-interest) endangers, through an immoderate pursuit of profit, the social fabric.

Smith's classical economics is lampooned by methodological individualism's impact in economics. For instance – and this is crucial for the 'Adam Smith–Karl Marx' synthesis Sen advances – Carl Menger suggests that Smith's work is rooted on Enlightenment principles. He believes that Adam Smith neglects the organic rootedness of economy in society, aiming instead at an abstract projection of human 'welfare'. For Menger, Smith's attachment to Enlightenment is tantamount to 'pragmatism'. Here, according to Menger, pragmatism carries the negative connotation of a sort of zealotry of amelioration and reform. Juxtaposing Smith to the 'Burke–Savigny' historical school Menger writes about the latter:

> The aims of the efforts under discussion here had to be, on the contrary, the full understanding of existing social institutions in general and of organically created institutions in particular, the retention of what has proved its worth against the one-sidedly rationalistic mania for innovation in the field of economy. The object was to prevent the dissolution of the organically developed economy by means of a partially superficial pragmatism, a pragmatism that contrary to the intention of its representatives inexorably leads to socialism.
>
> (Menger (1883) 1996, 158–159)

Menger's rebuttal of normativity in economics, including notions like a 'national economy' that he imputes to Adam Smith, provides a template for Sen's convergence thesis on Adam Smith and Marx. For if 'collective will' and conventional 'agreement' are seen as derivatives of individual interests, then the collective validity of social institutions, and the economy in particular, emerges as an unintended outcome of individually separate constituencies. Adam Smith's vision of the 'good' economy must, for Menger, incorporate some sort of collective planning, which throws Adam Smith's classical political economy straight into a socialist straightjacket. Menger's judgment is of major significance, because he grasps the axiological and normative elements of Adam Smith. These, as we know, inspire Sen to rediscover Adam Smith as an economist and moral philosopher in the outskirts of the economics canon, in spite of the fact that he is canonically considered to be the founder of economics. Scholarly work on Adam Smith on the wider nuances of the 'invisible hand' identifies latent ethical convergences with the Marxian critique of capitalism (see, for instance, Drosos 1996; Hill 2007).

Liberalism *and* socialism (II): CA and Hegel

Hegel is a philosopher whose thought on the economy provides us with a foundation to rethink the MM model and CA. Following Kant's realization of Reason in cultural formations associated with modernity, Hegel noted early on the alienating effects of capitalism. For example, in the *Jena Lectures on the Philosophy of Spirit*, young Hegel described in stark colours the alienation and misery of the industrial worker ((1805–1806) 1966, 166) through the lens of abstract value. In *The Philosophy of Right* Hegel's disaffection with the poverty that is generated in 'civil society' – a crucial intersubjective space of justice in the institutional logic of freedom in modernity – troubled many of his epigones. The most conventional approach sees Hegel's impasse as the starting point of Marx's analysis and critique of capitalism through the labour theory of value. Others though prefer to 'upgrade' Hegel's analysis and depart from its historical anchoring to the extent that it can be shown that Hegel's system leaves open the possibility of non-capitalist configurations of the economy (see for example, MacGregor 1984).

Not all Hegelian scholars though adopt this project of a 'Marxian Hegel'. Winfield (1990), for example, insists that the economy as a sphere of justice is conceptualized in terms of freedom as social interaction. Hegel is thus seen as the most powerful exponent of the idea that market economy fulfils genuine normative goals. Its ethical content is obviously not sufficient in itself. It operates under the vigilant supervision of the state, but in line with Hegel's system of social freedom, no institutional sphere monopolizes the content of justice. Rather, it is the entire exposition of institutional spheres of freedom (and this includes the economy) that serves as a template for a just society. This symmetrical account of spheres of justice removes the burden and blame to civil society for the alienation of justice that it causes. It is now on a par with similar pathologies in the family or the state.

Capital, as an irreducible component of the market economy, is for Winfield a pure form of mutual freedom of exchange and constitutes the sphere of transactions between all sorts of different agents under the freedom to exchange commodities. Capital is subject to historically contingent permutations (predatory capital, primitive accumulation, state capitalism, workers' self-management, speculative finance capital) but, like other institutional arrangements, its conceptual truth cannot be exhausted by any of these logical shapes of capital's expansion of profit. Instead, all market economies presuppose capital that is set in motion through the conventional agreement of its protagonists (producers and consumers, buyers and sellers) as a moment of their civil freedom to pursue their interests. Winfield condenses this point with impressive precision, as follows:

> What makes capital's quest for ever increasing wealth juridically indispensable is the conventional character of market need, which entails all the limitless multiplication and refinement of wants pointed out by Hegel. The market economy's self-determined pursuit of a conventional standard of living, where the choice of vocation, personal needs, and commodities is determined not by natural scarcity or psychological necessity, but by the concomitant willing of autonomous market agents, can only be realized if its economic institutions provide for a correspondingly free expansion of wealth. For this reason, capital, be it private, worker self-managed, or public, plays an essential role in enabling civilians to satisfy their freely chosen interests in reciprocity, even if no form of capital can alone insure that all market agents have an equal opportunity to do so.
>
> (Winfield 1990, 131)

Winfield makes several concessions on the historical specificity of capital's permutations, having been persuaded that Hegel's conceptual configuration of civil society maintains its validity as a capitalist formation at a high level of abstraction. This aligns with Sen and the significant enhancement of the freedom of the worker to sell his labour-power, an achievement of world-historical significance recognized also by Marx (Sen 1999a, 29–30). Essentially, therefore, on Winfield's account, capital's drive for profit does not bear an intrinsically coercive and exploitative relation to the freedom of the labourers. Although, for Winfield (1990, 121), capital accumulation can assume distorted forms, there is nothing in the logic of capital that contradicts the freedom of the economic agents. Whatever the outcomes of the decision to sell a commodity at a profit, at break-even point, at a loss or fail to sell, none of these belong to the minimal structure of capital; they all depend on the conventional decisions of the market players. Whatever evils befall markets, these, for Winfield, are 'externally' secreted into the minimal M-C-M′ (the transformation of money into commodities and the value-added transformation of the latter into more money) structure of capital.

Yet Winfield is not oblivious to the inequality and the injustices that the market mechanism is susceptible to. This acknowledgement makes him particularly attentive, following and reconstructing Hegel, to the problem that the market allocation of wealth inequality requires public supervision. However, whatever normative breadth and technical precision public intervention assumes, this corrective, too, is subject to the contingency of the infinite (re)arrangements of the conventions of market participants. Thus, the market that operates under a structure of reciprocity wrought by capital cannot be forestalled of normative outcomes and be relegated to a formal 'just economy', as is the case with Marxist accounts of it. Rather, its 'just' operation serves as a benchmark against intrusions from other spheres (e.g. political advantage, war, colonialism) that tend to make it appear as if it the market is responsible for a host of evil misuses of its efficiency (125–126).

At the other end, these Hegelian lessons that Winfield musters inform a central position of the argument we advance in this book – particularly in Chapter 6

– about Honneth's Hegelian accommodation of market economies into the institutional spheres of justice of a free society. A Hegel–Sen affinity on institutional economics has also been advanced recently. Hermann-Pillath and Boldyrev (2014) suggest that the duality of subjective motivations and revealed preferences is resolved if incorporated into the realm of Hegel's social ontology. This move considers the historically dynamic and intersubjectively validated process of mutual recognition within which individual preferences are articulated and externalized. Drawing on classical and contemporary sources, even from the area of neural science, the authors highlight a number of contemporary developments in economics that can be properly reconstructed within a Hegelian approach to human sociality. It is not my purpose to summarize these conclusions as my standpoint shares with these authors the Hegelian drive but tunes it to sociological theory. Amartya Sen's work figures in their exposition (Hermann-Pillath and Boldyrev 2014, 147–162) at the point when Sen's repulsion of a contractarian transcendental deduction of institutional spheres of justice yields a concept and use of rationality in the framework of 'realization-focused comparisons'. The thrust of the argument is that Sen's model of rationality, which adheres to the sympathetic capacities and informational broadening of the 'impartial spectator' is cut off from a theory of *Sittlichkeit*. Drawing on Hegel's well-known sympathies with classical political economy, the authors suggest that Adam Smith's 'spectator' is mediated historically and within the ladder of categorial–institutional–teleological (normative) exposition of modern spheres of social freedom. Thus, Sen is rightly taken to task at this point (148–149) because the universal broadening Sen himself advocates is premised on the very transcendental institutionalism' he *prima facie* rejects. I say *prima facie* because although Sen claims to 'pluralize' the West's appropriation of democracy, as we shall see later in the book, he nonetheless is quite cautious in denigrating modernity, despite its colonial past and its own internal history of dispossession and immense suffering (e.g. Holocaust, Gulag archipelago). In fact, it is the indispensability of those major social spheres of rights that make Hegel's model so compelling and, contrary to various adumbrations of his thought, quite open to experience, historical change, diversity and negativity. Regardless of how we think about the status of modernity, its institutional spheres are quite powerfully deduced by Hegel in conjunction with the historical transition to industrial capitalism and the emerging culture of rights. Although this work of Hegel's offers a philosophical traction of *Bildung* as the (painful) education of philosophical consciousness observing its own conditions of possibility, Hermann-Pillath and Boldyrev (161–162) read Hegel's process of *Bildung* in ways that incorporate the role-taking capacities (beyond professional skills) of associational life. In effect, this approach interrogates Sen's ideas of capability and functionings that presuppose the ethical will-formation of agents to choose from a set of functionings that are intersubjectively recognized and validated. So if we draw on Sen's repeated example about starvation as a capability deprivation (i.e. a person does not wish that he should starve) and starvation as a result of choice of a functioning (i.e. fasting or hunger strike) it needs to be recalled that both functionings are meaningfully recognized under a *Sittlickheit* that respects religious tolerance and responds with care and attention to the claims a hunger strike is expected to convey.

However, Sen is not oblivious to institutions. It is thus odd that Hermann-Pillath and Boldyrev silence the repeated calls for institutional formation of capabilities, as well as CA's attentiveness to the tensions between a cultural setting governed primarily by traditional values and the rights that govern modernity's *Sittlichkeit*, if by the latter we can understand the liberal democracy's attention to social justice. These points will be taken up in Part III of the book. It is crucial though to note that in response to the Marxist call to revolutionary abolitions of markets, Axel Honneth's reconstruction of the value of socialism under conditions of functional differentiation (i.e. Luhmann's self-making steering capacities of each social system, the economy included) aims at an understanding of moralizing the market, quite promising in CA terms. Drawing on socialism's rich history and the subsequent moral mediations between economy and society sought, for example, by Durkheim, Honneth gives a twist to socialism that, as he claims, maintains the concept's origins (i.e. 'the collective as the bearer of individual freedom') and replenishes it outside the logic of a revolutionary transformation of society. For Honneth,

> [the] conception shared by both Dewey and Hegel, according to which the only criterion for social improvement consists in the liberation from barriers to communication and from dependencies that prevent interaction, provides us with a theoretical instrument for casting the idea of social freedom both as a historical foundation and as a criterion for an experimental understanding of socialism.
>
> (Honneth 2017, 63–64)

Moralization of markets then is on Honneth's account incumbent on deliberative processes. These forge ever more inclusive frameworks from which socialists at given phases of the movement's critique of capitalism excluded themselves in becoming active participants since they jettisoned the vocabulary of liberal rights. In Honneth's reconstructed idea of socialism the moral diffusion of freedom across the spheres of 'emotional intimacy', 'economic independence' and 'political self-determination' seeks, as it were, to reconsider the logic of social reconstruction with sociological weapons drawn from Hegel, Durkheim, and Parsons in light of the challenges Luhmann's functional differentiation posed for old-fashioned normativism, Marxist or liberal.[17]

Liberalism *and* socialism (III): contemporary attempts at synthesis

As we reach the last sections of this chapter, the proposed 'fusion' between liberalism and socialism, which may have appeared scandalous or at least paradoxical, can be further elucidated. The aporia though is legitimate: How can a fusion between liberalism and socialism be sustained when, since the Industrial Revolution, liberal societies – in both the political and economic sense – have grown in unprecedented in intensity and sustenance ideological entrenchment with socialist critiques of capitalism? Surprisingly enough it a cursory remark by Sen that gives us a hint:

> Indeed, there is some truth even in the apparently puzzling claim made in *The Wall Street Journal* that Japan is "the only communist nation that works". This enigmatic remark points to the non-profit motivations underlying many economic and business activities in Japan.
>
> (Sen 1999a, 266)

The previous section served as a template for exploring this 'impossible' consideration. As both liberalism and socialism diversified, common areas started to emerge. Intersecting normative principles and goals (democracy, abundance, social justice, human rights) amplified bridges of dialogue and cooperation. It will though appear less offensive to our standard intuitions if, for example, we consider positions held by sociologists like Daniel Bell ((1976) 1996). He did not hesitate to call himself a liberal in politics, socialist in the economy, conservative in culture. And even Parsons' (1969, 465) more temperate but no less sanguine distance from standpoints of 'committed capitalism' or 'committed socialism' indicated both a fatigue with irreconcilable fixities but no less ambitiously a necessity (and faith) in overcoming them.

Even relatively early since Marx's legacy, the so-called revisionist project of social democracy challenged paternalistic implementations of Marx's penetrating analysis of capitalism. In itself this social democratic legacy is to a large extend to be credited to victories of social justice that tempered markets, without jettisoning though the radical potential of the Marxian project. Within this tradition surveyed by Berman (2006), Carlo Rosselli, along with Eduard Bernstein and Jean Jaurès among others, holds a prominent position because he prefigured this bridge in the shape of 'liberal socialism'. I shall not reiterate conclusions drawn from Berman's brilliant analysis. I only wish to note that, according to Rosselli, limiting freedom to the realm of procedural and legal capacities renders markets the main player for feeding human capacities. In order for liberalism (and its concomitant core value of democracy) to meet its own ideals, Rosselli contends that the democratic will-formation processes need to leave ever-greater spaces for autonomy, which intrinsically implies material preconditions for human capacities to flourish. Yet, ascribing to liberalism democratic accomplishments is not a cut-and-dry factum. Rather, it is a process that denotes a degree of freedom's consolidation that secedes from dualistic visions of society and thus pursues the socialist completion of liberalism under conditions of a '*pact of civility*' ((1930) 1994, 94 [original emphasis]). Rosselli appeals here to some sort of prepolitical–axiological core of liberty, conceptualized later as civil rights, which may be tweaked towards historically concrete political manifestations, yet its nearly natural law formulation is itself the product of civilization (95). Meaning, that some significant degree of historical coincidence between the content of liberalism and its form is discernible in modern society. Thus, as if employing a contemporary version of system differentiation, Rosselli chides those socialist struggles that feed on a decisionist demonization of the bourgeoisie and fail to understand that as a class it no longer operates as a 'uniform bloc' (96). This does not forestall the possibility of violent struggles. As Rosselli is clearly aware, liberal socialism's utopia could potentially be implicated in a world that requires struggle within the pact of civility and exceptional measures but only if this pact is transgressed by the bourgeoisie itself. Ultimately, 'the socialist movement is [...] the objective heir of liberalism: it carries this dynamic of liberty forward through the vicissitudes of history toward its actualization' (87).[18]

Other powerful proposals, like 'Marxian Liberalism' (Reiman 2014), extend the paths of a reconstruction of a just market tuning a Rawlsian theory of justice to Marx's objections against capitalism. Like Berman, Reiman's position is marked by the qualification 'as much as possible'. The upshot here is that the horizon of equality in an economy of associated producers and consumers bears pragmatically on current accomplishments. These exist both as theoretical toolkits (thus in the shape of collectively available knowledge) and, as we shall intimate later, in the form of viable policy proposals. Reiman's thought-experiment is powerful and pertinent. The wedlock he advances is one between John Rawls' liberalism and Marx's communism. Reiman is dissatisfied with much contemporary political philosophy that drifts from exploring mediations between these two extremely robust positions. This is so because the accomplishments of a capitalist market with the freedoms it provides to its agents obscure the violent moments in the extraction of surplus labour and, further, occlude (with sophisticated ideological mechanisms) the structural coercion that is in place. Marx's relevance, for Reiman, is in this sense undeniable. By contrast, the failures of Soviet Marxism reveal that any socialization or state-control of the means of production must be accomplished alongside maximum protections from coercion. Thus, negative freedoms need to inform from ground zero the model of Marxian Liberalism. This prerequisite is a necessary but not a sufficient condition for CA too. Within though the realm of the possible (as the thought-experiment is built with the current socioeconomic and political environment in mind, despite its future-driven prospects) efficient markets need to be animated by universal principles of justice, geared to those who happen to be worst-off, but freed from the democratically inept paternalism that could prove dangerous in 'punishing' those who are better off in terms of talents or effort.

Thus, from Rawls' liberalism, Reiman takes roughly the following features: a) the original position (albeit in a reconstructed form), b) the difference principle and c) Rawls' recognition of Marx's insights about the structural coercion of capitalism and its impact on non-owners of the means of production, even if Rawls ((1971) 1999) does not adopt Marx's labour theory of value. (It is no coincidence that Piketty ((2013) 2017, 610–611) brings CA and Rawls together on similar grounds.) To enable the Marxian Liberalism position to emerge as a potent and superior fusion, Reiman selects from Marx the following cardinal issues: a) the division of capitalist society between owners of the means of production and non-owners (and the structural violence entailed in this relation); b) the idea that capital is not a thing but a social relation; c) the deep-seated ideological framework that distorts this social relation and renders it visible in the inverted shape of a relation among discrete and independent individuals; d) the admission on Marx's part that capitalism signals the most progressive phase in the history of the human species' material reproduction; e) that the freedoms accomplished in capitalism along with a formal establishment of a system of justice both enhance and inhibit the agent's freedom in society; and f) although Reiman avoids using the phrase 'determinate negation', he proceeds along these lines when he retains both moments of capitalism's partial accomplishment of justice. Thus, in order to avoid freezing communism into a fixed state of affairs, he follows Marx's Kantian legacy in choosing to configure communism heuristically in terms of an ongoing struggle to combat injustices in capitalism. Reiman hopes that this relaxation of communism as an ideal but also as an ongoing project in socioeconomic reality justifies the 'as just as possible' title of his work, given the historical specificity of the project of Marxian Liberalism. Rather than eliciting a retreatist regress to Hegel's normative black hole of poverty in civil society, Reiman's qualification keeps open the possibility of a realistically possible future society of universal justice in line with the letter and spirit of Marx's idea of communism.

I need to insist a bit on this point and offer some further remarks that will gradually take us to Marxian Liberalism's relevance for CA. As Reiman continues, Marx's focus on the material conditions of liberty includes objects 'that enhance people's ability to act on their choices' (2014, 170). In a footnote in support of this approach Reiman cites Sen and the Universal Basic Income (UBI) advocate Philippe van Parjis (171n. 18). It is unfortunate that Reiman does not pursue further the relevance of a CA theory of justice to some of the premises of Marxian Liberalism. Such relevance can be discerned on numerous occasions in Reiman's exciting argument but the seeds of such fusion can be gleaned from Sen's critique of Rawls (and Nozick) when he questions the lack of importance both models attach to the risks of economic deprivations. Thus, Sen's sustained critique of complete rankings of principles of justice challenges Rawls' priority of personal liberty and wonders why 'intense economic needs, which can be matters of life and death, be lower than that of personal liberties?' (1999a, 64). Similarly, the entitlements Nozick's theory adduces are held to be bent only if 'moral horrors' arise, while other and very intense types of deprivations (e.g. endemic hunger, lack of medical care) can allegedly co-exist with libertarian conceptions of right (65–66).

The point at which the political theory of Marxian Liberalism transfers the validity of its theoretical reconstruction to sociology should, I think, be evident by the following long but important extract. Reiman suggests that the 'difference principle' sets the 'rightful pursuit of self-interest' at the point where the share of those worst-off is maximized, as those who are more talented and those who are less talented cannot attain this knowledge at the level of the original position. For Reiman:

> [The difference principle] sets [the maximum limit of rightful pursuit of self-interest] not at the point at which the more talented are capable of foregoing incentives, but at the point at which an actual social system, executed by humans as we know them, will work to maximize the share of the worst off.
>
> No doubt it will be difficult to determine this point in an actual economy. Societies will have to engage in experimentation with more and less inequality to see how much inequality really maximizes the worst-off share; and they will have to look seriously at the results of different experiments in different nations, and so on. But the principle is clear: That degree of inequality that actually works to maximize the share of the worst off is the maximum limit of the legitimate personal prerogative, the rightful range in which people may pursue their self-interest. It should be clear that this does not justify every grasping conduct, such as price-gouging or other practices, widely agreed even by capitalists to be unethical, and not necessary to the functioning of the system. It justifies the normal self-interested pursuit of incentives that makes capitalism work to raise the standard of living of society.
>
> (2014, 153–154)

The trial-and-error experimentation with degrees of inequality and human well-being is, for example, conquered by the work of Wilkinson and Pickett (2010). Societies with an eye attentive to the weakest pillar, whether opting for equality of incomes before taxes (as in Japan) or equality after taxes (as in Scandinavian economies) happen, as their study demonstrates, to score better in most of all relevant well-being indicators. Interestingly enough, Reiman makes talk about a 'normal self-interest', a qualification that has received ample reflection in sociology (e.g. Marx and Durkheim under Aristotle's heritage who opt for a *normal* development of human needs). (Similarly, Piketty's attention to inequality's – current and projected – rise points to the continued role of a 'hyperpatrimonial society', based on inherited wealth, next to the fuzzy relation of incomes to merit, in a 'hypermeritocratic society' of 'supermanagers' (2014) 2017, 331.) In fact, both communism and organic solidarity (for Durkheim, 'socialism', as he was allergic to the homogenizing tendencies of communism as understood by many a Marx epigones at the time), disallow such excesses, not paternalistically, but as the spontaneous outcome of a society patterned with a different division of labour based on justice. (In this sense, Nussbaum's articulation of her thick vague CCL resembles, as she admits, the outcomes of people's preferences in Scandinavian societies (Nussbaum 1990, 241–243)) and forms the backdrop of her fusion of liberalism with 'Aristotelian social democracy'.)

Pragmatic codas

As the groundbreaking study by Boltanski and Chiapello ((1997) 2007) showed in sociology, capital's gradual displacements of labour have followed the trail of the partial absorption of critique against capital, since the late 1960s. Critical sociology's arsenal thinned spectacularly as a result of its partial victories but also because of capitalism's capacity to process critique and, as if in a reentry operation, utilize it to energize itself anew and displace critique to other and uncharted fields. Boltanski and Chiapello's research programme has had purchase in CA-inspired critics of labour's gradual depletion by neo-management's self-corrigibility in the face of capital's crises and the novel projects of capitalism's self-regeneration (the 'new spirit of capitalism'). Both the capability for enhancing worker's voice at the workplace (e.g. Zimmermann 2012) and the invention of a new semantics of a politics of capabilities that can supplement the code of 'competences' that dominates neo-managerial approaches to employment and its evaluation (Zimmermann 2004), coalesce in the project of social dialogue in Europe with a view to accomplish both market efficiency and social justice. As suggested by Zimmermann (2018), CA and its pragmatist epistemology offers the possibility of investigating critically institutions, organizations and the individual in the plural shapes where claims to autonomy can have pragmatic purchase.

Workers' capability for voice in terms of autonomous collective bargaining, legal framework of industrial relations and social dialogue is proposed (Negrelli 2012) as a value that ought to be recaptured so that economic implosions, like the Great Recession, can be contained in a global system of multiple system differentiation. The deliberative ideal that figures here works as a functional and normative space within organizations, firms, trade unions, professional associations that can 'convert' workers' capabilities to functionings. This is a fruitful implementation of CA to the problem of an increasingly privatized working class where the capacity for voice is under duress and pressure, either direct or indirect, and frequently in the shape of a partial absorption of its demands as Boltanski and Chiapello (2007) have painstakingly demonstrated.

Instead therefore of interpreting CA as a refined neo-liberal tool for decentering critical attention to capital, its radical defenders focus on labour issues and seek to supplant workers with the capability for voice. Salais (2012), for example, goes as far as to make a thought-experiment about what social relations of labour would look like once CA has been fully endorsed in a society. Reading CA through Marx's fully flourished social individual, Salais interprets the logical consequence of Sen's *Development as Freedom* to be a society, radically transformed in ways where finance and money would be 'redefined as means for socio-economic ends' (2012, 230). The fusion of the different realms (a capacitated labour process and an informed citizen in what Salais names a 'situated state', a middle-range version of an interventionist and an absent state) fall under the crux of what he reads in CA to be its most promising potential, namely deliberative democracy. Regardless of the feasibility of the vision propounded by

Salais, his perspective shows that CA can neither be squeezed into the domain of neo-liberalism's reformist compass (the abstractions made by many such interpreters distort the deep axiology of CA and leave unaccounted many of its domains that lead elsewhere) nor be seen as an 'anywhere fits' toolkit.

In such proposals we again get a foretaste of latent intersections between liberalism and socialism at work. For example, Bauman contends that most of liquid modernity's challenges bear on the growing global inequality. The post-war era of 'reconciliation' between capital and labour, feeds, for Bauman, the currently momentous scale of inequality gaps with a utopian (this time realistic) project of mitigating it. Replenishing this critique of work in light of current findings about inequality must converse with the advocates of UBI. Implementation of UBI may be more easily said than done (see Kentish 2017) but voices in its favour grow. Adoption of UBI is likened not only to strengthening the minimum standard of decent living but ideally would extend to the institutionalized release from the necessity of labour of human capabilities in a periodic frequency. As Bauman claims:

> The UBI advocates, as much as for their predecessors, the designers of the welfare state that 'positive freedom' – i.e., the capability to self-assert and to follow one's choices – is, however, an indispensable concomitant of the 'negative' one, once it is recast as the warrant against rendering the latter a recipe for the destitution of a large number of society's members.
>
> (2017, 113–114)

While the shift to a politics of well-being can be susceptible to ideological distortions[19] the avenue opened up by Bauman or André Gorz so that formal entitlements can turn to a standing cultivation of human capabilities, figures as a promising recalibration of a nascent socialist morphology of market economies. UBI should not, of course, be seen as a panacea to the problem of poverty and to the unfreedom coupled to it. Rather, in a networked conception of capabilities (like Nussbaum's CCL) it would strengthen a person's capability to control her material environment. This leads Sen (1999a, 130), for example, to insist on public support for those unemployed since any 'disincentives' should be expected to be curbed by the fact that employment is valued over and above the income it provides. As such, it functions as a precondition for the flourishing of other capabilities in this list; it also propels further fructification of an agent's command of material resources. It is thus not unexpected that even in cursory fashion Sen (2009, 65) cites approvingly van Parjis on the UBI reforms.

Concluding remark

The normative detour to classical political economy attempted by Sen is, as I have indicated, a normativization of economic categories. This moral upgrading enunciated by CA relies heavily on Aristotle. Sen (1990) conceives CA as an implementation of the Aristotelian notion of potentiality, the latter being a central component of the reconstruction of individual happiness. He also emphasizes the widening of communicative channels between peoples but also, intra-societally, between social subsystems. For Sen (see, for example, 2006, 146–148) then, the globalization of trade and commerce is part of the tendency of markets to bind people from different locations and continents together and thus of increasing the scope of mutuality and justice. Ultimately, replenishing the market is crucially dependent on values, the role of which is for Sen 'extensive in human behavior' (1999a, 272).[20]

For all its merits, Sen's system operates within the parameters set by current market mechanisms. While wisely abstaining from any utopian projection, Sen's model abstracts from the systemic structure of global capitalism. His version of CA operates at a distance from the systemic social relations that give rise to (and are in turn reproduced by) the economic categories that abstract from the realization of Adam Smith's 'full man' or from Marx's 'species-being potentiality'. If, according to Sen's accommodation of Adam Smith, 'moderation' should be inculcated into the action-map of modern persons – presumably as the work of institutional socialization, education and sanctions – then moderation of market logics is still abstracted from the logic of capital and its uncharted flows of monetary transactions detached from real economies. In other words, Sen's CA fails to consider what Ronald Meek urges economists to do, namely to bring 'sociology back into economics' (1956, 317) patterned after what Marx's original attempt sought to accomplish in the sphere of the social relations of production, but is now urgently required 'in sensitive spheres like that of a theory of distribution where we most need to achieve it' (317). Similarly, CA, for all its pluralist scope and contextual agility, lags in the emphasis given to capitalism's intrinsic alienation and dispossession of workers at the 'genetic' moment when this is predicated on the 'silent' fact of primitive accumulation and thus to capitalist modernity's colonial history.[21]

If, as I maintain in this book, CA's 'methodologically individualist' immanent critique of *homo economicus* keeps fast into its emancipatory potential then it cannot cut all links from the Kantian regulative ideal of a 'categorical imperative' that permeates Marx's materialism, namely 'to overthrow all conditions in which man is a debased, enslaved, neglected and contemptible being [...]' (Marx (1843–1844) 1992, 251). And because man is still in a systematic risk of being plunged even deeper into debasement, deprivation, neglect and contempt, the conditions for this accumulation of suffering are still at work.[22] For Marx capitalist society 'is no solid crystal, but an organism capable of change, and constantly engaged in a process of change' (Marx (1867) 1990, 93). Today, this injunction, among Marx's many criticisms against hasty applications of the 'ideal' in history or formulaic proclamations of society's 'one-size-fits-all' solution that demands the abolition of capital, is given new impetus by Sen's CA.[23] Sen notes that it is a characteristic of freedom that it has diverse aspects that relate to a variety of activities and institutions. It cannot yield a view of development as freedom that translates readily into some simple 'formula' of accumulation of capital, primitive or modern, or of opening up of markets, or of having efficient economic planning (although each of these particular features fits into the broader picture). The overarching principle that brings these factors together is encapsulated in the last chapter of Sen's *Development as Freedom*, titled 'individual freedom as a social commitment'. What this individual freedom is, Part II of this book is about to explore.

Notes

1 In this context it is worth recording the idea that Sen's critique of economic rationality extends to an umbrella of a wider 'balance of reasons' (Morris 2010, 56) suitable to common sense as, for example, when humans cannot inflict pain on others at first sight but only on the preconditions of role-taking, identity training and mental and emotional conditioning (55n.24). This is the morale behind Kader Mia's untimely death. Such vivid imagery is theorized by neighbouring economist Vivian Walsh. Inspired by an episode from D.H. Lawrence's *The First Lady Chatterley*, Walsh confesses:

> to see someone dying slowly for want, as it were, of some constituent of the air a human being needs to breathe [...]; to watch helplessly the slow dying of such an expiring spirit is to be acquainted with scarcity. Once seen, it is never forgotten.
> (Walsh 1961, 31)

An empirically supported study (Anderson 2014) on suffering designates the broad scope of this concept and its regrettably wide gamut of experiences of pain. The typology of frames of suffering offered generates fruitful space for dialogue with CA.

2 Beyond this passing approving reference to Sen, Negri provides an intriguing conceptual modification of capital's valorization of labour. He thus creates a space for dialogue with CA, often obscured by Marxist and non-Marxist critiques of Sen. Although it cannot be expounded here – as its deeper implications concern Chapter 4 – Negri's concept of 'self-valorization' may be discussed strictly within the project of capital's domination over labour, something that only marginally takes the front stage in Sen. The possibility of self-valorization, which in effect stands for the subjective resistance against capitalism rather than the collective mobilization traditionally associated with orthodox approaches to class struggle, opens up a multitude of spaces both within and outside capitalism that lie beyond capital's valourization process. Negri is elliptical and unnecessarily obscure on this point but self-valourization (free time in weekends, in the workplace at the time where labour cannot be fully supervised by capital, in urban and other spaces seized for self-expression) figures as the capability of the subject to the 'auto-determination of its development' (Negri 1991, 162–163). Similar ideas are to be found in André Gorz (2010) who, like Negri, cites approvingly Sen. To be sure Sen's CA refrains from the maximalism of Negri's faith in the molecular revolution of the multitude. Still, CA contains in terms of its own pragmatic flexibility and contextual openness characteristics that resemble the multitude's capability-fulfilment as subjective positive resistance against capital or against other non-economic forms of domination. Both Negri and Gorz rely wisely on Marx's *Grundrisse* that comes to occupy a major place in Marxian scholarship, in that it reconstitutes the conditions of labour-power's fulfilment of human capacities. Salais' (2012, 233) Marxian reading of work through the lens of CA anchors it in a life-process and thus shares the deeply ontological features of this programme, regardless of the hesitation of CA scholars to develop further these features outside the comfort zone of human rights.

3 For instance, Bauman (2017) attempted to reserve – almost heroically – spaces of resistance and remoralization claims within the TINA ('there is no alternative') logic

of austerity politics and the ensuing neo-liberal dismantling of the commons. In the context of the crisis in Europe some of the discipline's most formidable exponents are ready to abdicate collective coordination of resistance. Thus, Claus Offe (2015) amalgamates the rejuvenation of the European project with realistic proposals for solidarity, still though condoning with iron realism his own version of TINA, namely a 'crisis of crisis management'. Even the extremely informed in empirical support resurgence of Critical Theory by Wolfgang Streeck, charts the transition from the tax state to the debt state and, currently, to the consolidation state but he, like Offe, focuses less on the perceived real possibilities of reconciliation between capital and labour (as in 1970s or in the last vestiges of welfare-state Scandinavian nations) and more on the irrevocable (as he sees it) implosion of capitalism (Streeck 2016; 2014).

4 Marx's intervention, as is also widely known, challenged the logical status of Hegel's exposition of institutional arrangements. The justice Hegel invoked was held by Marx to be purely formal. Capitalist social relations of production inflicted deep wounds on social integration (i.e. the alienation of workers in their everyday lived and future prospects) and system integration (the debatable 'reduction' of superstructure into the 'base' of market logics). In short, the form of value in capitalism makes the content of value (free social reproduction of human beings) dependent exclusively on economic institutions. To remove the formal actualization of values in society from the social spheres that surround the capitalist market is encapsulated with the problem of values being dependent on the law of value. This murky and difficult problem is not foreign to classical sociology (see Simmel (1900) 1990).

5 From the perspective of sociology of knowledge, Fourcade (2009, 157–158) locates Sen's CA in the tradition of British economics (and its attention to colonial history) which may account for the emphasis on ethical aspects of development. Her findings illustrate elective affinities in the two disciplines' focal concerns and thus, from this lens too, the hiatus between economics and sociology is held to be suspended.

6 Unfortunately, I lack the space to address the 'economy–society' interdependence through Max Weber's magisterial account. Although Weber is indispensable for the religious, legal, organizational, technical, and normative mediations of economy by society, the chief reasons for not engaging more forcefully with his work are: a) the fact that I find Parsons' Weberian heritage better equipped as an analytical tool in enabling the sociologist to deal with system differentiation; b) Parsons' advantage over the Weberian models is that the space in the social system for value-diffusion is more prominent in terms of amplifying, from Weber's historical sociology (e.g. the 'Protestant ethic' thesis), a specific subsystem of functional axiology; c) because the latter is ontologically fractured in Weber's theses on value-incommensurability (see Chapter 1), unlike Parsons' incorporation of the opposite approach to values as this was set by Durkheim (i.e. values belong to society as an object in historical movement and are thus binding at the point of societal development where they coincide with the subject's free capacity for valuations). This does not suggest that Sen's project of moralizing the economy disqualifies affinities to Weber's 'peace' prerequisites of 'economic action' (Weber (1922) 1978, 63). The question remains if prudential goals to economic action are inserted to the typical cluster exogenously or if the moral infusion of markets under secular value-sets intersects with the 'peaceful' presuppositions of capitalist action, presuppositions that require a logic of how Weber's various normative requirements intermesh with the economy under a *Sittlichkeit* conducive to individual (and economic) freedom.

7 Search for typologies about the 'economy–society' troubled relation are not foreign to sociology. Indicatively, Erik Olin Wright conceives it also in terms of 'vocabularies' and thus argues within ideal-types of capitalism, statism and socialism. He then proceeds in elaborating seven configurations of economy that liken with different degrees and complexity of directionality among social systems, the clusters of 'social power', 'state power' and 'economic power' in fostering different versions of

'economic activity' (Wright 2016a). In spite of his reticence on Parsons, Wright deploys three of the four functional imperatives, this time patterned after Weber. Adaptation (economic power), goal-attainment (state power) and social power (societal integration) are reproductions within the code of power (G). There is little space given to something akin to ethical imperatives (let us call them for the sake of argument, 'normative power'), an omission that is odd given the author's sustained emphasis on democracy and non-contractual values, as in Polanyi and Durkheim (Wright 2016b). The reliance on Weber's scheme of power explains the omission of values and the retrospective and external appendage to this model. Paradoxically, such 'radical' proposals under-theorize and under-operationalize the component of value-generalization in society, although their accounts presuppose it.

8 For Luhmann, the self-reference of each social system's steering capacities prescribes an autopoietic, as he coins it, process of each system's own reproduction. The economy as a social system is no exception. Like every other system it functions on the basis of a primary code that sets it in motion. The code 'profit/non-profit' is a type of semantics unique to the economy. Although the economy is loosely coupled to other systems this only implies that the economy 'sees' other systems through its own code; conversely, economic processes and the content of the economy is 'observed' by other social systems (political, religious, moral, aesthetic, legal) but this happens only through the lens of discrete self-referential systems.

9 For instance, Hayek's a-social language of 'capacities' (1967, 233) is premised on the scientific 'incapacity' to enquire into an actor's motives and justifications. Actual outcomes and preferences figure as the sole index of how the actor's merits are to be judged in terms of the value of her services. Hayek does not silence the gap between the actual monetary reward and the potentially incongruent with it degree of esteem that a person commands for her fellows. In perceiving this asymmetry between income and status Hayek is essentially undermining the welfare-state for its 'materialistic' world-view. Believing that a materialist blueprint of society is not a priori morally valid, Hayek repels recourse to a collective set of values that are conducive to non-material indicators of merit. He, however, keeps the materialist option open but now transfers the option for such reevaluation to the freedom society accords to the individual (235). If such non-material goals should be primed, isn't 'sacrifice' a cost in pursuing such individual remapping of valued priorities? Doesn't this sacrifice constitute a matter of individual responsibility in a free society? In turning socialist utopia (a society that does not prioritize material needs but aims at the fully-fledged development of human potentialities) on its head Hayek makes collective valuations derivative of the individual effort in producing valued goods and services for others. He thus hopes to render welfare-state beneficiaries social free-riders. Sensing the advent of social democracy, Hayek calls for 'a liberal Utopia' (194), a project, however, that does not seek to ratify the status quo (the latter marred by its own 'bad apples' of capitalist susceptibility) or to adhere to a 'diluted kind of socialism' (194) driven by an intellectual leadership of integrity unsusceptible to Sirens of 'power and influence' (194). The crucial question that arises now is that, following the neoliberal realization of Hayek's Utopia, less and less people are capable of considering the option to sacrifice material ends so that they can consider the options Hayek would assign to the domain of 'free' agency. But this condition of 'unknowability' of what is social that Hayek promotes in his expressed discontent on the meaning of the 'social' (237–247), seems to be suspended once a Utopia (i.e. a cognitive state of social being where all circumstances and variable are 'known') is mustered in defence of the 'free society' with the individual 'allowing to decide himself about his action' (244), since, paradoxically, all 'social' frameworks of actions remain inscrutable.

10 This idea of openness underlines Sen's conception of equality. When he asks 'equality of what?' Sen (1992) adduces two criteria that make equality an operational

concept. He has to rely on the need for carving an evaluative space so that equality is addressed in terms of the multiple focal variables that require scrutiny. He also argues that when a specific evaluative space is opened then particular and precise measurements of equality can be seen to emerge and to acquire merit in terms of broadening the conceptual base for addressing income inequality. Sen wants to avoid treating equality as some 'jack-of-all-trades' normative tool. Thus, CA on inequality is held to operate as a middle-range tool, equidistant from approaches to the issue of equality which in themselves are useful but should not be taken to exhaust an all-encompassing paradigm. In fact Sen argues with a sociological mind-set here when he warns against explaining away 'interpersonal comparisons' in measuring inequality. The two extremes he warns against stretch from a pragmatic approach that is driven by parsimony and thus risks occluding more complex analytical measurements than income inequality *stricto sensu*, and a grand narrative of equality that applies *tout court* to all people and ignores situational and other differences. Such a model of moralizing inequality conceptualization and measurement makes 'an easy transition between one space and another, e.g. from incomes to utilities, from primary goods to freedoms, from resources to well-being' (Sen 1992, 30). Again, he gleans inspiration from Marx's critique of seeing human beings 'only as workers' (Marx (1875) 1958, 24).

11 What Nussbaum aims to accomplish with an expanded CCL may bear on Sen's factors of contingency in measuring the relationship between income and individual freedoms. The five factors of 'parametric variation' discussed by Sen (1997, 385–386; 1999a, 70–72) include: a) personal heterogeneities, b) environmental diversities, c) variations in social climate, d) differences in relational perspective and e) distribution within the family. If the specific characteristics of each variation are considered, as Sen articulates them, then they come surprisingly close to Nussbaum's CCL. So, for example, factors (b) to (e) capture Nussbaum's normative expectations of capabilities of affiliation, natural habitat, and control over an economic and political environment. This type of conceptual unpacking engages factors of variation (and contingency) in the broadening of capabilities so that variation is curbed, not by recourse to some institutional or economic blueprint, but by considering the insertion of Central Capabilities into each domain. (This taxing problem that bears on fundamental assumptions about reality's contingency will reemerge at various points in the argument.)

12 Citing Japan's 'rule-based' behaviour as a counterpoint to the alleged 'free-market' efficiency of Japanese economy, Sen (1987a, 18n.15) widens the scope of what constitutes affluence and growth, repatriating genuinely sociological aspects of this high-trust society, and stressing facets of social conduct that denote adoption of an economic model within a wider template of values, cultural mores and etiquette. It is this call for embeddedness that Wilkinson and Pickett (2010) invoke in the empirically demonstrated superiority of Japan on lower inequality rates among affluent societies. Group loyalties entail a mixed picture of how self-interested and self-sacrificing behaviour interact. And group life pervades social life in its entirety, from family and peer groups, to professional organizations, firms, political parties or social movements, admittedly though with a surplus of paternalism. Sen adduces this 'intermediate' realm (1987a, 20) and in this sense he makes use of what is unusual in economics but constitutes standard approaches in sociology that see market transactions as intrinsically tied to a wider institutional net.

13 Sen's qualified but explicit critique of utilitarianism has invited lively debates (see Sen and Williams 1982). For Sen the impact of utilitarianism is not denied. In fact he considers utilitarianism to have the strengths of: a) consequentialism ('taking into account the results of social arrangements in judging them' (1999a, 60); and b) the attention it gives to the 'well-being of people involved when judging social arrangements' (60). Influential though as utilitarianism may have been in its different guises,

it suffers though from three broad defects: a) '*distributional indifference*' as it tends to ignore how happiness is being distributed, thus omitting from its explanatory map issues of 'inequality', b) '*neglect of rights and freedoms*' as these are valued only indirectly toward utility maximization and not intrinsically, and c) '*adaptation and mental conditioning*' which, for Sen, means that the conception of individual well-being is not rigorous enough, since it tends to neglect issues of false-consciousness and other adjustments of socially deprived individuals in unfavourable economic and other circumstances (62). Thus, the utilitarian model confronts its own horizon of limited applicability and normative coherence when it silences (under the scale of utilities) the 'destitute thrown into beggary, the vulnerable landless labourer precariously surviving at the edge of subsistence, the overworked domestic servant working round the clock, the subdued and subjugated housewife reconciled to her role and her fate' (1999b, 15). Sen moves even further in the broadened perspective offered, that, sociologically speaking, aims at bridging agency and structure. It thus converts commodity-characteristics to individual achievements with the awareness of the variety of factors (metabolism, body size, age, sex, activity levels, medical conditions and access to health care among others) that span biology as well as sociability (e.g. social conventions, affiliation, placement in the family) (17–18). This tension in the utilitarian tendency to reduce all preferences to utilities is also taken to task by Amitai Etzioni (1999). Etzioni's observations are launched from the perspective of 'socioeconomics' that challenges major precepts of neo-classical depictions of rational choice and is a variant of communitarianism with, however, a committed consideration to market efficiency. Yet, we should be cautious about the Etzioni–CA bridges. The communitarian ramifications of the former are not really compatible with core CA values like freedom and diversity (for a critique of Etzioni's communitarianism in general, see Nussbaum 2004, 56, 175).

14 Actually, Sen (1987c, 32–33) broadens, quasi-sociologically, the canvas within which utility preference can be transferred from a major determinant of the standard of living to a less crucial one. In brief, he alerts us to complex epistemological problems that confound any neat demarcation in how objective and subjective reasons for preferences relate to accepted social standards. Part of this disengagement of the standard of living from utilitarian models is that the agent is embedded in an ongoing process of self-evaluation. As a result of this evaluative standpoint, based on all sorts of factors (desires, choices, happiness), the relevance of a single set of utility rankings is called into question. The standard of living can be a matter of great esteem in a society that has accomplished literacy and rise of life expectancy. Conversely, it can be a matter of great urgency if its citizens are deprived of fundamental freedoms, like the freedom to access information. (Sen's discussions of the comparative merits between India and China resonate today about China's spectacular growth rates which, though, can be hugely misleading in the face of the 'Great Firewall').

15 Starting from 'behavioural ethics', the sociological tradition that includes Marx (even if he saw most of these ethical norms as formally valid only), Weber's ((1904–1905) 1968) 'Protestant ethic' thesis, Durkheim's call for moral conditions of contracts as a means for bringing closer 'economists and sociologists' ((1887) 1993, 58–77), and certainly Parsons' critique of utilitarian motivation in the famous convergence thesis of non-economic conditions of economic action (Parsons (1937) 1968a; (1937) 1968b), as well as the motivational complex of economic action with diverse normative shades (Parsons (1940) 1954), indicate a sociological discourse that saw capitalism to be entangled with values.

16 For all its merits CA ethical scope becomes transfigured, for Marxist critics, into just another subtle mechanism of control ('governability'), similar to Foucault's disciplinary discourses, which makes human beings 'takers' of policy than 'makers' of their won fulfilled lives. Critics, like Navarro (2000), question the open scope of Sen's capabilities and instrumental freedoms (an issue which will be taken up in

detail in Chapter 6) on the grounds that it lacks prioritization, understood here as priming the materialist preconditions of human life. It is thus suggested that Sen overpoliticizes the problem and findings on famines and squeezes it into the dualisms democracy (modernity)/non-democracy (modern dictatorships/tradition). Thus, significant differences within each political constellation obscure both significant accomplishments (e.g. on health services, for instance) in some dictatorships (like Cuba as opposed to Pinochet's Chile) or in democratic societies governed though by some version of socialism (Navarro 2000, 667–671). Still more vitriolic is the critique that chides Sen for his silence on the systemic corruption of advanced finance capitalism in liberal democracies that trumpet deliberation yet distort it by media selectivity and colossal power structures, both financial and political. In this line, Sandbrook (2000) labels Sen a 'pragmatic neoliberal'. Through this lens, Sen appears to be insensitive to the social embededdness of markets argument, advanced, according to Sandbrook, by Karl Polanyi. Sen's argument skirts, it is argued, the unprecedented concentration of corporate power in the contemporary era of global market expansion. Offering a telling list of capital's systemic corruption, Sandbrook (1078) suggests that Sen offers an apology for neo-liberalism that lags behind a critique of capitalism, anticipated and disdained also by its own apostles (i.e. Soros and Fukuyama). Sen is thus held to bear the errors of abstracting deliberative democracy and social progress from the power relations that currently mediate them. Others (Dean 2000; Menon 2002; Walby 2012) reiterate similar reservations. For all the scepticism expressed in such critical engagements with Sen, these suffer from a reluctance to dig deeper into the ontology of CA which, as I shall argue, in Chapters 3 and 4 aligns in many and unexpected ways with Marx's vision of the free human being. To argue, for example, as often happens, that Sen's CA is colonized by neo-liberalism is in itself an insufficient criterion in so far as Marxism too lacked the inbuilt protection against ideological and implementation deformations. It suffered equally in the hands of Soviet tyranny and by militant critics of Marx like Popper and Hayek. Rather, Sen's so-called individualist CA creates a wedge in neo-liberal discourse and forces its policy makers to take account of human flourishing even if, expectedly, it silences or relegates structural issues of unemployment and inequality. Yet as a dialogic space of accountability, even in such partial readings of it, CA can be of great help. One issue that many criticisms do not seem to notice is that when Sen is held to devote no space to struggle (see, for example, Dean 2000, 271–275) he nonetheless recognizes its political significance as a collective force of social change. Sen writes: 'In fact, the activism of opposition parties is an important force in nondemocratic societies as well as in democratic ones' (1999a, 156). Examples cited include 'pre-democratic South Korea' and 'Pinochet's Chile' (156). This does not read exactly as a neo-liberal apology, given also the fact that opposition is entangled with 'value formation' (156) and thus partakes of a historical openness to change in strengthening democracy. Many critics also fail to notice the chapter layout in Sen's manifesto of CA: *Development as Freedom*. The chapter on 'Markets, State and Social Opportunity' is followed by the one titled 'The Importance of Democracy'. In the latter Sen argues powerfully for many of the goals he is accused of having omitted. For instance, he demolishes the Asian market dogma that democracy is incompatible with growth (150), as in the case of Singapore, which as confirmed by Wilkinson and Pickett (2010), showcases growth rates that obscure Singapore's huge inequality. The same can be said about China today. Further, Sen – like Critical Marxism – warns about the dangers of treating either economic modifications blindly, in the absence of deliberation or, inversely, of treating democracy as a formal mechanism (155). In fact, Sen's injunction that political freedoms are pivotal not only 'in inducing social responses to economic needs' but in leading to a 'reconceptualization of economic needs themselves' (154) is identical to Marcuse's objection against a mechanical understanding of what the socialization of the means of production really means, if one is to avoid despotic and authoritarian travesties of Marx (see Marcuse (1941) 1977, 282–283). In the wedlock of Adam Smith and Karl Marx, Sen (1999a, 289) commends the founding axiological principle in Marxian philosophy of history that requires humans to become owners of the circumstances within which their lives unfold. Such textual support challenges the distorted picture of Sen that emerges from radical and conservative critics alike.

17 For Tony Smith (1990) who takes Winfield to task on the level of Marx's categorial exposition of capital, beyond the unequal opportunities given to those who hold economic power to 'crystallize' their status in terms of political power too, the state's dependence on capitalist accumulation – because of the need for revenues – implies that constraints posed by capital are far from negligible and beyond 'regulation' or 'moralization'. Writes Tony Smith with regards to 'capital strike':

> Investments funds would be hoarded, or devoted to speculation, or diverted to overseas investment, or dissipated in an orgy of luxury consumption. Such investment strike would bring the economy to a stretching halt. Unemployment would rise drastically. Numerous firms would go bankrupt. The limited fiscal resources of the state would be undermined. And so on.
>
> (1990, 204–205)

It is remarkable that the anomalies depicted here match the Great Recession. To my knowledge none of these structural aspects of capital's deformation of its own presuppositions are systematically addressed by Sen or Nussbaum. One exception though is the Fitoussi report co-authored by Stiglitz, Sen and Fitoussi (2009). In it, issues about market risks and 'bubble' profits indicate both measurement problems of what is 'one of the worst financial, economic and social crises in post-war history' (8). Better measures of an economy's 'balance-sheets' are held to be an important step in learning from the crisis. This injunction aligns with CA in its fundamental premises. Important among other issues here is the measurement of 'governmental output' in the promotion of well-being. (The report's working definition of well-being (14–15) is strikingly close to Nussbaum's CCL.) Interestingly enough the report functions as a forum for opening a discussion on (presumably, convergent or overlapping) 'societal values' (18). In terms of the centrepiece goal of 'quality of life' indicators, 'capabilities' figure as a prominent criterion for measurement. (42). Important with respect to our previous discussion about values, as well as the ensuing argument in Chapter 7, is the fact that the authors hold that there is considerable consistency on the value-judgments that support quality of life perceptions (44). Health, education, personal activities, political voice and governance, social connections, environmental conditions, personal insecurity and economic insecurity (44–54) indicate objective parameters of well-being.

18 As Berman is eager to clarify, placing Rosselli's social democratic revision of Marx into a wider political convergence in Europe, implies that contemporary versions of this possibility extend well beyond the scope of third-way politics (e.g. Giddens 1998). In the latter no serious objections were raised against markets in capitalism. Nor were systemic grounds for the social dislocation caused as the flipside to economic efficiency, seriously questioned. Liberal socialism, it should be added, has nothing to do with the hybrid concoction termed 'liberal communism', criticized by Žižek (2008).

19 CA has come under fire – as of deflection so to speak – due to fact that it has been 'absorbed' by the Equalities Review in the UK. Consequently, it is 'penalized' for providing a platform for neo-liberal normative agendas, at the same time as the criticism of its insufficient critical policy standpoint sets it up as part of a chain in the sequence of normative policy theories 'since Tawney and Titmuss' (Carpenter 2009, 369). Sen anticipates this type of formal stratagem when he writes that moving to a 'self-help' environment in Europe requires 'devising adequate policies for reducing

the massive and intolerable levels of unemployment' (1999a, 21) that hinder this vision. It is also important to consider, as Sen does, the limitations of focusing exclusively on income inequality and then extrapolating causal explanations with unemployment rates. Sen (94–95) presents the different cases of USA and Europe where the former is prepared – in terms of its 'social ethics' (95) – to accommodate high inequality rates but little unemployment, while Europe generates policies that aim at reducing inequality while tolerating high unemployment. In this sense Sen qualifies the role of capabilities in illuminating such 'asymmetries' that the exclusive focus on each indicator would most likely block from view. (For a different appreciation of the differences on inequality between the US and Europe, yet in the same spirit that invites comparative political economy, see Prasad 2012.) Sen though is close to Wilkinson and Pickett's findings about income inequality because the latter's metrics (Gini coefficient) eventually corroborate Sen's approach, in spite of his own methodological reservations against Gini coefficient. As they suggest: 'Where income differences are bigger, social distances are bigger and social stratification more important' (Wilkinson and Pickett 2010, 27). The social gradient they employ strongly correlates to inequality and when societies do demonstrate lower income inequality the tendency in most social gradients is one that conveys a measurable 'quality of life' improvement. The corrosion of quality of life is summarized succinctly by Wilkinson (2005, 201fig. 6.2) in a series of causal connections: greater income inequality *leads to* increased social distance between income groups, as these come to view themselves in 'us' and 'them' antagonistic categories, which *leads to* greater discrimination coupled to hierarchical values, which *leads to* increased status-competition and an emphasis on self-interest rather than cooperation, which then *leads to* poorer quality of social relations (i.e. Durkheim's well-known anomic loosening of the social fabric).

20 The interchange of economic rationality and the common good implicates, as I have tried to suggest in Chapter 1 and resume in the rest of the book, a Durkheimian understanding of what is precisely being shared by agents. Although Durkheim never surfaces in Sen, Rousseau's concept of the 'General Will' that influenced Durkheim does. In a joint article written with Runciman, Sen (Runciman and Sen 1965) treats, in the context of the Prisoner's Dilemma hypothesis, the 'general will' as the Pareto-optimal preference while the will of all would refer to particularistic goal-seeking preferences. Beyond the normative construal for economics that Sen would seek to supplant in order to instil the 'general will's' common good to the object of rational behaviour on the basis of individual preferences, his reconstruction of Rousseau's 'general will' is germane to the problem that concerns us here but is only implicit in Sen's and Runciman's challenging essay. As I lack the space to address this further, I can only suggest the fascinating discussion of the economic consequences of the general will that, unsurprisingly, culminates with a section on quality of life and capabilities, see Fridén (1998). On Durkheim's reading of Rousseau the ethical goal served by the general will (and on this Runciman and Sen agree as they subsume the 'general will' to 'social justice' (561–562)) must be added *synthetically* with a moral order that is 'consecrated' and 'superimposed' on the facts. For Durkheim, to 'effect this connection a new force is required, namely the *general will*' (Durkheim (1892) 1970, 103).

21 Bhambra's (2007) original account of an impure modernity as opposed to narratives of hierarchical rupture with tradition provides ample opportunities for rethinking the 'roots' of modernity. In her account liberal and Marxist economics from within classical sociology are taken to task for their (relative) paucity on capital's alleged 'pre-history' of dispossession, something that the author takes to lie within the very project of modernity itself. Drawing on the epistemology of 'connected histories' Bhambra broadens both the normative base of what modernity and industrial capitalism regarded as an 'individual right' (namely the right to hold property) and,

further, she aligns historical sociology's sight to an area that, as she claims, was blinded by Eurocentric bias. I shall return to this point about the merits of 'connected histories' in the last chapter; here it suffices to note that classical sociologists have not been entirely oblivious to this remarkably neglected feature of modernity's economic history. Oddly enough, in classical sociology, more nuanced than both liberals and Marxists was the reactionary sociologist Werner Sombart. Sombart ((1913) 1967) addressed primitive accumulation with regards to the demand for luxury in Europe. He is among the few to underscore, albeit briefly, 'forced labor' and 'slavery' (142). He also interpreted – based on empirical data – that the demand for luxury and the nearly exclusive subjugation of natives in the colonies had a distinctive feminine stylization in Europe. For Sombart it was the 'triumph of woman' (94–98) that reaped these surpluses of the dispossessed in a medieval consumer economy polished with a feminine lustre. Regardless of the validity of sources adduced by Sombart, which certainly call for further scrutiny, his thesis aims to dispel equations of colonial dispossession with patriarchy. Incidentally, Piketty ((2013) 2017, 151) confirms the drive to consumption in colonialist Britain and France but makes no further remark about gender. Sombart's explanatory categories are normatively defective and morally unacceptable today. Still, this dualism captures not only the racist pivot of his own focus on dispossession but also, conversely, in line with Scheler's *Ausgleich* whom Sombart cites ((1934) 1969, 184), it asserts that only 'by cooperation, by supplementing the unrepresentable parts of mankind, is it possible to develop the entire strength which resides within mankind as a whole' (184). This sort of 'overlapping consensus' as a process of 'balancing-out', articulated then by a deeply conservative sociologist, anticipates some of the dilemmas around methodological cosmopolitanism and the role nations can play in conducting a universal coordination of values, even if these should rightly move in the opposite direction of Sombart's political principles. Even though CA drew its inspiration from onerous deprivations mainly in the developing world, oddly enough it is relatively silent on capitalism's colonial history of dispossession. For example, Bauer (2000) – an economist whose work Sen welcomes – suggests that extreme poverty in certain regions has virtually nothing to do with the dispossession and plunder that was orchestrated by the West. Holmwood (2014), writing about inequality in Great Britain, underscores the colonial preconditions of primitive accumulation behind class analysis.

22 It is thus apt to recapitulate Sen's critique of utilitarianism through the lens of CA. Salient here is the concept of 'life' in Sen's recalibration of the 'standard of living':

> If the objects of value are functionings and capabilities, then the so-called 'basic' needs in the form of commodity requirements are *instrumentally* (rather than intrinsically) important. The main issue is the goodness of the life that one can lead. The need of commodities for any specified achievement of living conditions may vary greatly with various physiological, social, cultural and other contingent features, as was discussed in the first lecture. The value of the living standard lies in the living, and not in the possessing of commodities, which has derivative and varying relevance.
>
> (Sen, 1987c, 25 [original emphasis])

Thus, the entire project of economics, for Sen, is now aligned to a concept of radical, rather than basic, needs. This shift incorporates the 'living' dimension in its concrete functionings and modulations of capabilities. It thus takes up again the crucial question of the value of life and how it can be made worth living.

23 In this respect, and following the CA influence on UN Development Reports, Jolly (2010) is right to conceptualize normative declarations and accomplishments from the Versailles Peace Conference of 1919 and the commitment to social justice to the 2000 Millennium Summit in terms of Sen's 'broadening' perspective of sympathy.

Again, the reference to Kant's regulative ideal of peace here is not alien to the problem of the economy. In this sense, Honneth (2017) keeps sociology and socialism alive when the revisions he proposes are enunciated in the 'demand for the "social" contained in the very term "socialism"' (66), figured as a 'cosmopolitan' undertaking. (For Honneth (102), Piketty's proposal for a global tax moves in this direction.)

References

Anderson, Elizabeth. 1993. *Value in Ethics and Economics*. Cambridge, MA: Harvard University Press.

Anderson, Ronald. 2014. *Human Suffering and Quality of Life: Conceptualizing Stories and Statistics*. Dordrecht: Springer.

Arrow, Kenneth. 1977. 'Social Responsibility and Economic Efficiency.' *Public Policy* 21 (3): 303–317.

Bagchi, Amiya. 2000. 'Freedom and Development as End of Alienation?' *Economic and Political Weekly* 35 (50): 4408–4420.

Barry, Brian. 1970. *Sociologists, Economists and Democracy*. London: Collier- Macmillan.

Bauer, Peter. 2000. *From Subsistence to Exchange and Other Essays*. Princeton: Princeton University Press.

Bauman, Zygmunt. 2008. *Does Ethics Have a Chance in a World of Consumers?* Cambridge, MA: Harvard University Press.

Bauman, Zygmunt. 2017. *Retrotopia*. Cambridge: Polity.

Beckert, Jens. (1997) 2002. *Beyond the Market: The Social Foundations of Economic Efficiency*. Princeton: Princeton University Press.

Beckert, Jens. 2006. 'The Ambivalent Role of Morality on Markets.' In *The Moralization of the Markets*, edited by Nico Stehr, Christoph Henning, and Berndt Weiler, 109–128. New Brunswick: Transaction Publishers.

Beckert, Jens. 2009. 'The Social Order of Markets.' *Theory and Society* 38: 245–269.

Bell, Daniel. (1976) 1996. *The Cultural Contradictions of Capitalism*. New York: Basic Books.

Berman, Sheri. 2006. *The Primacy of Politics: Social Democracy and the Making of Europe's Twentieth Century*. Cambridge: Cambridge University Press.

Bhambra, Gurminder. 2007. *Rethinking Modernity: Postcolonialism and the Sociological Imagination*. Basingstoke: Palgrave Macmillan.

Boltanski, Luc, and Eve Chiapello. (1999) 2007. *The New Spirit of Capitalism*. London: Verso.

Boltanski, Luc, and Laurent Thévenot. (1991) 2006. *On Justification: Economies of Worth*. Princeton: Princeton University Press.

Bourdieu, Pierre. 2005. *The Social Structures of the Economy*. Cambridge: Polity.

Browne, Jude, Simon Deakin, and Frank Wilkinson. 2004. 'Capabilities, Social Rights and European Market Integration.' In *Europe and the Politics of Capabilities*, edited by Robert Salais and Robert Villeneuve, 205–221. Cambridge: Cambridge University Press.

Calhoun, Craig, and Georgi Derluguian, eds. 2011. *Aftermath? A New Global Economic Order?* New York: New York University Press.

Callon, Michel. 1998. 'An Essay on Framing and Overflowing: Economic Externalities Revisited by Sociology'. In *The Laws of the Market*, edited by Michel Callon, 244–269. Oxford: Blackwell Publishers.

Cameron, John. 2000. 'Amartya Sen on Economic Inequality: The Need for an Explicit Critique of Opulence.' *Journal of International Development.* 12 (7): 1031–1045.

Carpenter, Mick. 2009. 'The Capabilities Approach and Critical Social Policy: Lessons From the Majority World?' *Critical Social Policy* 29 (3): 351–373.

Dale, Gareth. 2010. *Karl Polanyi. The Limits of the Market.* Cambridge: Polity.

Dean, Hartley. 2000. 'Critiquing Capabilities: The Distractions of a Beguiling Concept.' *Critical Social Policy* 29 (2): 261–278.

Di Maggio, Paul. 1994. 'Culture and Economy.' In *The Handbook of Economic Sociology*, edited by Neil Smelser and Richard Swedberg, 27–57. Princeton: Princeton University Press.

Drosos, Dionysios. 1996. 'Adam Smith and Karl Marx: Alienation in Market Society.' *History of Economic Ideas* 4 (1–2): 325–351.

Durkheim, Émile. (1892) 1970. *Montesquieu and Rousseau: Forerunners of Sociology.* Ann Arbor: The University of Michigan Press.

Durkheim, Émile. (1887) 1993. *Ethics and the Sociology of Morals.* Buffalo: Prometheus Books.

Elster, Jon. 1982. 'Marxism, Functionalism and Game Theory.' *Theory and Society* 11 (4): 453–482.

Etzioni, Amitai. 1999. *Essays in Socio-Economics*. Berlin: Springer.

Feldman, Shelley. 2010. 'Social Development, Capabilities, and the Contradictions of (Capitalist) Development.' In *Capabilities, Power, and Institutions: Toward a More Critical Development Ethics*, edited by Stephen Esquith and Fred Gifford, 121–141. University Park: The Pennsylvania State University Press.

Foroohar, Rana. 2016. *Makers and Takers: The Rise of Finance and the Fall of American Business*. New York: Crown Business.

Fourcade, Marion. 2009. *Economists and Societies: Discipline and Profession in the United States, Britain, and France, 1890s to 1990s*. Princeton: Princeton University Press.

Fraser, Nancy. 2011. 'Marketization, Social Protection, Emancipation: Toward a Neo-Polanyian Conception of Capitalist Crisis.' In *Business as Usual: The Roots of the Global Financial Meltdown*, edited by Craig Calhoun and Georgi Derliguian, 137–157. New York: New York University Press.

Fridén, Bertil. 1998. *Rousseau's Economic Philosophy: Beyond the Market of Innocents.* Dordrecht: Kluwer.

Gellert, Paul, and Shelley Feldman. 2006. 'The Seductive Quality of Central Human Capabilities: Sociological Insights into Nussbaum and Sen's Disagreement.' *Economy and Society* 35 (3): 423–452.

Giddens, Anthony. 1998. *The Third Way: The Renewal of Social Democracy.* Cambridge: Polity.

Gorz, André. 2010. *The Immaterial.* London: Seagull.

Gould, Carol. 1978. *Marx's Social Ontology: Individuality and Community in Marx's Theory of Social Reality.* Cambridge, MA: The MIT Press.

Granovetter, Mark. 1985. 'Economic Action and Social Structure: The Problem of Embeddedness.' *American Journal of Sociology* 91 (3): 481–510.

Hardt, Michael, and Antonio Negri. 20o4. *Multitude: War and Democracy in the Age of the Empire.* New York: The Penguin Press.

Harvey, David. 2005. *A Brief History of Neoliberalism.* Oxford: Oxford University Press.

Harvey, David. 2014. *Seventeen Contradictions and the End of Capitalism.* London: Profile Books.

Hayek, Friedrich. 1967. *Studies in Philosophy, Politics and Economics*. London: Routledge and Kegan Paul.

Hegel, Georg W.F. (1805–1806) 1966. *Hegel and the Human Spirit*. Detroit: Wayne State University Press.

Hegel, Georg W.F. (1821) 1967. *Hegel's Philosophy of Right*. Oxford: Oxford University Press.

Hermann-Pillath, Carsten, and Ivan Boldyrev. 2014. *Hegel, Institutions and Economics: Performing the Social*. Abington: Routledge.

Hill, Lisa. 2007. 'Adam Smith, Adam Ferguson and Karl Marx on the Division of Labor.' *Journal of Classical Sociology* 7 (3): 339–366.

Hodgson, Geoffrey. 1994. 'The Return of Institutional Economics.' In *The Handbook of Economic Sociology*, edited by Neil Smelser and Richard Swedberg, 58–76. Princeton: Princeton University Press.

Holmwood, John. 1996. *Founding Sociology? Talcott Parsons and the Idea of General Theory*. London: Longman.

Holmwood, John. 2006. 'Economics, Sociology, and the "Professional Complex": Talcott Parsons and the Critique of Orthodox Economics.' *American Journal of Economics and Sociology* 65 (1): 127–160.

Holmwood, John. 2013. 'Public Reasoning without Sociology: Amartya Sen's Theory of Justice.' *Sociology* 47 (6): 1171–1186.

Holmwood, John. 2014. 'Beyond Capital? The Challenge for Sociology in Britain.' *The British Journal of Sociology* 65 (4): 607–618.

Honneth, Axel. 2017. *The Idea of Socialism*. Cambridge: Polity Press.

Jolly, Richard. 2010. 'Employment, Basic Needs and Human Development. Elements for a New International Paradigm in Response to Crisis.' *Journal of Human Development and Capabilities* 11 (1): 11–36.

Kalecki, Michal. 1943. 'Political Aspects of Full Employment.' *Political Quarterly* 14 (4): 322–330.

Kentish, Benjamin. 2017. 'Canadian Province Trials Basic Income for Thousands of Residents' *Independent*, 29 November. Accessed 27 August 2018. www.independent.co.uk/news/world/americas/canada-universal-basic-income-ontario-trial-citizens-residents-poverty-unemployment-benefits-a8082576.html.

Krippner, Greta. 2011. *Capitalizing on Crisis: The Political Origins of the Rise of Finance*. Cambridge, MA: Harvard University Press.

MacGregor, David. 1984. *The Communist Ideal in Hegel and Marx*. Toronto: University of Toronto Press.

Marcuse, Herbert. (1941) 1977. *Reason and Revolution: Hegel and the Rise of Social Theory*. London: Routledge and Kegan Paul.

Marx, Karl. (1875) 1958. 'Critique of the Gotha Programme'. In *Karl Marx and Friedrich Engels Selected Works in Two Volumes*. 13–48. Moscow: Foreign Languages Publishing House.

Marx, Karl. (1857–1858) 1973. *Grundrisse: Foundations of the Critique of Political Economy (Rough Draft)*. London: Penguin.

Marx, Karl. (1867) 1990. *Capital. Volume 1*. London: Penguin.

Marx, Karl. (1843–1844) 1992. 'A Contribution to the Critique of Hegel's Philosophy of Right. Introduction.' In *Early Writings*, 243–257. London: Penguin.

Marx, Karl, and Friedrich Engels. (1845) 1976. 'The German Ideology'. In *Collected Works, Volume 5 Marx and Engels 1845–1847*, 19–539. London: Lawrence and Wishart.

Meek, Ronald. 1956. *Studies in the Labor Theory of Value*. New York: Monthly Review Press.

Menger, Carl. (1883) 1996. *Investigations into the Method of the Social Sciences*. Grove City: Libertarian Press.

Menon, Nivedita. 2002. 'Universalism without Foundations?' *Economy and Society* 31 (1): 152–169.

Merkel, Wolfgang. 2014. 'Is Capitalism Compatible with Democracy?' *Zeitschrift für Vergleichende Politikwissenschaft* 8 (2): 109–128.

Merton, Robert. 1968. *Social Theory and Social Structure*. New York: The Free Press.

Mills, C. Wright. 1940. 'Situated Actions and Vocabularies of Motive.' *American Sociological Review* 5 (6): 904–913.

Morris, Chistopher. 2010. 'Ethics and Economics.' In *Amartya Sen*, edited by Christopher Morris. 40–59. Cambridge University Press.

Navarro, Vicente. 2000. 'Development and Quality of Life: A Critique of Amartya Sen's *Development as Freedom*.' *International Journal of Health Sciences* 30 (4): 661–674.

Negrelli, Serafino. 2012. 'Capability for Voice and the Deficit in EU Democracy.' In *Democracy and Capabilities For Voice: Welfare, Work and Public Deliberation in Europe*, edited by Ota De Leonardis, Serafino Negrelli, and Robert Salais, 119–139. Brussels: P.I.E. Peter Lang.

Negri, Antonio. 1991. *Marx Beyond Marx: Lessons on the Grundrisse*. New York: Automedia.

Nussbaum, Martha. 1990. 'Aristotelian Social Democracy.' In *Liberalism and the Good*, edited by Bruce Douglass, Gerald Mara, and Henry Richardson, 203–252. New York: Routledge.

Nussbaum, Martha. 2000. *Women and Human Development: The Capabilities Approach*. Cambridge: Cambridge University Press.

Nussbaum, Martha. 2004. *Hiding from Humanity: Disgust, Shame, and the Law*. Princeton: Princeton University Press.

Nussbaum, Martha. 2005. 'The Death of Pity: Orwell and American Political Life.' In *On Nineteen Eighty Four: Orwell and Our Future*, edited by Abbott Gleason, Jack Goldsmith, and Martha Nussbaum, 279–299. Princeton: Princeton University Press.

Nussbaum, Martha. 2007. 'On Moral Progress: A Response to Richard Rorty.' *The University of Chicago Law Review*, 74 (3): 939–960.

Offe, Claus. 2015. *Europe Entrapped*. Cambridge: Polity.

Parsons, Talcott. (1940) 1954. 'The Motivation of Economic Activities.' Ch. 3 in *Essays in Sociological Theory*. New York: The Free Press.

Parsons, Talcott. (1937) 1968a. *The Structure of Social Action. Volume I: Marshall, Pareto, Durkheim*. New York: The Free Press.

Parsons, Talcott. (1937) 1968b. *The Structure of Social Action. Volume II: Weber*. New York: The Free Press.

Parsons, Talcott. (1969). *Politics and Social Structure*. New York: The Free Press.

Parsons, Talcott, and Neil Smelser. 1956. *Economy and Society: A Major Contribution to the Synthesis of Economic and Sociological Theory*. New York: The Free Press.

Piketty, Thomas. (2013) 2017. *Capital in the Twenty-First Century*. Cambridge, MA: The Belknap Press of Harvard University Press.

Polanyi, Karl. (1944) 1957. *The Great Transformation: The Political and Economic Origins of Our Times*. Boston: Beacon Press.

Prasad, Monica. 2012. *The Land of Too Much: American Abundance and the Paradox of Poverty*. Cambridge, MA: Harvard University Press.

Prendergast, Renée. 2005. 'The Concept of Freedom and its Relation to Economic Development-a Critical Appreciation of the Work of Amartya Sen.' *Cambridge Journal of Economics* 29 (6): 1145–1170.

Prendergast, Renée. 2011. 'Sen and Commons on Markets and Freedom.' *New Political Economy* 16 (2): 207–222.

Putnam, Hilary, and Vivian Walsh, eds. 2012. *The End of Value-Free Economics.* London: Routledge.

Rawls, John. (1971) 1999. *A Theory of Justice. Revised Edition.* Oxford: Oxford University Press.

Reiman, Jeffrey. 2014. *As Free and as Just as Possible: The Theory of Marxian Liberalism.* Chichester: Wiley-Blackwell.

Rogan, Tim. 2017. *The Moral Economists: R.H. Tawney, Karl Polanyi, E.P. Thompson, and the Critique of Capitalism.* Princeton: Princeton University Press.

Rogan, Tim. 2018. 'Why Amartya Sen Remains the Century's Greatest Critic of Capitalism.' *Aeon,* 27 February. Accessed 5 November 2018. https://aeon.co/ideas/why-amartya-sen-remains-the-centurys-great-critic-of-capitalism.

Rosselli, Carlo. (1930) 1994. *Liberal Socialism.* Princeton, NJ: Princeton University Press.

Runciman, Walter, and Amartya Sen. 1965. 'Games, Justice and the General Will.' *Mind. New Series* 74 (296): 554–562.

Salais, Robert. 2012. 'Labour and the Politics of Freedoms.' In *Democracy and Public Capabilities For Voice: Welfare, Work and Deliberation in Europe*, edited by Ota De Leonardis, Serafino Negrelli, and Robert Salais, 227–244. Brussels: P.I.E. Peter Lang.

Sandbrook, Richard. 2000. 'Globalization and the limits of neoliberal development doctrine.' *Third World Quarterly* 21 (6): 1071–1080.

Sayer, Andrew. 2006. 'Approaching Moral Economy.' In *The Moralization of the Markets*, edited by Nico Stehr, Christoph Henning, and Berndt Weiler, 77–99. New Brunswick: Transaction Publishers.

Sayer, Andrew. 2012. 'Capabilities, Contributive Justice and Unequal Divisions of Labour.' *Journal of Human Development and Capabilities* 13 (4): 580–596.

Sen, Amartya. 1984. *Resources, Values and Development.* Cambridge, MA: Harvard University Press.

Sen, Amartya. 1985. 'The Moral Standing of the Market.' *Social Philosophy and Public Policy* 2 (2): 1–19.

Sen, Amartya. 1987a. *On Ethics and Economics.* Oxford: Basil Blackwell.

Sen, Amartya. 1987b. 'The Standard of Living: Lecture I, Concepts and Critiques.' In *The Standard of Living: The Tanner Lectures, Clare Hall, Cambridge 1985*, edited by Geoffrey Hawthorn, 1–19. Cambridge: Cambridge University Press.

Sen, Amartya. 1987c. 'The Standard of Living: Lecture II, Lives and Capabilities.' In *The Standard of Living: The Tanner Lectures, Clare Hall, Cambridge 1985*, edited by Geoffrey Hawthorn, 20–38. Cambridge: Cambridge University Press.

Sen, Amartya. 1990. 'Capability and Well-Being.' In *The Quality of Life*, edited by Martha Nussbaum and Amartya Sen, 30–53. Oxford: Clarendon.

Sen, Amartya. 1992. *Inequality Reexamined.* Cambridge, MA: Harvard University Press.

Sen, Amartya. 1993a. 'Markets and Freedoms: Achievements and Limitations of the Market Mechanism in Promoting Individual Freedoms.' *Oxford Economic Papers, New Series* 45 (4): 519–541.

Sen, Amartya. 1993b. 'Money and Value: On the Ethics and Economics of Finance.' *Economics and Philosophy* 9: 203–227.

Sen, Amartya. 1997. 'Income Inequality to Economic Inequality.' *Southern Economic Journal* 64 (2): 383–401.

Sen, Amartya. 1999a. *Development as Freedom*. Oxford: Oxford University Press.

Sen, Amartya. 1999b. *Commodities and Capabilities*. Oxford: Oxford University Press.

Sen, Amartya. 2002. *Rationality and Freedom*. Cambridge, MA: The Belknap Press of Harvard University Press.

Sen, Amartya. 2006. *Identity and Violence: The Illusion of Destiny*. London: Penguin.

Sen, Amartya. 2008. 'The Economics of Happiness and Capability.' In *Capabilities and Happiness*, edited by Luigino Bruni, Flavio Comim, and Maurizio Pugno, 16–27. Oxford: Oxford University Press.

Sen, Amartya. 2009. *The Idea of Justice*. Cambridge, MA: The Belknap Press of Harvard University Press.

Sen, Amartya, and Bernard Williams, eds. 1982. *Utilitarianism and Beyond*. Cambridge: Cambridge University Press.

Simmel. Georg. (1900) 1990. *The Philosophy of Money*. London: Routledge.

Smith, Adam. (1759) 1984. *The Theory of Moral Sentiment*. Indianapolis: Liberty Fund.

Smith, Tony. 1990. *The Logic of Marx's Capital: Replies to Hegelian Criticisms*. Albany: State University of New York Press.

Sombart, Werner. 1909. *Socialism and the Social Movement*. London: J.M. Dent & Co.

Sombart, Werner. (1913) 1967. *Luxury and Capitalism*. Ann Arbor: The University of Michigan Press.

Sombart, Werner. (1934) 1969. *A New Social Philosophy*. New York: Greenwood Press.

Stehr, Nico, Christoph Henning, and Weiler Berndt, eds. 2006. *The Moralization of the Markets*. New Brunswick: Transaction Publishers.

Stewart, Frances. 2010. 'Power and Progress: The Swing of the Pendulum.' *Journal of Human Development and Capabilities* 11 (3): 371–395.

Stiglitz, Jospeh, Amartya Sen, and Jean-Paul Fitoussi. 2009. *Report by the Commission on the Measurement of Economic Performance and Social Progress*, Accessed 11 October 2018. http://ec.europa.eu/eurostat/documents/118025/118123/Fitoussi+Commission+report.

Streeck, Wolfgang. 2014. *Buying Time. The Delayed Crisis of Democratic Capitalism*. London: Verso.

Streeck, Wolfgang. 2016. *How Will Capitalism End? Essays on a Failing System*. London: Verso.

Swedberg, Richard. 1994. 'Markets as Social Structures.' In *The Handbook of Economic Sociology*, edited by Neil Smelser and Richard Swedberg. 255–282. Princeton: Princeton University Press.

Walby, Sylvia. 2012. 'Sen and the Measurement of Justice and Capabilities: A Problem in Theory and Practice.' *Theory, Culture and Society* 29 (1): 99–118.

Walby, Sylvia. 2017. *Crisis*. Cambridge: Polity.

Walsh, Vivian. 1961. *Scarcity and Evil*. Englewood Cliffs: Prentice-Hall.

Weber, Max. (1904–1905) 1968. *The Protestant Ethic and the Spirit of Capitalism*. London: Unwin University Books.

Weber, Max. (1922) 1978. *Economy and Society*. Berkeley: University of California Press.

Wilkinson, Richard. 2005. *The Impact of Inequality: How to Make Sick Societies Healthier*. Abingdon: Routledge.

Wilkinson, Richard, and Kate Pickett. 2010. *The Spirit Level: Why Equality is Better for Everyone*. London: Penguin.

Winfield, Richard Dien. 1990. *The Just Economy*. New York: Routledge.

Wray, Randall. 2016. *Why Minsky Matters: An Introduction to the Work of a Maverick Economist*. Princeton: Princeton University Press.

Wright, Erik Olin. 2016a. 'Socialism and Real Utopias.' Ch. 4 in *Alternatives to* London: *Capitalism: Proposals for a Democratic Economy* by Robin Hahnel, and Erik Olin Wright. London: Verso.

Wright, Erik Olin. 2016b. 'Final Thoughts.' Ch. 6 in *Alternatives to* London: *Capitalism: Proposals for a Democratic Economy* by Robin Hahnel, and Erik Olin Wright. London: Verso.

Zimmermann, Bénédicte. 2004. 'Competences-Oriented Logics and the Politics of Employability.' In *Europe and the Politics of Capabilities*, edited by Robert Salais and Robert Villeneuve, 38–53. Cambridge: Cambridge University Press.

Zimmermann, Bénédicte. 2012. 'Having a Voice and Participating in a Company.' In *Democracy and Capabilities for Voice: Welfare, Work and Public Deliberation in Europe*, edited by Ota De Leonardis, Serafino Negrelli, and Robert Salais, 79–99. Brussels: P.I.E. Peter Lang.

Zimmermann, Bénédicte. 2018. 'From Critical Theory to Critical Pragmatism: Capability and the Assessment of Freedom.' *Critical Sociology* 44 (6): 937–952.

Žižek, Slavoj. 2008. *Violence: Six Sideways Reflections*. London: Profile Books.

Part II

Agency, alienation and emotions

3 From agency to capabilities

The capable social self

Preliminary remarks: CA and agency

The implications that stem from broadening economic action by recourse to capabilities call for a consideration of the problem of agency. In this chapter I argue that if properly assimilated into sociology, CA can contribute to sharpening, conceptually and empirically, the discipline's normative intuitions and theoretical paradigms, in order to configure a resourceful notion of agency aligned to a vision of a good society. Sen's idea of the 'capable agent', glued together from normative configurations drawn from economics and moral philosophy, has been partly anticipated by sociologists, particularly Parsons and Giddens. For example, Parsons' concept of 'capacity' provides an indication of the institutional patterns that can envelop the capability of action in collective values and norms. Giddens' recourse to the 'capability' of agency brings him close to CA, but not close enough, precisely because Giddens' actor is immersed in the routinized backgrounds that shape the horizon of intersubjectivity. Acting upon structures takes, for Giddens, an altogether different route from Parsons' normative institutionalism, a route that I find less persuasive, yet worthy of discussion because of the semantic affinity that Giddens shares with Sen on 'capability'. These sociological expositions of agency require, however, a far more normatively specified conception of the human than hitherto available in sociology. In this direction I shall attempt to recover normative elements from the tradition of natural law, hoping to persuade the reader that an essentialist bent in sociology and CA does not detract from pluralism and historical openness but, rather, constitutes their central axis.

I need to clarify that the following discussion about agency is conducted at a generic level of abstraction. The entire CA (e.g. Sen 1999, 189–203; Nussbaum 1999, 2000a, 2005; Nussbaum and Glover 1995) has made gender an integral focus of its theoretical architectonic and its policy breadth.[1] As my focus here is on anthropological dimensions of agency and its natural law reconsideration in sociology I use agency generically without offering insights on reconstructions of the sociological use of capabilities that are attentive to gender or, for that matter, to race, disability (on the latter, see indicatively, Hvinden and Halvorsen 2018; Kuklys 2005, 75–103; Nussbaum 2006, 96–223) and ageing (see Nussbaum and Levmore 2017).

Sociology has grappled with the problem of the agent's capability in various ways. Weber and Parsons advanced a theory of action that for many decades dominated theoretical paradigms in sociology. But also later in Giddens' (1984) notion of 'capability', Dahrendorf's (1979) 'life-chances' the theme of the actor's potential and actual ability to shape the social surroundings which render life worth living, as well as the formation of this ability by social structures and institutional role-complexes, constitutes sociology's epistemological presupposition in the absence of which it becomes increasingly difficult to conceptualize both communal and individual life. Also similar is the blend of sociology and philosophical anthropology in the configuration of the 'capacity to act' offered by Etzioni (1968, Chs.1 and 2), or in the pressing normative call for the 'return of the actor' (Touraine 1988, 2000) against institutions of domination. Other approaches to the problem of agency focus on the capability of the actor to respond creatively to the demands of the 'situation' (Joas 1996, 133),[2] hoping to promote agency as 'a creative and vital participant in the democratic debate' (Emirbayer and Mische 1998, 1013). Given the multiplicity of perspectives converging in the intuitive recourse to the idea of 'capacity', CA is only marginally identified as a promising ally to sociology (for exceptions see Lukes (2005, 117) and Sennett (2012, 29)). But let us look first at the core concept of capability to see if the potential to supplement current understandings of agency is sufficient.

Capabilities: a new framework for normative action?

There is no better place to commence than Sen's own programmatic words:

> I am using the term 'agent' [...] in its older-and 'grander'-sense as someone who acts and brings about change, and whose achievements can be judged in terms of some external criteria as well. This work is particularly concerned with the agency role of the individual as a member of the public and as a participant in economic, social and political actions (varying from taking part in the market to being involved, directly or indirectly, in individual or joint activities in political and other spheres).
>
> (Sen 1999, 19)

If we read this indicative passage with sociological paradigms in mind, the normative functionalism of Durkheim and Parsons addresses similar imperatives and conditions for agency. For Parsons, for instance, 'institutionalized individualism'means:

> a mode of organization of the components of human action which, on balance, enhanced the capacity of the average individual and of collectivities to which he belongs to implement the values to which he and they are committed. This enhanced capacity at the individual level has developed concomitantly with that of social and cultural frameworks of organization

> and institutional norms, which form the framework of order for the realization of individual and collective unit goals and values.
>
> (Parsons and Platt 1973, 1)

The 'interrelatedness' of functionings as well as the range of their assessment in society align with the normatively coherent notion of agency that the functionalist paradigm in sociology sees enmeshed in social institutions. Such normative patterns that have been consolidated in modernity[3] call for a reconceptualization of capable agency in this normative sense. For Parsons, prerequisites that are essential for any notion of agency's capabilities, like 'nutrition and physical safety' (1951, 28), are not to be seen as negative exigencies determined solely by necessity. Rather, these adaptive capabilities are sustained by the values of higher social system levels. Configured as 'minimum needs of individual actors' they 'constitute a set of conditions to which the social system must be adapted' (28). Sen's lifelong project of combating deprivations that bear on nutrition, physical safety, health, education, among other prime capabilities, is similarly triggered by wider institutional and normative expectations (Sen 1990).

At this point, the discussion on capabilities reveals a subtler theoretical texture. It comprises companion concepts, like 'agency' and 'well-being' that serve to fortify capabilities and to equip social science with a normative–empirical synthesis that can generate tangible enhancements of freedom across societies and cultures. Given the prolific writings in CA, I use as programmatic Sen's essay on 'Capability and Well-Being' (1993), although the classification he develops has been set forth in earlier writings (Sen 1985). The two principal categories of Sen's project are: (1) well-being and (2) agency. Dividing each to an 'achievement' and a 'freedom' variable, Sen (1993, 35) works out a fourfold classification based on the following distinctions: 'Well-being' is seen in terms of 'well-being achievements' (functionings) and in terms of 'well-being freedoms' (capabilities). Moving to our key concept, agency, its aspects of 'achievement' and 'freedom' are seen respectively as 'agency achievements' and 'agency freedoms'. The transition to the notion of agency and its central role in Sen's CA is schematically represented in Crocker (2008, 151) and Crocker and Robeyns (2010, 62) (see Figure 3.1).

Let us take a closer look at this conceptual breakdown. Turning to the normative category of agency, Sen places under (a) agency-achievement the processes by which persons decide what they wish to pursue in terms of valued

Figure 3.1 Well-Being and agency

	Well-Being	*Agency*
Achievements	Well-Being Achievements (Functionings)	Agency Achievements
Freedom	Well-Being Freedoms (Capabilities)	Agency Freedoms

Source: Crocker (2008, 151); Crocker & Robeyns (2010, 62).

goals; (b) agency-freedom is defined as the 'freedom to achieve whatever the person, as a responsible agent, decides he or she should achieve' (Sen 1985, 204). The qualification of 'responsibility' here requires further commentary. Sen, having accommodated institutional constraints on agency freedom as well as opportunities to expand it (Sen 1999, xi–xii), seems to preserve an enabling, but normatively residual, mode of agency in his scheme.

CA scholars Crocker and Robeyns (2010) muster textual support from Sen's many writings and they flesh out what we might call the 'thick' version of agency from which its fundamental elements can be sliced off. According to these authors (80–83), four, seemingly irreducible, coordinates of Sen's agency are: (i) self-determination, (ii) reason orientation and deliberation, (iii) action and (iv) impact on the world. The prerogative of self-determination is normatively the most crucial component of agency. We can surmise that Kant's idea of autonomy lies behind Sen's use of self-determination and thus the hard core of agency is one that ascribes to the agent the a priori modality of being 'able to act otherwise' as a practical implementation of freedom. *Reason orientation* seems also Kantian in origin. It constitutes purposive activity based on critical scrutiny and deliberation over a course of action, its purposes and goals. *Action* is defined by Crocker and Robeyns obliquely. It is argued that action is the condition or process whereby 'the person performs or has a role in performing X' (80). This compact way of putting it takes us into the heart of theories of the sociological dimensions of action but is wanting in terms of the analytical elements of the action-pattern, the performative turn of a theory of 'cultural pragmatics' (Alexander 2004) and, more importantly, it says very little about role placements and role dispositions. This is at least one aspect of the concept of agency where CA reveals its sociological deficit. At the same time it needs to be recognized that CA accommodates society and the influence of roles. These are initially conceived in terms of three sets of conversion factors: the 'individual' ('personal conversion factors like metabolism), 'society' (social conversion factors like social norms, power relations, societal hierarchies) and 'nature' (environmental conversion factors like geographical location and climate) (see Crocker and Robeyns 2010, 67–69; Robeyns 2005, 99 and, for a slightly different version, Sen 2004, 332–333n. 29). These conversion factors (or conversion processes) are held to create enabling possibilities for mediating agency and structure (see, for example, Hvinden and Halvorsen (2018) and their implementation of CA-conversion processes to the field of disability studies.) The fourth dimension of *impact on the world* makes the normative load of Sen's conception of agency particularly resonant: 'Greater freedom enhances the ability of people to help themselves and also to influence the world, and these matters ("the 'agency aspect' of the individual") are central to the processes of development' (Sen 1999, 18). (This last point is pertinent to my upcoming discussion of Giddens.) To counter potential charges of formalism and any detestable outcomes that may emanate from the abstract use of the term 'capability' (i.e. the military 'capability' to engage in genocide),[4] Sen (1993, 30), fully aware of this risk, unfolds the analytical patterns of the term capability and its companion concept of agency.

Nussbaum on her part elucidates further those capabilities that are 'most clearly involved in defining the minimum conditions for a life with human dignity' (2006, 166).

In Chapter 1 I drew some parallels between Max Scheler's hierarchy of values (lexical ordering in current scholarly turf) and Nussbaum's CCL. At this stage, and before I take up the problem of agency and its natural law foundations, it is important to mention that the project of a hierarchy of values or human needs is not at all a remnant of a bygone philosophical era. It is the great merit of CA scholar Sabina Alkire (2002) to have tabulated various overlapping lists of valued needs and capabilities. I do not have the space to discuss these lists, from which Scheler is absent, even as a precursor to this project.[5] My contribution from the perspective of sociology is to argue that if this project is held to be relevant and subject to future scholarly debate in political and moral philosophy, sociology in the Schelerian scheme had already anticipated its overarching logic.

Nussbaum introduces further distinctions within capabilities. These appear initially as a triptych of 'basic capabilities' (e.g. the human capacity for imagination), 'internal capabilities' and 'combined capabilities' (Nussbaum 1999, 44–45; 2000a, 84–85). In a slightly modified shape (Nussbaum 2004, 344–345), they reappear as 'inner' capabilities (i.e. the agent's readiness to take up valued functionings), 'external' capabilities (i.e. those social and environmental conditions that enable the prepared agent to actualize capabilities) and as 'combined' capabilities (i.e. the coordination of 'inner' and 'external' as the political goal per se). The implication is that the normative notion of agency would be hard to conceive in the absence of a CCL. Let us recall the list's basic capabilities: 1. Life; 2. Bodily Health; 3. Bodily Integrity; 4. Senses, Imagination, and Thought; 5.Emotions; 6. Practical Reason; 7. Affiliation; 8. Other Species; 9. Play; 10. Political and Material Control over One's Environment. Such capabilities are not met at a single level of human togetherness. Some (i.e. 1 to 5, 8 and 9) can be seen as priming the embodied self's scope of action, while others (6, 7, 10) extend further to structural matters, encompassing the wider political, economic and moral order of society. A schematic division like this runs the risk of reproducing all the tensions generated by 'self-society' or 'action-structure' schemes (Archer 2000; Elder-Vass 2010; Holmwood and Stewart 1991);[6] for it is immediately apparent that the capability for play, for instance, presupposes rational socialization processes and institutions on the level of capability 10 (e.g. a democratic constitution that safeguards play against child labour). Or, to take another example, the essential capability of life (capability 1) is itself an institutional value for societies nourished in the ideals of human dignity, equality and justice, all of which are derivative of capability 10. On the approach I adopt in this book and reconsidering the irreducible ethical constitution of the human being in terms of the capacity to be free, examined though through the lens of a social ontology (i.e. the assumption that being human entails the social development of universal attributes, like capabilities, and thus remains an open project of reciprocal, relational and just expression of freedom's niche *qua* capabilities), the matter is put with clarity by Carol Gould. Her argument in favour of a social ontology and ethical foundationalism draws, among others, on the deep and complex entanglement of life and freedom. In confronting this question, she deserves to be quoted at some length. She writes:

> One may begin by saying that in a certain sense human life and freedom are generically identical, if one takes life not simply as a state of being, but as an activity characterized by choice. Clearly, however, one may distinguish life in the sense of biological existence from freedom and see it as a necessary condition for the free activity of human beings, since one has to be alive in order to act. Yet, to understand this biological existence as *simply* a matter of organic life would be to lose its distinctive character as *human* biological existence, or its value as human life, that is, as the existence of that kind of living being whose nature it is to exercise free choice. Thus life may be understood not as a separate precondition of agency but rather as ingredient in it and as expressed or realized in human activity. The value of life, like that of freedom, is thus affirmed in the very activity of human beings. Since life too is a necessary condition for the possibility of any other value – for without it there would be no agency – it also is a primary value.
>
> (Gould 1988, 130–131)

As the reader will recall from Chapter 1 the a priori value of a human life worth living is a core principle of CA. Interrogated in Gould's robust statements are many things at once. a) the biological precondition of life as a historically validated value if the human being is not to be relegated to that status of the subhuman (the odious consequences of which Nussbaum scrutinizes, as we shall discuss in Chapter 5);[7] b) the necessity of configuring a transcendental solution to the problem of agency, if transcendentalism in the Kantian sense, as I think the case is here, enquires into the *conditions of possibility* for something to be and to become; c) if this is the case, life (along with its biological materiality but not exclusive to this) is elevated to the (political–axiological) content of (just) social arrangements; d) this is the reason behind Gould's further reconstruction – which I cannot expand upon here – of the ontological foundation not only of freedom but also of 'other principal values of the social ethics', which include 'equality, reciprocity, and democracy' and are ontologically grounded in the 'nature of human activity itself' (131). Evidently, the lacuna in the CA edifice – more in Sen, less in Nussbaum – is the reluctance to consider both some sort of lexical ordering in the transcendental sense (as I intimated in my use of Scheler, although I do not propose *that* specific hierarchy) and the logic of institutions as spheres of justice in democratic societies. This last point about the 'social ethics', invoked here by Gould and somehow mildly recognized by some CA scholars (e.g. Robeyns 2005, 109–110), reveals the urgent need to recover of the Hegelian project of *Sittlichkeit* in a contemporary sociological theory of justice (more about this in Chapter 6.)

Natural law, human agency and CA

I have intimated that notions of agency like those forged by CA (reached after the imperative to study famines (see Drèze and Sen 1989)) and their intersection with sociology's rich contributions entail a materialist and natural law substratum that should not be lost from the horizon of any pluralist and pragmatic undertaking in our complex world. For Sen the search for a meta-value of this sort is not precluded in making moral judgments. His claim is actually that it is not required in order for such judgments to be morally assertive. This argument will be elaborated in Chapter 4, yet I need to point out that in suspending the quest for complete rankings in moral judgments, Sen merely suspends this 'biological' or 'ontological' foundation as a complete and a priori requirement for such judgments to gain in moral legitimacy.

Notwithstanding this important move that uncouples binding moral judgments from 'foundationalism', it is my contention that CA resides, as nearly every normative discourse today, on normative elements that owe to the rich tradition of natural law. In particular, the CCL comes very close to a reformulation of natural law normativity.[8] If this is the case, how can any natural law foundation of social theory allow us to rehabilitate binding notions of what it means to be human? How can the natural law idea of human dignity inform contemporary projects, including CA, which embrace relationism, pragmatic situatedness and plural attention to 'difference' and local struggles?

There is no need, mainly for reasons of space, to embark on a survey of natural law. Daniel Chernilo (2013) has contributed greatly to reinstalling to natural law its long lost relevance for a contemporary normative sociology. He has provided a comprehensive account of classical sociological theory's deep entanglement with natural law theory. Thus I shall not reiterate most of the natural law continuities that he discerns. For Chernilo:

> [a]lthough natural law ideas keep playing a relevant role in modern society – justice, fairness, equality, freedom, human rights are not values we want to do away with – changing socio-historical circumstances mean that new normative challenges emerge for and from them.
>
> (2013, 38)

Chernilo's qualified approval in reconstructing natural law takes its cue from Habermas whose claims about the unfinished project of modernity is prompted by the challenge to combine the human foundation of freedom in a canopy of legitimation forged through deliberate and intersubjectively coordinated criteria of democratic will-formation and validity.

With this proposed paradigm shift in normative accounts in social theory I suggest, in line with Chernilo's proposed reconstruction of universality in social theory, that CA reopens the case of natural law with more promising potential than current sociology's stagnant normative coordination of its own plural voices. Nussbaum accepts this legacy when in light of 'staggering' economic and other inequalities in 'basic life chances', the 'capabilities approach, which in many ways revives the Grotian natural law tradition, provides more useful guidance' (2006, 20–21). Let us enquire a bit further to this natural law tradition by connecting it to the category of agency.

A noteworthy attempt to rehabilitate the metaphor of 'creativity of action' (Joas 1996) as a guiding thread of sociology and one that is conventionally attached to 'agency' includes the category of 'life' as one among its many historically gleaned permutations. Joas understands the category of life solely in terms of *Lebensphilosophie*, which, of course, is accurate if evaluated as an intellectual trend that exerted some influence on classical sociology. He tends though to occlude the Hegelian heritage that, as Marcuse has shown, found its way via Dilthey in neo-Kantian strands of sociology. For the argument I advance here and, as in Joas, aims at replenishing this neglected dimension (indeed, ultimate precondition) of agency, normative shades of 'Life' deserve reexamination. It is no accident that the recuperation of 'Life' as an ontological bedrock of our sociality and as a key element in normative excursions to the project of a good and just society utilizes, as Gould intimated, Hegel and Marx. For instance, Marx is not merely adhering to a materialist view of nature as many commentators have shown through careful textual exegesis. His writings invite the category of 'life' as a species-being ontological foundation that, of course, is formed according to historical transformations in the social relations of production. Marx's most evocative connotations about human freedom from alienation and, antithetically, the dramatic imagery of working conditions described in *Capital* contain an unambiguous anchoring in the human life-process. In fact, as Henry ((1973) 1986), an important Marxist scholar, has persuasively argued, Marx is never ontologizing labour but, rather, he subsumes it to serve 'life' and its motility in history. Although the problem of life's alienation as capability deprivation will be taken up in Chapter 4, it is of utmost significance to highlight once more the natural law foundation of the Marxian project. Henry writes:

> After having stated that life as the presupposition of history implies drinking, eating, and the production of material life, and after having designated this production as the 'first historical act', Marx adds, 'and indeed this is an historical act, a *fundamental condition of all history*'.
>
> That life constitutes the fundamental condition of all history, it's a *priori* necessary condition or, as we may again say, its transcendental condition, that it is, consequently, to be understood as a metahistorical condition, in no way signifies that it is situated outside history. Transcendental condition signifies a condition immanent in everything it makes possible, an internal condition, an essence, and, finally, a substance. [...] How can life at one and the same time belong to history and not belong to it? For life, belonging to history means being in every instance in it, at every moment *or rather in every individual* the condition for an effective production, a production made necessary by this

> life and for it. Not belonging to history means: this condition for all history is not something that could be submitted to history, carried along and finally abolished by it; it is not an historical state, that is to say, precisely, a state of things in the process of transformation, slated, finally, to disappear. *The repetition alike unto itself, against the background of its own proper essence, of individual phenomenological life and of its fundamental determinations, the indefinite repetition of desire, need and of labor – this is what, as the always new and always present condition, allows there to be history.*
>
> (Henry (1973) 1986, 92–93 [original emphasis])

I have quoted Henry at some length because he captures well the a priori value-judgments that, as we insisted, inform sociology and operate behind the back, so to speak, of the discipline's criteria of value-relevance. In this passage, elements of Marx's natural law[9] are theorized with a view to recognize the dual relation between life and history, which informs, as we saw in Chapter 1 on values, also Durkheim's moral sociology. The Marxian discourse of species-being (itself taken from Hegel[10]) provides ample proof that his critique of capitalism remained committed to this dual (history/natural law) view of species-life (see, for example, Marx (1861–1863)1988, 245).[11]

Yet, sociologists have underplayed the normative dimension underneath agency and have, prematurely, as it seems, repelled a normative philosophical anthropology that seeks not only to explore the human as a rational and cognitive being (Landmann 1974) but also to engage with the normative problem of human nature. Likened to a theory of social action (Honneth and Joas 1988) philosophical anthropology discloses to sociologists those aspects of agency that form conditions for theories of social integration. (For a contemporary shift to this debate, see Chernilo 2017 and Joas 2013.) Habermas (2010), for his part, repels a 'retrospective charging of human rights' (466), yet he insists that conceptual connections between human rights and morality are couched in human dignity. Faithful to his Marxist background, Habermas locates the elevation of human dignity to the status of a value that infuses human rights in history's indignities and the 'plethora of experiences of what it means to be humiliated and be deeply hurt' (468). Interestingly, the trail from natural law and the permutations that give it a sociological dimension configured as 'utopia' has another formidable supporter. Interested primarily in the legalization of the natural law tradition, Habermas is never blind to the necessity of the warm streams, as Bloch ((1961) 1987) would say, of the tradition of natural law to dry up the dynamism of the human capability to stand upright.

It is though the late thought of Daniel Bell that provides sociology with the means to rethink the natural law tradition in light of a critique of contemporary disjunctions among institutions and values. In the 1996 afterword to *The Cultural Contradictions of Capitalism* ((1976) 1996a) Bell takes issue with postmodernism and the withering of binding norms, which have generated a discourse driven by various (occasionally very sophisticated) rejections of universal values. In that afterword Bell (1996b, 298n.18) had announced that he was working on a manuscript that would liken natural law to utopia. In that unpublished manuscript titled 'The Re-birth of Utopia: The Path to Natural Law', Bell (1996c) offers a systematic justification for reconsidering the normative potential of natural law. Compared to *The Cultural Contradictions of Capitalism* the novel dimension now is natural law's link to utopia. Bell revisits the themes of natural law taking recourse to distinct 'cosmographies' (coherent world-views), which at different eras sought to provide a foundation for meaning and solace to human lives afflicted with tragedy and violence. It is beyond the scope of this discussion to probe deeper into these cosmographies (namely, the classical world of Greece, Christianity and modernity). What is clearly evident from Bell's concern is that the question 'what it means to be human' (4) is surging, given the acute problems that afflict the contemporary world. For Bell, the diremptions of modernity call for a 'philosophical anthropology' (4) and thus require a reconsideration of natural law, this time though not as an a priori constitution of the human but rather as an ongoing and incomplete 'normative foundation of human rights' (4).

Given recurring problems of dissensus (due to conventional 'language-games' or ineluctable value-wars), reconstructing natural law, for Bell, requires three modalities, or 'tiers' as he puts it: First, a quest for ontology figures as a valid requirement, if the motley of contemporary cultural disjunctions and epistemological confusion is to be mitigated. A human ontology would supplant us with a foundational realm from which 'normative judgments' can be recovered and adduced. Although this factor is far from complete, Bell provides us with significant hints about the common humanity entailed in each. For one thing he offers a not so cryptic solution to the problem of incommensurability of perspectives when these get organized around a particular culture or a historical era. Speaking of our ability to 'rotate the pictures to see the entire gestalt' (40), Bell, we may surmise, intimates the possibility of coordination of these 'different' and seemingly incompatible 'cosmographies', as he puts it, as if they were mutually complementary pieces in a single vision of our humanness. This process of reactivating natural law is justified if natural law is conceptualized as an ongoing, incomplete and constantly enriched project. Bell does not wish to stick to natural law as a 'transcendent' or a 'transhistorical' ontology, although the 'common humanity' that we all share constitutes indeed this ontological substratum. Rather, tying natural law to sociology exhibits for Bell the human 'capacity to fulfil' the 'reciprocity' upon which membership in a community is incumbent. Criteria of membership that Bell sketchily lists, include 'to meet others without shame at one's estate, to have a necessary self-esteem, to be treated with equal dignity and respect, is a condition of being human and feeling human' (41–42). Evidently, this normative discourse is in accord with the basic contours of CA.

Second, a set of normative rules is identified by Bell in terms of 'responsibility and rights' (42). Although he devotes only a short paragraph in the manuscript on this second criterion of 'utopia', this juncture is essential for the argument we advance in this book. Both responsibility and rights possess, for Bell, 'objective validity'. In tune with his proposed reconstruction of natural law, both are held to be 'constitutive of the human condition'. Conversely, if suspended, they unleash, first, social discord (anomie captures better I think this state of affairs) since no member of the community considers the moral and ethical repercussions of her actions and, second, they imply heteronomy; no self-determination is possible without a niche of rights and entitlements. What is crucial to underscore here is that to support his point Bell cites Putnam's rejection of the fact/value distinction and, below Putnam, Amartya Sen's argument about the explanation of famines due to a 'collapse of entitlements' (42).

Finally, a consideration of 'substantive outcomes' enables Bell to reserve a place in this new ontology for empirical and historical contingency. As different claims of justice are raised, the normative principles invoked by Bell can operate as templates for mutual coordination so that historicism and relativism, rather than figuring as the end of the moral constitution of humankind, become deferred to the beginning (40). Natural law appears thus as the 'utopia without illusions' anchored in the 'ontological fact' of human 'potentiality' (45). We can conceive its possibility given, at least, the minimum fact that 'moral conduct is universal', a fact though that points to a secular 'beyond', namely the utopia without illusions.

I commented on Bell not so much for the fact that a major contemporary sociologist pondered with such clarity and verve on issues of normativity in a relatively unknown manuscript – in itself a finding of significant interest – but, mainly, because he must have been among the earlier sociological interlocutors with Sen to have urged the discipline's scholars to consider the line of thought, which digs deeper into the multilayered humanness through the lens of human dignity. Although some reluctance (Nussbaum 2004, 308) is understandable because no normative programme would wish to open the Pandora's box of human nature essentialism (see, for example, Nussbaum 2011, 28), abstaining completely from this move runs the risk of making a leap onto ethical presuppositions that bear little to the natural law foundation that CA seems to acknowledge as one of its sources of inspiration. This is particularly pronounced when CA recognizes essential elements of human life that are 'compatible with the continued' membership of a being into the 'human kind' (Nussbaum 1999, 39). Inevitably, therefore, the natural law intimations of CA take us to the area of human rights. This has been a point of controversy between CA scholars and sceptical, albeit sympathetic, critics of human rights. I shall only deal here with the basic morphology of CA on human rights.

Excursus on human rights

Sen (1999) tackles three broad areas of critique against human rights: (1) the *legitimacy* critique challenges the natural law justification of human rights. It asserts that such rights qualify as ethical entitlements and thus they require legal encoding and institutional legitimation; (2) the *coherence* critique suggests that rights ought to be supplemented by agency-specific duties if they are to acquire concrete substance; (3) finally, the *cultural critique* adopts a relativist standpoint and questions the universality of values that figures as a necessary adjunct to any notion of human rights. Since there is no universal culture, the criticism goes, human rights collapse under the sheer weight of cultural diversity and incommensurability.

Sen takes to task the three critiques. He recognizes that any prelegal justification of human rights – like those couched on natural law – is insufficient. He prefers to conceptualize rights as 'claims, powers and immunities [...] supported by ethical judgments' (1999, 229). Reversing the critique's claim, Sen argues that rights are identified most clearly in those cases where legal enforcement is inadequate. In doing this Sen does not rest content with a standpoint that regards value-formation (i.e. human rights as values) a process that springs from negation, that is, from a moment of claim-violations. Rather, he demonstrates the inadequacy of a 'legal enforcement' approach in, for example, cases of the 'right to respect'. What I think is missing here for this sketchy defence is the idea that claims arise out of some infringement. This infringement may be prelegal (in the Hobbesian sense) as it may bear on violations of the body, of an agent's capability for voice and dissent, of control of productive resources. Out of this primordial infringement, human rights take up the positive claims of natural law, which extend to the social contract. In this direction it is rightly pointed out that, for Sen, empowerment of the individual is central to CA, the latter being 'anti-sacrificial by nature' (De Munck 2018, 931). (This anti-sacrificial character of capability empowerment avoids the defects of a rigid value-hierarchy – as in Scheler – which entails the partial sacrifice of a lower value if higher values are to be felt in full.) According to De Munck (2018) the advantage of Sen's theory of human rights is that they are coded as values and thus disable interpretations that align with methodological individualism. To withstand the force of the coherence critique that requires duties as logical supplements of rights, Sen resorts to Kant's idea of 'imperfect obligations' and essentially introduces an 'as if' requirement. Although no particular agency can be assigned the task of promoting human rights, the addressee of the claim could be any rational being, 'as if' it was her duty to treat people as bearers of human rights. In addressing the merits of the cultural critique Sen (1999, 231–240) emphasizes the capacity for transpositional scrutiny. We shall discuss this issue later in the book but for Sen (2005) the idea is first to challenge the popularity of cultural critique on factual and historical grounds (like, for instance, in debunking the monopoly of freedom and tolerance as exclusively Western values, bringing to the fore non-Western affirmations of them). At the other end, sequestered accounts of 'Asian values' are equally held in check in terms of extremely biased recourse to Asian traditions that neglect what those traditions share with 'non-Asian' culture.

Sen sees no incompatibility between holding on to universal assumptions about human rights and adjusting these to imperfect orderings, local variation and different policy agents and processes. Human rights rise initially as 'ethical demands'. But ethical demands claiming what? To tackle this question, Sen abstracts towards the content of what enables this ethical demand to become a normative claim. This content of freedom is the 'subject-matter of human rights'

(Sen 2004, 319). As an ethical claim human rights summon the other to cooperation and aid. Sen does not use the word 'summons' and it is beyond the scope of this discussion to elaborate its importance. It implicates though a claim to recognition that the agent of human rights 'counts' and she is thus entitled to help and support when those features of her life that are violated (i.e. the 'process' aspect and the 'opportunity' aspect of freedom). For example, the freedom of movement is a substantive aspect of freedom as an end in itself but it needs to be coupled to the opportunity (i.e. the capability) to command an adequate income. The latter will enable a person to travel or take the bus rather than being able to move but lack the capabilities to convert her movement across places into the lifestyle she chooses to value and to pursue.

Legislation is for Sen (2004) one route to take; but given various contingencies that eschew the positivity of law, public discussion and activism can play a major role in promoting human rights. At this juncture Sen takes recourse to the space opened by historical contingencies when institutional prerequisites for economic and social freedoms are only partially in place. He opts for a pragmatic broadening of current arrangements so that the zone of what is unrealizable or pending in terms of institutional adequacy be prevented from serving as an apology for the non-realizability of human rights (320). Finally, the universality of human rights is not so much an issue of intersection of interests (as these would also include deeply authoritarian states) but, rather, 'an interactive process' based on free dissemination of information and 'uncurbed opportunity' to deliberate on the contending issues at hand. It seems that Sen places this last criterion of deliberation in the domain of undistorted communication but it is not at all clear at what level of actual deliberation nation-states or international organizations can be engaged in a type of dialogue that abstracts to a considerable degree from geopolitical claims, economic interests and ideological commitments. For Habermas, the positivity of law can convert the claims of the life-world (i.e. Sen's invocation of 'pressure' from public reasoning (2004, 356)) into media-induced information so that the legal system can activate the 'mediating' space for a potential or actual dispute to be converted into a mutually accepted topic for a discussion driven by mutual tests for genuine criticism (i.e. criticism in line with the validity-claims suggested by Habermas).

Thus, Sen provides us with a broader and deeper idea of individual agency freedom. In line with his commitment to non-dualism he takes issue with the famous dichotomy of freedom espoused by Isaiah Berlin. The latter's 'negative' view of freedom from interference aligns, for Sen (1990, 49) with a libertarian waiving of restrains. Yet, the 'positive' aspects of freedom are seen as mere derivatives of negative freedom. For Sen this indicates a spurious relationship between the two 'moments' of freedom, if seen to be exclusive and monophonic. Actually, the reverse tendency may call for equal weight. In this case, blockades on the positive freedom to live a comfortable life in stable employment and having access to food may instantiate conditions equally harmful as those that Berlin assigns to the class of negative freedoms. Thus, in the much cited biographical testimony of Kader Mia's death (50) although the negative freedom to be able to live was breached by assault, the reverse holds just as well: He was driven to a hostile area in India where Muslims were discriminated against (with result to have been stabbed to death) because in the community in which he lived he had no access to work. Kader Mia's poverty is clearly not an infringement on his negative freedom but a deprivation of his positive freedom to have the capability to choose the lifestyle he had reason to value. The implications of seeing these two 'moments' of freedom outside their conceptual and practical interlacing is, for Sen, 'not only ethically incomplete, but can also be socially disjointed' (50). Implicitly at least, yet unequivocally, Sen recognizes both an ethically integrated theory of freedom with practical implications that translate into social dislocations and conflicts of sorts beyond those – citing Dahrendorf here (54) – that stem from conflicting claims by categories and classes of people 'in modern society' (54).[12]

From capacity to capability (I): Parsons and Sen

I contend that Parsons' work provides the normative opportunity for a connection between agency and capability in this context of modern society for two reasons: first, because he renders the notion of 'capacity' central to social action and traces its enrichment from the personality to the system level; thus, he grapples directly with philosophical anthropology as his essays on the human condition (Parsons 1978) demonstrate; second, because, the idea of capacity is configured not only negatively as capacity-deprivation but also as a 'condition' for the actor's participation in 'full citizenship' (Parsons 1977, 338). If seen in the context of modernity, then what we encounter here is a form of social ontology, one that informs normative conceptions of the human potential and makes the latter derivative but also co-constituting of social institutions and processes.

For our purposes, therefore, it is Parsons' thought which tells us best what this institutional adaptation of agency can be. Parsons offers a template for a theory of social institutions and role-complexes, upon which the capable actor's goal orientations are normatively grounded and evaluatively sanctioned. Parsons' analytic rigour reconsiders aspects of the problem of evaluative action, a problem central to Sen's approach. Let us, briefly, recall the contours of Parsons' theory of action. Parsons distances 'action' from utilitarian interpretations of neo-classical accounts of economic action and thus anticipates the reservations of CA expressed against the limitations of similar models of rational choice in economics. While, as have seen, commentaries have discerned complications in the mutual adaptation between economics and sociology, it is evident that both Sen and Parsons bring forth the evaluative dimensions of economic action and thus introduce to such models institutional factors, most notably, norms and values. Sen's argument in terms of economic policy is often held to be rooted in classical accounts to agency. As he admits:

> In our normal lives, we see ourselves as members of a variety of groups-we belong to all of them. A person's citizenship, residence, geographic origin,

> gender, class, politics, profession, employment, food habits, sports interests, taste in music, social commitments, etc., make us members of a variety of groups. Each of these collectivities, to all of which this person simultaneously belongs, gives her a particular identity. None of them can be taken to be the person's only identity or singular membership category.
>
> (Sen 2006, 5)

Not only is this claim incompatible with the utilitarian identity of a person in the market, but, additionally, it affirms the social richness of situations, against the charges which impute to Sen a neglect of sociality. Sen reaches this goal by attaching a hitherto unnoticed normative load to agency, while Parsons, although not indifferent to this, normatively speaking, ambitious notion of agency, prefers to integrate it into a wider social system and to deduce logically the normative presuppositions and validity of 'economic action' (the gist of the 'convergence thesis'). For Parsons, norms, as well as collectively held values, shape communal patterns of agency. These patterns of choice (known as 'pattern-variables', the validity of which has not gone unchallenged in subsequent commentaries of Parsons) are mediated by the 'effort' exerted by agents as they attempt to creatively transform situational constraints and opportunities (Parsons (1939–1940) 2010, 72–73n. 42). However, the pattern-variables form only general frames within which role-complexes become consolidated in social institutions. In this function they set the parameters for the coordinated action of individuals holding statuses and acting on the basis of the status-emanating respective roles. Evidently, for Parsons' institutional point of view, the capability of the actor is bounded by normative opportunities and constraints and is thus anchored in social institutions; at first glance we encounter an incompatibility with Sen's individualist point of view. Nevertheless, as Sen tells us in the extract about the diversity of the self, the agent is placed within a complex web of social memberships. The question that surfaces is if these social memberships carry a normative content (i.e. if they enhance capabilities they *ought to*) and whether this content can be patterned in specific types of institutions, mitigating the involuntary dimension in the actor's 'effort' to attain valued goals.

As generally known, Parsons' unit-act served as a model of analytical reduction of the action system into its ultimate foundations. For Parsons the system of action comprises: (1) an agent, (2) goals, (3) opportunities and (4) a normative orientation. Sen's approach – he nowhere adduces Parsons – has a different vantage point, yet its own essential premises invite us to take the unit-act's parameters into consideration. The agent's capability constitutes for Sen the equivalent of the 'actor' in Parsons. Actors are endowed with physiological, personality and cognitive capacities, which form the 'materialist', so to speak, prerequisite for any expressed will to activate any subsequent 'means-ends' sequence. Functionings (the lifestyles agents have reason to value) operate in close analogy to the agent's goals. In the form of lifestyles valued by agents, such goals carry a marked voluntaristic dimension consisting of the agent's selection of an evaluative/instrumental criterion merely by virtue of the fact that a goal has been selected and affixed in the agent's efforts to accomplish it. Conversion factors (personal, environmental, social) seem to act like opportunities, which for Parsons tend to be both enabling and constraining. Of course, any such schematization on Sen's part demarcates the level of agency from conversion factors of a person's characteristics. If the agent and her personal factors are to be distinguished, as Sen suggests, then agency has to be transferred to a meta-level of human potentiality which as I have argued is most powerfully configured in Hegel and Marx (and the Aristotelian legacy they share with CA) As for Parsons' normative orientation, Sen's CA would have to be considered at the level of human rights. It cannot entail societal values as these seem to operate on a lower level of abstraction since they form part of conversion factors. Schematically, the parallel between the two action-systems appears as shown in Figure 3.2.

Moreover, like Sen, Parsons (1951, 49) sees instrumental goal orientation as achievable only under the guidance of an 'evaluative primacy'. Parsons believes that the normative coordinates of actors in exercising their wills and capabilities under a commonly defined set of norms need not entail always a maximal value-convergence. Rather:

> an agreement of practical moral attitude in the relevant situations is sufficient. But some minimum of practical agreement as to the "rights" of other members of the collectivity is essential. This is, in fact, an aspect of *common* value-orientation, an integration on the level of moral sentiments.
> ((1939–1940) 2010, 116 [original emphasis])

Parsons' point about the practical appreciation of 'rights' is arguably a direct attempt to theorize social action by recourse to an explanatory and normatively binding framework. What makes Parsons' solution a persuasive one is that he sets, like Adam Smith and CA, the institutional presuppositions of these 'rights' as functional conditions for action. With his last reference, therefore, to 'moral sentiments', Parsons draws from the same normative pool as Sen often does, namely Adam Smith. For Parsons:

> gratification needs have alternatively possible objects presented in the situation. Cognitive mapping has alternatives of judgment or interpretation as to

Figure 3.2 Amartya Sen's aspects of agency configured after Parsons' functional imperatives.

	Talcott Parsons (Action-System)	*Amartya Sen on agency*	
L	Normative Orientation	Human rights	**L**
I	Opportunities	Conversion factors (personal, environmental, social)	**I**
G	Goals	Functionings	**G**
A	Actor	Agent's capabilities	**A**

> what objects are or what they 'mean'. There must be ordered selection among such alternatives. The term 'evaluation' will be used to define this process of ordered selection. There is, therefore, an evaluative aspect of all concrete action orientation.
>
> (Parsons 1951, 7)

This value-dimension enriches significantly the concepts of economic rationality. For Parsons and Sen rational economic action is embedded in orderly institutional arrangements patterned after collectively validated values. With respect to the moral dimension of social cohesion, Parsons ((1939–1940) 2010, 138–139), like Sen and Nussbaum, visualizes 'expressional' patterns of action like 'play', 'art', 'affective attitudes' ('love', 'friendship') and 'disinterested scientific truth' as essential contributors to the equilibrium of the action system; implicitly at least, what is posited here is a minimum of institutionally processed capabilities upon which the degree and value of the expressional patterns of action are incumbent. These expressive elements figure also in Nussbaum's CCL (i.e. capabilities 4, 5 and 9).

Drawing on the work of T.H. Marshall on citizenship, Parsons delineates further the conditions under which inclusion in the system of rights is premised on pluralism rather than assimilation. In the seminal essay on the Negro American, Parsons analyses the process of inclusion with the aid of the action dimension of 'capacity'. Although not stemming directly from the 'unit-act' as in Parsons' early phase, the notion of 'capacity' figures as a derivative of the democratic process of inclusion typical of 'advanced societies'. In explicating Marshall's idea of social rights Parsons writes:

> The social component does not concern the opportunity to express and implement the rights derived from the societal values so much as the resources and capacities necessary for this implementation. In this connection the societal community defines and presents standards for the allocation of resources to the community as a whole and to its various subsectors. The obverse of this allocative function, is the definition of the terms on which capacities, as matched with opportunities, can be involved in the process of inclusion.
>
> (1969, 260)

Even though 'capacity' appears in Parsons' systems theory in a cybernetic sense (Parsons and Smelser 1956, 49), it retains an agent-centric normative core, one that suffuses Parsons' exposition of the action system and its normative ideal of 'institutionalized individualism'. It is thus not surprising that the connection of CA to social rights with regards to T.H. Marshall pioneering work has not gone unnoticed (see Browne, Deakin and Wilkinson 2004, Holmwood 2013).

The terminological turn towards capacities signals a progressive problem shift in the Parsonsian scheme, one, which I believe, can make us more attentive to its fruitfulness if we attach to the admittedly underdeveloped notion of 'capacity' the concrete contents implied in the normatively more solid pattern of 'capability'.[13] Parsons gets us closer to this fusion when he writes next that 'the underlying capacity of the units, especially individuals and their families, to function effectively in the environment in which they are placed' concerns, primarily, 'health and education' (1969, 261). Institutions are thus seen as capacity-steering mechanisms normatively oriented to enhance the respective capabilities of the actor. Parsons, for instance, holds that the actor's capacities and that of the system to (partially) correspond. The interchanges among the AGIL subcomponents highlight the mediating channels and processes that cement the various subsystems. Sen, for his part, repels such analytical apriorism, but introduces similar intimations when he identifies (1999, 10) a set of 'rights and opportunities' (e.g. political freedoms, transparency guarantees, economic facilities, social opportunities), that are instrumental in advancing the 'general capability of the person'. Sen's semi-pragmatic approach leaves open the mode by which these rights will be implemented and realized in concrete sociohistorical conditions. Nevertheless, as I shall argue in Chapter 6, the moral content of these rights is derived from modern society's institutional arrangements (Sen 1999, 38–40) like the ones fashioned after Parsons' AGIL categories and has been preceded by Hegel and Durkheim.

With respect to opportunities in society, Parsons holds that 'capacities' are central to institutionalized individualism in terms of the capability to accomplish socially worthy goals:

> Since opportunity for the individual is such an important condition for achievement, this is one of the main points at which the universalistic principle leads to the ideal of '*equality of opportunity*'. The other main one is with respect to the training element of capacity. This issue is one of the most important meanings of *individualism* in our society. It concerns the right of the individual to a fair chance to show what he can do in effective achievement rather than a simple freedom to 'do what he pleases' so long as he respects the corresponding rights of others. His freedoms are necessary conditions of acting *responsibly* in terms of the values.
>
> (Parsons 1991, 58–59 [original emphasis])

Transferring, as Parsons does, the notion of 'change' into the individual capacity requires the shift to capabilities. Giddens provides it when he theorizes agency as the 'capability to act' but he does so sporadically and at the cost of discarding the normative parameters discerned in Parsons.

From capacity to capability (II): Giddens' wanting normativity

Tilting the emphasis to routinized action, as Giddens does, has an immediate advantage: It addresses the actor's resourcefulness to act (by recourse to pregiven structural properties) and extends this idea to the theme of the actor's ontological security, positioned in the matrix of social roles. This ontological security – a metaphysically loaded term, at odds with Sen's humbler concept formation – constitutes a core component of CA. CA supplements the ontological security of agency in that, by eliciting intersubjectively sanctioned value-choices, actors draw on normative patterns, by recourse to which agency acquires those features that can generate a competent, morally reflexive and freely chosen goal orientation that can impact social life. With this provision in mind, it is worth looking at what Giddens writes:

> Action depends on the capability of the individual to 'make a difference' to a pre-existing state of affairs or course of events. An agent ceases to be such if he or she loses the capability to 'make a difference', that is, to exercise some sort of power [...] Expressing these observations in another way, we can say that action logically involves power in the sense of transformative capacity. In this sense, the most all-embracing meaning of 'power', power is logically prior to subjectivity, to the constitution of the reflexive monitoring of conduct.
>
> (1984, 14–15)

What Giddens tells us here is that an agent's action instantiates transformative outcomes on the level of intersubjective relations, which in Giddens' structuration scheme takes the form of tacit manoeuvring against systems of action. I will leave aside for a moment the intimation that the 'to make a difference' clause adds a moral dimension in structuration theory and introduces, as claims to esteem and recognition, system properties in Giddens' model. Giddens admits it when he understands, albeit momentarily, capability as 'autonomy' (156). Still, one cannot extrapolate from Giddens' anti-Parsonsianism the normative content that a determinate connotation of autonomy would normally require. The abstractness imputed to Parsons is not compensated by the allegedly concrete but normatively opaque 'logic' of social institutions that Giddens offers as an alternative. In fact, a Parsonsian lineage survives in other formulations of the self's capacity to make a difference. Thus, Giddens writes that:

> the *autotelic self* [...] refers to a person able to translate potential threats into rewarding challenges, someone who is able to turn entropy into a consistent flow of experience. The *autotelic self* does not seek to neutralize risk or to suppose that 'someone else will take care of the problem'; risk is confronted as the active challenge which generates self-actualization.
>
> (Giddens 1994, 192 [original emphasis])[14]

Moreover, Giddens lodges capability in the organization of collective life, conducive to 'a way that the individual is *capable* – in some sense or another – of free and independent action in the environments of her social life' (1991, 213). This use of the concept of capability points to aspects of agency-empowerment, which form the prelude to Giddens' own proposal of life-politics. Evidently, it constitutes also an identifiable ingredient of Sen's programme. To be sure, Giddens tells us here something important and relevant to CA, especially in the 'some sense or another' intimation; unfortunately, this intimation is insufficiently developed in Giddens' own use of 'capability': If capability is held to form a central component of agency, then Giddens would have to widen the normative scope of choices implied by the capable actor. The direction to be pursued is precisely that of specifying the types of choices that individuals are capable of making. This opening into the empirical, Giddens' project lacks. For if agency's capability is to count as essential for the drive and will of the self 'to make a difference' then a supplement from the domain of normative theories of socialization and interaction must be sought – which at points Giddens indeed provides – in conjunction with a theory of institutional arrangements drawn from sociology's explanation of modernity. Although such arrangements would be driven, as Sen also argues, to the logic of 'individualism as a social commitment' (Sen 1990), the crucial commitment that is missing from both Giddens and Sen is the institutional normativism that would enable both to benchmark societies' development of capabilities.[15]

Haunted by the spell of formalism once Parsonsian institutions are emptied of content, Giddens feels compelled to reinsert into the formal project of 'life-politics', the normative substance that capability ought to have carried with it in the context of structuration theory. To be sure, the disruption of the mundane world of routinized trust is given voice in Giddens' theory when he deploys the device of 'critical situations' (1979, 123–128; 1984, 60–63). The increase in anxiety, either through the elimination of the performative 'front' and 'back' regions, or through the reduction of the agent's 'transformative capacity', is addressed at the level of the most extreme deprivation and mortification of the self. Given these risks for the actor, Giddens, unexpectedly, does not theorize the 'empowerment' steps that may lead to the agent's 'capability to make a difference'. He thus misses the opportunity to rethink the notion of routine as ethically adequate and action-enabling social arrangements. This happens because the notion of capability he resorts to is tethered to the formalism of routinized resources emptied of normative content. In contrast, a capabilities-based reconstruction of agency would preserve Giddens' insights but would not hesitate to fortify, normatively, the capability of the agent. This repair would retain essential normative qualities (i.e. life, autonomy of the body, control of material resources among other capabilities) of what capability can mean in addition to contextual concreteness. Moreover, it would preserve an open range for capabilities' expansion, precisely because contextualist accounts of the self, retain empirical relevance and historical force. Rather, therefore, than conceding to the relativistic consequences of a contextualist account, a renovated notion of agency based on capabilities would call for the implementation of the capability of the self to 'make a difference' in producing and reproducing resourceful routines. This time though on the condition that such routines are worthy of preservation in the binding sense of acting as markers of the capability and freedom to make valued choices. Such an approach to structuration would be premised on the condition that routines are themselves benchmarked in terms of their enabling–constraining ratio for the freedom of the actor. For this to happen the theory in question would have to extract from social reality a set of institutional 'capabilities' conducive to consolidating the self's transformative capacity. Such prerogatives seem to call for a more explicit formulation of the normativism implicit in the sociological category of agency's capability with which Giddens is working.

Our attempt to probe deeper into the hitherto available notions of capacity in sociology reflects the antinomy that stems from Giddens' need to preserve autonomy in action while, at the same time, he repels the institutional and role-specific presuppositions for this autonomy. He thus upholds, nominally only, the capabilities referent assumed by his social-theoretical analysis. In contrast, for Sen, this methodological step is taken in the direction of moving beyond the constraints of the situation. This, he believes, can be attained through a rational process of 'comparative broadening', which not only adduces new information for the local agent but prompts her to rationally justify why existing practices and belief-systems may have to be partially retained, in spite of empirical and normative anomalies, revised, or even discarded altogether because of such anomalies.

Enriching agency

What is then our proposed categorial reconstruction of agency? Caught between two important versions of agency, namely Parsons' accentuation of capacity within his general system of action and Giddens' references to capability in the domain of routinized agency, Sen's idea of capability can render concrete the abstractions entailed in these two formulations of agency. This is accomplished with two categorial adjustments (summarized also in Figure 3.3).

Sociology's shift to capabilities elicits a definition of actors' capacities with greater chances of becoming concretely operational than the one provided by Parsons. Unlike capacities, thinking in terms of capabilities prompts us to look at what actors can really achieve in specific situations; these though require some normative specificity in terms of wider contexts and systems and under the umbrella of some basic capabilities. It makes a lot of difference if the categories we use capture simply the potential of agents to escape premature morbidity or to achieve sources of self-esteem beyond conspicuous consumption or if they allow us to conceptualize and simultaneously measure their actual capabilities to achieve these valued choices. While talk about potentialities is by no means insignificant or caught in abstract theorizing, the aim of social theory can be better served by categories that focus on the social processes that actually impede or enable real persons, groups and entire categories to enhance basic and other capabilities.

Second, the shift to capabilities confirms Giddens' powerful intuition. Yet, Giddens offers an impoverished notion of agency because he undertheorized the normative thrust of the idea of 'capability'. I argued that his contribution is important in that it brings onstage the actor's capability in terms of the freedom

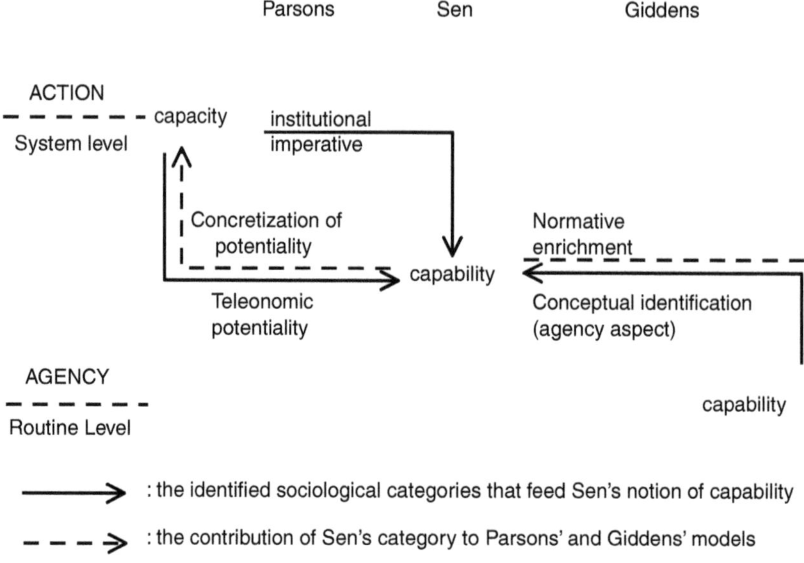

Figure 3.3 Reconstructing agency as capability: linkages among Parsons, Sen and Giddens.

of agency. Abstract 'capacities' or routinely sanctioned 'capabilities' constitute a normative starting point and an important one for purposes of developing a general theory of action or for defending the horizon of ontological security for the actor. Nevertheless, the normative thread that underpinned Parsons impressive attempt leads us to some notion of capability, deduced from roles, statuses, social institutions and systems (AGIL). And this is why, for all his faults, Parsons is still needed: The thread from Parsons' abstract notion of capacity does not, therefore, lead to Giddens' but to Sen's capabilities. Sen has shown with ample biographical, empirical and conceptual tools how routines can incapacitate actors and can blatantly violate their horizons of ontological security. In this shift towards 'capability' sociology needs to guard itself against slipping into esoteric entrenchments of agency (see the topical complaint by Barnes 2000, 154–155n.10). It also needs to recouple the pragmatist call for a situated positional objectivity, pluralism and freedom as interaction (Zimmermann 2006) or as situated agency (Hobson 2013) beyond the moral compass of the person's capabilities, to functional and 'material' prerequisites that CA is designed to accommodate.

The limitations of the current discussion of agency in sociology can be overcome, I claim, at the juncture when the recurring usage of the term 'capacity' can be systematically transformed if recourse to CA could reset the parameters for a new normative foundation behind any version of agency. In Parsons, this vision of capacity, no matter how abstractly formulated, can be viably likened to the normative programme of capabilities, aiming at a social self, free of major deprivations and sufferings. As Parsons writes:

> If the problem of suffering comes to focus in human exposure to the impact of deprivation independent of individual agency, and that of evil, in exposure to that of consequences independent of active intentions, that of capacity focuses on the fact that, however much we may *want* to do something, we may be prevented to incapacity from actually doing it.
>
> (1978, 79 [original emphasis])

Internal to Parsons' system is therefore a moral foundation of human essence when, in passages like this, his philosophical anthropology identifies serious deprivations on 'teleonomic capacity'. While Parsons transfers the problem of capacity deprivation to the sphere of existential suffering, he nonetheless acknowledges that these deprivations that bear on human health become more acute in a society 'with an activistic orientation' (79). 'Activistic' patterns of action based on common value-orientations that inform institutional means need not necessarily be seen as fixed modernist arrangements that lock agency into a competitive system of rewards. This proves a narrow perspective on the moral investment of institutions, the latter seen by Durkheim, Parsons and many others as the key to a sociological understanding of agency. Rather, as Nussbaum notes, in an 'aspiring society':

> the conception of the human being that lies at the heart of the political conception involves both striving and vulnerability. Human beings are not just passive recipients of fortune's blows. Instead, they are active beings who pursue aims and who seek lives rich in activity.
>
> (2013, 120)[16]

This philosophical and normative conception of what it means to be human is the running theme and connecting motif between sociology and CA. Parsons' and Nussbaum's versions of normativity are thus on the par: 'Agency and support are connected: it is on account of their capacity for activity and striving that human beings are entitled to support for their vulnerability' (Nussbaum 2013, 120).

It is this assumption that encourages us to see capability as the bedrock of agency. Freedom couched in the 'capability' to 'act otherwise' makes little sense if capability is weakly or nominally defined. The normatively solid conception of this 'capability' to practice our freedom in society reintroduces the necessity to take up again the Parsonsian mapping of the normative patterns which amplify actors' capabilities to choose the lifestyle(s) they have reason to value. Why this prerogative precludes choices of nominal 'freedom' or of 'abstract' and even of 'malign' capabilities is evident by the normative ontology of CA – shared also by thinkers like Parsons – in the absence of which living together becomes an impossible undertaking. Sen is very clear about this:

> Even the identity of being human – perhaps our most basic identity – may have the effect, when fully seized, of broadening our viewpoint correspondingly.

> The imperatives that we may associate with our humanity may not be mediated by our membership in smaller collectivities such as specific 'peoples' or 'nations'. Indeed, the normative demands of being guided by 'humanity' or 'humaneness' can build on our membership of the wide category of human beings, irrespective of our particular nationalities, or sects, or tribal affiliations (traditional or modern).
>
> (Sen 2009, 142)

This quote shows also that despite Sen's reluctance to commit himself to pursuing the argument from human nature, there is actually very little that separates Sen from Nussbaum on human nature. Instead of the CCL, Sen invokes three human capacities: the ability to understand, to sympathize and to argue (Sen 2009, 415). In effect, practical reasoning, sympathy, public deliberation are transferred to a conversion level for which the CCL may be promoted. Yet, they are posited as irreducibly human and widely shared. It would be hard to accept today, given sociology's increasingly public voice,[17] that sociologists can possibly justify action-patterns that fall short of most of the capabilities outlined in Nussbaum's list, especially since sociologists from all schools look primarily at action in modern society and must presuppose some essential normative features of it (even when they embark on the luxury of postmodernist critique). It would be even harder, based on the actual entitlements of agents, to make sufficient sense of action and its transformative capacity without regard for the capabilities set controlled by the 'humaneness' of an actor, her membership in a group, a region or for that matter a nation.

Notes

1 On the other hand, feminism, at least up to the early 2000s when CA had already articulated its basic premises, did not consider CA as a programme with much potential. For example, in the four-volume edition titled *Feminism: Critical Concepts in Literary and Cultural Studies* only one contributor (Soper 2001) discusses CA. It is also no coincidence that this one occasion is a qualified consideration of human nature, which concerns us here too. Nussbaum's liberal feminism and the essentialist reconstruction she proposes has been the subject of constructive criticism in feminist literature. Unsurprisingly, the target is Nussbaum's argument for universal essential capabilities (in the CCL). (For this debate see Nussbaum 2001; Quillen 2001, but also Lawson 1999; Robeyns 2003.) Oddly enough the counterproposal that surfaces in some of these critiques (e.g. Quillen 2001) points to relational epistemologies and conceptions of the human which are held to fit contemporary discourses tuned to pluralism and cultural difference. While Nussbaum retorts (2001) by recourse to psychology's findings (e.g. Winnicott) it needs to be underlined that relationism is quite a modernist, if not classical Greek, idea that stems from Plato, Aristotle, all the way to Hegel, Simmel, and Durkheim. I do not reproach Nussbaum or her critics for neglecting this trajectory in the neighbouring discipline of sociology but I argue that the so-called non-foundational problem of relationism gets us back to the Hegelian problem of the just ordering of freedom in modern institutional arrangements. Similar problems about social totality afflict Flax's informed criticisms of Nussbaum (Flax 2000a; 2000b) when she asserts initially a standpoint that lacks an external vantage

point of objectivity and is thus embedded in 'existing social relations' (Flax 2000a, 27), while she then adheres to a version of the *hiatus irrationalis* claiming that 'incommensurable differences is an ethical commitment' (28). The possibility of internal relations, as in Hegel, that include also 'incommensurability' as a partial, even if necessary standpoint, is explained away and this omission is also reproduced in Nussbaum's (2000b) response to Flax.

2 To be sure, the 'imaginary capacity' (Castoriadis 1987, 127) from which Joas draws inspiration, and through which the subject opens a realm of future possibilities may indeed constitute a core component of the human psyche. It thus may contribute to a philosophical anthropology of the type envisaged by Castoriadis' attempt to ground agency in some originary faculty of the imagination. In a loose way the centrality of imagination towards an emancipatory function is pertinent to the capability of imagination in Nussbaum's CCL. Without the capacity for imagination, agents cannot construct a vision of an actual life situation in accord with their valued lifestyles. Thus, for the agent to be capable of formulating a project certain ethical-practical conditions need to be in place. The CA paradigm makes room for the faculty of the senses and the imagination, but, freed from Castoriadis' quasi-vitalist twist.

3 Douglas and Ney (1998, 58–73) offer a sympathetic critique of CA. They argue that it neglects cultural resources in how individuals pattern their choices. But is this the case? Sen and Nussbaum assess capability empowerment against the backdrop of cultural resources. What they accommodate is both a democratically achieved model of capabilities but, also, an internal to cultures mode of giving voice to capability deprivations, imposed on segments of a society's population by cultural barriers. For this argument against cultural relativism, see Sen (2002, 476–477) and Nussbaum (2000a, 48–49).

4 This is a virtually intractable problem in CA if the latter is seen as a system of moral communication based on the concept of capability (and its opposite which denotes a lack of capability). This distinction does not seem sufficient without essentialist further qualifications. If this is the case, then within the foundational category of CA too, there seems to be a blind spot as soon as qualifications have to be accommodated. As a blind spot it can only be accepted because it is the condition (a CCL) of selection for observation (i.e. further distinctions among trivial and non-trivial capabilities). (This was Lask's problem of *hiatus irrationalis* that surfaced in Chapter 1.)

5 Alkire (2002, 78–84) draws 39 lists (!) of human development dimensions from different disciplines. Looking closely at the different classifications one cannot fail to notice two crucial things: first, that for many of the scholars discussed in her book the lists are axiological and concern values (see, for example, Davitt's value areas, Grisez, Finnis and Boyle's basic human values, Goulet's values which are sought by all, Griffin's prudential values, Lasswell's human values, Max-Neef's axiological categories, Qizilbach's prudential values for development, Rokeach's terminal values, Schwartz's and Diener's value-based quality of life index (all authors and lists discussed and presented in Alkire 2002, 25–84)). Automatically, the explicit invocation of values in the context of listings (lexical or not) tells us that, at the very minimum, claims and expectations of delineation of human values and hierarchies are far from being obsolete. In this sense, Scheler's vision is immediately rendered apposite, given the fact that the values of sensibility, utilitarian values, vital values, spiritual values, values of the holy, capture to a remarkable extend the items listed. One could observe, of course, a tendency of greater overlap with most of Scheler's values, except the values of the holy. This should not be surprising given our predominantly secular age, although Scheler's vision relaxes the latter in the cosmopolitan ethics he advocated. Second, looked at through the lens of Parsons' AGIL, the concentration across all four functional modalities in terms of the physiological system, the personality system, the social system and the cultural system is truly remarkable. Added to those lists with explicit value-dimensions, others, which

include Maslow, Fromm, Nussbaum, Rawls and Sen among others spread similarly across the AGIL components. When I mention correspondences I do not assume 'perfect' pairings. Instead, what I claim is that substantively, all these different listing corroborate two different a priori and axiomatic orderings of values and functional prerequisites in sociology, both of which are unjustly neglected. Thus, the basic building blocks in Scheler and Parsons' architectonics prove resilient and explanatorily fecund and thus justify the operationalizations and reconstructions of them that inform CA and other normative projects of development. In this sense they are transcendentally binding, as the array of the items listed by Alkire indicates.

6 I am not sure how CA would respond to issues of validity of dualistic categories. It seems, however, that Archer's reenchantment of 'being-human' (2000) bypasses all too easily, the realist challenges that CA sets for sociology, although Archer seems to welcome a list of properties constitutive of human nature, especially as she sides (2000, 42) with Norman Geras' reconstruction of human nature based on Marx's species-being categories (see Chapter 4), the latter constituting a major source of inspiration at least in Nussbaum's CA. As such, these capabilities cut across the diverse 'normative circles' (Elder-Vass 2010, 115–143) that make up an individual's intersectional placement in societies. Although the agent's 'sophisticated practical consciousness' (something akin to 'practical reasoning' in the CCL) is posited as a prerequisite for contexts of 'complex normative intersectionality' (133) both the historical anchoring (i.e. modernity) that makes this possible and a further specification of how the agent's own powers are equipped, regardless of the particular intersection of normative circles to which they belong, remains undertheorized in terms of a human ontology, part of which is the normative quality of sociality (e.g. sympathy is a case in point).

7 Amid poststructuralist and posthumanist representations of the human as 'irrelevant' (ironically, from the perspective of bourgeois modernity, rather than from hunger-stricken parts of the developing world), CA returns to the urgent issue – as documented by Sen (1981) – of the satisfaction of this, most 'egotistical' need. While Sen is careful not to ignore the difficulties in metrics and social variations in determining the biological fact of malnutrition, he nonetheless does not find this fact's incompleteness alarming any more than all the other concepts related to issues of deprivation – rather incomplete themselves, like inequality or poverty – halt scientific scrutiny and policy intervention. (The dialectical phrase that something can indeed be 'salvaged' from the biological fact's looseness (Sen 1981, 13) is another index of the 'deontological' elements in CA.) In fact, this biological fact is transferred to the evaluative space of scrutiny that concerns social relations of production. For Sen, '[o]wnership of food is one of the most primitive property rights, and in each society there are rules governing this right' (45).

8 Nussbaum may be eager to dissociate her CCL from a metaphysical justification. Of course a lot depends on how metaphysics is defined and utilized. The ontological foundation of CCL assumes also a hardly unnoticeable philosophical anthropology. In an Aristotelian reformulation of the CCL the designations 'The Constitutive Circumstances of the Human Being (or: the Shape of the Human Form of Life)' includes features like: mortality, the human body, capacity for pleasure and pain, cognitive capacities, early infant development, practical reason, affiliation with other human beings, relatedness to other species and to nature, humour and play, separateness, strong separateness (Nussbaum 1990, 219–226). All build an anthropological architectonic of what it means to be a human being capable to aspire to a good life (Nussbaum 1992). Sen, for his part, accepts the idea of an approach to rights seen as 'intrinsic' to the human being but couples it to an indispensable consequentialism (see, for example, his discussion on reproductive rights and coercion in Sen 1999, 211–213).

9 In a letter to Kugelmann, Marx retains the content of the concept of value in the shape of 'natural law'. Marx writes: 'Natural laws cannot be abolished at all. The

only thing that can change, under historically differing conditions, is the form in which those laws assert themselves' (Marx (1868) 2010, 68). (Further discussion about the 'natural', 'social' and 'normative' status of any natural law foundation of the CA is deferred to Chapter 4.)

10 As Marcuse ((1932) 1987) has systematically shown, this dual ontology of Life and its implication with reality as the condition for history is patterned after Hegel's placement of 'Life' in the *Science of Logic*. It conceives Life as motility in freedom's realization in history. If one ponders on the often-abstruse formulations of Hegel and Marcuse's nuanced reading of it Life exists as the original ground that splits consciousness into subject and object. This bifurcation generates, as Hegel argues, philosophy but also through its negative positing of negativity (the 'other' that I am now set against and strive to transform it through my will) initiates the 'ought' as life's movement beyond itself, namely into intersubjective systems of attaching to life, affirming or negating principles. That even the utmost negativity cannot erase the 'dignity' of life is continuously asserted by Hegel who writes that 'the ugliest of men, or a criminal, or an invalid, or a cripple, is still always a man. The affirmative, life, subsists despite his defects, and it is this affirmative factor which is our theme here' (Hegel (1821) 1967, §258A). For this radical notion of life, see (Gangas 2019).

11 Nussbaum's CCL derives in some respects from the reformulation of natural law by John Finnis. He also developed a list of the basic forms of human good: (i) Life, (ii) Knowledge, (iii) Play, (iv) Aesthetic experience, (v) Sociability, (vi) Practical reasonableness, (vii) 'Religion' (Finnis 1980, 81–99). Finnis, like Nussbaum, understands these values as fundamental and irreducible. Finnis, unlike Scheler, for example, denies some sort of objective a priori hierarchy of these values. So even the value of life can be suspended in the case of altruistic action or war. This concession carries, I am afraid, a significant dose of formalism. This is evident in the cases of altruistic action: a person's life is sacrificed to rescue another life! If understood solely individually then life may appear as part of the compromise one can indeed concede. Yet, if Life is read ontologically and according to its diversification along the several shapes of human togetherness (group life, community, nation, humanity) then its individual surrender is not tantamount to a total negation. What is important I guess here is a sociological input to natural law about the flexibility of prioritizations in the scale of human sociality. This would preclude an aggressive war from claiming authenticity in terms of serving Life – as it would tend to subjugate the lives of millions to a higher religious, geopolitical, cultural or communitarian ideal – but not a defensive war the content of which is the life of humanity as a global moral ideal served and sustained by the democratic nations.

12 Other critiques of human rights, such as the 'institutionalization critique' advanced by Onora O'Neill require a correspondence between rights and precise duties, making thus institutionalization processes a condition for human rights. Similarly, the 'feasibility critique' takes to task the unlikely possibility for any full realization of human rights for all. I have covered Sen's epistemological approach in the previous chapters. His response (Sen 2009, 381–385) mobilized first the linkage of rights to both perfect and imperfect obligations. Second, he argues that human rights improvements on what we in sociology understand as social integration should be seen as a replenishing force that can improve the institutional arrangements, which, rightly argued by O'Neill, must have the primary role in the promotion and realization of human rights. Regarding feasibility the response is really less demanding for Sen. The lack of guarantees of full accomplishment of human rights can hardly be defended as a sound and persuasive reason for aborting this or other normative programmes. (Similar objections concern various proposals for the alleged non-feasibility of communist or socialist modification of the economy. We have seen some in the previous chapter; others reemerge in Chapter 6.)

13 Alan Gewirth accounts for the shift from 'capacities' to 'capabilities'. The idea of 'capability' conveys constitutive values of humanness and is thus better suited to be retranslated to actual functionings in society (1998, 63n.5). Thus, I follow Gewirth in rejecting a terminological conflation between 'capacity' and 'capability'. We have seen that CA draws cautiously and eclectically from pragmatism. Dewey's criticism of the term capacity as abstract possibility is pertinent here because Dewey challenges the adequacy of the category of capacity when severed from activity. He writes: 'If capacity is itself definite activity and not simply possibility of activity, the question arises why we conceive of it as capability, not as complete in itself' (1893, 656). Dewey's objection has to do with the fact that capacities give up the problem of mediation and risk adumbrating a concept of idealized human essence. For his part, Ricoeur considers this problem when he adduces CA in terms of a theory of recognition. Sen, according to Ricoeur, provides the 'anthropological base from which stems the pivotal idea from the power to act' (Ricoeur 2005, 148). The teleological presuppositions of CA in line with Ricoeur and the 'politics of living together' based on a view of human beings as ends are rightly stressed by Déneulin and McGregor (2010). In the domain of policy and peace process, see, indicatively, Hodgett (2008).

14 This dimension of the self's sociality and sense of responsibility is contrasted by Giri (2000, 1008), for example, to Sen's more individualized notions of the self. Giri (1015) is right, I think, to draw our attention to an ontological ground of justification something that is occluded in pragmatist or rational-choice accounts of agency. Yet the links to Parsons that I suggest provide opportunities for such ontological enrichment but, unlike Giri's suggestions, these should draw on the social ethics heritage of sociology rather than on those traditions that reject it.

15 Ballet, Dubois and Mahieu (2007, 192), for example, find wanting an extension of CA to the institutional level, drawing mainly on the ethical grounds of responsibility. Ferreras (2012) on her part proposes a problem shift from individual capabilities to how these are coordinated in groups. She thus suggests and empirically demonstrates for service workers in Belgium the salience of this shift from individual to group capabilities.

16 This connection to human aspiration has been noted by Appadurai (2004). Claiming to carry influences by Sen's CA, Appadurai makes the logically preceding step with respect to the category of 'capability' and considers anew the category of 'capacity'. In Appadurai's modification, capacity is theorized at a meta-normative level. Appadurai thus builds on the cultural 'capacity to aspire'. Roughly speaking, this capacity to aspire is culturally encoded and is presented by Appadurai as a culturally steering capacity that enables people to have a voice, to criticize, to participate in decision-making process; in short, to recall Nussbaum, to be able to form a practical conception of the good. Appadurai focuses on the poor in order to justify the validity of the capacity to aspire so that the poor and the excluded form a credible balance between patience and emergency as they are those whose lives are jeopardized by emergency projects of globalization. In calling the capacity to aspire a 'meta-capacity', Appadurai claims to provide a missing supplement in Sen's idea of capabilities. He writes:

> The capacity to aspire provides an ethical horizon within which more concrete capabilities can be given meaning, substance, and sustainability. Conversely, the exercise and nurture of these capabilities verifies and authorizes the capacity to aspire and moves it away from wishful thinking to thoughtful wishing. Freedom, the anchoring good in Sen's approach to capabilities and development, has no lasting meaning apart from a collective, dense, and supple horizon of hopes and wants. Absent such a horizon, freedom descends to choice, rational or otherwise, informed or not.
>
> (Appadurai 2004, 82)

One can justify Appadurai's transference of 'hope' to a realistic setting provided by culture so that deliberative mechanisms become culturally activated and thus enhance consensus among the poor. A reservation one may voice against Appadurai's corrective is that although the idea of the capacity to aspire highlights, as a 'meta-capacity' the need to sensitize the shared cultural sensors on which the poor necessarily depend so that development projects and policies based on CA assume a firm and pragmatic anchoring, the cultural validities that will funnel the capacity for aspiration and voice are not sufficiently articulated in terms of a normative content. While it is urgently important to utilize a given culture as a short-circuit 'currency' that can bring the poor into effective dialogue with those who are better off (and thus bind the latter as they are also culturally bound to the shared ways that the poor may activate) and thus make them able to 'circulate' their claims, the opposite move of cultural broadening by reference to broader alliances begs the question of how a culture will be tweaked so that its capacities for voice are strengthened. Important in this direction is the connection of the 'capacity to aspire' with the 'informational broadening' advocated by Sen and the implications for 'the human right to research' (Borghi 2018, 915). Generally, some sort of 'abstract' values like the ones that Nussbaum discussed must also act as counterforce to what can be culturally inert. Yet, Appadurai makes an important step in reminding to Marxian projects of emancipation that values, norms and traditions can no longer be conspicuously ignored as co-forces of alleviating poverty. The Parsonsian legacy in modernization theory as for example in the World Values Survey has not gone unnoticed by CA theorists. One of the major CA scholars, Sabine Alkire (2008, 267–269) provides relevant data that demonstrate conversions of cultural values with common denominator well-being in terms (e.g. 'mass liberty aspirations') modulated like CA.

17 Burawoy devotes a footnote to CA (2005, 23n.9) in order to welcome the relaxation of ideological rigidity in economics; he rightly perceives this polyphonic shift as a potential bridge with sociology. As I lack the space to compare CA to Burawoy's 11 theses on public sociology I shall limit myself to the following remark which concerns agency, which can be compromised by the risk of 'faddishness' (Thesis VI, 15–17). 'Faddishness' is not only a vice that Burawoy's critical social science needs to protect itself from. (For an accommodation of faddishness as fashion, this time to genuinely ethical democratic goals, see Lipovetsky 1994). In fact, Sen's examples about the capability to assume a decent attire in public (drawn from Adam Smith) and Nussbaum's case in point of Vasanti whose enhancement of capabilities included also the capability to enjoy 'dressing well', reveal that faddishness can serve ethical goals. Of course, the examples offered deal with appearance and fashion as adjuncts to a decent life and not to some sort of 'trendy' capability fad. As Nussbaum writes about Vasanti: 'Her sari is a lovely color of bright blue; like most poor women in India, she does not allow poverty to restrict her aesthetic imagination' (2011, 10). Lipovetsky, for his part, provides a role to fashion similar to Hegel's 'cunning of reason'. He argues that fashion is not intrinsically likened to a social collapse of values:

> '"All I did", declared Bob Geldof, organizer of Band Aid, "was make famine fashionable" – in other words, he broadcast a painless, optional, emotional and circumstantial ethics, an ethics adapted to the new individualist culture and stripped of regular, maximalist, sacrificial commandments.
>
> (Lipovetsky 1994, 249)

Similarly, CA should not shy away, if and when it becomes 'trendy', from the risk that its goals may suffer colonization by the 'system' logic (e.g. fashion-driven superficial lifestyles) if this 'pollution' is the cost it must bear in order to gain purchase in the 'life-world'. In fact, Sen has Bob Geldof in mind as an exemplar of sensitizing public opinion about poverty in Africa and the need for a humane treatment of poor nations' past debt (Sen 2006, 195, n.5).

References

Alexander, Jeffrey. 2004. 'Cultural Pragmatics: Social Performance Between Ritual and Strategy.' *Sociological Theory* 22 (4): 527–573.

Alkire, Sabina. 2002. *Valuing Freedoms: Sen's Capability Approach and Poverty Reduction.* Oxford: Oxford University Press.

Alkire, Sabina. 2008. 'Subjective Measures of Agency'. In *Capabilities and Happiness* edited by Luigino Bruni, Flavio Comim, and Maurizio Pugno, 254–285. Oxford: Oxford University Press.

Appadurai, Arjun. 2004. 'The Capacity to Aspire: Culture and the Terms of Recognition.' In *Culture and Public Action*, edited by Vijayendra Rao and Michael Walton, 59–84. Stanford: Stanford University Press.

Archer, Margaret. 2000. *Being Human: The Problem of Agency.* Cambridge: Cambridge University Press.

Ballet, Jérôme, Jean-Luc Dubois, and François-Régis Mahieu. 2007. 'Responsibility for Each Other's Freedom: Agency as the Source of Collective Capabilities.' *Journal of Human Development* 8 (2): 185–201.

Barnes, Barry. 2000. *Understanding Agency: Social Theory and Responsible Action.* London: Sage.

Bell, Daniel. (1976) 1996a. *The Cultural Contradictions of Capitalism.* New York: Basic Books.

Bell, Daniel. 1996b. 'Afterword: 1996'. In *The Cultural Contradictions of Capitalism.* 283–339. New York: Basic Books.

Bell, Daniel. 1996c. 'The Re-birth of Utopia: The Path to Natural Law.' *Daniel Bell Personal Archive.* Collection no. 18559, Box 53, Folder 12 (courtesy of Harvard University Archives Harvard University Archives).

Bloch, Ernst. (1961) 1987. *Natural Law and Human Dignity.* Cambridge, MA: The MIT Press.

Borghi, Vando. 2018. 'From Knowledge to Informational Basis: Capability, Capacity to Aspire and Research.' *Critical Sociology* 44 (6): 899–920.

Browne, Jude, Simon Deakin, and Frank Wilkinson. 2004. 'Capabilities, Social Rights and European Market Integration.' In *Europe and the Politics of Capabilities*, edited by Robert Salais and Robert Villeneuve, 205–221. Cambridge: Cambridge University Press.

Burawoy, Michael. 2005. 'For Public Sociology.' *American Sociological Review* 70 (1): 4–28.

Castoriadis, Cornelius. 1987. *The Imaginary Institution of Society.* Cambridge: Polity.

Chernilo, Daniel. 2013. *The Natural Law Foundations of Modern Social Theory: A Quest for Universalism.* Cambridge: Cambridge University Press.

Chernilo, Daniel. 2017. *Debating Humanity: Towards a Philosophical Sociology.* Cambridge: Cambridge University Press.

Crocker, David. 2008. *Ethics of Global Development.* Cambridge: Cambridge University Press.

Crocker, David, and Ingreyd Robeyns. 2010. 'Capability and Agency.' In *Amartya Sen*, edited by Christopher Morris, 66–90. Cambridge: Cambridge University Press.

Dahrendorf, Ralf. 1979. *Life Chances: Approaches to Social and Political Theory.* The Chicago: University of Chicago Press.

De Munck, Jean (2018) 'Human Rights and Capabilities: A Program for a Critical Sociology of Law.' *Critical Sociology* 44 (6): 921–935.

Déneulin, Séverine, and Allister McGregor. 2010. 'The Capability Approach and the Politics of a Social Conception of Wellbeing.' *European Journal of Social Theory* 13 (4) 501–519.

Dewey, John. 1893. 'Self-Realization as the Moral Ideal.' *The Philosophical Review* 2 (6): 652–664.

Douglas, Mary, and Steven Ney. 1998. *Missing Persons: A Critique of Social Sciences.* Berkeley: University of California Press.

Drèze, Jean, and Amartya Sen. 1989. *Hunger and Public Action.* Oxford: Clarendon Press.

Elder-Vass, Dave. 2010. *The Causal Power of Social Structures: Emergence, Structure and Agency.* Cambridge: Cambridge University Press.

Emirbayer, Mustafa, and Ann Mische. 1998. 'What is Agency?' *American Journal of Sociology* 103 (4): 962–1023.

Etzioni, Amitai. 1968. *The Active Society: A Theory of Societal and Political Processes.* New York: The Free Press.

Ferreras, Isabelle. 2012. 'The Collective Aspects of Individual Freedom: A Case Study in the Service Sector.' In *Democracy and Capabilities for Voice: Welfare, Work and Public Deliberation in Europe* edited by Ota De Leonardis, Serafino Negrelli, and Robert Salais, 101–116. Brussels: P.I.E. Peter Lang.

Finnis, John. 1980. *Natural Law and Natural Rights.* Oxford: Oxford University Press.

Flax, Jane. 2000a. 'On Encountering Incommensurability: Martha Nussbaum's Aristotelian Practice.' In *Controversies in Feminism*, edited by James Sterba, 25–46. Lanham: Rowman and Littlefield.

Flax, Jane. 2000b. 'A Constructionist Despite Herself? On Capacities and Their Discontents.' In *Controversies in Feminism*, edited by James Sterba, 47–57. Lanham: Rowman and Littlefield.

Gangas, Spiros. 2019. 'Simmel, Marx and the Radical Concept of Life: A Hegelian. Approach'. *Dissonância: Critical Theory Journal.* Advance Online Publication. www.ifch.unicamp.br/ojs/index.php/teoriacritica/article/view/3452/2635.

Gewirth, Alan. 1998. *Self-Fulfillment.* Princeton: Princeton University Press.

Giddens, Anthony. 1979. *Central Problems in Social Theory: Action, structure and Contradiction in Social Analysis.* Berkeley: University of California Press.

Giddens, Anthony. 1984. *The Constitution of Society: Outline of the Theory of Structuration.* Cambridge: Polity Press.

Giddens, Anthony. 1991. *Modernity and Self-Identity: Self and Society in Late Modern Age.* Stanford: Stanford University Press.

Giddens, Anthony. 1994. *Beyond Left and Right: The Future of Radical Politics.* Cambridge: Polity Press.

Giri, Ananta. 2000. 'Rethinking Human Well-Being: A Dialogue with Amartya Sen.' *Journal of International Development* 12 (7): 1003–1018.

Gould, Carol. 1988. *Rethinking Democracy: Freedom and Social Cooperation in Politics, Economy, and Society.* Cambridge: Cambridge University Press.

Habermas, Jürgen. 2010. 'The Concept of Human Dignity and the Realistic Utopia of Human Rights.' *Metaphilosophy* 41 (4): 464–480.

Hegel, Georg W.F. (1821) 1967. *Hegel's Philosophy of Right.* London: Oxford University Press.

Henry, Michel. (1973) 1986. *Marx: A Philosopher of Human Reality.* Bloomington: Indiana University Press.

Hobson, Barbara. 2013. 'Introduction: Capabilities and Agency for Worklife Balance – A Multidimensional Framework.' In *Worklife Balance: The Agency and Gap, Capabilities*, edited by Barbara Hobson, 1–31. Oxford: Oxford University Press.

Hodgett, Susan. 2008. 'Sen, Culture and Expanding Participatory Capabilities in Northern Ireland.' *Journal of Human Development* 9 (2): 165–183.

Holmwood, John. 2013. 'Public Reasoning without Sociology: Amartya Sen's Theory of Justice.' *Sociology* 47 (6): 1171–1186.

Holmwood, John, and Alexander Stewart. 1991. *Explanation and Social Theory*. Basingstoke: Macmillan.

Honneth, Axel, and Hans Joas. 1988. *Social Action and Human Nature*. Cambridge: Cambridge University Press.

Hvinden, Bjorn, and Rune Halvorsen. 2018. 'Mediating Agency and Structure in Sociology: What Role for Conversion Factors?' *Critical Sociology* 44 (6): 865–881.

Joas, Hans. 1996. *The Creativity of Action*. Chicago: The University of Chicago Press.

Joas, Hans. 2013. *The Sacredness of the Person: A New Genealogy of Human Rights*. Washington: Georgetown University Press.

Kuklys, Wiebke. 2005. *Amartya Sen's Capability Approach: Theoretical Insights and Empirical Applications*. Berlin: Springer.

Landmann, Michael. 1974. *Philosophical Anthropology*. Philadelphia: The Westminster Press.

Lawson, Tony. 1999. 'Feminism, Realism, and Universalism'. *Feminist Economics* 5 (2): 25–59.

Lipovetsky, Gilles. 1994. *The Empire of Fashion: Dressing Modern Democracy*. Princeton: Princeton University Press.

Lukes, Steven. 2005. *Power: A Radical View*. London: Palgrave Macmillan.

Marcuse, Herbert. (1932) 1987. *Hegel's Ontology and the Theory of Historicity*. Cambridge, MA: The MIT Press.

Marx, Karl. (1861–1863) 1998. 'Economic Manuscript of 1861–63: A Contribution to the Critique of Political Economy.' In *Karl Marx and Friedrich Engels Collected Works, Volume 30*. London: Lawrence and Wishart.

Marx, Karl. (1868) 2010. 'Marx to Ludwig Kugelmann. London 11 July 1868.' In *Karl Marx and Friedrich Engels Collected Works, Volume 43. Letters 1868–1870*. London: Lawrence and Wishart Electric Book.

Nussbaum, Martha. 1990. 'Aristotelian Social Democracy.' In *Liberalism and the Good*, edited by Bruce Douglass, Gerald Mara, and Henry Richardson, 203–252. New York: Routledge.

Nussbaum, Martha. 1992. 'Human Functioning and Social Justice. In Defense of Aristotelian Essentialism.' *Political Theory* 20 (2): 202–246.

Nussbaum, Martha. 1999. *Sex and Social Justice*. New York: Oxford University Press.

Nussbaum, Martha. 2000a. *Women and Human Development: The Capabilities Approach*. Cambridge: Cambridge University Press.

Nussbaum, Martha. 2000b. 'Essence of Culture and a Sense of History.' In *Controversies in Feminism*, edited by James Sterba, 59–64. Lanham: Rowman and Littlefield.

Nussbaum, Martha. 2001. 'Comment on "Feminist Theory, Justice, and the Lure of the Human".' *Signs* 27 (1): 123–135.

Nussbaum, Martha. 2004. *Hiding from Humanity: Disgust, Shame, and the Law*. Princeton: Princeton University Press.

Nussbaum Martha. 2005. 'Women's Bodies: Violence, Security, Capabilities.' *Journal of Human Development* 6 (2): 167–183.

Nussbaum, Martha. 2006. *Frontiers of Justice: Disability, Nationality, Species Membership*. Cambridge, MA: The Belknap Press of Harvard University Press.

Nussbaum, Martha. 2011. *Creating Capabilities*. Cambridge, MA: The Belknap Press of Harvard University Press.

Nussbaum, Martha. 2013. *Political Emotions: Why Love Matters for Justice*. Cambridge: MA: The Belknap Press of Harvard University Press.

Nussbaum, Martha, and Jonathan Glover, eds. 1995. *Women, Culture, and Development: A Study of Human Capabilities*. Oxford: Clarendon Press.

Nussbaum, Martha, and Saul Levmore. 2017. *Aging Thoughtfully: Conversations About Retirement, Romance, Wrinkles, and Regret*. Oxford: Oxford University Press.

Parsons, Talcott. 1951. *The Social System*. New York: The Free Press.

Parsons, Talcott. 1969. *Politics and Social Structure*. New York: The Free Press.

Parsons, Talcott. 1977. *Social Systems and the Evolution of Action Theory*. New York: The Free Press.

Parsons, Talcott. 1978. *Action Theory and the Human Condition*. New York: The Free Press.

Parsons, Talcott. 1991. A Tentative Outline of American Values. In *Talcott Parsons: Theorist of Modernity*, edited by Roland Robertson and Bryan Turner, 37–65. London: Sage.

Parsons, Talcott. (1939–1940) 2010. *Actor, Situation and Normative Pattern*. Wien: LIT.

Parsons, Talcott, and Gerald Platt. 1973. *The American University*. Cambridge, MA: Harvard University Press.

Parsons, Talcott, and Neil Smelser. 1956. *Economy and Society: A Study in the Integration of Economic and Social Theory*. London: Routledge and Kegan Paul.

Quillen, Carol. 2001. 'Feminist Theory, Justice, and the Lure of the Human.' *Signs* 27 (1): 87–122.

Ricoeur, Paul. 2005. *The Course of Recognition*. Cambridge, MA: Harvard University Press.

Robeyns, Ingrid. 2003. 'Sen's Capability Approach and Gender Inequality: Selecting Relevant Capabilities.' *Feminist Economics* 9 (2–3): 61–92.

Robeyns, Ingrid. 2005. 'The Capability Approach: A Theoretical Survey.' *Journal of Human Development* 6 (1): 93–114.

Sen, Amartya. 1981. *Poverty and Famines: An Essay on Entitlement and Deprivation*. Oxford: Clarendon Press.

Sen, Amartya. 1985 'Well-Being, Agency and Freedom: The Dewey lectures 1984.' *The Journal of Philosophy* 82 (4): 169–221.

Sen, Amartya. 1990. 'Individual Freedom as a Social Commitment.' *New York Review of Books* 37: 49–54.

Sen, Amartya. 1993. 'Capability and Well-Being.' In *The Quality of Life*, edited by Martha Nussbaum and Amartya Sen. 30–53. Oxford: Clarendon Press.

Sen, Amartya. 1999. *Development as Freedom*. Oxford: Oxford University Press.

Sen, Amartya. 2002. *Rationality and Freedom*. Cambridge, MA: The Belknap Press of Harvard University Press.

Sen, Amartya. 2004. 'Elements of a Theory of Human Rights.' *Philosophy and Public Affairs* 32 (4): 315–356.

Sen, Amartya. 2005. 'Human rights and Capabilities.' *Journal of Human Development* 6 (2): 151–166.

Sen, Amartya. 2006. *Identity and Violence: The Illusion of Destiny*. London: Penguin.

Sen, Amartya. 2009. *The Idea of Justice*. Cambridge, MA: The Belknap Press of Harvard University Press.

Sennett, Richard. 2012. *Together: The Rituals, Pleasures and Politics of Cooperation.* New Haven: Yale University Press.

Soper, Kate. 2001. 'Naked Human Nature and the Draperies of Custom.' In *Feminism: Critical Concepts in Literary and Cultural Studies. Volume I*, edited by Mary Evans, 253–267. London: Routledge.

Touraine, Alain. 1988. *Return of the Actor: Social Theory in Postindustrial Society*. Minneapolis: University of Minnesota Press.

Touraine, Alain. 2000. *Can We Live Together? Equality and Difference*. Stanford: Stanford University Press.

Zimmermann, Bénédicte. 2006. 'Pragmatism and the Capability Approach: Challenges in Social Theory and Empirical Research. *European Journal of Social Theory* 9 (4): 467–484.

4 From alienation to capability deprivation

Reconstructing a sociological concept

Why alienation? Some conceptual limitations

Among sociology's normative narratives, alienation figures as one of the most captivating, influential and contested. Anchored in Hegel and Marx, the idea of alienation generated valuable theoretical and empirical tools for explanation as well as offering a normative critique of modernity. Drawing on various motifs of Hegel's thought, Marx offered a fresh and ideologically groundbreaking formulation of alienation, especially in the manuscripts of 1844. He depicted the processes of alienated labour that deprive workers from essential attributes of the human species; by recourse to these damaged features of human sociality he sought to envision society's emancipation from the commodity form of labour. Since then the political use of the concept of alienation within social theory, especially in the light of Marxian or Hegelian paradigms (e.g. Lukács (1966) 1975; Taylor 1979), yielded a theory of social crisis which stressed diremption and conflict within capitalist modernity. The repercussions of this conflict on human beings and on social relations became the focal point of alienation scholarship (indicatively only, see Geyer 1996; Geyer and Schweitzer 1981; Honneth 2008; Israel 1979; Jaeggi 2014; Schacht 1970; Seeman 1959). However, the Marxian paradigm saw its explanatory potential severely compromised as advocates of the idea of alienation expanded its diagnostic scope in a way that was often contrary to what constituted the ethical hard core of Hegel's and Marx's respective projects. The orthodox critique of alienated labour in capitalism gave way to theories of an instrumentally reified and one-dimensional modernity, which sought to renovate the alienation problematic from the perspective of Weber's disenchantment thesis, reinforcing the perception of capitalism's instrumental grip over labour. As a result, in an effort to preserve the idea of 'crisis' in capitalism few options were reserved by these approaches for a non-revolutionary, yet radical amelioration of society. It is not, of course, that these arguments are no longer relevant. Rather, the problem in many alienation narratives of Marxian origins (i.e. Mészáros 1986; Ollman 2001; Schaff, 1980) comes from magnifying the crises tied to capitalism and from subsuming under capital's spectral powers all facets of human action and sociality. As a result of proliferating a sharp and adversarial 'system versus anti-system' category-building but without identifying intermediate levels of normativity between these extremes, Marxian alienation theories reinforced the idea of capitalism's discontents and became even further removed from the explanatory and policy-building functions in line with what the dialectical concept of alienation demanded.

To be sure, Marxian sociology has opened up several emancipation sites pertinent to the worker's experience of everyday life. It thus showed great intuition for those central components of human activity marred by serious deprivations in the domain of the commodity form of labour. A typical case is Henri Lefebvre. He argues that the alienated condition is experienced as 'deprivation' at different degrees of abstraction and intensity by both the bourgeois and the worker ((1947) 1991, 143). The impact for a theory of alienation is, according to Lefebvre, evident in its everyday-life dialectical particularization. The upshot here is that, following Lefebvre, alienation's corrective should be conceptualized as a 'particular' response to real and concrete instances of alienated relations and experiences. Such 'alienation/disalienation' dialectical movement enables Lefebvre to dissociate alienation from the matrix of capitalism's systemically perpetuated alienation(s) and to track its impact on concrete life. The trouble, however, with this approach is that it is still attached to explanatory abstraction because it keeps theorizing the content of alienation in a multitude of contexts which, in their causal and contextual diversity, seem to resist being explained by the very concept of alienation to which they are held to belong, namely the alienation of capitalist society. As a result, Lefebvre ends up in the acceptance of alienation's 'infinite complexity' ((1961) 2002, 209).

I do not wish to deny the richness of the concept of alienation. In sociological theory, and beyond Marx's use, 'alienation' has been addressed by the normative functionalism of Merton and Parsons, or even by the interactionist approach to performance advanced by Goffman. Even more, the breadth of this formidable concept in the areas of psychoanalysis, existential philosophy, philosophical anthropology, reactionary social theory and Critical Theory, reflects a trustworthy reflex among intellectuals regarding modernity's problems, which extends its reach even to the human condition (Arendt, Heidegger). All such paradigms, however, address alienation under different and often mutually exclusive banners, fragmenting and alienating the very discourse of alienation. Indicative here, is the perplexing remark by a major scholar of alienation, that '*there is no such thing as alienation.* Neither is there any such thing as S-alienation, or O-alienation. But there *are* myriad alienations-alienations that have existed, that do exist, and (no doubt) that will come into existence [...]' (Schacht 1994, 34 [original emphasis]).[1] This explanatory opaqueness is reinforced by Schacht's claim that 'there is nothing wrong with the practice of using the term 'alienation' in the characterization of the various phenomena in question, both experiential and social-relational – even if there is no compelling reason to retain and expand it either' (34). I find such conceptual diversification unsatisfactory. I tend, therefore, to follow Lukes (1967) in his claim that when alienation can mean anything from bureaucratic disenchantment, to a psychological condition of isolation, or to societal malintegration, 'then the time has come either to abandon the concepts or return to their origins for guidance' (1967, 76). My approach seeks precisely to combine these two options offered by Lukes. I return to the concept's Marxian origins in order to reconstruct it with reference to a new strand of social theory. What, therefore, I aim to achieve in this chapter is to cast doubt in the future of the concept of alienation, at least in the shape of an all-encompassing calculus of social pathology.

Unlike other obituaries on alienation (see, for example, McClung Lee (1972, 125) who proposes 'relative deprivation' as an alternative route to capture alienation impact), this chapter advances the argument that this concept's implicit normative goals can be served better by other theoretical and empirical means. To be fair, therefore, to Schacht, we need to note that he does point to a route of reconstruction similar to the one I am proposing when he contends that the future of alienation lies in value-theory and the 'quality of life' theory (Schacht 1994, 141). He also writes that, 'the notion of *self-realization* may be recast in terms of some configuration of realized human possibilities constituting a form of selfhood proposed as especially worth attaining, owing to the character and quality of human life associated with it' (150 [original emphasis]). This better conceptual tool, I suggest, is already available in CA.[2] As I argue, CA attaches deprivation to a more open character of capability, and of what can count as capability deprivation; it thus provides a wider policy scope obscured by alienation's emphasis on negation and its attachment to radical politics. It illuminates further a variety of sites that can serve as the battleground against inequality, violence, deprivation and social exclusion without recourse to transcendental proofs or to revolutionary agency, but still positing a firm moral core from which these deprivations can be justly and effectively confronted.

To counter these shortcomings of a radical view of alienation, I will advance the claim that Sen's idea of capability deprivation can renew alienation approaches because it serves better the goal of 'de-alienation'. To be sure, Sen grounds his project primarily on economics and hence many of his categories remain sociologically underdetermined (social capital is a case in point[3]). While this limitation cannot be taken further in this chapter, it is worth looking, however, at alienation through the lens of capability deprivation in order to resurrect a declining narrative of sociology and thus to renew its relevance for social problems.

Why CA? Elements of a new research programme for alienation

Instead of drawing on the semantics of many alienation theories, CA sets the parameters for salient achievements and values that are central to human life. Marxists pursue a similar trail when they amplify the notion of radical needs (as, for instance, in the work of Agnes Heller).[4] Still, this terminological amplification does not allow for explanatory clarity and keeps Marxism tethered to the core argument of capitalism's intrinsic pathologies. Capabilities renew – but by no means discard – the Marxian emphasis on 'needs'. The latter's passive connotations give way to the enabling dimensions contained in the term 'capability' (Sen 1984, 513–515), although 'needs' are retained within CA as an auxiliary rather than as a central concept. Similar is the clarification offered by moral philosopher Alan Gewirth on the 'capacity' – 'capability' ambiguity. For Gewirth, 'alienation presents a serious challenge to capacity-fulfillment' (1998, 119). While capacity captures potentiality in a rather indeterminate fashion, capability, as Gewirth admits, is tied to constitutive values and is better retranslated to actual functionings in society (63, n.5). For Lukes too, the key Marxian question about the social preconditions needed for the well-being of human lives, is taken up by the 'most promising attempt to work out such an account', namely 'the so-called 'capabilities approach'' (2005, 117). Flowing, therefore, from the Aristotelian legacy in Hegel and Marx, capability retains the dimension of potentiality and its philosophical justifications; however, it adds to it the social mode that activates it in reality, by rendering it subject to social benchmarks and metrics on health, disability, education and gender, among others (see Brighouse and Robeyns 2010, 129–235). In this sense, capability is still in tune with the Marxian project of praxis, although it does not delimit the latter in the domain of marginal resistance to an alienated system. Instead of positing a systemic benchmark (i.e. non-capitalist society) as a condition for theorizing and measuring justice, injustices, exclusions as well as other deprivations are interpreted by CA via normatively committed and empirically richer sets of capability deprivations.

To be sure, capability deprivation seems to occupy a secondary theoretical role in Sen's normative programme as he is more concerned to identify and combat deprivations that plague individuals, groups, communities and countries without, however, being required to provide a general theory of deprivation (Sen 1983, 2009). He does, however, offer an explicit indication of it when he claims that this approach 'concentrates on deprivations that are *intrinsically* important' (Sen, 1999b, 87 [original emphasis]). I thus draw on Sen's argument about 'poverty as capability deprivation' (Sen 1999b, 87–110) but I take the liberty to expand its normative basis of capability deprivation beyond poverty. As I will show later, these intrinsically valuable capabilities can be collected across Sen's work, but, as we have already seen, it is Nussbaum's CCL (see, for example, 1998, 324–336) that roughly corresponds to Aristotelian and Marxian reconstructions of the socially rich self.[5] Capability empowerment carries forward the concrete shape of unalienation for each individual to the extent that each person is called upon to express her individuality in a society that offers ample opportunities for lifestyles people have reason to value. For instance, it may not be coincidental that Sen (1999b, 23–28, 170–175) uses the term 'alienation' when in *Development as Freedom* he discusses famines. It is not coincidental either that the discussion centres on mid-nineteenth century famines in Ireland. The focus is on the expropriation of Ireland by Great Britain and not so much some alleged shortage of food in Ireland. He not only invokes, among others, the Marxist scholar Terry Eagleton and momentarily Friedrich Engels, but comes to the conclusion that the 'market forces would always encourage movement of food to places where people could afford to pay a higher price for it' (172). This is of course not a source of anathema for markets tout court but rather a call to a serious consideration of political, economic and cultural factors that play a role in the cause and prevention of famines. The 'cultural alienation' in the shape of divisive hierarchies (more about this in Chapter 7) that denigrated the Irish is also an index of the non-exclusivity of economic factors alone. Push-factors that stem from culture or politics – as is the case with authoritarian regimes and the large-scale famines which afflicted their populations – act as catalysts for the market forces to suffocate (USSR, China) or operate on their own devices outside every other social consideration (Ireland) (see also Drèze and Sen 1989).

It is not uncommon for Marxian theorists of alienation, even for those of a dialectical and critical orientation, to see liberal institutions as ideological apparatuses, which perpetuate global market domination. Normative integration is thus deferred to the consciousness of the proletariat or to non-identity politics. Despite the appeal of such arguments, these hide from view intermediate institutional constituencies, which, instead of being seen as incidents of false-consciousness, allow, under CA, democratic deliberation, mutual criticism and corrigibility of standpoints to emerge as critical weapons against oppression, exclusion and false-consciousness. Thus, the vision of a better society is unhooked by the exponents of CA from categories that carry the estrangement/disenchantment fusion. As total categories the latter come to negate the very normative vision Marx wished them to serve. In Alfred Schmidt's words:

> Marx gave up using such terms as "estrangement", "alienation", "return of man to himself" as soon as he noticed that they had turned into ideological prattle in the mouths of petty-bourgeois authors, instead of a lever for the empirical study of the world and its transformation.
>
> (1971, 129)

If we disregard a bit Schmidt's intemperate tone, we can promisingly extract CA from the very heart of what Schmidt holds Marx's real ambition was: namely, to develop empirically fruitful concepts with a view to bring about a change in those social relations that foster alienation, rather than, as Sayer (1987) judiciously demonstrates, of advocating perfunctory abstractions for social change fashioned as moral polemics. Continuing to work within the programme of the critique of political economy, but dislodging it from the narrative of alienation, Marx in *Capital*, for instance, shows how important the content of alienation is in its empirical relevance. The sections on the Factory Acts (Marx, [1867] 1990, Ch.15) with the numerous inspectors' reports cited one after the other display graphically the impact of alienated labour on the mental and bodily capabilities of workers under capitalism. This episode in Marx's mature works may perhaps explain the shift to systematic political economy analysis in the absence of an equally well-shaped normative category that could have served as a substitute for alienation then. Ultimately, such a reading of Marx may share many of the principles of the theory and policy synergies forged by Sen, which renew radicalism, precisely because they account for problems and solutions in macro and micro levels, in both the developed and the developing world. It thus goes to show that the shift to political economy analysis forged by late Marx may converge with the tendency, often understated in CA, to incorporate larger frameworks of capability strengthening or deprivation into its conditions of growth. As Sen also notes (1984, 282n. 13), Marx's rejection of 'crude communism' was couched on the dialectical commitment of retaining the accomplishments of the civilizing tendency of capital. CA makes room for wider aspects of inequality, including class, gender, religion, ethnicity, without subsuming them under a single cause of deprivation (Sen 1992). In spite, however, of the differences on the degree and cause of alienation they attribute to capitalism, alienation theories and capability deprivation approaches share essential ethical claims and it is worth probing into points of convergence.[6]

Decompressing alienation: the essentialist (re)turn in CA

Whether intended or not, the premises in any theory of alienation must somewhere rely on moral essentialism. Alienation, as a defective form of species-being sociality, presupposes a conception of some socially unalienated condition, which sociology needs to conceptually recover and reconstruct. Essentialisms of this sort have been under fire and even sympathetic critics have had to revise drastically or even drop altogether the ambitious normativism with which every theory of alienation, explicitly or implicitly, has been imbued. To be sure, many of the critiques of essentialism aim to dispense with it completely, and seek instead to relocate its claims to some sort of normative theory with a contextual foundation in history. This type of approach, fashioned more by Sen and less by Nussbaum, champions openness in terms of the normative core of human dignity and claims to incorporate in explanation the challenges posed by an ever-expanding cultural diversity. The difficulties (or challenges) in explanation for a normative project toying with essentialism are not dissimilar for the advocates of a strictly pluralist and contextual approach to norms and values. For the particular context within which capabilities or some other normative ground become configured has to be treated too as a 'universal'; whether one starts from particular contexts and moves towards universal foundations or, inversely, from some 'universal' normative essence, like human dignity, and moves towards the particular manifestations of it, the trail seems to me to lead to the same problem, namely the elimination of human suffering and misery. In this sense, moral essentialism is far from being obsolete; rather, it can be realigned to contemporary normative theory via CA.

For this to become more obvious we need to recall our discussion of natural law in Chapter 3. There, we saw that elements of natural law are implicit and presupposed in modernity's attachment to values like human rights, human dignity, equality, justice and universal peace. Far from being bourgeois remnants, normative ideas couched in natural law played a significant role in Marx. For example, in the form of Marx's species-being potentiality Marxian scholars, like Heller (1972) and Márkus ((1966) 1988), have rescued philosophical anthropology from its conservative and even reactionary load, highlighting the importance of radical needs that underline the development of the social individual. Horkheimer, for his part, chided philosophical anthropology's abstract constitution of the human, yet he identified as 'anthropological' *par excellence* the problem of human freedom, stated in terms of capacities: 'how can we overcome an inhumane reality (since all human capacities that we love suffocate and decay within it)?' ((1935) 1995, 160).[7] And, of course, these Marxian analyses disentangle the key normative question for philosophical anthropology, namely 'what it means to be human?' from any search for constant, primordial and a-social human attributes (I shall return to this shortly in the excursus below).

Foundational and anthropological elements in Marx are mediated by social relations but it would be an error to assume that these are excised from Marx's social ontology altogether. For example, the work of Norman Geras promotes through careful textual analysis a reading that shows Marx's appreciation of natural capacities, close to a conception of a human nature, shared to some degree by the entire human species. Geras, correctly I think, argues that universal human capacities can be perfectly compatible with the social configuration they assume in history. Using language as an example Geras (1983, 48) offers a nuanced extrication of universal capacities from Marx's texts and sketches human needs (72–73) along the lines of 'capabilities of human species' (81–82). Conjoining the problem of the thwarting of human capabilities to the countless deprivations of millions on the planet, at least on the level of basic human needs, such as hunger and access to health (105), Geras concludes that if:

> new relations and practices are thought able to have the effect in question [socialist effect on social relations, S.G.], human beings must be assumed capable, if only in the "right" circumstances, of developing the necessary qualities. These must be capacities potentially available to members of the human species.
>
> (109)

Geras recaptures here the Hegelian solution to the 'is'–'ought' dichotomy. He entertains not only the availability of the capability to a different relationship of affectivity and social cooperation among humans but also the possibility that a jointly developed social form is feasible and, even by Marx's own empirical standards of describing and explaining capitalism, partially in place.[8]

Excursus on alienation without essentialism: a critique

It is generally accepted and easily discernible that one crucial – maybe the most crucial – divergence between Sen and Nussbaum concerns the necessity of a CCL, although Sen (1998, 303–305) admits that there is no objection on his part if such path is taken to complete CA. We have seen that his reservations do not challenge the possibility or moral worthiness of a CCL but simply its necessity. Further, this debate raises the additional question if recourse to essentialism is a prerequisite for the entire project of CA. To the extent that CA addresses – less explicitly but certainly implicitly – issues of alienation, the question of essentialism must be taken up again.

In Chapter 3 I suggested that the current non-foundational approaches to normative issues are characterized by a mismatch in that they presuppose a conception of a living individual who, as Bloch ((1961) 1987, 2) suggested, once 'alive must will' to continue living with others and thus to persevere in the ensuing clash of wills. This was the problem of order addressed by Hobbes and Hegel, for example, albeit in markedly different trails of resolution. How can alienation critique align itself with weapons that escape from the Critical Theory orthodoxy of instrumental rationality's and capitalism's grip over free agency? To be sure little has been accomplished on this front since several decades now. Within this climate on stagnant accounts of alienation, Rahel Jaeggi's recent work (2014) offers a refreshing and highly sophisticated reconstruction of alienation. While there is plenty to applaud in Jaeggi's shift of alienation critique away from essentialist presuppositions, the disengagement she proposes is far from ubiquitous. I shall thus take up facets of her argument that bear on the CCL and its consequences for unalienation.

Jaeggi is adamant on the inadequacy of alienation critique's return to a human essence from which normative judgments can be drawn. Nussbaum is cited sporadically as a representative, albeit sophisticated, of a renovated essentialist project of ethics (Jaeggi 2014, 29–30, 227). In order to make the concept alienation productive a paradigm shift seems to be required, one in which no 'appeal to metaphysically grounded (substantial) ethical values' (32) would be needed. Nor it would be needed an anchoring to 'the happy life' or 'the good life'. Rather, for Jaeggi:

> [unalienation] would refer to a certain way of *carrying out* one's own life and a certain way of *appropriating oneself* – that is, a way of *establishing relations* to oneself and to the relationships in which one lives (relationships that condition or shape who one is.
>
> (33 [original emphasis])

It is odd to notice initially that all the elements Jaeggi excises as 'banal' remnants in essentialism are encrypted here too. The critical question 'alienation from what?' is elided the more alienation, as Jaeggi admits, is presented as a 'disruption' or as a 'relation of relationlessness'. This happens because, quite plausibly, Jaeggi suggests that the major motifs of alienation do not convey absence of relations but only defective relations in society. Similarly, the 'essence' so often claimed to be recovered as authentic is being articulated in social terms and standpoints (of a person's inability to appropriate one's life).

I shall not discuss at great length the many merits of Jaeggi's original and fascinating reconstruction. I shall only limit myself to a few remarks that I find pertinent to the thesis I advance here. Defined as a 'relation of relationlessness', alienation for Jaeggi hopes to abandon strong essentialist justifications or ones that envisage some perfect match between the self and social institutions. Alienation's 'potential would then lie not in the possibility of providing a robustly substantial ethical theory but in being able to criticize the contents of forms of life precisely without needing to appeal to ultimate, metaphysically grounded (substantial) ethical values' (33). On the one hand, like previous approaches to reconstructing alienation, the proposed trail is expected to halt appeals to 'ultimate values'. Appeal to values is tantamount to metaphysics. On the other hand, the merits of the reconstructed category are held to provide us with the means 'to criticize the contents of forms of life'. Oddly enough, the second qualification appeals to the contents of life. What are these? Answers from the neo-Kantian sociology and philosophy specify them in terms of values, no matter what justification different authors offer. For Scheler though, as we have already showed, life is anchored in those a priori contents that constitute human essence as a being that is open to the world and appropriates its forms of values. What seems to be proposed here is a self-referential (since no appeal to essences is conceded) concept of alienation free of appeal to foundations. It posits a criterion that somehow allows us to define certain types of relating to others 'alienated' or 'unalienated', yet with no teleological inscription other than the normatively vague goal of people appropriating their lives and world. No wonder then that issues of 'mere survival' (30) are treated as peripheral to the proposed reconstruction's standpoint. In the antipodes of this marginalization of human materiality, essentialist categories are placed immediately front stage. Such, for instance, is the recourse to Tugendhat's 'functional capacity' to will; or, in Jaeggi's words, 'I want to be able – freely – to will' (34).[9] In fact, in the encapsulation of the formal model of what constitutes alienation through the negative lens of impediments to the capacity to will, the essentialist – indeed the most metaphysical of all – category of capacity (with a long heritage from Aristotle to Hegel) is repeatedly mustered (see, indicatively, 200).

Promulgating the duality of social roles (they are held to be both 'enabling' and 'constraining') (92) Jaeggi's reconstruction of alienation recoils in the *hiatus irrationalis*. A role is held to constrain me because it abstracts from my wholeness. But on this account it is also enabling because it renders possible my sociality. Jaeggi, of course, wants to posit sociality as the totality out of which nothing (no essence) exists. In effect this resembles a Durkheimian approach but without Durkheim! Having established the self's capacity to appropriate the world via the range of distinctions the self is called to handle in a diversified set of roles, Jaeggi's account falls short of the fact that the essence of the self represents the world in consciousness as something outside consciousness. Thus, whether the self divides – ontologically – the world into projects in society and nothingness, or in 'essence' and 'existence' or between 'individual' and 'society', the crux of the matter is that the self can appropriate the world by sublating some of these distinctions. Jaeggi's critical target is the quest for some allegedly true and authentic self behind artificial social roles or some essence outside the historical contingency of existence; her standpoint occludes, however, the mediations between essence and existence by many of the authors criticized (i.e. Marcuse (1936) 1968). Jaeggi is thus *forced* always to 'reply' to some alleged 'essence', while essence is close to the arguments she articulates as an 'essence' (there is always something 'mine' in my participation and performance of roles, as George Herbert Mead conceived the social self) that opens for itself possibilities for self-realization in social existence.

What also adds an essentialist dint is the economic–theological phraseology used to denote 'unalienation'. This appears as an act of 'balancing-out', as Jaeggi writes (64, 176), of inner oscillations and ambivalences. Scheler's normative trope (i.e. 'balancing-out') in resolving the ethics of the ecumenical person amid conflicts and alienations of sorts is now problematized in the domain of the self's compensation of projects and praxis. But if this notion of ersatz sublation (i.e. the balancing-out) can work for the unalienated self why isn't the balancing-out process at work when confronted to the indubitable non-social properties and potential of the human being? Isn't this what Marx's vision of unalienation emphatically presupposed and sought to mediate (and elevate) through social relations of production based on the freedom of associated producers? Either society (as the community of spirits) is the totality from which I abstract (but then some notion of reconciliation to that of Absolute Spirit would still be pending) or, alternatively, society is transposed to the mysteriously resourceful bootstrap capacity to engage in infinite problem-solving and project-appropriating but with no essential capacity to structure this motility of being around a centre (i.e. labour, freedom etc.). This was pragmatism's difficulty as it was addressed in Chapter 1. The self-centred part of the self is, to be sure, no mystical shell; yet, the self abstracts from social relations and posits itself as a claim for his realizable will, or potential, independently of current arrangements. It is this 'valence' of the self, i.e. the claims that the self makes in being recognized in the projects she wishes to pursue, that makes 'essence' an essential category. The 'surplus' that enables the self to proceed with this abstraction – while being placed in society and 'acting' on the world – is how essence is conceptualized. And precisely because somewhere (i.e. Society) there is a 'surplus' can 'balancing-out' claims be articulated and conquered by the agent. It is just that this surplus requires to be conceived as something 'other' than the self, something that is owed to those capacities and actions of the self that did not pay off and thus placed the agent 'in debt'. (The analogy with the self, made in layers but no core and resembles the onion, contrasts negatively with the notion of the earth's axial movement as argued in the image of 'true infinity' in Hegel's *The Phenomenology of Spirit*, which makes movement possible precisely because there is a 'core' ((1807) 1977, §169).) The important conception 'of a unity-creating self that appropriates its various possible roles and dimensions, as well as its attitudes and desires, and works through and integrates different experiences' (Jaeggi 2014, 192) requires the 'center', the 'core' as it were, that makes praxis a normative possibility. If the process of finding oneself in the world is both 'constructive' and 'reconstructive', as Jaeggi correctly intimates, then what needs to be rendered sharper is the metabolic moment of the relational social self. This metabolic component (as I have discussed in Chapter 3 on agency and natural law) requires scrutiny in terms of actors' own claims upon an 'essence'. In debunking essentialism individuals are held to be constructing their identity as they go on. This process entails resourceful but also alienating steps of making oneself authentic by carving out options in life with which the agent can identify, become affectively involved, and manage (201). (A risk for the critical potential in Jaeggi's reconstruction is the uncanny resemblance of these features of unalienation to structural-functional models of conformity and social control, like those advanced by Travis Hirschi.) The 'Münchausen effect' depicted here has implications that are indeed palatable to CA in terms of the ongoing process of constructing, reconstructing and managing one's identity. What is presupposed though in such a conception is that it is not only skilled but, additionally, normatively charged. This is so because what is claimed in the process of reconstruction (what one may call 'broadening') are also capabilities of practical reasoning, bodily integrity and sets of substantive and instrumental freedoms that make this self-management possible. Yet, the container view of the self (an authentic and expressive inner core), as Jaeggi rightly criticizes, is nothing other than the self's motility in the world. Presented as an abstraction the container view of the self is a form of recalling the capacity or capability resources that are stifled in a social role, a group, an organization, a life-project. But what makes the self 'move' in society is not only the power of critique but the reservoir of attributes and capacities that can serve as essentialist 'hooks' to any project of self-realization in light of critique's disclosure of defects. One cannot pull herself up by her own bootstraps. Nor do human beings exist in the fantastic Münchausen world where a Baron can rescue himself from drowning by pulling himself up, nor for that matter, ships build themselves in the ocean. The self that is debunked here constitutes, rather, the bundle of biological, psychological, cognitive and moral capacities (e.g. like the capacity for sympathy) that constitute the *movement* of appropriation. To suggest that the self is what one *does* in society is correct but it is not necessarily a negation of essentialism. Formally, at least, one can just as well suggest that the self is what one sees, hears, tastes, smells, touches or, like Scheler, how the self 'feels' the value-contents of the world (aesthetic, ethical, juridical, holy, vital, utilitarian values and so on.) All such capacities for projects (biological, psychological, social, cultural) constitute an 'essence'. When people get a sense that they are drained, they – correctly – convey a sense of capacity-exhaustion as a result of role-conflicts or role-strains. The self is both given and in the making, especially as the projects of the self's doing entail not just diversity and intractable features but also remarkable convergences, borrowings, cooperative networks, and universal properties (e.g. all societies value longevity).

Jaeggi's existential reconstruction is remarkably nuanced but – if it aims to belong to Critical Theory – it needs to recover both a theory of needs (or capacities – which it nonetheless concedes) and a theory of social relations, especially if the latter prove for millions of people to be detrimental to the very capacity for having a project and *owning* it. Given such deprivations the 'balancing-out' capacity can take the shape of a bourgeois luxury (as this is premised on the freedom in society to engage with diverse projects) or of desperate resentment. Evidently, Jaeggi's proposed reconstruction of alienation critique is conducted, if we translate it into CA terminology, on the level of *functionings* (lifestyles chosen by people) rather than the more fundamental ground of *capabilities*. The latter is though closer to the pool from which the Marxian view of alienation hoped to replenish and CA aspires to provide for every human being. In this sense Jaeggi concedes the radical and universal precondition for the freedom to own a life-project that the original theme of alienation sought to capture. Having silenced its own, rather strong, metaphysical presuppositions (as the 'balancing-out' recalls both the promise of religious compensation for those whose projects are undermined and a form of 'exchange'), Jaeggi's notion of alienation requires the supplement she recognizes in the conclusion, namely the theory of *Sittlichkeit* conducive to people's capacity to appropriate the world. In addition, it also requires a more 'essentialist' moment that is no other than articulating what exactly is being valued as a resource in the process of appropriation. In fact, this requirement for a balanced ownership of one's life through project ownership is not foreign to CA. Discussing consumption, for example, David Crocker theorizes well-being and consumption in terms of 'balancing acts' (1998, 374) of the self against one-sided pursuits of well-being and happiness. Crocker's argument is tailored to operate beyond fixed hierarchies of preferences and visualizes a model of human pursuit outside logics of 'sacrifice' of one's well-being, should higher goods (e.g. artistic perfection, professional excellence) are deemed worthy of pursuit. Interestingly enough, Crocker utilizes a conceptual apparatus close to the one adopted by Max Scheler. Considering the logic of 'balancing-out' when, for example, the pursuit of 'one valuable capability, especially when chosen and enjoyed, compensates' (375) for the limited cultivation of others, Crocker insists that the option of a non-sacrificial possibility of enjoyment of a major capability is a real possibility in society informed by the 'ideal of balance'. This ideal, if we read between the lines, aligns with the Marxian request for an all-round development of human capabilities. (For Crocker through his apprenticeship with the Praxis Group, these ideas gain purchase from the perspective of a theory of praxis based on the realization of human optimal potentialities. See Crocker (1983); Marković (1974, 64–67).)

CA offers I think this possibility of essence's 'remembrance' when the CCL provides conditions for self-realization that are also a-social (as in the case of 'feral children' who have no self but do have capacities for symbolic interaction), as well as thoroughly social (the capability of bodily integrity or of practical reason or of the capability of recognition *qua* affiliation or of the capability to have control over ones' political and material environment – the latter three all varieties of 'appropriation'). In fact, for, Jeaggi 'the distinction between self-realization and alienation can be described as a distinction between intrinsically and instrumentally valuable relationships or ways of life' (207). The intrinsic value invoked here is not far from the substantive freedoms and functionings in CA. This is indeed what the essentialism of CA also suggests. An issue to consider though is if Jaeggi's arch-distinction between self-realization and alienation regresses into dualism of value-rationality and instrumental rationality, transposed now into the individually authentic project-formation in the world. Would this be an 'essentialist' dualism? (Essentialist dualisms, for example, *pace* Durkheim are dualisms that reproduce the originary distinction between 'sacred' and 'profane'.) Transferred to the domain of the social self, is self-realization a self-understood projection of the human onto the world that operates pretty much along the lines of an ahistorical conception of labour? (For psychological research findings that demonstrate the merits of a CA theory of human flourishing and self-determination and thus redraw our attention to human nature without though neglecting society or culture, see Vansteenkiste, Ryan and Deci (2008)).

Nussbaum (1992) has anticipated many of these issues, particularly the imputation to CCL of some sort of 'essentialist' realism. Indeed any recourse to this domain *beyond* how human beings act and what humans do in in real contexts is rejected by CA. (However, the persistence of religiosity in contemporary affluent societies should be taken into consideration by non-paternalist defences of essentialism.) In fact, the invocation of essentialism bears on the broad consensus of recognizing each other as human, in communicating – mostly successfully – with other people in different cultural settings among other intuitively obvious facts. It can even be suggested that Nussbaum launches a functionalist response, which poses the question of what remains, as part of our essential humanness, once the properties associated with her CCL are being removed. Jaeggi's account of alienation does not of course lead to the simulated world of 'Textualité' that Nussbaum (1992, 241–242) associates with deconstructions of human essence. For Nussbaum, the model of essentialism that she primes is 'internal', i.e. without an anchoring in a metaphysical foundation. Although one should be cautious about any premature debunking of metaphysics, 'internal essentialism' broadens the foundations of what counts as a human being and thus 'excludes' far more exclusions than those that can be 'accommodated' in non-essentialist invocations of some 'essence': playful, spoken, noble, slavish, simulated, irrelevant, parodic (Nussbaum 1999). This lack of a meta-value set – what internal essentialism is all about – can yield serious deformations of our sociality. I do not suggest that Jaeggi takes necessarily this trail – or even that her account leads in any immediate way to it – but in her radical bracketing alienation is normatively weakened and, in spite of Jaeggi's critique of postmodern identities, the normative foundation of what it means to be human is unnecessarily emaciated. In fact, Jaeggi is closer than she herself thinks to Nussbaum essentialist negation of metaphysical realism. Thus, for Nussbaum, the much-derided 'nature' is not some sort of 'external' point of reference that would offer ethical validation. Rather:

> [h]uman nature cannot, and need not, be validated from the outside, because human nature just *is* an inside perspective, not a *thing* at all, but rather the

> most fundamental and broadly shared experiences of human beings living and reasoning together.
>
> (Nussbaum 1995, 121 [original emphasis])

Thus, the self-relation that Jaeggi and Nussbaum argue for is enveloped in socially accomplished yet open to collective frameworks of acting in relation to others.

Alienation from what? Deprivation from what?

A first attempt at decompressing alienation through CA is to render explicit many of its unarticulated premises. The question 'alienation from what?' asked by sociologists and philosophers can be reformulated as 'deprivation from what'? According to most alienation narratives, alienation signifies bifurcation and contradiction between social entities, which deserve to exist in an interdependent and cooperative arrangement. This dialectical interdependence corresponds, if we follow Hegel, Marx and Durkheim, to social arrangements and institutions founded on freedom, autonomy and justice. Because deprivation carries a normative adjunct capable of entering actors' experiences in a variety of ways (contingent on cultural identity, historical heritage, institutions and international relations), it no longer mystifies the normative 'essence' that had always been presupposed by alienation approaches. Rather, CA informs us about the degree and type of deprivation that is likely, if and when it occurs, to foster alienation. It is not therefore alienation that generates deprivation, but rather it is the agency's socially derived capability deprivation that yields the experiential consequence of alienation.

If we briefly revisit the analytical categories of alienation theory as developed by sociology (e.g. Seeman 1959) we see that these are configured as an interrelated set of core deprivations: powerlessness, meaninglessness, normlessness, estrangement and social isolation. Calibrated into the conceptual scheme of capabilities, powerlessness signals deprivation from the capability of control over one's material and political environment, meaninglessness captures deprivation in terms of dissociation from affiliations and sociability as an outcome of substantive powerlessness, normlessness can be seen as a consequence of deprivations in the capabilities of practical reason (i.e. the self proves incapable of forming and planning a conception of the good in the absence of fair normative networks) and affiliation (as the actor fails to fulfil self-esteem and recognition in ways other than norm-breaching ones, or experiences as meaningless a reality where such norms are poorly validated in everyday life). Estrangement and social isolation constitute also substantive deprivations from our sociality, cut off from recognition and esteem-securing social groups, roles and qualifications. These convey to the self the sense of fulfilment and the cognitive confirmation that she counts according to her contributions to collectively valued goals, but also *substantively* as a human being capable of choosing, forming and transforming preferred lifestyles and goal sets.[10]

Decompressing alienation's normative potential forces us to rethink it in terms of Marx's admirable formulations and see if the normative premises he implied but did not develop further in his mature work, allow our proposed reconstructions. Marx seems to make room for what later developed as CA when he writes in the *Grundrisse* that 'the capability to consume is a condition of consumption, hence its primary means, and this *capability* is the development of an individual potential, a force of production' (Marx (1857–1858) 1993, 711 [original emphasis]). In the famous passage on alienation and the manifold development of human potential once labour and leisure fully mediate each other, Marx makes interesting use of how capital inverts the activities of the socially rich self, like theorizing, learning, or engaging in art, capturing it as a capability inversion (Marx (1844) 1992, 361), hence, I add, as capability deprivation. At crucial points Sen makes use of Marx on how, for example, commodity fetishism can be avoided as Marx would have hoped through functionings (Sen 1999a, 19), or on going beyond class analysis as Marx had also suggested (Sen 2009, 247), or even on Marx's not infrequent affinity to the 'libertarian concentration on freedom' (Sen 1999b, 29). It is also clear that for Marx, as for Sen and Nussbaum, these capability inversions *qua* deprivations constitute serious injuries and deformations of the socially capable self, that is, of species-being. Capability deprivation needs to be seen then in terms of updated continuity rather than radical departure from the Marxian idea of alienation. Now, this capable social self implies the formation of capability and freedom across a variety of institutional arrangements and social spheres (i.e. the mediation between ethics and the economy). In this respect, Sen's CA shows sensitivity to reality's indeterminacy and pluralism as well as to the public realm of deliberation, combining piecemeal acts of democratic broadenings with pragmatic problem-solving. These are factors sufficient to distance Sen from revolutionary projects, 'spontaneous' acts of resistance or abstract applications of democratization. Instead, as I argue here, the structure of his categories runs across the reform/revolution dualism. For the alienation approaches which connect Marxian critique to instrumental rationality, both revolution and reform remain impossible undertakings when, for example, revolution is transferred to voluntarist capacity for resistance or to scattered anti-system collectivities, while the reform alternative, often equated with pragmatism, counts by orthodox and Critical Marxism's standards, as an instance of instrumental reason's domination. For Sen, by contrast, the reformist project is the one that gains considerable appeal, flexibility and scope because it makes room for intermediate institutional levels, in order for agency freedoms and achievements to materialize. Drawing on what was discussed in Chapter 2, Sen's comment does not repel liberalism's achievements as a result of reformism. Rather, while it identifies the deeply alienating effects of much of liberalism's mechanisms and institutions, it focuses instead on aspects of public reason and public policy, which remain underdeveloped by standard accounts of alienation and inequality.

These intermediate levels of public reasoning and institution-built freedom within the historical formation of contemporary (capitalist) societies are not entirely disregarded by Marxian thinkers. André Gorz, for instance, who offers fresh insights onto the Marxian theory of (un)alienated free labour brings to the fore the wider set of capabilities Marx had associated with the emancipation of labour from capital. Gorz identifies sites where discursive deliberation led to significant accomplishments, as, for example, in the dissemination of 'co-operative networks' (1999, 107) like the Local Exchange Trade Systems (LETS) in North America and Europe. For Gorz, welfare and labour-related achievements in Scandinavian societies are tantamount to less alienation, allowing people sufficient degrees of self-actualization, since 'free time enables individuals to create capacities (of invention, creation, conception and intellection) which give them a virtually unlimited productivity [...]' (92). Like Gorz, who calls for a redefinition of wealth on the basis of Sen's approach (Gorz (2003) 2010, 111, 136–137n.3), Nussbaum and Sen repeatedly invoke the quality of life metrics of Scandinavian societies in unison with ongoing research on that front (e.g. Erikson 1993; Wilkinson and Pickett 2010), with a view to enrich well-being indicators via CA. In fact, Nussbaum admits (1990, 241) that Scandinavian welfare-indicator lists are strikingly, but unsurprisingly, similar to the Aristotelian list and to her version of it that we have already cited. They are tantamount to fusion of liberalism and social democracy (Nussbaum 1990).[11]

Reconfigured as 'Gross National Happiness' (Gorz (2003) 2010), the idea of human development should take the shape of 'an *intelligent society* in which the full development of each person's abilities is everyone's aim' (109 [original emphasis]). Harnessed to CA, Marxian critique recovers not only the jettisoned project of the human species-being that young Marx thought was partially fulfilled under capitalism; it also replenishes its contemporary subversive potential. Thus, the transformation into a knowledge society means for Gorz that knowledge (the source of value and profit) eschews the quantification upon which abstract labour resides. Rather:

> [this knowledge] covers – and refers to – a wide diversity of *heterogeneous* capacities, including judgment, intuition, aesthetic sense, level of education and information, ability to learn and to adapt to unforeseen situations, which are capacities themselves brought into play by heterogeneous activities ranging from mathematical calculation to rhetoric and the art of persuasion, from techno-scientific research to the invention of aesthetic norms.
>
> (35–36 [original emphasis])

If we revisit momentarily the famous, so-called 'utopian', passage in *The German Ideology* we read:

> whereas in the communist society, where nobody has one exclusive sphere of activity but each can become accomplished in any branch he wishes, society regulates the general production and thus makes it possible for me to do one thing today and another tomorrow, to hunt in the morning, fish in

> the afternoon, rear cattle in the evening, criticize after dinner, just as I have a mind, without ever becoming hunter, fisherman, shepherd or critic.
>
> (Marx and Engels (1845–1846) 1976, 47)

Such passages inform Sen's approval (1987c, 37n.18; 1992, 41n. 8) of Marx's celebration of the (social) freedom of persons to be capable to choose the life-styles (qua functionings) that inform the vision of a future society. They are also considered to present a comprehensive view of freedom as opposed to libertarian emphasis on negative freedom. Thus, the problem is not that my capabilities are implicated in hard work, as all the aforementioned activities undoubtedly require (on this passage and the voluntary aspect of work, see Karatani 2003, 345n. 22). Rather, it is the abstract form of labour that renders these activities subject to an economic codification of the purpose they serve, tied to necessity. Like Gorz's critique of the end of the proletariat, so Sen (1992, 119–121) draws from Marx the insight that class-relations should not become the single evaluative space for inequalities. This does not dispense with class analysis but requests instead that given existing diversities within a class different foci broaden the scope of human agency. In this sense Amartya Sen accommodates quality of life and basic needs approaches to the paradigm shift on CA-inspired studies of inequality.[12]

Interestingly, if we seek this welfare analogy to Sen's approach within classical sociology, this must be located not in Marx but in Durkheim's more affirming explanations of modernity, which the conflation of anomie with alienation renders obscure. I do not refer here to the invocation of a collective subject like Society rejected by Sen's endorsement of Marx's similar objections (Sen 2009, 245) on the grounds that it constitutes an abstraction set against real individuals in their contextual and empirical concreteness. On this item both Marx and Sen err for reasons I discussed in Chapter 1. With Durkheim bearing the burden of sociological criticism, it is rather constraining to understand Society only as a reified abstraction. Rather, as I have suggested, it is Durkheim's moral conception of economic institutional arrangements, like the division of social labour with the non-contractual values of trust, cooperation, well-being and justice, that can be considered a normative barrier against anomie. Durkheim's logic, which is neither against markets per se, nor indifferent to the anomic (alienated) consequences of an abstract and nominal division of social labour, is close enough to Sen's contemporary critique of the limitations of current economic categories (e.g. Pareto optimality, neo-Malthusianism, rational choice) (Sen 1987a). Durkheimian scholars have picked up the affinity between Durkheim and Sen towards the development of adequate theoretical foundations guided by Sen's idea of 'individual freedom as social commitment' (Sen 1990; Cladis 1992, 286, 292) that transcends the communitarianism/liberalism dualism and the ethics/economics divide (Steiner 2002, 96n.1). Through this optic the very individual dignity both Marx and Sen celebrate and struggle to upgrade is itself the core moral content of Society, if the latter is not approached in conventional terms but as an sequence of those complex arrangements that enable individuals to raise claims to justice and also to attain them.

Precisely because deliberation within civil society is crucial in forming the capability to broaden the sphere of choices we have reason to value, Sen revisits the Marxian theme of false-consciousness. As false-consciousness is a central pillar of Marx's theory of alienation it is worth addressing it. Far from ascertaining a ubiquitous defect in agents' perspectives on their own class situation (Marx, Lukács), Sen aims to account for those agents and collectivities, which, at a given time, may become subjected to systematic cognitive distortions and intersubjective deformations stemming from the force of traditional beliefs and practices, religious fundamentalism, as well as from their class situation but never because of the latter's sheer primacy. Sen calls this defect, 'solitarist illusion' (Sen 2006, 178) and 'objective illusion', namely, a 'positionally objective belief [...] mistaken in terms of transpositional scrutiny' (Sen 2009, 163). Sen eschews, however, the Marxian strategy of deducing the corrective to false-consciousness by appeal to the logical exposition of capital or, as Lukács would have it, through the objective positionality of the proletariat and its true consciousness of that exposition. Moving beyond illusions entails actual 'comparative broadenings', which in their turn are premised on economic, cultural or educational opportunities and come about too by 'shared frustrations' on global risks, which 'unite rather than divide' (Sen 2009, 173). Sen resorts to the motif of 'crisis' here – although never to that idea only – and thus activates a crucial Marxian notion, albeit in reconstructed form. Both as opportunity and crisis problem-solving this broadening makes use of Adam Smith's impartiality clause and in far less explicit and unacknowledged terms of the Hegelian 'reach of reason', especially when Sen refers to collective learning 'from past mistakes' (Sen 2009, 47). As we saw in Chapter 1 comparative broadenings reveal, therefore, another tool that ties Sen to the dialectical tradition, in the form of the capability to broaden one's perspective, since broadening follows not from unreflective allegiance to the authority of an (external or internal) interpretive scheme, but rather it signals the adoption of the new interpretive scheme which stems from acts of self-criticism and mutual corrigibility of standpoints. As Sen puts it, 'what needs curing is not just 'too little market' or 'too much market', but 'too little market' in some areas and 'too little *beyond* the market' in others' (Sen 1997, 27). With no need to preclude spectacular reconstructions of the market based on justice Sen, as a consequence of his consequentialist approach to markets, uses capabilities as the common denominator of both alternatives.

Sen attacks dualism further when he claims that decision-making 'with unresolved conflicts is part of a more general problem, viz., decision making with *incomplete* rankings [...] [which] may have to be faced even with *one* ultimate principle of valuation' (Sen 1985a, 179 [original emphasis]). Value-conflicts do not constitute, therefore, an irreducible element in reality. They can be coordinated within partial rankings as these differ in terms of scale and type of capability strengthening and which are 'assertive' or non-assertive about their incompleteness at no cost of conceding the legitimacy of the actor's or the group's moral standpoint. These partial orderings are configured by Sen as 'closed incompleteness' because they allow continuous and pragmatic informational broadening. By contrast, 'open incompleteness', reflects models that, like alienation theories, denigrate all sorts of social improvements simply because they are figured within capitalism. The latter 'incompleteness' becomes thus, significantly marred by its pragmatic shortcomings and by its neglect of the public sphere's problem-solving capacities. When Sen refers to 'assertive' incompleteness he suggests that no further process of completing value-orderings may be possible (thus, in the famous example of the Buridan ass, one of the two haystacks should be preferred even if there may be no perfect haystack). Non-assertive incompleteness by contrast aspires that incompleteness in rankings is in principle subject to completeness. Value-conflicts thus tend to appear as irreconcilable along models of 'closed incompleteness', yet this does not render responsible decision-making impossible. (There is, I think here, a Weberian colouring of ethics of integrity amid value-wars, where each value-standpoint in question 'asserts' completeness of rankings.)

Reconstructing alienation as capability deprivation: 'back' to value-formation!

Alienation is perceived by normative theories as a disentanglement of fact from value. Similarly, Marxist critics have rendered the problem of values commensurate to the law of Value. As we have seen in Chapter 1, Sen and Nussbaum opt for a different trail. Unlike advocates of a free-market economy they incorporate values and ethics into economics and unlike staunchly materialist advocates of Marxism they wisely proceed by disengaging the problem of values from capitalism's subsumption of human values to the law of Value. In other words, values offer the teleological standpoint of critique against conceptions of the economy that draw on different versions of utilitarianism. What an idealist vision of economics, and society as a social system, can also offer is to construct material interests as objects of collective values.[13]

Although never explicit, what lurks in the background of Sen's model is the idea that values, apart from their intrinsic coherence and merits, can be seen also as 'conditions' for social reproduction, if the latter are correlated to the enrichment of the life of each person.[14] Now the so-called value-neutral condition for broadening values and valued choices must be a valued choice itself. Moreover, as Sen contends:

> [if] individuals do, in fact, incessantly and uncompromisingly advance only their narrow self-interests, then the pursuit of justice will be hampered at every step by the opposition of everyone who has something to lose from any proposed change. If, on the other hand, individuals as *social persons* have broader values and objectives, including sympathy for others and commitment to ethical norms, then the promotion of social justice need not face unremitting opposition at every move.
>
> (Sen 1990, 54 [emphasis added])

We should add that given modernity's growing interdependencies, this broadened perspective is a condition for waiving barriers to merely self-interested goals and aspirations. Elsewhere, Sen (1999c) puts flesh on the bones of this condition when he connects democratic deficits with calamities like famines, or when in the face of global risks he defends 'democracy as a universal value' rendering it a condition for economic development and a value in itself: Looking at it, that is, in terms of its intrinsic, instrumental and constitutive merits or, additionally, in terms of democracy's configuration through global diversity as opposed to being formed exclusively through Occidental values.

As we have already discussed, the problem here is that countering injustice and removing inequalities and exclusionary practices cannot presuppose a fully developed and absolute value-hierarchy from which normative claims can unambiguously be gauged.[15] Returning for a moment to the capabilities-based response to social choice, it is worth recalling how the incompleteness clause addresses the problems that stem from the invocation of a normative grand narrative, like justice or from the negative corollary of alienation that we discuss in this chapter. Sen is adamant on this point:

> Indeed the insistence on the completeness of judgments of justice over every possible choice is not only an enemy of practical social action, it may also reflect some misunderstanding of the nature of justice itself. [...] The recognition of evident injustice in preventable deprivation, such as widespread hunger, unnecessary morbidity, premature mortality, grinding poverty, neglect of female children, subjugation of women, and phenomena of that kind does not have to await the derivation of some complete ordering over choices that involve finer differences and puny infelicities.
>
> (1999b, 254)

These incomplete value-rankings dispense with a normative super-pathology, like the standard account of alienation, which 'in the last instance' traces most forms of deprivation to the commodity form of labour. However, although Sen welcomes relative deprivation theories, he mediates their input with an 'absolute view of poverty' when, for example, he translates the absolute approach in the field of capabilities into the relative approach in the 'space of commodities, resources and incomes in dealing with some important capabilities, such as avoiding shame from failure to meet social conventions, participating in social activities, and retaining self-respect' (Sen 1984, 343) (a recognition motif in Honneth's theory of alienation). The focus on poverty, as he stresses, by no means underplays the inequalities of capabilities, or the variation in how a society, or in how within a society, commodities become converted into capabilities. This is another aspect in Sen's relaxation of dualisms (i.e. primacy of absolute or relative deprivation) when by shifting the terms of the debate and looking at the particular loci in which the category of deprivation can be shown to be problem-solving relevant.[16] Looking at rights as capabilities, enables Sen to avoid freezing values outside the practical and deliberative intra-communal or inter-communal nexus but at the cost of not clarifying sufficiently capability's moral core.

Because Sen must reckon with a normative core of the capable self once he has admitted reality's irreducible pluralism, he needs to reinsert into his normative framework a set of interrelated concepts of justice, rights, entitlements, functionings and capabilities. Notwithstanding his assurances for categorial modesty, he visualizes partial orderings of values (or capabilities) but seeks simultaneously the 'totality of entitlement relations' (Sen 1983, 155; Crocker 2008, 71) upon which, for instance, a person's ability to command adequate food to avoid starvation is incumbent. On the same issue, Nussbaum recovers the missing and insufficiently worked out normative core in alienation theories. She extends the programme's hard core when Sen's more elaborate theory of partial orderings and incompleteness gets in the way of offering a clearer view of the capable self upon which it is premised. As Nussbaum claims, the 'thick vague essentialism' of networking capabilities, in the absence of which, or in their presence below or excessively beyond functional and ethical capability thresholds, human lives become severely damaged and demeaned, secures revisability as a response to various contextual and historical contingencies (the 'vague' aspect). Thus, human capabilities comprise the multifaceted and rich social self, denoted by human dignity in line with what the young Marx had sketchily adumbrated but sociological theories of action have gradually demoted. Capabilities do not abstract from particular identities; on the contrary, the latter are constituted through the resourceful self that is implied in them. Levels of diversity as to how agents deliberate in what values they choose cannot erase the fact that lack of any of these 'functional capabilities' subtracts from 'humanness' (Nussbaum 1990, 225). This critical departure from Sen is corroborated by Nussbaum when she claims that Sen's notion of capability is normatively wanting, calling this omission 'a big mistake' (Nussbaum 2012, 134). This is, again, a natural law intimation very similar to Bloch's Marxist imperative for 'production according to one's capabilities' (Bloch (1961) 1987, 221).[17]

Because CA addresses power relations when it views agency as empowerment, its normative core sustains unambiguous correspondences with alienation and resistance projects. But on top of this continuity with alienation motifs, it also provides a better inventory of what sociology needs to accomplish in terms of polishing its normative theoretical models. As I argued, CA can help us to renew the concept of alienation by lowering the bar in terms of the latter's overly ambitious explanations of social problems. Alienation seems ill-suited to serve explanation when it tends to subsume the variation of mediations between property and freedom to a radical view of power and domination and when it refuses to uncouple capability deprivations from ideological and explanatory frameworks that lack realism. As Sen puts it, 'different people can have quite different opportunities for converting income and other primary goods into characteristics of good living and into the kind of freedom valued in human life' (2009, 254). A complementary function of each concept for explanation might be vindicated by the fact that, as we have seen, alienation already breaks up into subtler notions; but capability also may have to be expounded to address those structures and institutions that breed deprivation, through the cluster of neighbouring to alienation concepts (like, anomie) from a macrosociological perspective on social problems. This last point is intimated by Putnam and Walsh when they raise a crucial claim against the hitherto developed scope of CA:

> What we *do* find missing is an explicit analysis of the structures of production and *reproduction* that goes with the class-based deprivations and exploitations described. Where is the *surplus* that results from the deprivations? How much of it is devoted to luxurious waste – which Smith deplored – and how much to setting to work industrious people so as to produce more of the necessaries and conveniencies needed by the poor and deprived?
>
> (Putnam and Walsh 2012, 222)

Their question is topical and urgent. And the way they cite Sen immediately after their substantive question reveals the latter's (Sen 1999b, 14) reluctance to consider the issue of growth in terms of 'primitive accumulation'. But this does not lead straight into the idea of alienation as we already know it. Where it does lead is its CA reconstruction, like the one intimated in the context of Hegel's victims of structural inequality – the 'rabble' – by Allen through the lens of capability: 'Whereas the moral character of the rabble may be that of decline and depravity, it is for Hegel no less than Sen the result of "their being deprived of all the advantages of society"' (Allen 2006, 504).

Notes

1 The reader should note that S-alienation stands for subjective alienation. This type reflects mainly psychological perceptions or feelings about an (alleged) alienated social relationship. Such a social relationship can be approached as O-alienation (objective alienation) expressed as a 'lack of integration' of individuals' activities with the 'conventions and expectations of groups and with the laws and institutions of the socio-politico-economic order in which they live' (Schacht 1994, 20–21).

2 To my knowledge, there are scant references to Sen through the lens of alienation. One is to be found in Richard Schmitt (2003, 116–118), who criticizes Sen for not offering sufficient insights to 'internal', rather than 'external' constraints on freedom. This is perplexing, since Schmitt, in the same section, makes use of the idea of capability to refer to the agent's internal potential to make use of available freedoms. Dean (2009), for his part, charges Sen with neglect of Marx's non-capitalist idea of work. Sen's work is held to elide issues of alienation. As this chapter shows, not only is Sen's full attention given to those who are blithely dispossessed but it also provides fruitful hints for reconstructing alienation a concept which is not problem-free in sociology. Another critic writes: 'In Sen's vocabulary, alienation can be perhaps translated as a systematic failure to attain the functionings a human being requires to be fully human' (Bagchi 2000, 4418). Bagchi helps us here to convert alienation to the conceptual toolkit of CA. Indeed, alienation from functionings (i.e. from the lifestyles people have reason to value) is a promising attempt at renewal. It should normally correspond to alienation from species-being, i.e. from the potential of human beings to pursue those lifestyles that would concretely enunciate their species-being

in the world of the production of objects. Thus alienation from 'functionings' must entail the experience of one's species-being as an abstract possibility tethered to the necessity of labour. But this type of alienation is derivative of deeper moments of human unfreedom and although I do not necessarily take issue with this aspect of Bagchi's critique, 'alienation as capability deprivation' addresses those real deprivations in terms of what lies beyond the control (the freedom) of people for choices to retain the meaning and exhilaration associated with life in free societies. The tension between 'Sen the moral philosopher and Sen the economist' (4418) requires resolution but I do not think that the resolution lies only in deepening the reasoning of CA to the institutional nexus of inequality and exploitation associated with capitalism. The reverse reasoning can muster plausibility. The utopian aspect in Sen that Bagchi correctly intuits as 'the end of alienation', may be served better if utopian empowerment via capabilities brackets the Marxist algorithm with respect to capitalism's domination over people. Along with pursuing the moralization of markets, and hence their transformation in the countless instances of alienation across the macro, meso and micro levels, such concrete empowerment reserves by that very act the project of emancipation. The law of Value is too undifferentiated to enter people's consciousness as the exclusive guardian of human freedom. CA, instead, accomplishes the differentiation that is required to consider utopia as a battle on all fronts and particularly on the Kantian front where freedom matters the most, namely in people's empirical lives and trajectories of life-choices and chances.

3 Sen (2009, 255) makes room for the social capital problematic, the shortage of which leads to forms of capability deprivation. Social capital, however, is elusive by sociological standards too (see Bourdieu 1986). Ironically, it is Fukuyama (1995, 26) who, having Sen in mind, makes a more resourceful gesture, grasping 'social capital' as 'a capability that arises from the prevalence of trust in a society' ranging from the family and secondary groups to inter-group relations.

4 Agnes Heller is one of the few Marxian scholars who sought to revive the discourse on values within a Marxian framework. Undaunted by axiology's dubious neo-Kantian heritage Heller struggles to isolate the principle axiological concept in Marx's critique of capitalism, in order to reconstruct a binding, yet open value-theory. This is connected to the problem of values in Marx that I addressed in Chapter 1. Heller believes that Marx's pivotal value-judgment is 'abundance' (*Reichtum*). She reconstructs this value-content using as aids the idea of 'normality'. The notion of normality is derived, she claims, from Marx's writings and it entails the form of social organization that enables the free development of human potentialities (Heller 1972, 19). Heller envisages a Marxian theory sensitized to the type of individualism associated with the value of the personality and argues that the true content of species-being categories includes the development and enrichment of 'personality-values'. For Heller, 'the wealth of personality depends on how universal it is (in terms of its needs, feelings, types of activity, capacities); and, finally, how free it is, i.e., how fully can it realize its potentialities?' (1972, 45). Although this is not the place to explore the mechanics of Heller's exposition, it is important to note that the value of the personality that she contemplates entails a person both capable and in need. The CCL seen as a template of 'universal values' corresponds roughly to Heller's ideals as well. A shift to the problem of radical needs is among the ingenious modification CA makes with regards to Marxian normativity. In this sense, Hamilton (1999) is correct when he suggests that CA is a fruitful reconstruction of a theory of true needs free of the paternalism so often associated with Soviet orthodoxy or the total occlusion of people's true interests as in the Frankfurt School approach to alienation. Yet, to invoke true interest today would have to involve values at risk and broader value-formation as a result of public deliberation on individual capabilities, on the social spaces where these are aired and on what sort of systemic barricades are still at work for a wider purchase of human flourishing to be feasible.

5 This also explains why moral essentialism is hard to dispense with. Nussbaum notes that the content of capabilities is missing from Sen's model, and against Sen's own intentions, leaves capabilities 'up-for-grabs', an omission with potentially hazardous consequences for women's deprivations (Nussbaum 2005, 48). We have assessed in the previous chapter the natural law grounds for a return to a human ontology. It is worth recalling that Marxists do not necessarily cede from natural law theories. Such is, for instance, Ernst Bloch's corrective to alienation where he, like Marx, and anticipating Sen, discusses unalienation in terms of production according to 'one's capabilities' ((1961) 1987, 221). The ultimate common value for all human beings is, for Bloch, *orthopedia* (human dignity); such capability to walk upright against violence and exclusion is configured by Crocker as the 'ultimate freedom to exercise our agency', therefore, as '[…] a meta-capability' (2008, 223). Nussbaum, too, envisions CA 'being defined in part in terms of dignity' (2011, 63). Although he does not explicitly bring the two together, Lukes (1985, 69–70) makes some sharp remarks on human rights and discusses at a glance Sen and Bloch on the compatibility of Marxist utopia with human rights. He also (Lukes 2008, 129–135) promotes Nussbaum's CCL as the most fecund and feasible response to moral relativism. This recollection of Bloch's metaphysics of hope is anything but merely tangential to CA. Linked to the human desire for fulfilment, hope becomes the instance of 'transcending' social infirmities, initiating possibility of praxis. Within the Marxian vision of the unalienated human person in a society where fulfilment is institutionally inscribed and processed, Sen, in nearly theological rhetoric, like Bloch, writes:

> It is not only that a poor person can offer less money for what he or she desires compared with a rich person, but also that even the strength of the mental force of desiring is influenced by the contingency of circumstances. The defeated and the downtrodden come to lack the courage to desire things that others more favourably treated by society desire with easy confidence. The absence of desire for things beyond one's means may not reflect any deficiency of valuing, but only an absence of hope, and a fear of inevitable disappointment.
>
> (Sen 1987b, 10–11)

Nussbaum in her recent book on fear, concludes with a section on hope, drawing largely on Kant's idea of hope as a 'practical postulate'. However, she, unnecessarily I think, reproduces dualism when she writes that '[u]topianism is a forerunner of despair, so faith and hope need to find beauty in the near' (2018, 215). If read as a Hegelian injunction to find the good in the misery of the present, then hope's actuality is powerfully retained. If though her statement is intended as a rejection of utopianism in general, it will need to be recalled that utopianism is entangled in the real. As Bloch's monumental reflections on hope have shown, what we cherish nearly in every art-form today is the outcome of hope in utopia. There is no a priori reason why this utopia should not feed spaces of hope in actuality. In this direction, CA is mentioned in positive light by Erik Olin Wright (2010, 13–14), although he still feels uncomfortable with human flourishing as an 'essence', invoking instead some sort of multidimensional complexity in what counts as human flourishing.

6 In reflecting on the vision of unalienation, another Marxist scholar warns against Marxian notions turning to formulaic schemata. Locating capabilities at the heart of Marx's project, Adam Schaff, writes on unalienated 'universal man': 'For this to be something more than an empty slogan, it is necessary to create the objective conditions for the *all-sided* development of man's capabilities and skills' (1980, 262 [original emphasis]). This Marxian moral universal, CA unpacks and transforms into workable indicators against social inequality bracketing the revolutionary scope of radical social theory. It thus converts the idea of 'all-sided development of man's capabilities' into a research programme for a new humanism in social science.

7 To my knowledge, one of the very few commentators addressing explicitly the anthropological consequences of CA in accord to Marx's is Giovanola (2005). The question put at the end of her essay aligns with my interest in these anthropological aspects and, interestingly enough, there is a hint too about twentieth-century Catholic thought – yet Scheler is not being mentioned – and personalist ethics. Can, as its author invites us to consider, 'the CA's underlying philosophical anthropology' become the focus of 'capability literature?' (266). (The current and previous chapter of my book attempt to carry forward this task.) For her more recent expansion in this direction, strictly though in the Aristotelian–Marxian legacy, see Giovanola (2009). Liberal critics of CA have also recognized categorial tensions in the absence of metaphysics in CA. Although I do not share the political conclusions of their critique, Den Uyl and Rasmussen (2009) have a point when they repeatedly point to the implicit but repelled 'teleological anthropology' (890) in the CA without which the pragmatic realism *pace* Putnam that Sen and Nussbaum endorse remains without a foundation.

8 A nuanced extension of Geras' argument that aims too to provide a groundwork that transcends dualisms is provided by Fracchia (2005) who posits as the first incontrovertible materialist fact human corporeality. Fracchia does this by deploying both the backward-looking view of the human being adopted by Darwin and the forward-looking objectification process associated with Marx's writings about the flourishing of embodied human agency. Unearthing Marx's corporeality he is forced to formulate the materialist first fact in prose that makes recourse to capacities and capabilities:

> But behind changing capacities such as the specific character of technology, it is the set of corporeal capabilities that establishes the possibilities for humans to make their own histories; and beyond the changing limits of inherited socio-cultural conditions, it is the set of corporeal constraints, the needs and limits embedded in human corporeal organization, that prevents humans from making their histories as they please, that imposes limits on the variability of human cultures and on human malleability. A taxonomy constructed according to this principle must delineate *both* the capacities *and* the constraints embedded in the corporeal organization of *Homo sapiens*.
>
> (Fracchia 2005, 43 [original emphasis])

Because it conceives corporeality as a limit concept too, Fracchia's inspired exploration of the corporeal a priori reproduces necessity and freedom (the latter as the capability aspect of the body and the social environment that extends its self-development). Yet, Fracchia's asymmetrical implementation of human corporeal dispositions downplays the phylogenetic dimension of our species' incompleteness, which for him is 'Whiggish' (37–38n. 10). This is at odds also with Marx's conception of modernity's partial actualization of social universality. Fracchia's argument reproduces the 'enabling'-'constraint' dualism within corporeality when he admits that Marx's concept of *Anlagen* (2005, 45–46) is implicitly subdivided to 'corporeal capabilities that enable people to make their own history, and the corporeal constraints that prevent them from doing so as they please' (46). Any talk of capabilities carries with it man's history of 'pain' in the shape of human confrontation with negativity, whether this is the negativity of natural calamities or the negativity of coercion and violent death in the hands of other people. This is one occasion that binds the human species together in a universal thread of seeking to escape our ineluctable entanglement with pain (for this catalogue of human culture's prehistory of pain see our discussion of Nussbaum and Nietzsche in Chapter 5). This materialist foundation of life is captured by Marx and Engels:

> The first and most important of the inherent qualities of *matter* is *motion*, not only *mechanical* and *mathematical* movement, but still more *impulse, vital life-spirit,*

> *tension*, or, to use Jacob Bohme's expression, the *throes* [Qual] of matter. The primary forms of matter are the living, individualizing *forces of being* inherent in it and producing the distinctions between the species.
>
> (Marx and Engels (1845) 1956, 172 [original emphasis])

This remarkable passage not only confirms the natural law aspects of human motility as Life but denote also its ontological implication with pain and suffering (of our living material side) via this reference to Christian mysticism (Böhme). As I argue, CA is hard to sustain if its pragmatism is detached from this ontological foundation that unites matter and spirit in the bifurcation that makes humans historical beings. It is further evident that the historical task of 'redeeming' and 'sublating' pain by minimizing its impact on life, involves not merely the necessity of labour but also its regrettable necessity through the lens of surplus-value. 'Methodological pragmatism' is argued to operate without recourse to values (St. Claire, 2010, 109–115) but although it is rightly asserted that 'facts, values and practices' emerge simultaneously (114), the prime fact of human motility as the human dignity of orthopedia – the goal of CA, *par excellence* – is abstracted as a single, presumably, contingent value, rather than as development ethics' a priori with the institutional qualifications this requires. As a second-order approach, however, 'methodological pragmatism' has much to offer. To his credit Bull (2007) discerns the motif of life (although he draws on other writers beyond Marx) and likens CA to biopolitics. He is also correct I think to claim that 'Sen and Nussbaum present the capabilities approach as being equivalent to (and perhaps a substitute for) the projected path of human development envisioned by communism [...]' (Bull 2007, 22). If I argue in favour of reclaiming the legacy of 'Life', even at the level of abstraction dealt with by Hegel, it is because Life preserves both the ontological possibility of human flourishing as 'motility' and as the sublation of negativity which itself generates. At the same time it keeps intact the memory of a 'worthwhile life' (Sen 1999b, 294) in times when lives still suffer massively from the worst deprivations. Nussbaum's Aristotelian expertise leads her also to the concept of life as she likens it to human capabilities (see Nussbaum 1995).

9 For Tugendhat, agency's self-consciousness and self-determination is defined through an act of responding to the practical situation. Tugendhat (1986, 172–173) conceptualizes the practical situation as summoning the agent to a 'yes' or 'no' standpoint to action. Rather than calling for exclusively instrumental responses, the practical situation carries, for Tugendhat, several stages that lead to a composite set of 'moments' in building the concept of a self-conscious and autonomous self (in other words, and by Sen's standards, a capable self). I lack the space to address these but although Tugendhat aims to disclose only the formal responsibility to one's self and to the other as a formal condition for the good life to materialize, his rendition tells us something significant about both the compressed philosophical justification of Sen's capability.

10 Blauner's sociological study on a variety of labour sites relaxes the conflict aspects of alienation and confirms our hindsight when, as he claims, the 'valuable humanistic tradition of alienation theory [...] view all human beings as potentially *capable* of exercising freedom and control, achieving meaning, integration, social connection, and self-realization' (1964, 187 [emphasis added]).

11 This raises the complex and contested problem of development and societal evolution. This is not the place to embark on the highlights of such complicated debate but since we talk about Scandinavian quality of life indicators it is worth noting that even moderate critics of over-reliance of welfare indicators recognize that a functional approach to societal development requires such mediation with welfare indicators. Important here is the contribution of Dahlström (1974). I shall only single out this scholar's remark that evolutionary theory itself is premised on some 'meta-assumptions' (7) drawn from humanist social science. While overuse and over-reliance

on these 'functional' dimensions tends to idealize (and distort) welfare accomplishments, the lesson that emerges is that given the complexity, diversity and crisis of development, functional and welfare approaches need to work in concert. Although Dahlström does not argue his case from a partisan normative standpoint, to his credit he recognizes the 'the value nature of the social dimension' (18). This congruence and sensitivity is served as I argue by CA. Interestingly enough, something like a list of welfare dimensions figures here (18), too, anticipating the CCL. The fact that such lists based on human needs were inspired by Maslow's hierarchy (1943), as Dahlström tells us (18), is from a historical perspective slightly regrettable given sociological paucity on the subject of human needs. My emphasis on Max Scheler's anthropology of value-modalities in the constitution of the human works also as a reminder of sociology's neglected accomplishments. A truly excellent account of the ethics of human development that not only relies on Sen but articulates with passion and erudition the imperative of 'alliances' among different philosophies or social theories with a common foundation on human needs is Gasper's *The Ethics of Development.* Gasper brings together, among others, Gorz, T.H. Marshall and, as I argued in Chapter 3, Talcott Parsons (Gasper 2004, 151–152).

12 In the Fitoussi report, its authors (Stiglitz, Sen and Fitoussi 2009) broaden the notion of economic well-being in ways reminiscent of Gorz and, of course, Marx. They write:

> Time spent on generating income (market or non-market) provides the means to buy goods and services to meet our needs, in addition to a range of non-market returns. Time available for leisure affects well-being in more direct ways. It follows that changes in the amount of leisure over time, and differences between countries, represent one of the more important aspects for comparative assessment of economic well-being. Focusing only on goods and services can bias comparative measures of well-being towards the production of goods and services. This is of particular concern as the world begins to come to terms with environmental constraints: it will not be possible to increase the scale of economic production, especially of goods, beyond limit. Taxes and regulations will be imposed that will both discourage the production of goods and change the way they are produced. It would be a mistake, beyond the decrease of production and consumption as they are currently recorded, not to consider that an increase in leisure time can benefit well-being.
>
> (2009, 131)

Although a complex variable to measure, it is generally accepted that societies with more room for leisure are deemed to be 'better-off' (134) in quality of life terms. For the centrality of time in Marx, see Postone (1993).

13 Marcuse admitted the operation of values in directing, teleologically so to speak, material interest so that a mechanical (or instrumental) implementation of the socialization of the means of production (as in USSR and the then entire Eastern bloc) is eliminated as a possibility. See Marcuse ((1941) 1977, 282–283). Marković (1963), whose thought as part of the Praxis Group influenced a major scholar of CA, David Crocker, rehabilitates the problem of values into Marxist theory not only to counter the shallow determinism of Marxist orthodoxy but also to build the moral dimension of Marxist ethics around the notion of 'disalienation'; particularly fruitful may prove the device of *ceteris paribus* 'tacitly assumed preferences' in favour of peace, freedom, action based on the fulfilment of human capacities and justice, which form 'generally accepted human evaluations' (Marković 1963, 20–21). Elsewhere, Marković (1974, 12–16) discusses human ontology on the basis of eight central 'human capacities' in an intriguing overlap with the CCL. (Capabilities constitute the normative mechanism that builds on these tacit preferences, taking into full considerations the abstract and contingent shape of their validity and implementation.)

14 Marxist philosophical anthropology shares this hierarchical provision with strands of normative functionalism (Parsons). The extension of the category of the violations of the conditions for life from a Marxian perspective has been pursued by Psychopedis (2000). The Kantian move in his version of opening Marx to other normative paradigms considers the a priori presupposition of freedom in terms that delineate the conditions for the flourishing of human life. His exposition ties well with the core of Sen's project: Values become formed at the moment of crisis (i.e. when the 'conditions of life' become threatened and rendered precarious). By 'conditions of life' Psychopedis understands micro-relationships of friendship and love, but extends the scope of the category and makes it inclusive of the a priori of human life and health as well as of wider social relations of 'freedom, justice, knowledge and aesthetic' judgment (90–91). Values mediate history insofar as they are formed through crisis; it is their mediation by crisis that invests human demands with the energy that warrants exit from inhuman relations. Unlike many Marxists who interpreted the ideal's application in history in deterministic terms, Psychopedis does not recede from the problems that Weberian relativism addressed and we noted in Chapter 1. Rather, he attempts to rework critically the idea of indeterminacy. Seen in this light, indeterminacy is theorized *simultaneously* as both freedom and exploitation: As exploitation, it is reflected in the forms of social crises that stem from a social division of labour founded on conflicting interests, injustice and exploitation; as freedom, it engages determinate values like solidarity, equality and justice. It is in this sense, as Psychopedis argues, that 'critical investigation of the question of values reveals something apparently worth questioning – values do not oppose the element of indeterminacy; on the contrary they are constituted through it' (2000, 97). Placing this insight within the purview of Kant's critical philosophy, Psychopedis draws a Marxian theme from idealism, claiming that

> every relation of exploitation and domination [...] is not necessary but exists as contingency. Underdetermined are the relations that humiliate, alienate and exploit human life. Thus determination can only be located in the rational critical thought and free action that ends humiliation (thus negating indeterminacy) (97).

Embedded in this normative demand, the concept of value becomes a material force, nuanced, however, to the critical aspects of idealism that inform Kant and Hegel. Psychopedis writes that, 'a *value* is the *resistance* offered to the conditions of life infringed upon by the coercive and exploitative organization of society' (2007, 109 [emphasis added]). Hence the openness to empirical contingency championed by Sen. Values, therefore, need not be set up as closed moral grids, but as relatively open (albeit binding) networks mediated by practical acts of defiance against oppression. Freedom is thus conceived as a relational value (see Sen 1999b, 37).

15 Alienation theories are often vulnerable because, like their opponents, they reduce complexity. This is not a Luhmann-inspired objection only, to how a system can silence contingency resorting to tautologies and paradoxes but, rather, one that takes complexity seriously from a normative and a systemic point of view. As suggested within the context of development ethics, blaming or praising

> such large formations as capitalism, socialism, industrialism, globalization, or Northern and Western imperialism commits fallacies of hasty generalization and over simplification that deter examination of the complex of causes that are both specific and alterable in the short, medium, and long run.
>
> (Crocker 2008, 287n. 29)

16 The Sen–Townsend exchange (Sen 1985b; Townsend 1985) exemplifies theoretical and empirical tensions between sociology and CA, none of which is beyond recuperation. Townsend has a point when he couples Sen's notion of agency to the model of

individualism 'rooted in neo-classical economics' (Townsend 1985, 668). While Sen too acknowledges the 'social nature of needs' (1985b, 675) his scheme is indeed vulnerable to the criticism of underplaying the impact of society but not exactly for the reasons advanced by Townsend. Rather, as much as needs are social, it is the intimation of a theory of the 'capable' institutions to respond to these needs that is pending in Sen. This crucial step will be taken up in Chapter 6. Townsend, for his part, reifies the 'social nature of needs' and thus occludes the species-being category that Sen's account of human needs entails. Rightly, Sen invokes the 'irreducible core of absolute deprivation' (Sen 1981, 22). My interpretation of this absolute core adds another 'anthropological' layer that Sen prefers to avoid, either because he does not wish to regress to some sort of 'universalism of needs' type of argument or simply because he does not believe it, either empirically or in terms of relevance. I think it would be odd to exclude the biological minimum here, which Sen (22) does not deny, but his understanding of what 'absoluteness' is all about is illuminating as it cuts across the binary 'relative-absolute' deprivation. Writes Sen:

> The characteristic feature of 'absoluteness' is neither constancy over time, nor invariance between different societies, nor concentration merely on food and nutrition. It is an approach of judging a person's deprivation in absolute terms (in the case of poverty study, in terms of certain specified minimum absolute levels), rather than in purely *relative* terms vis-à-vis the levels enjoyed by others in the society.
>
> (Sen 1985b, 673)

In fact, the reference to 'absoluteness' strikes the reader as a deprivation of something (food, health, shelter, esteem) that is absolutely valued. Its disvalue is experienced as an absolute deprivation irrespective of relative weights of that deprivation in a society.

17 For the ontological foundations of the idea of capability – upon which Bloch's ideal of human dignity is premised – one would need to revisit Hegel. For Hegel, human development has two moments: 'The first is what is known as capacity, power, what I call being-in-itself (*potentia, δύναμις*); the second principle is that of being-for-itself, actuality (*actus, ενέργεια*)' (Hegel (1819–1831) 1955, 20–21). The foundational constitution of humanness as viewed by Hegel's ontology of freedom's realization in history and the 'we' shapes of this freedom in social institutions add to contemporary notions of agency a normative load that is difficult to discharge, regardless of the complexity (and alienation) of freedom's realization in history. For an excellent discussion of this idea, see Marcuse ((1932) 1987). In the quoted extract, analysed by Marcuse, Benhabib translates *Vermögen* as 'capability' (see Marcuse (1932) 1987, 178). Hegel's distinction between these two stages resurfaces in Sen's demarcation between 'capability' and 'functionings'. The former concept refers to the ethical imperative of cultivating capabilities with which human beings are endowed; the latter captures the realization of capabilities in actual lifestyles, that enable persons to feel at home in the social milieu they live in and pursue their freely taken choices and decisions. This level of functionings was, I repeat, Jaeggi's focal concern in a renovated alienation critique that omitted capabilities not only as presuppositions for any chosen (and owned) functionings but also as ends in themselves. They are the matrix of human nature. Even more impressive though is Hegel's designation of the content of the just state: 'the final end of the state and the social life of men is that *all* human capacities and *all* individual powers be developed and given expression in every way and in every direction' (Hegel (1823–1829) 1975, 48). In spite his reservations for an essentialist argument, Sen (1984, 310) concedes that 'digging' for a foundation is not incompatible with the moral backdrop of a theory, which, like his own, addresses rights, entitlements, freedoms and capabilities.

References

Allen, Michael. 2006. 'Hegel between Non-domination and Expressive Freedom: Capabilities, Perspectives, Democracy.' *Philosophy and Social Criticism* 32 (4): 93–512.
Bagchi, Amiya. 2000. 'Review: Freedom and Development as End of Alienation?' *Economic and Political Weekly* 35 (50): 4408–4420.
Blauner, Robert. 1964. *Alienation and Freedom*. Chicago: The University of Chicago Press.
Bloch, Ernst (1961) 1987. *Natural Law and Human Dignity*. Cambridge, MA: The MIT Press.
Bourdieu, Pierre. 1986. 'The Forms of Capital.' In *Handbook of Theory and Research for the Sociology of Education*, edited by John Richardson, 241–258. New York: Greenwood.
Brighouse, Harry, and Ingrid Robeyns, eds. 2010. *Measuring Justice: Primary Goods and Capabilities*. Cambridge: Cambridge University Press.
Bull, Malcolm. 2007. 'Vectors of the Biopolitical.' *New Left Review* 45: 7–25.
Cladis, Mark. 1992. *A Communitarian Defense of Liberalism: Emile Durkheim and Contemporary Social Theory*. Stanford: Stanford University Press.
Crocker, David. 1983. *Praxis and Democratic Socialism: The Critical Social Theory of Marković and Stojanović*. New Jersey: Humanities Press.
Crocker, David. 1998. 'Consumption, Well-Being, and Capability.' In *Ethics of Consumption: The Good Life, Justice, and Global Stewardship*, edited by David Crocker and Toby Linden, 366–390. Lanham: Rowman and Littlefield.
Crocker, David. 2008. *Ethics of Global Development*. Cambridge: Cambridge University Press.
Dahlström, Edmund. 1974. 'Developmental Direction and Welfare Goals. Some Comments on Functionalistic Evolutionary Theory about Highly Developed Societies.' *Acta Sociologica* 17 (1): 3–21.
Dean, Hartley. 2009. 'Critiquing Capabilities: The Distractions of a Beguiling Concept.' *Critical Social Policy* 29 (2): 261–278.
Den Uyl, Douglas, and Douglas Rasmussen. 2009. 'Liberalism in Retreat.' *The Review of Metaphysics* 62 (4): 875–908.
Drèze, Jean, and Amartya Sen. 1989. *Hunger and Public Action*. Oxford: Clarendon Press.
Erikson, Robert. 1993 'Descriptions of Inequality: The Swedish Approach to Welfare Research.' In *The Quality of Life*, edited by Martha Nussbaum and Amartya Sen, 67–83. Oxford: Oxford University Press.
Fracchia, Joseph. 2005. 'Beyond the Human-Nature Debate: Human Corporeal as the Organisation 'First Fact' of Historical Materialism.' *Historical Materialism* 13 (1): 33–61.
Fukuyama, Francis. 1995. *Trust: The Social Virtues and the Creation of Prosperity*. London: Hamish Hamilton.
Gasper, Des. 2004. *The Ethics of Development*. Edinburgh: Edinburgh University Press.
Geras, Norman. 1983. *Marx and Human Nature: Refutation of a Legend*. London: Verso.
Gewirth, Alan. 1998. *Self-Fulfillment*. Princeton: Princeton University Press.
Geyer, Felix, ed. 1996. *Alienation, Ethnicity, and Postmodernism*. Westport: Greenwood Press.
Geyer, Felix, and David Schweitzer, eds. 1981. *Alienation: Problems of Meaning, Theory and Method*. London: Routledge and Kegan Paul.

Giovanola, Benedetta. 2005. 'Personhood and Human Richness: Good and Well-Being in the Capability Approach and Beyond.' *Review of Social Economy* 63 (2): 249–267.

Giovanola, Benedetta. 2009. 'Re-thinking the Anthropological and Ethical Foundation of Economics and Business: Human Richness and Capabilities Enhancement.' *Journal of Business Ethics* 88 (3): 431–444.

Gorz, André. 1999. *Reclaiming Work: Beyond the Wage-Based Society*. Cambridge: Polity Press.

Gorz, André. (2003) 2010. *The Immaterial*. London: Seagull.

Hamilton, Lawrence. 1999. 'A Theory of True Interests in the Work of Amartya Sen.' *Government and Opposition* 34 (4): 516–546.

Hegel, Georg W.F. (1819–1831) 1955. *Lectures on the History of Philosophy*. London: Routledge and Kegan Paul.

Hegel, Georg W.F. (1823–1829) 1975. *Aesthetics: Lectures on Fine Art, Vol. I*. Oxford: Oxford University Press.

Hegel, Georg W.F. (1807) 1977. *Hegel's Phenomenology of Spirit*. Oxford: Oxford University Press.

Heller, Agnes. 1972. 'Towards a Marxist Theory of Value.' *Kinesis* 5 (1): 7–76.

Honneth, Axel. 2008. *Reification: A New Look at an Old Idea*. Oxford: Oxford University Press.

Horkheimer, Max. (1935) 1995. 'Remarks on Philosophical Anthropology.' Chapter 6 in *Between Philosophy and Social Science: Selected Early Writings*. Cambridge, MA: The MIT Press.

Israel, Joachim. 1979. *Alienation. From Marx to Modern Sociology: A Macrosociological Analysis*. Boston: Allyn and Bacon.

Jaeggi, Rahel. 2014. *Alienation*. New York: Columbia University Press.

Karatani, Kojin. 2003. *Transcritique. On Kant and Marx*. Cambridge, MA: The MIT Press.

Lefebvre, Henri. (1947) 1991. *Critique of Everyday Life. Volume 1: Introduction*, London: Verso.

Lefebvre, Henri. (1961) 2002. *Critique of Everyday Life. Volume II: Foundations for a Sociology of the Everyday*. London: Verso.

Lukács, Georg. (1966) 1975. *The Young Hegel. Studies in the Relations between Dialectics and Economics*. Cambridge, MA: The MIT Press.

Lukes, Steven. 1967. 'Alienation and Anomie'. In *Philosophy, Politics and Society*, edited by Peter Laslett and Walter Runciman, 75–96. Oxford: Basil Blackwell.

Lukes, Steven. 1985. *Marxism and Morality*. Oxford: Oxford University Press.

Lukes, Steven. 2005. *Power: A Radical View*. London: Palgrave Macmillan.

Lukes, Steven. 2008. *Moral Relativism*. London: Profile Books.

Marcuse, Herbert. (1936) 1968. 'The Concept of Essence'. Chapter 2 in *Negations: Essays in Critical Theory*. Boston: Beacon Press.

Marcuse, Herbert. (1941) 1977. *Reason and Revolution. Hegel and the Rise of Social Theory*. London: Routledge and Kegan Paul.

Marcuse, Herbert. (1932) 1987. *Hegel's Ontology and the Theory of Historicity*. Cambridge, MA: The MIT Press.

Marković, Mihailo. 1963. 'Marxist Humanism and Ethics.' *Science and Society* 27 (1): 1–22.

Marković, Mihailo. 1974. *From Affluence to Praxis: Philosophy and Social Criticism*. Ann Arbor: The University of Michigan Press.

Márkus, György. (1966) 2015. *Marxism and Anthropology*. NSW, Australia: Modem-Verlag.

Marx, Karl. (1867) 1990. *Capital, Volume I.* London: Penguin.

Marx, Karl. (1844) 1992. 'Economic and Philosophical Manuscripts.' In *Early Writings*, 279–400. London: Penguin.

Marx, Karl. (1857–1858) 1993. *Grundrisse*. London: Penguin.

Marx, Karl, and Friedrich Engels. (1845) 1956. *The Holy Family or Critique of Critical Critique.* Moscow: Foreign Languages Publishing House.

Marx, Karl, and Friedrich Engels. (1845–1846) 1976. 'The German Ideology.' In *Collected Works. Volume 5*. London: Lawrence and Wishart.

Maslow, Abraham. 1943. 'A Theory of Human Motivation.' *Psychological Review* 50 (4): 370–396.

McClung Lee, Alfred. 1972. 'An Obituary for 'Alienation'.' *Social Problems* 20: 121–127.

Mészáros, István. 1986. *Marx's Theory of Alienation*. London: Merlin Press.

Nussbaum, Martha. 1990. 'Aristotelian Social Democracy.' In *Liberalism and the Good*, edited by Bruce Douglass, Gerald Mara, and Henry Richardson, 203–252. New York: Routledge.

Nussbaum, Martha. 1992. 'Human Functioning and Social Justice. In Defense of Aristotelian Essentialism.' *Political Theory* 20: 202–246.

Nussbaum, Martha. 1995. 'Aristotle on Human Nature and the Foundations of Ethics.' In *World, Mind and Ethics: Essays on the Ethical Philosophy of Bernard Williams*, edited by Jimmy Altham and Ross Harrison, 86–131. Cambridge: Cambridge University Press.

Nussbaum, Martha. 1998. 'The Good as Discipline, the Good as Freedom.' In *Ethics of Consumption: The Good Life, Justice, and Global Stewardship*, edited by David Crocker and Toby Linden, 312–341. Lanham: Rowman and Littlefield.

Nussbaum, Martha. 1999. 'The Professor of Parody: The Hip Defeatism of Judith *The* Butler.' *New Republic* 22: 37–45.

Nussbaum, Martha. 2005. 'Capabilities as Fundamental Entitlements: Sen and Social Justice.' In *Capabilities Equality: Basic Issues and Problems*, edited by Alexander Kaufman, 44–70. New York: Routledge.

Nussbaum, Martha. 2011. *Creating Capabilities.* Cambridge, MA: The Belknap Press of Harvard University Press.

Nussbaum, Martha. 2012. 'Tragedy and Human Capabilities: A Response to Vivian Walsh.' In *The End of Value-Free Economics*, edited by Hilary Putnam and Vivian Walsh, 130–135. London: Routledge.

Nussbaum, Martha. 2018. *The Monarchy of Fear: A Philosopher Looks at Our Political Crisis*. Oxford: Oxford University Press.

Ollman, Bertell. 2001. *Alienation. Marx's Conception of Man in Capitalist Society*. Cambridge: Cambridge University Press.

Postone, Moishe. 1993. *Time, Labor, and Social Domination: A Reinterpretation of Marx's Critical Theory*. Cambridge: Cambridge University Press.

Psychopedis, Kosmas. 2000. 'New Social Thought: Questions of Theory and Critique.' In *The Politics of Change: Globalization, Ideology and Critique*, edited by Werner Bonefeld and Kosmas Psychopedis, 71–104. Basingstoke: Palgrave Macmillan.

Psychopedis, Kosmas. 2007. 'On the Logic of the Realization of Reason in Society and History.' In *Terror, Peace, and Universalism. Essays on the Philosophy of Immanuel Kant*, edited by Bindu Puri and Heiko Sievers, 93–110. New Delhi: Oxford University Press.

Putnam, Hilary, and Vivian Walsh. 2012. 'The Fall of Two Dichotomies, and the Need for a Macro-theory of Capabilities.' In *The End of Value-Free Economics*, edited by Hilary Putnam and Vivian Walsh, 214–225. London: Routledge.

Sayer, Derek. 1987. *The Violence of Abstraction: The Analytic Foundations of Historical Materialism*. Oxford: Basil Blackwell.

Schacht, Richard. 1970. *Alienation*. New York: Anchor Books.

Schacht, Richard. 1994. *The Future of Alienation*. Urbana: University of Illinois Press.

Schaff, Adam. 1980. *Alienation as a Social Phenomenon*. Oxford: Pergamon Press.

Schmidt, Alfred. 1971. *The Concept of Nature in Marx*. London: New Left Books.

Schmitt, Richard. 2003. *Alienation and Freedom*. Colorado: Westview Press.

Seeman, Melvin. 1959. 'On the Meaning of Alienation.' *American Sociological Review* 24 (6): 783–791.

Sen, Amartya. 1981. *Poverty and Famines: An Essay on Entitlement and Deprivation*. Oxford: Clarendon Press.

Sen, Amartya. 1983. *Poverty and Famines: Am Essay on Entitlement and Deprivation*. Oxford: Oxford University Press.

Sen, Amartya. 1984. *Resources, Values and Development*. Cambridge, MA: Harvard University Press.

Sen, Amartya. 1985a. 'Well-Being, Agency and Freedom: The Dewey Lectures 1984.' *The Journal of Philosophy* 82 (4): 169–221.

Sen, Amartya. 1985b. 'A Sociological Approach to the Measurement of Poverty: A Reply to Professor Peter Townsend.' *Oxford Economic Papers* 37 (4): 669–676.

Sen, Amartya. 1987a. *On Ethics and Economics*. Oxford: Basil Blackwell.

Sen, Amartya. 1987b. 'The Standard of Living: Lecture I, Concepts and Critiques.' In *The Standard of Living: The Tanner Lectures, Clare Hall, Cambridge 1985*, edited by Geoffrey Hawthorn, 1–19. Cambridge: Cambridge University Press.

Sen, Amartya. 1987c. 'The Standard of Living: Lecture II, Lives and Capabilities.' In *The Standard of Living: The Tanner Lectures, Clare Hall, Cambridge 1985*, edited by Geoffrey Hawthorn, 20–38. Cambridge: Cambridge University Press.

Sen. Amartya. 1990. 'Individual Freedom as a Social Commitment.' *New York Review of Books* 37: 49–54.

Sen, Amartya. 1992. *Inequality Reexamined*. Cambridge, MA: Harvard University Press.

Sen, Amartya. 1997. 'Radical Needs and Moderate Reforms.' In *Indian Development*, edited by Jean Drèze and Amartya Sen, 1–32. Delhi: Oxford University Press.

Sen, Amartya. 1998. 'The Living Standard.' In *Ethics of Consumption: The Good Life, Justice, and Global Stewardship*, edited by David Crocker and Toby Linden, 287–311. Lanham: Rowman and Littlefield.

Sen, Amartya. 1999a. *Commodities and Capabilities*, Oxford: Oxford University Press.

Sen, Amartya. 1999b. *Development as Freedom*, Oxford: Oxford University Press.

Sen, Amartya. 1999c 'Democracy as a Universal Value.' *Journal of Democracy* 10 (3), 3–17.

Sen, Amartya. 2006. *Identity and Violence. The Illusion of Destiny*. London: Penguin Books.

Sen, Amartya. 2009. *The Idea of Justice*. Cambridge, MA: The Belknap Press of Harvard University Press.

St. Claire, Asunción Lera. 2010. 'A Methodologically Pragmatist Approach to Development Ethics'. In *Capabilities, Power, and Institutions: Toward a More Critical Development Ethics*, edited by Stephen Esquith and Fred Gifford, 96–120. University Park: The Pennsylvania State University Press.

Steiner, Philippe. 2002. 'Division of Labour and Economics.' In *Durkheim Today*, edited by William Pickering, 87–106. New York: Berghahn Books.

Stiglitz, Jospeh, Amartya Sen, and Jean-Paul Fitoussi. 2009. *Report by the Commission on the Measurement of Economic Performance and Social Progress*. Accessed

11 October 2018. http://ec.europa.eu/eurostat/documents/118025/118123/Fitoussi+Commission+report.

Taylor, Charles. 1979. *Hegel and Modern Society*. Cambridge: Cambridge University Press.

Townsend, Peter. 1985. 'A Sociological Approach to the Measurement of Poverty – A Rejoinder to Professor Amartya Sen.' *Oxford Economic Papers* 37 (4): 659–668.

Tugendhat, Ernst. 1986. *Self-Consciousness and Self-Determination*. Cambridge, MA: The MIT Press.

Vansteenkiste, Maarten, Richard Ryan, and Edward Deci. 2008. 'Self-Determination Theory and the Explanatory Role of Psychological Needs in Human Well-Being.' In *Capabilities and Happiness*, edited by Luigino Bruni, Flavio Comim, and Maurizio Pugno, 187–223. Oxford: Oxford University Press.

Wilkinson, Richard, and Kate Pickett. 2010. *The Spirit Level: Why Equality is Better For Everyone*. London: Penguin.

Wright, Erik Olin. 2010. *Envisioning Real Utopias*. London: Verso.

5 The Capability Approach and the sociology of emotions

Emotions, suffering and the fragility of the social self

The two previous chapters explored the sociological resonance of agency and the benefits that can accrue for sociology if a normatively fortified notion of the person takes on board the conceptualization of agency in CA. I defended this reformulation of agency in CA drawing also on sociology's configuration of a social self. It was evident that this conception of the social self, apart from being grounded in the phenomenological and behavioural roots of symbolic interactionism, carried an additional normative load. This load, I suggested, has had a positive and a negative impact. The positive shift pertained to ontological considerations about what it means to be human; the negative conception of a social self, though not fully detached from the ontological baseline that I somehow heretically sought to resuscitate, derived from the suffering endemic to the human condition. In this chapter I extend both the positive and negative trajectories of the social self to the domain of emotions. A first justification for this decision is Nussbaum's CCL. She devotes a large bulk of her work to the normativity of emotions (Nussbaum 2001, 2004, 2013, 2016, 2018). Before I address the sociologically more relevant aspects of her work about emotions, I need to highlight briefly the sociological context that will serve as a template for the ensuing discussion.

A suitable starting point is a fundamental assumption that undergirds modernity. The moral individualism that furnished Durkheim's account of organic solidarity opens itself to diverse trajectories. While we lack the space to discuss these in detail, the sphere of individuation proved a recurring coda of nearly all social institutions in modernity. For Durkheim even 'religion' (the morally denser social configuration of solidarity) inscribed in its core value the dignity of the individual. Drawing on the ideals of the French Revolution the realization of individual freedom was of course hewed on socially validated rights yet it is beyond dispute that it propelled an unprecedented concern with the 'care of the self'. From Simmel's sharp analyses of the modern style of life and its cultivation of particularistic forms of individualism, Weber's retreat to the heroic integrity of individual character vis-à-vis a demonically efficient instrumental modernity, to contemporary accounts of the diverse ways of the self's presentation in a no longer solid but liquid everyday life, the focus continues to be the self and the realization (even self-management) of individual potentialities. Strengthened by technological extensions of our sociality (e.g. social media and communications) we now feel capable of taking the risk of extending our front-stage appearance to ever-wider circles of consociates.

Notwithstanding the many advantages this seemingly infinite drive to self-expansion has, the ensuing aggrandizement of individual particularity seems to come at some cost. Sanguine voices address the challenges for the social self that stem from relative deprivation and from ever-rising income inequality that gets 'under the skin' (Wilkinson and Pickett 2010; Bude 2018).[1] In this climate of 'liquid modernity', what Bauman calls 'adiaphorization' (indifference) is growing into something more than the self's defence against modernity's over-stimulation. A common denominator in all such narratives is that the modern self has a taut relation to collective emotions. As part of the controversy between liberalism and communitarianism, the notion of an exceedingly, and socially sanctioned, capable self seems to come up against its own limits. For now the issue is not so much the instrumentalization discourse that pessimist social theory alarmed intellectuals and lay persons alike, but, rather, the perplexing realization that the fragility of the self stems, somehow, from its own empowerment. This paradoxical intuition is aptly captured by Heinz Bude:

> A number of studies have been dedicated to the psychological effects of the spread of the other-directed character in societies such as ours. All of them describe the change in the individual, from a focus on conquest to a focus on empathy, as a shift in an existential question – namely, from 'what I am allowed to do?' to 'what am I capable of doing?' […] The sensitive self […] which seeks feedback and acknowledgment from others as it strives for self-realization, moves within the 'social construction of reality' right from the start. This self takes it for granted that its concept of itself is shaped only through its interaction with others. However, my fellow humans not only support my self-image, they also threaten my possibilities. The associated feeling of depressive inadequacy is aptly described by metaphors such as being suffocated, entangled, and engulfed. The pivot from the corset of permission to the mobilization of capability affects key concepts in communal life.
>
> (2018, 67–68)

The list of sociological sources invoked by Bude is rich and need not be reproduced here. Riesman's 'other-directedness', Sennett's 'corrosion of character', Giddens' 'transformation of intimacy' as well as the climate of a culture of narcissism that was adumbrated by Christopher Lash qualify as a diagnostic capital hard to ignore. Currently, this climate becomes even more attentive to a self-contained and 'resourceful' self in the face of reality's structural strains like, for instance, in the trends towards 'coaching' (see Bauman 2017a, 129–130). This paradox of a 'capable' yet fragile self is also confirmed by psychology (Ehrenberg 2010).[2]

It is Nussbaum's work that rehabilitates emotions into normative accounts of the social self. Her *Political Emotions* (2013), on which I will chiefly focus, furnishes CA with an emotional discourse and is often triggered by Kant's problematic of 'radical evil' (on the latter see Bernstein 2002; Neiman 2002) and the human propensity (indeed 'freedom') to prefer it. This inscrutability of the problem of evil Nussbaum aims to relativize. Arguing that public emotions of love and solidarity can be cultivated so that the evil part of the human self that thrives on other people's subordination and humiliation can be significantly tempered, Nussbaum makes a case for the social mediation of emotions.[3] Channels of 'processing' evil tendencies come from the pool of loving emotions in the human reservoir of instincts and from appropriate institutional frameworks that nourish them. Drawing mainly on social psychology and less on sociology Nussbaum (2013, Ch. 7) tackles the themes of the empathetic drive that social and developmental psychology has conceptualized, following Donald Winnicott, of the human 'capacity for concern'; the drive and essential component of the human condition called 'play' (again, her scientific evidence draws on Winnicott); the emotional reaction of disgust, when the latter is modelled to stigmatize others parcelling them into neat and subordinate categories (Goffman 1963); and the much discussed topic of conformity, in-group thought, peer group pressure and uncritical obedience to authority. (Here she draws from the pool of experiments by Solomon Ash and Stanley Milgram, which corroborate Arendt's thesis of the 'banality of evil'.)

I shall not probe into the details of Nussbaum's reading (2004) of Winnicott, whose findings she rightly connects to the social forces of love and recognition initiated by the roles and nourishment of caregivers. These align with Axel Honneth's work on normative emotions. Honneth (1995, (2010) 2014a), too, traces in the work of Donald Winnicott, John Bowlby and Jessica Benjamin the emotional substratum of prime trust that binds human beings in interactive nexuses of relationships of mutuality. And although Nussbaum never thematizes intersubjective recognition, it is clear that the process of engaging the 'other' as an object of worth and respect, as a being with a just claim to a life worth living is coloured by claims to recognition (Nussbaum 2004, 188). The difference that I stress, and makes perhaps CA wanting in terms of systematic presuppositions of the aspiring 'just society', is the reluctance to connect the social spheres of such healthy reciprocity. (One such attempt is made by Gasper and Truong (2010) but then again outside any institutional coordinates, although the 'streams' of development ethics of care that they chart is in all respects important.) This gap is what separates CA from contemporary reconstructions of a logic of institutional spheres of freedom. Let us then start exploring the overlap between CA and sociology on the politics of emotions.

'Capable' emotions and the good society (I): the politics of emotions

For Nussbaum, the focus on emotions is not only enunciated in the agent's capacity for a range of feelings, both positive (love, esteem, respect, sympathy, compassion) and negative (envy, fear, disrespect, shame, resentment); it is also registered in society's collective sentiments and in the symbolic formats that trigger the emotional capacities of the self. In *Political Emotions* (2013) Nussbaum suggests that emotions are relevant as public foci instantiated and cultivated in many different ways and in support of diverse political principles (from liberal democratic to fascist ones). The sociological twist in her argument concerns the public coordination of emotions in a number of ways: first in how a society commissions positive and negative emotions to its members in an organized fashion; or, antithetically, through conspicuous social omissions that trigger cumulative and diffuse negative emotions like, for example, retreatist moral apathy; second, any social order depends for its legitimacy on strong evaluations made by its members. People may think and judge a social order as legitimate or 'good' but this cognitive judgment is never entirely free of emotional anchorings on love, respect, awe and reverence. Nussbaum's focus on John Stuart Mill and Rabindranah Tagore reserves as common denominator not only the liberal humanism that she thinks is the political configuration suited to accommodate best plural identities but, additionally, the fact that both writers were inspired by Auguste Comte's religion of humanity. In sociology Comte's normativism found its formidable reconstruction in Durkheim's moral sociology. Both placed collective sentiments that enveloped a nation as a just moral order within a cosmopolitan horizon of possibility, founded on moral individualism and on the choices people have to shape the milieu they have reason to value. (I shall take up Durkheim later in this chapter.)

Among Nussbaum's other inspirations are Kant, Rousseau and Rawls. The 'political' underlining of emotions bears for Nussbaum on the problem of a just society conceived by those writers. It also clothes with emotional fabric the fact that 'living together' (Nussbaum 2008) is not a merely functional possibility or social interaction. Rather, it is informed by genuine normative feelings of mutual respect. To deduce the 'evaluative content' of emotions that serve a just political order, yet outside any culturally particularist monopoly is Nussbaum's ambition:

> My solution to this problem is to imagine ways in which emotions can support the basic principles of the political culture of an aspiring yet imperfect society, an area of life in which it can be hoped that all citizens overlap, if they endorse basic norms of equal respect: the area of what Rawls has called the 'overlapping consensus.
>
> (Nussbaum 2013, 6)

One thing that requires sociological recoding here is Nussbaum's admission that this overlapping space is one of the 'fundamental principles and constitutional ideals' (7). Thus a meta-level of coordination of citizens' commitment to a liberal culture that does not collapse under the freedoms it secures and provides for its citizens must be one of collective valuations. In their turn, these collective valuations must somehow gain purchase not only in people's minds but in their hearts too. This value-diffusion (associated by Talcott Parsons with the functional prerequisite of 'latent-pattern maintenance') is initially of concern to our 'consociates' (the nation) and secondarily to our 'contemporaries'. The latter category, particularly through the universalist content of 'love' (reconstructed outside primary group relations), sets the tone of wider configurations in solidary human togetherness, beyond the nation-state and thus is suitable only for a cosmopolitan ethic. It is in this sense that Nussbaum understands the 'political'. As she writes, the 'idea of the political, however, is understood in an inclusive way, as comprising all those institutions that influence people's life chances pervasively and over the entire course of their lives (John Rawls's notion of the "basic structure")' (16). These basic structures are on a first, strictly analytical level, tantamount to an agent's habitus (Bourdieu) or to an agent's capability to make choices along pattern-variables, themselves prescribed by social norms that cut across the available pairings of role dispositions, such as diffuseness versus specificity, achievement versus ascription, self-orientation versus collective-orientation, universalism versus particularism, affectivity versus affective neutrality. These pairings, which come from Parsons (1951), imply that emotions are cultivated, channelled and expressed in ways that can be legitimately sanctioned, even if they can challenge aspects of social order (as, for example, in the function of 'rationalized deviance' of profane humour's parody of the political establishment). On a second and more auspicious level these institutions constitute themselves ethical shapes that actualize the self's freedom. This essentially Hegelian approach to institutions that informs normative functionalism will be taken up in Chapter 6, although it is worth noting that it looms sociologically in rather unspecified terms in Nussbaum's defence of such institutional arrangements. The 'political' thus, since it permeates social life in its entirety, must be coded as a force that binds people to a just social order (and thus unites people under a common set of values). By contrast, the 'political' can unbound sentiments from the fundamental social relations (e.g. such is the argument in sociology about instrumental reason); it can decouple citizens from their very source of being, which is no other than the validity of their manifold social memberships (as in Habermas' notion of the life-world). To avoid charges of formalism here it is worth recalling that the order that deserves our devotion in emotional elation is one that requires several qualifications, condensed in the 'public culture of liberty, equality, and fraternity' (30).

Nussbaum renders Comte (with the appropriate critical distance at points) a programmatic thread for her book:

> Engaging with Comte will prove valuable for our project, since he responds with detailed proposals to the need I have identified – for a public culture based upon love and extended sympathy, which can support the goals of a just society and ensure the stability of its commitments.
>
> (58)

I shall leave aside for a moment the impression that nearly all the ingredients Nussbaum finds palatable in Comte were later upgraded by Durkheim, one of his best disciples. For the moment, let us encapsulate what Nussbaum retains from Comte (see indicatively, Comte 1975):

a The Kantian heritage and Comte's belief in the universal human morality. Genuine moral actions cannot be grounded on self-serving goals and Comte attaches to this a firm sociological ground.
b Part of her sociological recall of Comte suggests that he never divorced (contrary to much textbook orthodoxy) scientific judgments from their normative foundation. This foundation inheres in the object itself, namely society.
c In studying society and feelings of love and sympathy Comte begins from intimate social formations (i.e. family) before he extends these moral currents to wider social groupings, culminating with the nation in a form of morally grounded patriotism. (This 'exposition' of morality Kant only dimly foresaw with regards to social institutions; this project was carried further by Hegel, Durkheim, Parsons and currently Honneth.)
d In spite of Mill's criticisms of Comte, which Nussbaum mostly shares, she finds merit in Comte's desire to extend public rituals in order to solidify in human habits the love of the nation and as its corollary the sympathetic broadening towards our human fellows.

Notwithstanding this Comtean influence, Nussbaum (2013) finds in Mill and Tagore sanguine correctives to some of the myopic grandeur of Comte's project. These correctives are: the cultivation of sympathy under the auspices of a general religion, which enables individuals to visualize and set goals outside themselves; the disembarking of transcendent notions of immortality (a happy and fulfilled life may have no need to a notion of immortality, other than the one that sees oneself and her accomplishments continuing in the lives of her successors);[4] the diffusion of emotions across genders; the loosening of any moral fundamentalism (as in Comte's repulsion of heterodoxy); the deliberative scope given to education; and last but not least the contextual space of traditions, rituals, beliefs and values from which the quest of universality can expand and align with similar projects from different contexts.[5]

I lump together all these criticisms of Comte – via Mill and Tagore – not because they do not deserve detailed scrutiny but because, for the economy as well as substance of the argument, they have all been (critically) incorporated in Durkheim's projection of a just society in the shape of organic solidarity. This sociological reconstruction of an imperfect, 'aspiring' as Nussbaum prefers to call it, society is based, as I have argued in the previous chapters, on principles, implicit or explicit, of a humanist ontology. Nussbaum herself begins her chapter on Tagore's sympathetic revision of Comte with an epigraph from the former's work. This states that man's refusal to 'remain a four-footed creature' is an index of man's inherent potential for 'insubordination' (82). This 'permanent gesture', as the same passage reads, is taken up further by Nussbaum, albeit momentarily, in order to highlight that, for Tagore, the 'erect posture of the human body' (88) is an indication of the capacity (and freedom) to create new norms that refuse to abide by servitude and slavery. (Ernst Bloch's natural law project of 'orthopedia' that, as we suggested in Chapters 3 and 4, serves as the ultimate imagery of corporeality of a radical anthropological foundation that initiates the capacity to be free, comes immediately to mind.) Let us approach this goal following the reverse trail of negative emotions. I shall not follow Nussbaum's classification on negative emotions in all its rich exposition. Rather, the clusters of negative emotions that I shall introduce highlight in broad strokes the relevance for sociology of her discussion about emotions and norms.

Negative emotions unbound (I): disgust and shame

Beyond their ethical implications, Nussbaum treats negative emotions often in the context of legal controversies. For lack of competence I shall not address these arguments in any detail. Some sociologically relevant dimensions though are worthy of commentary.

It is to Nussbaum's credit that neither emotions nor compassion as their normative centrepiece are portrayed as risk-free emotional upheavals of the self. Rather, although part of human nature, some emotions can be intensely corrosive when sociopsychological circumstances do not keep them in check or, conversely, when they fail to be diverted to constructive criticism and self-criticism; or, even, when, because of such inertia of criticism, they stifle effort at self-fulfilment in the manifold opportunities offered in a just society patterned along the principles of political liberalism. Nussbaum's CCL is not designed as a full account of human nature and its positive capabilities. Human nature includes an array of negative emotions that if unchecked can translate into a heavy toll of suffering. There are also parts of human nature that are profane and scatological, which as Durkheim had argued, have indispensable functional value for human health. Nussbaum qualifies the recognition of these profane aspects when she promotes a society capable of humour and rationalization. Thus, as we have been discussing in our defence of human nature, the issue is less if such as an entity exists, but rather if what we know about it (its cooperative and corrosive potentials) continues to be relevant. Nussbaum's CCL shows us what components in human essence can envelop and nourish the ways in which we can abstract from our profane needs and unconscious drives, gain some partial control over these, and thematize them in the diverse ways in which human beings can look ironically and sarcastically at the human condition.[6]

In this context Nussbaum relies on Mary Douglas ((1966) 1985). The implication of the distinguished anthropologist's study on society's symbolic, functional and moral boundaries is taken to be far too contextually spread and thus cannot be particularly useful when invoked in the courtroom cases Nussbaum examines. She finds that disgust is a problematic emotion, insufficient in itself to denote offence taken and justify legal sanctions, often premised on the logic of classificatory anomalies. In taking distance from Douglas, Nussbaum recognizes the functional role of disgust, yet she rejects the cognitive, moral and systemic status of disgust as an anomaly that is imputed to it by Mary Douglas. On this point, she is more in line with Durkheim (an influence of Mary Douglas) who accommodates pathology in broader terms than what the category of anomaly would concede. In explaining his much debated theses on the normality of crime, Durkheim makes an analogy with disgust: 'Are there not distasteful functions in the physical organism whose regular exercise is necessary for individual health? Do we not dislike suffering? Yet an individual who did not experience it would be abnormal' ((1895) 1966, xxxviii). As is well known, Durkheim's point was that crime (and by extension the 'profane' elements of life) qualified as a pathological phenomenon only if its frequency and intensity exceeds the functional and moral conditions of a society's reproduction. This relativistic formulation is curbed to some degree, implicitly only, when Durkheim demarcates, but unfortunately does not pursue further, what society regards as normal. He thus makes the distinction between a normality of 'fact' (*normalité de fait*) and a normality of 'right' (*normalité de droit*) (59, translation amended, see also (1895) 1988, 152).[7] According to Durkheim, this shift is tantamount to a movement of consciousness from the 'externality' of the social fact as thing to the conception of the latter as a component of consciousness. Imprinted into the logic of society and thus overcoming relativism, the first type of normality aligns with the 'external' validity of collective consciousness in mechanical solidarity (e.g. a current 'duplication' of mechanical solidarity within organic solidarity is the communitarian turn of modernity's liberal democracies). Conversely, suffused by just principles of social order, organic solidarity generates social facts based on the normality of right (this is, as I contend, the logical and normative equivalent of liberalism in Nussbaum). It is not that mechanical solidarity does not have room for difference. It does. What makes it mechanical is the external mode by which that social order's elements relate to each other, thus seeing deviance from the 'norm' in terms of anomaly and threat to social cohesion. This is a crucial point to remember because when Nussbaum rescues disgust as a functional modality that prevents us from regressing into the profane and merely animal aspects of our human constitution (history is replete with diminutions of the 'other' through imagery and rhetoric that energized disgust), she does so from the perspective of the core values of a liberal society that makes room for dissent. These spaces for freedom of the individual give even to 'disgust' a voice in the courtroom, yet with, as Nussbaum demonstrates, fallacious reasoning. This reasoning makes itself vulnerable to arguments that have, all too often and tragically in history, resorted to disgust to denigrate the 'other' to the status of the subhuman, the filthy, the polluted. For our purposes Durkheim too connected the familiarity with the profane facets of the human being with the very substance of ethics (the realm of the sacred)![8]

To be able to stand beyond the classifications of sacred–profane or purity–danger requires, as Goffman (1974) has impressively shown, a mediating frame. The 'meta-frame', so to speak, which Nussbaum adumbrates has room for irony, parody, sarcasm, dissent. For Nussbaum (2004, 59–60, 76) far from being value-neutral, a liberal (modern) society is one based on the core value of respect for the fact that 'reasonable disagreement' about ultimate values is an irreducible ingredient of public life. Nussbaum's liberal society generates all sorts of diverse frames that act as refractory and deflective devices that mediate the continuum between conformity and deviance. The task, of course, is how well these frames function as 'evaluation spaces' of our profane reality and whether these frames set the profane object (e.g. sex, defecation, fetishism, violence, death) into a broader context of meaning, so that ultimately the frontal dimension of the object is immersed into the back-stage information density of the frame. By contrast, the legal injunction against disgust or the moral outrage of suspending 'frames' in how negative emotions are addressed in public life, pose a serious risk for societies as they create pools of pent up frustration and fundamentalist de-differentiations in intersubjective relations and the meanings that sustain them.[9] Given Nussbaum's calls to placing 'disgust' in proper frames (e.g. children's toilet training, the cultural intermixing of the attractive and the disgusting in sexuality) the argument she advances against extirpating disgust from public life's thematizations is essentially Durkheimian and quite resonant for institutional arrangements in liberal modernity, although she is careful to distance herself from linear and Eurocentric accounts of disgust's marginalization (see her critique of Norbert Elias' 'civilizing process' thesis (Nussbaum 2004, 115–116)).

Nussbaum's reservation against the functional and legal role of shame in mitigating acts of deviance and crime moves along the same lines. As with disgust, Nussbaum seems to endorse a symbolic interactionist framework for understanding deviance. That Goffman's (1963) work on stigma figures so prominently (Nussbaum 2004, 250–271), is one index of her insistence on the 'political' construction of normality and deviance, a distinction that appears as hierarchical, exclusive and ultimately corrosive. Nussbaum's reluctance to consider functionalist explanations (mostly conflated with Etzioni's communitarian curbing of important liberties) prevent her from exploring the richer meanings of normality. Furthermore, conflict-theory perspectives surface sporadically in her work only as a categorial area (the poor, the unemployed) for prospective stigmatization and not as a deeper challenge to the economic structures that render people vulnerable to social stigma. We should not however ignore the fact that Nussbaum is attentive to issues of 'materiality' (344). Whether in the form of non-embarrassment about bodily decay and disability, in the form of coping and containing disgust and shame at bodily functions, or even in the Marxian sense of a theory of needs, materiality is front stage in her account: First, as an effort to neutralize legal and popular invocation of the profane aspects of the human body so that people cannot suffer legal and tacit sanctions by recourse to this factor (rather than the criminal intent); second, when societies are egregiously lacking the appropriate values, institutions and culture for priming the 'sacred' aspects (i.e. human dignity) for every single individual in their vicinity. Then the safety valves and diverse options liberal societies reserve for coping with disgust and shame give the latter an undue role in marking 'us' versus 'them' boundaries and thus of a de facto normality that stigmatizes, humiliates and excludes (on the trail from inequality to toxic emotions, see Wilkinson 2005, 201, figure 6.2).

One issue, as we already noted, is the way in which Nussbaum understands key notions of normative functionalism. The 'normal' is rightly associated with the 'normative' (Nussbaum 2004, 217–218, 255). Yet this conflation is utilized as an opportunity to relax the rigidity of the distinction between the 'normal' and the 'unusual'. The Goffmanesque reading Nussbaum adopts leads her to the critical scrutiny of covert, complex, sophisticated but ultimately flawed justifications of shaming as a mechanism of deterrence, retribution and rehabilitation. What though is recurring as a blind spot in CA is the notion of the normal in the sense ascribed to it by Durkheim's conception of Society as the ultimate realm of valuation of the very principles Nussbaum harnesses on the liberal society. Thus, her understanding of ultimate values (328) forfeits the ultimate grounding of values in the very idea of human dignity that her liberal society aims to protect, envelop and cultivate. If shame and disgust should be acknowledged as ingredients of the human condition – in all probability unlikely to be completely extinguished, as they also fulfil positive functions in society – then a society 'based on the idea of human dignity and on social relations characterized by reciprocity and mutual respect' part of which includes 'respect for differing conceptions of the ultimate good in human life' (321) must always prime citizens' right to this fundamental liberty and never let shame or disgust occupy the basis for dealing with legal matters.

This ultimate rejection of shame as a ground for legal justification and action against those whose acts 'offend' the 'norm' should not be taken to imply that shame is evacuated from any moral functions. Drawing on sociology again and commenting on Barbara Ehrenreich's *Nickel and Dimed* (2002), Nussbaum (212) connects shame to the complicity one may feel when reading the stories of lowly-paid jobs, abysmal working conditions, abuse at work as 'exchanges' for a barely acceptable living standard for millions of American women and men. Consequently, a 'winner-take-all' mind-set in the US (200) where health and will to perfection reach fantastic proportions, is also one that is more likely to suffer, since for all those 'others', disability, racial, ethnic or class identity translates all too easily into collective perceptions of ascribed and irrecuperable deficits. Such one-dimensional collective validations of acceptable goals hide alternative ways of opening spaces for people's capabilities, resulting often in conformist adaptations of someone's identity as a ticket to normality (as Nussbaum notices (292) acting 'white' is a typical syndrome). With this point in mind it is clear that Nussbaum's vision of a liberal society remains quite radical in its implications when value asymmetries augment the distance between core societal principles and established means to achieve self-flourishing. Although initially deep structures of power remain unaddressed in her account, rigid identity building (like the idea of the 'perfect' White Anglo-Saxon Protestant adult) depends on 'constructed' classifications, as those which – again via Goffman's (1963, 135–139) distinction between public/private, normal/stigmatized realms – Nussbaum (312) displaces in the domain of 'fictions'. Here we encounter

Nussbaum's radical theoretical intimations that, if taken to their logical conclusion, challenge the deepest and most embedded classifications of modern society. At the same time the difficulties that stem from this universe of 'social construction' begin to appear. Nussbaum has to posit some meta-classification from the standpoint of which we can observe socially corrosive and ethically demeaning classificatory matrices and distinctions like those she so robustly challenges. Because Nussbaum does not consider the possibility that classifications can possess an unconditional normative validity (without this the liberal society she defends cannot prime human dignity as a moral code that keeps in check subclassifications) she gives up the merits of normative functionalism, many of which are presupposed in the normatively muscular but transcendentally mute CA.

Negative emotions unbound (II): envy and *ressentiment*

Drawing mainly on John Rawls' discussion of envy in the last sections of his *Theory of Justice* ((1971) 1999) Nussbaum focuses on those conditions that render envy a negative emotion. The wider pool from which envy emanates is not judged to be a spring of merely negative feelings or outcomes in the human tendency to compare ourselves to others. Nussbaum contends that:

> [e]mulation and resentment are both healthy emotions in a decent society: the former encourages the individual to be better, and the latter encourages the society to be better. Envy has no such constructive function, and while it can spur individuals on to hard work and personal achievement, its rancor can indeed prove harmful.
>
> (2013, 342)

The deep-seated roots of envy are not denied by Nussbaum even in the ideal conditions of 'the most decent and just society' (342).[10]

The structurally embedded problem of 'ressentiment' is put forward with clarity by Max Scheler:

> *Ressentiment* must therefore be strongest in a society like ours, where approximately equal rights (political or otherwise) or formal social equality, publicly recognized, go hand in hand with wide factual differences in power, property, and education. While each has the 'right' to compare himself with everyone else, he cannot do so in fact. Quite independently of the characters and experiences of individuals, a potent charge of *ressentiment* is here accumulated by the very *structure of society.*
>
> (Scheler (1915) 1961, 50 [original emphasis])

Modern society's differentiation of functions, organizational complexity and occupational specialization mitigates social gaps because it brings people closer in the interdependence wrought by advanced division of labour; second, because in such a pluralistic and differentiated social system 'no single scale is relevant for all' (Nussbaum 2013, 344). This last point bears on the Weberian theory of social stratification when, for instance, high status may abhor class privileges, although both can enjoy high placement in social stratification. The upshot here is that, through the lens of the Weberian hostility to issues of justice, Rawls' appeal to internal moderation in social spaces that may incite undue envy blurs the criteria for hierarchical orderings of valued class, status and power. This happens, we can surmise, for all those reasons that normative functionalism calibrated as a just relation of interdependence and relative autonomy among different subsystems. This is the track I shall elaborate in the next chapter. Suffice to add here that the syndrome of envy must be tackled in the continuum that begins with the placement of envy as an ineradicable feature of the human psyche and society and the vision – from Marx to Rawls – that 'what a social system must not do clearly is to encourage propensities and aspirations that it is bound to repress and disappoint' (Rawls (1971) 1999, §81). The first approach is taken by the still unsurpassed sociological compendium of envy by Helmut Schoeck (1969) who traces envy across cultures and different historical epochs. The second approach leads us to the sociology of structural-functionalism. Both Merton and Parsons conceived of the problem of envy and its derivatives (rancor, resentment). The former is forced to visualize a society of less distance – in terms of viable and fair opportunities – between societal values (goals) and the institutionalized opportunities (means) to achieve them, and hence to contain envy's toxicity. Parsons, too, grasped the problem as an acute threat of modern, highly competitive societies, geared to individualism (on global individualism's costs on emotions, see Bauman 2017a, 99–100; Elliot and Lemert 2009). The syndrome of 'winners/losers' and a concomitant 'sour grapes' mentality on the part of the latter make the modern society's 'genuine standards of fair competition' the 'critical problem' (Parsons 1954, 330).

Operating through the filters of any sort of 'impression management' technique that internet users may put up as front-stage performance hoping to maximize trust and sincerity in communication, *ressentiment* proliferates through the spectre of anonymity. Nussbaum (2010b) approaches through the lens of *ressentiment* the problem of internet slander, threat and generally of objectifying the other behind the veil of simulated and anonymous identities, especially when this 'other' are women. She draws on *ressentiment* through the reciprocal tie that binds two parties together in what at least one party regards to be a deeply unequal and unworthy relationship, even if the latter is confined to secondary and large impersonal groups rather than threatening primary ones where the emotional stakes are usually higher. For Nussbaum, Nietzsche's notion of 'slave morality' finds its technically possible release of *ressentiment* in the anonymous virtual plateaus of the internet. Thus, celebrities and people of high status can (eventually) be 'subordinated' via the imaginary (yet real in its consequences) universe of 'compensation' for missed opportunities, ascribed deficiencies, unbridgeable value-wars. As Nussbaum notes (2010b, 78), to effect a strike, the slanderer (who is interested not simply in a private fantasy of omnipower but in actually hurting the 'victim') has to operate in a zone of feasibility where minor celebrities would 'depend' on reading the libellous or pornographic content, while the very rich and famous would not obviously bother.

Returning to the inbuilt in human beings 'primitive shame', Nussbaum recognizes its sociological tuning when it allows persons to relate to others in a mutually coordinated test of the reality principle. She perceived though the same risks that we gleaned from the work of Simmel, Scheler, Bude and Ehrenberg – although none of these authors are mentioned in her article – when societies cultivate an excessive perception of independence and individual 'self-sufficiency'. For Nussbaum:

> A social fact that augments shame is the tendency of some societies to define the ideal adult as self-sufficient, independent, lacking in deep needs with respect to others. In many societies, such pictures are held out to young people—but far more often to males than to females (82).

The fiction of cutting loose from all attachments and (inter)dependence, cultivates a perception of a self, similar to the egoistic syndrome that Durkheim feared about modernity's centrifugal cost for human autonomy. In commenting on a review of the volume (Levmore and Nussbaum 2010) where Nussbaum's chapter appears, Bauman (2017b, 27) adds to the concern over the surging anonymity of offence Arendt's reminder about diffuse and floating responsibility, a problem that surfaces in Nussbaum's accounts on Ash, Milgram, and Zimbardo. Nussbaum's immanent critique of Nietzsche culminates as follows:

> Above all, however, what we really need is what Nietzsche, I am sure, would have hated most of all: a true 'slave revolt,' a 'revaluation of values' that would put the 'morality of pity' (i.e., a morality centrally based upon compassion for weakness and suffering) in place of the will to power as a key social aspiration. Or, even more radically, a revolution that would show that the need to dominate is a form of weakness, the ability to allow another person to be whole and real a sign of strength. *Pace* Nietzsche, this 'slave revolt' would not be inspired by ressentiment. It would be an attempt to undo the work of ressentiment, and it would be inspired by compassion, respect for the dignity of each human individual, and a sense of human interdependence.
>
> (2010b, 86 [original emphasis])

Nussbaum offers here an interpretation of Nietzsche based on immanent critique and reconstruction. She is right, I think, to champion a 'slave revolt' that has transcended *ressentiment*, based on the liberal society's reciprocal emotions and the value of human dignity. She is though wrong in her overall appreciation of Nietzsche, not only here but on other occasions too (e.g. Nussbaum 1997b) where Nietzsche's virtues as a political thinker are limited to the domain of emotion. It needs to be taken into consideration that Nietzsche has suffered from the poststructural confiscation of his thought. As a result, normative readings of Nietzsche have been occluded by hegemonic poststructuralist approaches. Thus, against this current, Nietzsche's political thought hides other dimensions. For example, the idea that modern civilization 'shall perish through the lack of slavery' (Nietzsche 1872) imparts to Nietzsche a concern for the real conditions of slavery (and this is what he learns from classical Greece, namely that art is implicated in its process of production with pain and misery of all who slavishly laboured for its production)[11] as opposed to ideological illusions that are promulgated by liberals and socialists alike who both tend to regard slavery as a thing of the past. Similarly, Nietzsche's hostility to compassion stems from the fact that the latter serves as a surrogate for solidarity by those who are reduced to 'slavery' (i.e. the capability deprivations that Nussbaum has in mind). It is a surrogate emotion because a true release of solidarity would imply revolutionary praxis. If this is a valid trail of thought, then benign emotions may just as well assume the function of 'state apparatuses': In their act of forging micro-solidarities they can undermine the structural deficits of solidarity and thus restrict it only to the civic friendship that Nussbaum adduces, or limiting it to the field, as Kant thought, of artistic perfection.

'Capable' emotions and the good society (II): empathy or sympathy?

Nussbaum defines human empathy as 'the ability to imagine the situation of the other, taking the other's perspective' (2013, 145). For her part, sociologist Candace Clark (1997) links empathy to the type of 'mental interaction' (34) that enables a person to reconstruct the physical constitution, the cognitive frame of mind and the emotional condition of other actors. Weber's more nuanced methodological prescription of *Verstehen*, namely to identify social patterns (crystallized in ideal-typical constructs) within which actors' own intended meanings are being articulated, is generally bracketed by Clark as she focuses on physical, cognitive and emotional empathy. Her explanation is helpful though because she stresses our biological capacities to register empathy with others on these levels, but also because she regards empathy as a necessary ingredient for sympathy, reserving for the latter the sociological value of human connectedness in societies based on ethical emotions. I shall use the latter understanding of empathy (more in line with Mead's notion of the 'generalized other') as the necessary, yet not sufficient, condition for sympathy, which entails identification with the suffering of others and is thus an ethical emotion. Following Adam Smith ((1759) 1984, 43), the 'word sympathy in its most proper and primitive signification, denotes our fellow-feeling with the suffering' rather than with the enjoyment of others. Nussbaum recognizes though that empathy retains diverse shades of meaning. Using the normatively loaded sense of empathy as the ability to identify with another person's suffering has a major advantage over the Weberian methodology of *Verstehen*. Used heuristically, empathy enables us to recognize others as valid foci of human experience, even if their acts are ethically abominable. Indeed this sort of empathy is mistakenly limited to a Weberian methodology *stricto sensu.*[12]

The neo-Kantian heritage that forms the backdrop of the Weberian recourse to interpretive understanding as a result of the deeper epistemological deficit in the *hiatus irrationalis* omits the phenomenology of sympathy in the work of Max Scheler. For Scheler:

> the *essential* character of human consciousness is such that the community is in some sense implicit in every individual, and that man is not only part of society, but that society and the social bond are an essential part of himself; that not only is the "I" a member of the "We", but also the "We" is a necessary member of the "I"
>
> ((1912) 1954, 229–230 [original emphasis]).[13]

Against sociological approaches (Turner 2010) that reduce normativity to the neurological facts that make empathy possible,[14] research findings suggest that empathy has also a dark side. As celebrity psychologist Steven Pinker notes, aside from the fact that empathy is parochial and grandiose in its ambitions (would we really need or have the extraordinary emotional resources to grapple with distant suffering?), its impact requires support from abstract principles and norms. As he writes:

> Mirror neurons notwithstanding, empathy is not a reflex that makes us sympathetic to everyone we lay eyes upon. It can be switched on and off, or thrown into reverse, by our construal of the relationship we have with the person.
>
> (Pinker 2011, 591)[15]

Nussbaum (2013, 146) also emphasizes the insufficient scope of empathy versus compassion, particularly because of the instrumentalization risks entailed in an over-reliance on empathy (e.g. the lawyer who resorts to empathy in order to confuse witnesses). Instead thus of directly empathizing with someone's plight – and Adam Smith has famously questioned this potential when he noted that our shock at a major calamity in China is quickly 'switched off' by the most minor of misfortunes in our closer milieu – the normative demand could be reformulated as: 'Treat everyone in such a manner as if she would deserve your empathy'. The prerogative here refers to the demand for institutional arrangements and just norms the actuality of which would render empathetic epiphanies, as Pinker calls them, tangent on policies, norms and abstract values. The demand for institutionalized values of justice, equality, freedom and solidarity incorporate the goals of empathy but refuse to accept the superhuman burden placed on the empathic agent. Thus, institutional normativism can be read now as an 'as-if' regulative recalibration of empathy. If institutions are marked by substantive and not merely formal justice, it is as if I could empathize with someone's plight or deserved claims to justice by virtue of this someone's humanness.

The 'as-if' modality we suggested, if it is to affect those at great distance from us, requires some idea of how emotions could be institutionally engineered. As Nussbaum's keen defence of emotions admits, benign emotions that strengthen solidarity, love, peace and justice among other ethical goals are better served within 'just' patterns of action. Nussbaum writes:

> When you feel sympathy for the poor, it is fine to view that as occasion for philanthropy, but it is better to use that energy to create a decent tax system and a set of welfare programs. Emotions in this way operate at two levels. Once laws and institutions are reasonably just, emotions sustain them. But they also create motivations to improve those laws and institutions. When that happens, we might say that the institutions themselves embody the insight of emotions.
>
> (2013, 135)

This is the task of the next chapter: That is, to justify sociologically this bridge where justice moves from emotions to institutions and, furthermore, to probe into Nussbaum's defence of social justice in a 'society that is already pretty good' (136). What does this value-judgment about the solidified worth of stable patterns of social life mean, sociologically speaking, for the institutions CA defends?

In fortifying the nation as a living and spiritual entity Nussbaum (210–211, 225) cites approvingly the French philosopher Ernest Renan and his famous treatise on the nation. In conjunction with those facets of Comte's sociology that Nussbaum finds attractive for CA, the configuration of patriotism, solidarity and inclusive nation points to Durkheim's sociology. The points of convergence between Durkheim's organic solidarity and Nussbaum's accommodation of patriotism in the aspiring just society that she visualizes are too many to keep ignoring. Durkheim's thought owes to Renan (Peyre 1960) more than his own expressed antipathies (Durkheim (1885) 1975, 374) betray. The upshot here is that, like Durkheim – and Hegel before him – Nussbaum seeks to preserve a differentiated unity of collective sentiments (the nation). This configuration hits two birds with one stone: It is modelled with sufficiently pluralistic scope and particularistic channels for expressive love and solidarity, yet it also cultivates a patriotic love for the nation that is no way incumbent upon similar collective sentiments held by other nations. There is, in other words, a latent pact of solidarity based on universal values of justice, equality and inclusion that make the aspiring just society a nation of cosmopolitan ethics. The role of feelings (and not only of abstract normative principles) in shaping the collective trust of social members is channelled through religious moments of collective effervescence, which traverse not only the rituals most commonly associated with civil religion but extend to secular celebrations of togetherness. For Nussbaum, these episodes of collective love for the nation retain the pleasure principle, so to speak, of early childhood development as a catalyst for intersubjective trust. Beyond institutional processes and safety valves that preserve legitimation, emotional identifications carry a eudaimonistic dimension and thus attach citizens to a collective ideal that they produce and reproduce. Of course, both the religious and secular domains of ritualistic celebrations are subject to shallow demotions and glamorous inflations. (From the cathedrals of consumption and the tourist gaze to local folklore festivities and art-house film festivals, the distance is considerable.) Durkheim would in all likelihood acknowledge the non-elitist and democratic spirit of those collective rituals that strengthen and uplift people when these ideals (as particularistic expressions) function to cherish values, broader than individuals and link together past, present and future orientations of the community in diffuse channels that reach the entire social body. The objector who may see in these values – over and above the individual – an unconditional glorification of collective identity and thus discern authoritative seeds, would need to jettison the normative presuppositions inserted by Durkheim when the latter defends the collective validity of organic solidarity. These presuppositions require particularity (hence they accommodate pluralism), yet aspire for justice and equality.

The Homeric beasts of Scylla and Charybdis that Nussbaum adumbrates address issues that troubled Durkheim too. For Nussbaum, Scylla includes the 'dangers of misplaced and exclusionary values', the 'imposition of ritual performance' on minorities and the 'excessive emphasis on solidarity and homogeneity that threatens to eclipse the critical spirit' (2013, 207). Charybdis, too, poses a serious barrier to proper patriotism, because it makes values far too abstract and diffuse and thus introduces through the back door 'watery motivation'. By this phrase, which Nussbaum (219) cites from Aristotle, one perceives the risk of transferring care to every citizen in the polis and thus diluting the factor of 'ownership' that makes individuals spirited and passionate about goals they have reason to value. 'Watery motivation' is tantamount to excessive impartiality and it is Habermas, who, for Nussbaum, represents this position, as he neglects to deploy a sufficiently motivated love for the nation *as if* it were the entire humanity.[16] Thus, the Habermasian institutionalism lacks the eudaimonistic channels of coordinating values to the actual citizens' flesh-and-blood lives and life chances. The parade of historical figures and leaders (like Washington, Lincoln, MLK, Gandhi or Nehru), emblems, monuments and anthems, allows Nussbaum to construct the material foundation that keeps a nation's memory alive and ready to replenish collective sentiments. This argument is also Durkheimian enough and opens up the sociological debate about the symbolic construction of memory. Nussbaum does not ignore the malign turn that such classifications of ideal and material culture can take under contingent historical circumstances. She regards, however, the societal carving of collective struggles, sacrifices and heritage in rituals and monuments as capable of providing flesh on the bone of ideals, even if those extend to actors, communities outside the geopolitical contour of a nation, and embrace humanity, as well as, even, the future generations. What demarcates Nussbaum's excursus on the visibility of patriotism from conservative or even reactionary theses is its universalistic ethic of peace and solidarity. This vision of justice that renders bellicose interpretations of emblems obsolete operates through the lens of a sort of ecumenical vision of solidarity ebbed in time with the maximum of international cooperation and adjustment. Thus, the collective ideal that she defends is never severed from the normative backbone of its core values, which is no other than the imperative of human flourishing. Because the vision of patriotism that she enunciates takes a leap backwards into the struggles and sacrifices in the making of national identity, it inevitably bumps on the seemingly only metaphysical question that requires a compensation for those whose lives were lost: winners and losers, aggressors and peacemakers. The division between purity and danger that intensified under eras of collective effervescence and heightened moral confusion is not merely suspended when the forces of justice and peace redraw political classifications. Now, the inclusive pattern of ideals, presumably if one talks about liberal democracies today, has to incorporate not merely current dissenters but also the lineage of those who represented the bellicose moments of danger. This progressive shift in inclusiveness may have to involve reparations and a genuine pardon for crimes committed and sufferings that were imposed on people whose inclusion is part of an aspiring society. Forgiveness, not merely as a Christian modality but as a logical step that recognizes the partiality and errors of one-sided categories that elicited escalation of subordination, exclusion, segregation, ethnic cleansing or genocide, figures as the trope for any broadening (pragmatic but also normative) that unites rather than divides people. Thus, in order to accomplish the broadening of identities in an inclusive patriotism, the love of the nation must deploy a surplus evaluation, one that somehow maintains *this* or *that* nation as a 'homeland' for humanity. While this is a geographical impossibility and is thus practically unreachable, yet, as Durkheim's work on religion intimated, it was conceptually inscribed into the very core of religious totemism in tribal societies. For Durkheim, it is modernity's organic solidarity that encapsulates this collective version of a categorical imperative:

> If each state has as its chief aim, not to expand, or to lengthen its borders, but to set its own house in order and to make the widest appeal to its members for a moral life on an ever higher level, then all discrepancy between national and human morals would be excluded. […] The more societies concentrate their energies inwards, the more they will be diverted from the disputes that bring a clash between cosmopolitanism – or world patriotism, and patriotism […] As long as there are States, so there will be national pride, and nothing can be more warranted. But societies can have their pride, not in being the greatest or the wealthiest, but in being the more just, the best organized and in possessing the best moral constitution.
>
> ((1890–1900) 1992, 74–75)

This projection of patriotism of a non-belligerent calibre combines a realist with an idealist trajectory for collective solidarity. As Nussbaum writes:

> Independence, as Nehru constructs the story of the new nation, is also no occasion for warlike self-assertion. For the idea of an exclusionary and

> warlike India, an image cherished by many of his countrymen, Nehru substitutes the idea of an India at work, characterized by incessant labor and striving toward the goal of eradicating human suffering – not only in India, but everywhere.
>
> (2013, 247)

Thus, in spite of emphasis on a particular nation designed under the universalistic ideal of justice, the content of which is freedom (at least in the Hegelian version I find to be better suited for this discussion), Nussbaum's trail cuts short this love for humanity from even more radical foundations. These are not altogether absent in Nussbaum. In a sense, there can be nothing more radical as a normative goal than the sort of cunning of love that Nussbaum's project on emotions champions. This love of the city 'gets under one's skin' and binds a social fabric in 'many different and incompatible ways' (393) weaving for people's short *durée* a common future. The common weal of humanity must rely not only on the overlapping consensus among communities and traditions; a vast domain of human accomplishment risks being rendered residual and thus open to merely particularistic or fundamentalist (as we shall see shortly but also in Chapter 7) regenerations of solitarist identities.[17]

Sympathy figures as a basic building block of Sen's version of CA. Most notably Sen (1982) aims to demonstrate the irrationality and explanatory poverty of the so-called rational economic man. For Sen the individual is not an isolated entity incapable of acting in consideration of those intermediate spaces (groups, institutions, community). Rather, individuals are capable of sympathy (Sen rebuts the doxastic reduction of sympathy to a form of self-interest) and capable of acting on the basis of moral commitments. Particularly on the latter, Sen adheres to the tactic of accommodating a free-floating moral commitment that can inform a person's preferences without thus being caught between the pincers of egoism and some sort of universal morality. In *The Idea of Justice*, Sen devotes considerable space to those motifs of extended sympathy. Indeed, in an almost Hegelian trope, Sen talks of the 'reach of reason' (2009, 46) and considers Adam Smith's impartial spectator as a heuristic device that initiates a cross-cultural learning process of mutual corrigibility of standpoints. Particularly telling is the occasion where this broadening is initiated from those nations that have committed crimes against humanity (e.g. Japan) or have caused other forms of major harms to fellow beings elsewhere. Learning, the function of guilt, empathy, sympathy, critical scrutiny of self, as well as forgiveness (the latter also as a 'logical' transcendence of error and not merely emotional healing of intersubjective wounds) figure as multiple elements in this process of reason's extended reach. This extended reach raises the capacity of individuals to 'observe' the plight of others in ways that cannot be accommodated by a vision of human beings that is governed exclusively by *amour de soi*. Thus, Sen (185) discerns in Adam Smith three possibilities of a broadened view of human behaviour: 'sympathy', 'generosity' and 'public spirit'. Taking up the sequence from Smith to Rawls, Sen adduces sociology and its findings about social cooperation. Not only is cooperation conceived as a social necessity, but also it is held to emerge from the will of individuals themselves. This recurring and central premise in the social contract tradition does not enjoy a Hobbesian interpretation in Sen, but, rather, moves in the opposite direction, the one that Durkheim designed as a response to the Hobbesian problem of order. The force of affective sentiments that Durkheim's findings and theoretical elaborations reveal captures the normative glue of the collective, beyond the functional and utilitarian justifications for human interdependence.

But this overcoming of unfreedoms is couched on a sympathetic capacity with regard to being interested (rather than disinterested) in what happens around us, particularly when it comes to the plight and suffering of fellow human beings. This sympathy requires demystification. As Sen suggests against narrow utilitarian conceptions of human psychology, the 'effectiveness of the press and news media' (1990, 54) is premised (indeed rendered possible) on the assumption (actually a fact of the human condition) that people are not indifferent and care for others. To be sure, ideological forms of 'caring' for the suffering of others are currently at work in the same media environment that includes manipulative filtering of relevant information. Yet the valence of sympathy is neither exhausted in narcissistic simulacra of humanitarian faddishness or be dissolved into a postsocial 'care for the self'.[18] Rather, the media's capability to steer public sentiments and indignation serve as a catalyst for realizable conversion of these moral sentiments of outrage to pressure on governments, to activism, to collective mobilization, to new legislation.

The social self and cultural problems of identity

What is the implication of sympathy as an act of identity broadening? Sen, particularly in his writings on cultural identity, tackles the proclivity of cultural blindness for the agent's understanding of her identity. The negative implication of such reductionism truncates the agent's capability to take the standpoint of others, an essential component of our constitution as a socially interacting persons.[19]

In a candid self-description Sen unfolds the plural identities a person may hold:

> I can be, at the same time,' he writes 'an Asian, a Bengali with Bangladeshi ancestry, an American or British resident, an economist, a dabbler in philosophy, an author, a Sanskritist, a strong believer in secularism and democracy, a man, a feminist, a heterosexual, a defender of gay and lesbian rights, with a nonreligious lifestyle, from a Hindu background, a non-Brahmin, and a nonbeliever in an afterlife (and also, in case the question is asked, a non-believer in a "before-life" as well).
>
> (2006, 19)

The richness of ascribed and achieved statuses that Sen adduces here captures what for many people comprises a status-set with diverse audiences as addressees.

The social self, as a holder of these plural identities and memberships, learns to coordinate the different sets of expectations, adjusting them to each sphere of sociality. Thus, it is expected that the agent is capable (and willing) to try and take on board many roles in society and to sensibly protect his status-set and personality from identity-insurgencies generated by competing status groups. Juggling the many identities that constitute our status-set in society, indeed enjoying the very learning process of competent participation across diverse social memberships, must presuppose objective possibilities that are in place and encourage this socially rich self to emerge and to flourish. Indeed Sen (177–178) has sociology in mind when he seeks to augment the consideration of 'social context' and 'situatedness' to include the multiple affiliations and loyalties a person has in a nexus of 'plural social relations' beyond the social constructionist view and its impoverished ethical implications for agents' freedom.

This problem of identity-holding is nonetheless tangential to social classifications and to relative degrees of flexibility societies allow in how boundaries are crossed, overlap and become retrieved. Criticizing the idea that tradition is a consensus-modelled form of identity-fixity, Nussbaum repeats Sen's autobiographical thought-experiment, defining herself as a '[...] woman and feminist, philosopher, runner, music-lover, Jew, Chicagoan, friend of India, friend of Finland, social democrat' (Nussbaum 2003, 63). The point behind this listing is to illustrate what countless cases of people may regard at a given point as a salient feature of their identity, yet other than their ethnocultural identity, which tends to confiscate difference and internal dissent. Dispersion of categories of belonging enables us, according to Nussbaum, to energize dissent at the moment when traditional ethnocultural groups mask their artificial and socially constructed identity. Issues of power and 'in-group–out-group' boundaries give rise to classificatory matrices that can often lock people to a single status (ascribed or achieved). What is thus being deferred from an agent's possibilities for affiliation is some bridge-building with other categories that appear initially as contenders or as indifferent bystanders of the identity in question. The strategy here is a different application of the informational broadening approach endorsed by Sen. Seeing people – positively or negatively – as bearers of a single identity (something akin to what in sociology is called a person's master-status) limits the informational basis of what they have reason to value from the bundle of identities they hold or the identities they aspire to achieve. Sociologists have always been drawn to the embededdness of tacit rules of everyday life. In pursuing this shift to micro-contexts, various strands of sociology (symbolic interactionism, ethnomethodology, phenomenological sociology and the sociology of knowledge) showed impressive sensitivity to the problem of boundaries, to the semantics of purity and danger with which these are clothed, and to their functional significance and normative validity.

Sen's and Nussbaum's exercise is instructive and supplemented by sophisticated and sober argumentation. It concerns the capacity to dissent against powerful structures and the capability to abstract towards other identities one holds dear, as well as the capability to transcend boundaries and thus refashion aspects of personal identity. This move is, I think, a first-order observation – extremely valuable as it deals with actual lives and real constraints faced – that seeks to demarcate the space of dissent within the person's plural identities when congealment of a single status occludes other needs, capabilities and rights in a person's current and projected functionings. Sociology's contribution could supply the second-order observation that probes into the patterns of social life and the ensuing classificatory schemes that affect people's lives as powerful symbolic frameworks. It is evident that Sen's and Nussbaum's examples work as abstractions from modernist preconditions. It is thus hardly surprising that the capability to manage, in a non-adversarial mode, the self throughout these plural memberships presupposes that the social matrix that gives rise to, and makes available, these memberships, can reflect something of this free coordination into those structures of thinking and acting that tend to be seen as sufficiently durable. (This is the sense in which we shall discuss 'capable institutions' in the next chapter.)

An impressive case in point here is Goffman. If the learned competence to hold and adjust plural identities constitutes the mode with which the self realizes her anchoring in the spatial and historical context (her 'thrownness' of 'being-in-the-world', so to speak, but also the potential to meet situation exigencies to which she can meaningfully relate), the sustenance of these identities must incorporate recognition from others. The audience's relevance orientation to the identity-role that is played out at the 'front stage' is, as we know, configured by Goffman as a socially skilled exercise of both pragmatic problem-solving and normative constraint. Thus, for Goffman:

> [society] is organized on the principle that any individual who possesses certain social characteristics has a moral right to expect that others will value and treat him in an appropriate way. Connected with this principle is a second, namely that an individual who implicitly or explicitly signifies that he has certain characteristics ought in fact to be what he claims to be.
>
> (1959, 24)

This truthfulness on the part of the agent as a carrier and performer of identities has the status of a 'moral demand'. Goffman tells us that it is mutually binding for the situation to be successfully defined and not being called continuously to doubt. Bracketing this radical doubt qualifies for Goffman as the a priori that gives social life the sense of a skilled and reciprocally negotiated back-and-forth in how identities are drawn in front of an audience.

If plural identities constitute the bulwark against fundamentalism and its violent erosion of the social, then this possibility needs to be sought elsewhere. The appropriate problem area is one that thematizes the question: How these identities operate at a sufficiently frictionless degree of coordination in a society with multiple points of intersectional contact among agents and groups of different identities? Beyond the tacit skill of applying roles to many situations and adjusting these to multiple audiences, being able to 'measure' the audience's resourcefulness and will to relate with what is at stake in a performance, institutional prerequisites have to convey the sense that reality (i.e. the classified space which serves as the intersubjective platform for identity formation and its empirical 'testing') is not up for grabs; nor is it a simulacrum or a linguistic game. Thus, unsurprisingly perhaps, the sociologist of dramaturgical performance is also the one who defends the objective features of reality and their salience in functionally maintaining the structural properties that are necessary for the enactment of identities (see, for example the criticism of the Thomas theorem, in Goffman 1974, 1–2).

The dramaturgical analogy brings up the problem of play not solely as a human attribute of practical and imaginative experimentation with the world's possibilities outside the constraints of necessity. An ineluctable feature of the early stages in socialization, play figures also as an irreducible inscription in a free society's ways of coping with its own imperfections and pretensions of closure and perfect integration. The capacity for play that appears also in Nussbaum's CCL constitutes a major motif of sociological discourse that makes Nussbaum's silence puzzling. On the level of child socialization, Mead considers the play stage and the game stage not merely as 'technical' stages in role learning that prepare the road for the child's consciousness conquering the stage of 'generalized other'. Even more ambitiously than Mead, it was Georg Simmel who considered play an essential form of human sociation. This inculcates the city-dweller with tolerance but also with positive appreciation of 'difference' and 'otherness', crucial elements for Nussbaum's liberal society, based on civic friendship (inclusive also of the generosity that mediates disgust with irony and humour as playful forms of dissent.)

But even less impressionist sociologists like Durkheim accommodated play in ways that CA could find instructive. It is often overlooked that Durkheim's so-called solid institutionalism retains an inbuilt sphere of playfulness that protects social morality from rigidity against playful aspects of life, which may be mocking, dissident or, in short, profane. The distinction (unfortunately underdeveloped by Durkheim himself) between *vie sérieuse* and *vie légère* (see Pickering (1984) 2009, 352–361) captures this symbiotic duality between the institutional, so-called 'serious' social facts, and those 'lighter' aspects of human life in society that construct our mundane, fallible and playful everyday life. Durkheim is thus quite conscious of the risk of too much integration. He emphatically warns against an overly serious, even self-righteous so to speak, morality. This excessive moralization of social life, as he claims, would pose a threat to morality itself. It is crucial to see how he puts it:

> Morality cannot excessively govern industrial, commercial functions, etc. without paralyzing them [...] Thus, to consider wealth as immoral is not less deadly an error than to see in wealth the good par excellence. There can, then, be excesses of morality from which morality, indeed, is the first to suffer [...]
>
> ((1893) 1960, 239)

Thus, the perception that Durkheim upholds some sort of rigid moral supervision of social life is contradicted not only in this passage but by the entire moral edifice of modern society that he envisages. A few lines later, focusing on play, Durkheim suggests:

> In general, the same may be said of all aesthetic activity; it is healthy only if moderated. The need of playing, acting without end and for the pleasure of acting, cannot be developed beyond a certain point without depriving oneself of serious life. Too great an artistic sensibility is a sickly phenomenon which cannot become general without danger to society. The limit beyond which excess begins is, of course, variable, according to the people or the social environment.
>
> (239–240)

The relevance of the aesthetic (playful) dimension in our discussion indicates that the collective capacity for self-mockery aligns with Nussbaum's vision of liberal democracy. The normative and systemic requirement here is that such a collective understanding of play should balance the criteria of the judicious deconstruction of self and society's ideals from *within* the core values of modernity – and not through some external vantage point of particularized 'difference', as is the trope of poststructuralist thought – even if these are taken to task by modern agents at different degrees of deconstructive (or reconstructive) intention and intensity. Thus, the capacity to keep fast to a sense of cognitive, emotional, psychological and social coherence of the multifaceted self is premised on balancing such immanent diversity – as Sen and Nussbaum admit for themselves – around a central core of what in each particular self makes one capable of coordinating such different dimensions in human personality.

Similarly, Sen's autobiographical identity pun beds down well with Mead's idea of the social self. For Mead, we

> divide ourselves up in all sorts of different selves with reference to our acquaintances. We discuss politics with one and religion with another. There are all sorts of different selves answering to all sorts of different social reactions. It is the social process itself that is responsible for the appearance of the self.
>
> (1934, 142)

Although Mead is concerned here with elevating the self beyond (but also including) the biological or psychological constitution of human personality, the reference to multiple audiences captures two things at once: first, the objective differences in the habitus of each agent at a given type of social setting and the unique biography that, consequently, emerges. (In this sense it possesses an unmistakable pragmatist sobriety on how people from different contexts are addressed.) Second, and beyond this, this skilled performance of the self is derivative of a structurally differentiated social system. In fact this 'functional differentiation and social participation in the full degree is a sort of ideal' attained in the human community that organizes itself under the 'ideal of democracy' (326). Mead articulates this process, arduous to be sure, in terms of evolutionary advanced social systems that use as repositories of the social self's mutability of role-taking and identity-holding, institutions, which in themselves not only provide the broad brush for human innovation, capability and flexibility but should be seen 'like individual selves' (262). As I argue, CA can render more explicit such coupling of identity – differentiation in modernity without risking a lapse into institutional essentialism or cultural evolutionism. In the previous discussion on emotions, the liberal society Nussbaum defended required a justification of 'human dignity, which lies at the core of *modern* notions of human rights' (Nussbaum 2004, 343 [emphasis added]). This normative anchoring in modernity is a pressing need because when the pragmatic context of justification is abstracted from a normative core that connects a pragmatically stabilized intersubjective sense of 'we' (e.g. something akin to a life-world) to normative ideals like justice, the outcome could be a paradoxical validation of those static discourses of justification that pragmatism renders open to reconstruction.[20]

As Mead contends, this process of socialization involves a broadening in terms of the self's positioning towards the 'content and values of the object'; as the self develops, to abandon the process of broadening of the new self to the 'field of values' governed by the old self is tantamount to 'selfishness' (Mead 1913, 378). Mead is not naïve to regard the evolution of the intersubjective social self in terms of a complete detachment from the old self (as we know from Freud the unconscious repository of the old self's experiences can exert chronic impact). Rather, as I believe is also the crux of Sen's autobiographical thought-experiment, Mead considers growth as 'partial disintegration' of the singular identities of the self in what is a reflexive 'reconstruction of the social world' (379–380) and consequently the new self's positioning towards this novel problem shift but also object shift. This learning process CA has maybe in mind in order to defer the blindness of referring the rich social self to a single and beyond revision identity. The difference is that Mead accommodates the social configuration of modernity as a historical transcendental condition for the capability of the self to engage in these crucial steps of self-reform in light of the contingent human diversity and the social permutations of it to which modern society attends to as part and parcel of its own logic of reproduction. This is what the next chapter is all about.

Notes

1 For others, far more hostile to the Faustian illusion of a self who is free of communal boundaries, the individual search for uniqueness is part of instrumental reason's ruse. For instance, Heidegger's 'anyone-self', Jünger's 'worker–soldier' still feed sociological critiques of 'working and soldiering' (Bauman 2017a, 111) as the new prerequisites for social membership with the cult of bodily rituals that sustain it. As we shall see later in the discussion on moral boundaries, their transcendence through

mixed types of the human and the technical, like those favoured by reactionary modernism, has not gone unnoticed by CA. Nussbaum (2004, 109) comments briefly but aptly on Ernst Jünger's image of the 'worker–soldier' as an elitist corrective to Occidental nihilism. She rightly discerns the virile ethic of Jünger's steel-like 'overman' whose denial of femininity is forged in line with a critique of the Weimar denigration of Jews and other enemies (not necessarily human but still 'feminine' in their structure, like the parliament). Of course, the Spartan imagery Jünger's eloquence conjures through the worker–soldier is one that fits now all genders and races. This happens because of the technological denial (effacement) of the face through the ubiquitous 'mask' of the bourgeois and proletariat worker alike, the latter looking like soldiers in uniform. On the whole Nussbaum extrapolates from Jünger the virile 'German' type of *übermensch*, while for Jünger ((1932) 2017) the worker–soldier or the (wo)man of steel is intrinsic to modernity's metaphysics of nihilism (see also Nussbaum 2001, 346–347).

2 We can add to this list Simmel's realization that the differentiation of a modern style of life as a consequence of the progressive liberation of human life from the constraints of collective moorings requires, paradoxically, a repository of hostility. This, for Simmel ((1908) 2016), is explained by the taxing social recognition requirements placed upon the self by modern life and its large pool of possibilities. It is this pragmatic and evolutionary adaptation that makes Simmel sceptical about modernity's capacity to heal the wounds it inflicts on the liberated individual. It is also one that informs his dialectical sociology, which sees group life to be only partially capable to contain its own reversals, whether these include conflict, subordination, exclusion, secrecy and estrangement.

3 What the accumulation of negative emotions tends to show is a marked decline in levels of trust. The rise of populism in Europe (Brexit, Orbán) and in the United States (Trump) enhanced the sense among sociologists that fear is gaining ground not just as an inner feeling of helplessness and fragility (Bude 2018) but as a collective impression of decline in political public discourse and society at risk. It is also identified (Bauman 2017b) as a derivative of explicit discourses of fear instigated by governments with Foucauldian–Schmittian predilections: to dismantle trust in the system (e.g. 'checks and balances'), to legitimize new forms of Caesarian leadership and to boost and refine a surveillance regime, all under the burgeoning narrative of 'securitization'. The negative spiral of fear-induced political rhetoric and the risk of seeing people's lives and neighbourhoods confiscated by fear troubles Nussbaum anew. I say anew because since 9/11 Nussbaum had expressed her alarm at the 'axis of evil' burgeoning rhetoric and the hints to a society based on the reified worship of collectivity as in George Orwell's Oceania (Nussbaum 2005). Such political order, through which complex reality appears in binary and adversarial opposites, is one that thrives on cultivating narcissism rather than a common humanity that includes incompleteness, fallibility, recognition and capacities for sympathy. Commenting on the political climate in the US following Donald Trump's Presidential victory, Nussbaum (2018) grabs the opportunity to address fear. She continues her previous work on emotions as fear, envy, anger and disgust are now compounded into a niche of negative emotions (though some as we have shown and Nussbaum admits too, are functional in certain respects). The result is an image of the human being in a state of fear as if existing in narcissistic 'monarchical' isolation. In spite of fear's entanglement in the human condition, it is human sociality that curbs it and nourishes its containment under relations of love, sympathy and social commitment to reasoned argumentation. Aptly, against the matrix of a monarchy of fear, Nussbaum cultivates the garden of 'democratic reciprocity' (2018, 31). In fact Nussbaum (2005, 295–296) likens this culture of fear and narcissism to clashes between ideal and real culture in the US or even to democratic societies' own implication with the massive suffering of those others it sets up as 'them'. To remedy fear (and the anger that may ensue) Nussbaum

draws on the emotional attachments in the family, school, involvement with legitimate activities, such as sport, and even strong beliefs about what we owe to our nation (2018, 148–151, 242–243) funnelled through institutions like national civil service. (The pattern here has a curious resemblance to Travis Hirschi's Social Control Theory.)

4 We should not neglect the Kantian formulation of this idea. For Kant,

> reason does not itself work instinctively, for it requires trial, practice and instruction to enable it to progress gradually from one stage of insight to the next. Accordingly, every individual man would have to live for a vast length of time if he were to learn how to make complete use of all his natural capacities; [...]
>
> (Kant (1784) 1970, 42–43)

Kant's regulative idea of the immortality of the soul aims to mitigate this problem and transpose its solution to the realm of culture. What Nussbaum and the entire CA see as 'unacceptable' in the sheer necessity of dying (i.e. from premature morbidity, sweatshop labour, racial and ethnic conflicts and other sorts of human calamities and disasters) is the project that ties Freud to Marx. For Marcuse, the 'necessity of death does not refute the possibility of final liberation. Like the other necessities, it can be made rational – painless. Men can die without anxiety if they know that what they love is protected from misery and oblivion' (1962, 216). Within Nussbaum's analysis (2013, 73–74) the necessity of death and the void it creates cannot be fully compensated by rational religion as, even Mill, as a critic of Comte, admitted. Thus, the so-called sublation of all religion to reason, even if ever effected, will contain a trace of loss that is beyond full compensation (in the theological sense) not only for those loved ones but also for the countless losses during the 'prehistory' of Reason.

5 Thus, the partial observations that lead to the overlapping consensus are equivalent to the 'phenomenon' of the 'thing-in-itself', namely observation itself. Nussbaum for her part aims to circumvent this problem by recourse to Socratic dialogues (2010a, Ch. 4).

6 Returning, for a moment, to the representation of standing upright (see Chapters 3 and 4) the human species' evolutionary dissociation from the animality of smell and thus of disgust, Nussbaum (2004, 90) musters Freud's explanations before addressing society's classification and moral boundaries.

7 Elsewhere Durkheim ((1892) 1970, 102–103) draws on Rousseau about the vertical link of organic to mechanical solidarity. He writes this invoking Rousseau's understanding of the 'state of nature' as a de facto order, as opposed to the *de jure* moral order. The latter is consigned into the sphere of Society's legitimacy, that is, the 'general will'.

8 He writes:

> Ethics [...] operate in the realm of action, which either gets to grips with real objects or else loses itself in the void. To act morally is to do good to creatures of flesh and blood, to change some feature of reality. In order to experience the need to change it, to transform it and to improve it, it is necessary not to abstract oneself from it; one must rather stay with it and love it despite its ugliness, its pettiness and its meanness. One must not avert one's gaze from it in order to contemplate an imaginary world, but on the contrary keep one's gaze directed steadily towards it.
>
> (Durkheim (1938) 1977, 207)

This remarkably dialectical and Christian passage suffuses Durkheim's entire programme of moral sociology and proves, once more, the accommodation of the 'negative' in the moral constitution of the human being under organic solidarity. The latter is not yet a fully unfolded configuration, if its historical actualizations still entail stigma, capital punishment and elevation of disgust from its heuristic role to one that is ascribed to categories of people whose status and dignity is for that matter relegated to the 'subhuman'.

9 The infamous illustration here in the history of ideas is De Sade but it can also affect the very Enlightenment principles a society beholds, as, for example, has been the case with serious stigmatization of sex-workers ('petite Jasmine' case) in Sweden's otherwise feminist 1999 Sex Purchase Act.

10 This last comment shares the realization that the drive to comparison with others is insatiable and while it can be significantly curbed it can never be altogether extinguished. Durkheim, for example, protected the 'ideal' from any facile identification with a society so perfectly coordinated that individuals would lack the human capacity to slip from the correct norm even for menial flaws. Before him, Rousseau spoke about the Janus-faced drives of *amour propre*, which he regarded not only as the cause of the evil of inequality but, as Neuhouser brilliantly shows (2008), also as the remedy for man's exit from *amour de soi* (which stands roughly for self-interest). After Durkheim, Axel Honneth (1995) buttressed the Hegelian theory of recognition with a rich body of psychological and sociological evidence. The struggle of recognition that he reconstructed gave credence to the function social arrangements can play in tuning, positively or negatively, those channels of opportunities and spheres of individual fulfilment and contentment that make a person 'rich' or 'poor' in self-confidence, self-esteem and self-respect. The latter triptych is held to offer emotional buffers against the toxicity of envy.

11 Georg Simmel contends that 'Nietzsche's law of history and philosophy is that the human being could not develop to his great power and sublimity without the most severe process of selection and trials without much recklessness and cruelty' (Simmel (1907) 1986, 166). The reference to the sublime aspects of human perfection recalls Kant and Simmel indulges himself in bringing Nietzsche close to, and not only against, Kant. Indeed Kant had already grasped – before Marx and Nietzsche – those unworthy conditions of human perfection of aesthetic faculties (see Kant's almost proto-Marxian formulations in Kant (1790) 1986, §83, about the misery and oppression of the lower classes with regards to culture's accomplishments). (I owe the links between Kant and Nietzsche as well as the attention it should be given to the latter's 1872 manuscript *The Greek State* to Kosmas Psychopedis.). In disqualifying Nietzsche as a coherent political thinker, Nussbaum sets up seven thresholds for Nietzsche's qualification. Paradoxically, violence and the idea of power – pillars of Nietzsche's thought – are omitted. A reading of *The Greek State* would automatically rectify this tarnished image of Nietzsche as adumbrated by Nussbaum. On compassion, therefore, when Nietzsche writes that '[b]eggars ought to be abolished: for one is vexed at giving to them and vexed at not giving to them' ((1881) 1982, §185), the compassionate standpoint rightly breaches the 'vexed at' standpoint but the 'symmetry' between the two standpoints towards beggars is made an occasion for configuring a society without the indignity of pauperism and beggary. It is beside the point to collect further evidence of Nietzsche's subtle dialectical travail on human morality (as a counterweight to Nussbaum's anti-Enlightenment Nietzsche (Nussbaum 1997b, 12)) (see his approval of 'moderation' (Nietzsche (1878) 1994, §464 and, just before this, of Voltaire's 'temperate nature' that, as opposed to Rousseau, should adduce us to recall the '*spirit of enlightenment and of progressive development*' (§463, original emphasis).)

12 The physical, cognitive and emotional fabric is considered in its diverse shapes of 'appearance' and interestingly enough the three shapes of empathy correspond to the three moments of the subjective mind (anthropology, phenomenology of mind, psychology) in Hegel's Part Three of the Encyclopedia. For the accommodation of sympathy in the Hegelian methodology, see the fascinating work by Katrin Pahl (2012).

13 The significance of Scheler's theory of sympathy for CA has only sporadically been addressed (Anderson 2003, 243; Nussbaum 2004, 174), particularly with a view to

showing that sympathy for the plight of others is not an extension of the sympathizer's egoism. Given the Schelerian idea of convergence in the ecumenical project of *Ausgleich* (the balancing-out of different perspectives) (more about this in Chapter 7) it is helpful to note that Nussbaum's version of a liberal correction of past mistakes does not endorse the 'get even' interpretation of what 'balancing-out' could regress to. Rather, she underscores – against the tendency to undermine Westernization by Afrocentric curricula – a logic of inclusion and 'related histories' (Nussbaum 1997a, 179) against reproducing a new partitionism against the West. Ally in her sharp vision is the heritage of Du Bois (see Nussbaum 1997a, 148–185).

14 Unfortunately I lack the space to engage with Turner's extremely nuanced and sophisticated exposition. I shall only point to the fact that having dismissed without much consideration natural law (2010, 48), Turner seems to succumb to the limitation from which natural law theories suffer: namely, thinning the normative core in order to accommodate universality. After a formidable exposition of defective family-resemblances among diverse justifications of normativity Turner affirms as valid Brentano's *Evidenz*, viz. 'as evidence to everyone' (205). The naturalist bedrock here is that if we follow one another such 'followership' must be traced causally to the 'primitive capacity' (204) to follow one another and to act based on the feedback that is generated by social interaction (205). But Turner is involved here in a mystification like the one he imputes to normativism (provocatively termed by him, 'normative fundamentalism'). For if we follow one another, what is it exactly that we follow? Do we follow some sort of 'residue' that feedback loops based on the double contingency in communication stabilize as 'social interaction'? And how much slice of reality is required for coordinating action that requires as an 'explanandum' the 'historical' fact (Weber's 'irrationality of life', Simmel's 'life, Lask's 'reality') that inserts into empathic evidence an indispensable sociality, irrespective of cultural diversity and specificity? Such sociality may just as well operate in experience, this time normative though, because the reasons imputed by agents to make intelligible their act of following, presuppose a 'looking-glass' effect (Turner (2010, 179) rightly invokes Cooley's trope). Agents do not resort to the immediacy of empathy but make empathy derivative of sympathy (the inductive and normative fact of living together in the way used by Durkheim, that is as 'affective bonds' and not as 'compassion').

15 Again this critique bears on Turner's recourse to neuroscience. When, for example, Turner invokes children's empathetic understanding based on the capacity to mimic, this naturalistic explanation of the inbuilt capacity to empathize is expected to hold without any normative inculcating having taken place. Yet, from the findings of relational psychoanalysis (Jessica Benjamin) and attachment theory (John Bowlby) we also know that the mimicry of the infant's gesture cannot initially be coordinated unless it is enveloped in the tacit sphere of expected reciprocation by the caregiver. The non-empirical comfort zone of the expectation (belief) in the reciprocation is neither normatively nor empirically founded. Rather, it is both. Turner leaves open the possibility of mutual corrigibility of standpoints following error removals, which, however, all refer to the naturalistic cause of the empirical facts adduced by a direct observational understanding. Turner writes:

> We have no privileged access to meanings that we can expressivistically articulate, because there is nothing like this – no massive structure of normative practices – to access. Instead we try to follow our fellow beings and their reasoning and acting, including their speaking: we make them intelligible.
>
> (2010, 165)

A few sentences later Turner concludes that, justification 'is just another piece of behavior: the child learns that saying "Why, mommy, why?" gets a reaction' (165). It needs to be noted that the child's utterance contains an implicit meaning because semantically the question is meaningless unless that, in the child's learning process of following fellow human beings, this utterance embeds, as a consociate signifier, the tacit knowledge that the 'why?' obliges the other to a response. Internal to the utterance 'mommy' is the child's expectation that the 'other' is summoned (and thus obliged) to reciprocate with meaning; a meaning that is authoritatively (yet, legitimately in the child's eyes) anchored in the affectionate sphere that buttresses meaning to the utterance, both in terms of role-expectations ('Mommy') and in terms of the intersubjective horizon of truthful communication (the child's 'why' is premised on the intuitive expectation of the validity of the parent's superior point of view). Such Meadian and Hegelian reconstruction of the Mirror Neurons System Model (see Marchetti and Koster 2014) indicates that the presence of the 'other' is necessary for cognitive development not merely in terms of physical presence, but mainly through a series of acts of intentional recognition of the subject as a 'self-conscious self' (Marchetti and Koster 2014). The child may not be in a position to check the normative features of the role (as the stage of the 'generalized other' has not yet been conquered) but she nonetheless rightly grasps as normatively correct the necessity of a reply. This primordial trust in the other is part and parcel of the child's utterance towards 'Mommy'.

16 Nussbaum is justified in critiquing Habermas' neglect of emotions in his proposal for 'constitutional patriotism'. Yet Habermas' vision of a Federation of European States – patterned after the models of US and Switzerland – aims at establishing an 'overlapping consensus' on human rights, where the relation between different traditions would also relativize them as solitarist undertakings of building a national identity (Habermas 1994, 27). This Nussbaum does not deny. The corrective move she suggests aims to funnel the constitutional patriotism of this overlapping consensus into collective representations, which can be vivid enough for the people who from the particular vantage point of view will be summoned to uphold human rights. One alternative solution to Nussbaum's reservations would be the strengthening of what Honneth – following Kant – understands as 'historical symbols' (Honneth (2011) 2014b, 335) of universal struggle. Events, like for instance the French, the American, the Haitian or the Indian revolutions, can serve as particularistic symbols of vivid collective effervescence under the banner of which other nations identify and solidify their warm streams of patriotism. Currently, the World Wide Web can create networks knit by an international symbol of solidarity. Usually this emerges bottom up from all those millions of world citizens who feel indignation against acts of terrorism in any part of the world and reset their Facebook profiles with the national flags of the attacked nation. Essentially, Nussbaum's recall of love becomes more relevant as a Durkheimian move that aims to replenish the vital streams of collective values of justice and patriotism. The periodic illuminations of love preserves in us 'that passionate and quasi-erotic emotion, if trust is not to become a lifeless simulacrum' (Nussbaum 2013, 318).

17 Crucial to the cultivation of sympathy is the function of (liberal) education. We cannot enter this rich domain but a few words will suffice I think to highlight the strong currents that exist between CA and Durkheim's moral sociology. Crucial to both is the child's ability to broaden a perspective on life, becoming thus capable of abstracting from the inevitable egoism that humans retain for individual well-being, group solidarity or national pride. Clearly, group membership is not enough. It can also trigger selfish and possessive sentiments so that our entire identity is suffused with the particularist value-system and the practices for the group in question. Coming to terms with one's self and gaining self-control and confidence about one's practical reasoning requires knowledge of moral and anti-moral emotions. The consequences of the latter trouble Nussbaum. Drawing, among others, on Milgram's and Zimbardo's experiments on unreasoned obedience, she sees the normative task of education across a springboard (Nussbaum 2010a, 45–46) that: a) enables students to gain empathetic understanding (this is not a panacea for morality, as she admits, but

it creates an indispensable space for parity as opposed to instrumental diminutions of the 'other'; b) accept that we are needy creatures so that our incompleteness ceases to be a source of shame; c) develop a capacity for sympathetic concern with the plight of others, no matter the distance; d) avoid binary thinking that perceives and treats minorities or other groups as agents of social 'pollution'; e) use teaching to counter stereotypes and prejudices by recourse to real facts about minorities, including also a single culture's internal diversity (Nussbaum 2006, 390–391); f) promote accountability; g) promote critical thinking so that dissent is possible against groupthink and peer pressure; and h) instruct pupils about justified reasons with regard to the moderate recourse to negative emotions (i.e. fear, anger, disgust) (Nussbaum 2004, 31–37). Similar prerequisites of the liberal education championed by Nussbaum safeguard us against the vices of chauvinism, arcadianism (i.e. romantic idealization of the past), and scepticism (see Nussbaum 1997a, 130–139). Drawing on what we have been arguing all along, namely that from the perspective of sociological theory CA articulates normative positions not far from Durkheim, it is helpful to recall that Durkheim drew extensively on the potential of 'moral education'. Like Nussbaum's turn to liberal education as a bulwark against the profit motive infiltration in US education, so was Durkheim's turn to education prompted by the risks of anomie (see Durkheim (1925) 1973).

18 As Chouliaraki (2013, 194–196) argues, within the context of mediatized humanitarianism, the road opened by Sen's reactivation of a politics of sympathy offers one viable mode of thinking about human problems outside the rigid dualisms of neoliberal colonization of humanism and, inversely, of narratives that subsume media under reification.

19 The interchangeability of standpoints, that sociologists like Simmel, Schütz and Garfinkel associated with the very possibility of our everyday-life routines and sociality, constitutes the practically skilful mode of interaction that shapes society and gives it the possibility of being lived as a continuous stream of acts, exchange of meanings and communicative possibilities. In its durable and routine unfolding, social life is absorbed, lived and reflected by the agent who, depending on the cultural setting and social dispositional load that he carries, his 'habitus' so to speak, maintains the sense of a coherent self, capable of relating to others in space. Moreover, the agent becomes capable of reconfiguring the evolution of these spatially coordinated social relations as essential ingredients of his biography, which in effect captures the unity of the uniquely lived social self in instituted social relations in time (history).

20 Looking by recourse to a pragmatic methodology at contexts of moral justifications in how agents draw upon to defer and neutralize anger, crisis and conflict, Boltanski and Thévenot ((1991) 2006) provide a useful typology (see Figure 5.1).

The interesting thing to notice here is that the pragmatic toolkit of critique, which, generally, holds a priori or even 'totalizing' critical discourses (e.g. The Frankfurt School) to be obsolete is faced with what is the recurring Achilles' heel of pragmatic sociology. The reluctance to retain what pragmatism may have discerned as the outcome of a melioristic approach to policy and problem-solving in general, runs the risk on hitting on already available conceptual categories. In other words, pragmatism's non-foundational tendencies can be prone to a big pragmatic mistake. The case of Boltanski and Thévenot is instructive because they adduce typical justification bedrocks on controversies among actors that take recourse to axiological notions of worth, which though emanate from different regimes of organization and semantics. As shown in Figure 5.1 these presuppositions of the common good upon which justifications rely can be converted to a cybernetic hierarchy one that fuses Parsons' system theory and Scheler's personalist ethics. This uncanny convergence with Scheler can be evinced in the exemplars of the person. In an essay titled 'Exemplars of Persons and Leaders', Scheler (1987, 127–198) deducts phenomenologically the paradigmatic moral exemplars, filtered by social roles across different historical

Figure 5.1 Luc Boltanski's polities of worth and Max Scheler's ideal exemplars of Persons configured after Parsons' functional imperatives

	Max Scheler (Ideal Exemplars of Persons)	*Luc Boltanski (The Polities of Worth)*	
L	Values of the Holy (The Saint)	The Inspired Polity (The Saint/The Artist)	**L**
I	Spiritual Values (Aesthetic – of Justice – Scientific) (The Genius)	The Renowned Polity (The Esteemed Person)	**I**
G	Vital Values (The Hero)	The Domestic Polity (The Elderly One); The Civic Polity (The Representative of the Collective)	**G**
A	Utilitarian Values (The Leading Mind of Civilization, The Master in the Art of Living)	The Commercial Polity (The Rich) The Industrial Polity (The Effective Professional)	**A**

circumstances. While I lack the space to engage on this affinity, it is indicative of the recalcitrance of a priori categories that operate as it were behind the back of pragmatic contexts of justification. Elsewhere, Boltanski justifies the selection of this orderly pattern as follows:

> Each of these regimes of justification is based on a different principle of evaluation which, envisaging beings in a determinate respect (i.e. also by excluding other types of qualification), makes it possible to establish an order between them. This principle is called the *principle of equivalence* because it presupposes reference to a form of general equivalence (to a standard) without which comparison between beings would be impossible. We can then say: in such and such respect (e.g. effectiveness in an industrial polity), the people put to the test turned out to possess more or less value. *Worth* is our name for the value attributed to people in certain respects when it results from a legitimate procedure.
>
> (2011, 167n. 29 [original emphasis])

The pragmatic paradigm shift that Boltanski inaugurates is, for all its novelty, anchored in 'traditional' concepts such as 'value' and 'worth'. As has been obvious thus far from my argument, 'tradition' here is far from a derogatory configuration. Rather, it encapsulates the unutilized repositories of theory (in sociology or philosophy, for example) that surfaces, 'spontaneously' and 'creatively', from the pragmatic construction of the 'new' conditions, situations, or contexts of social life.

References

Anderson, Elizabeth. 2003. 'Sen, Ethics, and Democracy.' *Feminist Economics* 9 (2–3): 239–261.

Bauman, Zygmunt. 2017a. *Retrotopia*. Cambridge: Polity.

Bauman, Zygmunt. 2017b. *A Chronicle of Crisis 2011–2016*. London: Social Europe Edition.

Bernstein, Richard. 2002. *Radical Evil: A Philosophical Interrogation*. Cambridge: Polity.

Boltanski, Luc. 2011. *On Critique: A Sociology of Emancipation*. Cambridge: Polity.

Boltanski, Luc, and Laurent Thévenot. (1991) 2006. *On Justification: Economies of Worth*. Princeton: Princeton University Press.

Bude, Heinz. 2018. *Society of Fear*. Cambridge: Polity.
Chouliaraki, Lillie. 2013. *The Ironic Spectator: Solidarity in the Age of Post-Humanitarianism*. Cambridge: Polity.
Clark, Candace. 1997. *Misery and Company: Sympathy in Everyday-Life*. Chicago: The University of Chicago Press.
Comte, Auguste. 1975. *Auguste Comte and Positivism*, edited by Gertrud Lenzer. New York: Harper Torchbooks.
Douglas, Mary. (1966) 1985. *Purity and Danger: An Analysis of the Concepts of Pollution and Taboo*. London: ARK.
Durkheim, Émile. (1893) 1960. *The Division of Labor in Society*. New York: The Free Press of Glencoe.
Durkheim, Émile. (1895) 1966. *The Rules of Sociological Method*. New York: The Free Press.
Durkheim, Émile. (1892) 1970. *Montesquieu and Rousseau: Forerunners of Sociology*. Ann Arbor: The University of Michigan Press.
Durkheim, Émile. (1925) 1973. *Moral Education: A Study in the Theory and Application of the Sociology of Education*. New York: The Free Press.
Durkheim, Émile. (1885) 1975. 'Organisation et Vie du Corps Social Selon Schaeffle. In *Textes: 1. Éléments d'une Théorie Sociale*, edited by Viktor Karádi, 355–377. Paris: Les Éditions de Minuit.
Durkheim, Émile. (1938) 1977. *The Evolution of Educational Thought: Lectures on the Formation and Development of Secondary Education in France*. London: Routledge and Kegan Paul.
Durkheim, Émile. (1895) 1988. *Les Règles de la Méthode Sociologique*. Paris: Flammarion.
Durkheim, Émile. (1890–1900) 1992. *Professional Ethics and Civic Morals*. London: Routledge.
Ehrenberg, Alain. 2010. *The Weariness of the Self: Diagnosing the History of Depression in the Contemporary Age*. Montreal: McGill-Queen's University Press.
Ehrenreich, Barbara. 2002. *Nickel and Dimed: On (Not) Getting By in America*. New York: Henry Holt & Company.
Elliot, Anthony, and Charles Lemert. 2009. *The New Individualism: The Emotional Costs of Globalization*. London: Routledge.
Gasper, Des, and Thanh-Dam Truong. 2010. 'Development Ethics through the Lenses of Caring, Gender, and Human Security.' In *Capabilities, Power, and Institutions: Toward a More Critical Development Ethics*, edited by Stephen Esquith and Fred Gifford, 58–95. University Park: The Pennsylvania State University Press.
Goffman, Erving. 1959. *The Presentation of Self in Everyday Life*. London: Penguin.
Goffman, Erving. 1963. *Stigma: Notes on the Management of Spoiled Identity*. New York: Simon and Schuster.
Goffman, Erving. 1974. *Frame Analysis: An Essay on the Organization of Experience*. Cambridge, MA: Harvard University Press.
Habermas, Jürgen. 1994. 'Citizenship and National Identity.' In *The Condition of Citizenship*, edited by Bart Van Steenbergen, 20–35. London: Sage.
Honneth, Axel. 1995. *The Struggle for Recognition: The Moral Grammar of Social Conflicts*. Cambridge: MA: The MIT Press.
Honneth, Axel. (2010) 2014a. *The I in We: Studies in the Theory of Recognition*. Cambridge: Polity.
Honneth, Axel. (2011) 2014b. *Freedom's Right: The Social Foundations of Democratic Life*. Cambridge: Polity.

Jünger, Ernst. (1932) 2017. *The Worker: Dominion and Form*. Evanston: Northwestern University Press.

Kant, Immanuel. (1784) 1970. 'Idea for a Universal History with a Cosmopolitan Purpose.' In *Kant: Political Writings*, edited by Hans Reiss, 41–53. Cambridge: Cambridge University Press.

Kant, Immanuel. (1790) 1986. *The Critique of Judgment*. Oxford: Clarendon Press.

Levmore Saul, and Nussbaum Martha, eds. 2010. *The Offensive Internet: Speech, Privacy and Reputation.* Cambridge, MA: Harvard University Press.

Marchetti, Igor, and Ernst Koster. 2014. 'Brain and Intersubjectivity: A Hegelian Hypothesis on the Self-Other Neurodynamics.' *Frontiers in Human Neuroscience* 8: 11.

Marcuse, Herbert. 1962. *Eros and Civilization: A Philosophical Inquiry into Freud*. New York: Vintage Books.

Mead, George Herbert. 1913. 'The Social Self.' *The Journal of Philosophy* 10 (14): 374–380.

Mead, George Herbert. 1934. *Mind, Self and Society*. Chicago: The University of Chicago Press.

Neiman, Susan. 2002. *Evil in Modern Thought: An Alternative History of Philosophy.* Princeton: Princeton University Press.

Neuhouser, Frederick. 2008. *Rousseau's Theodicy of Self-Love: Evil, Rationality, and The Drive for Recognition.* Cambridge: Cambridge University Press.

Nietzsche, Friedrich. 1872. *The Greek State.* Unpublished manuscript. Last accessed 23 September 2018. http://nietzsche.holtof.com/Nietzsche_various/the_greek_state.htm.

Nietzsche, Friedrich. (1881) 1982. *Daybreak: Thoughts on the Prejudices of Morality.* Cambridge: Cambridge University Press.

Nietzsche, Friedrich. (1878) 1994. *Human, All Too Human*. London: Penguin.

Nussbaum, Martha. 1997a. *Cultivating Humanity. A Classical Defense of Reform in Liberal Education.* Cambridge, MA: Harvard University Press.

Nussbaum, Martha. 1997b. 'Is Nietzsche a Political Thinker?' *International Journal of Philosophical Studies* 5 (1): 1–13.

Nussbaum, Martha. 2001. *Upheavals of Thought: The Intelligence of Emotions*. Cambridge: Cambridge University Press.

Nussbaum, Martha. 2003. 'The Complexity of Groups: A Comment on Jorge Valadez.' *Philosophy and Social Criticism* 29 (1): 57–69.

Nussbaum, Martha. 2004. *Hiding from Humanity: Disgust, Shame and the Law*. Princeton: Princeton University Press.

Nussbaum, Martha. 2005. 'The Death of Pity: Orwell and American Political Life.' In *On Nineteen Eighty Four: Orwell and Our Future*, edited by Abbott Gleason, Jack Goldsmith, and Martha Nussbaum, 279–299. Princeton: Princeton University Press.

Nussbaum, Martha. 2006. 'Education and Democratic Citizenship: Capabilities and Quality Education.' *Journal of Human Development* 7 (3): 385–395.

Nussbaum, Martha. 2008. 'Living Together: The Roots of Respect.' *University of Illinois Law Review* 5: 1623–1641.

Nussbaum, Martha. 2010a. *Not For Profit: Why Democracy Needs the Humanities.* Princeton: Princeton University Press.

Nussbaum, Martha. 2010b. 'Objectification and Internet Misogyny.' In *The Offensive Internet: Speech, Privacy and Reputation*, edited by Saul Levmore and Martha Nussbaum, 68–87. Cambridge, MA: Harvard University Press.

Nussbaum, Martha. 2013. *Political Emotions: Why Love Matters for Justice*. Cambridge, MA: The Belknap Press of Harvard University Press.

Nussbaum, Martha. 2016. *Anger and Forgiveness: Resentment, Generosity, Justice.* Oxford: Oxford University Press.

Nussbaum, Martha. 2018. *The Monarchy of Fear: A Philosopher Looks at Our Political Crisis.* Oxford: Oxford University Press.

Pahl, Katrin. 2012. *Tropes of Transport: Hegel and Emotion.* Evanston: Northwestern University Press.

Parsons, Talcott. 1951. *The Social System.* New York: The Free Press of Glencoe.

Parsons, Talcott. 1954. *Essays in Sociological Theory.* New York: The Free Press.

Peyre, Henri. 1960. 'Durkheim: The Man, His Time, and his Intellectual Background.' In *Essays on Sociology and Philosophy by Emile Durkheim* et al., edited by Kurt Wolff, 3–31. New York: Harper Torchbooks.

Pickering, WSF. (1984) 2009. *Durkheim's Sociology of Religion: Themes and Theories.* Cambridge: James Clark & Co.

Pinker, Steven. 2011. *The Better Angels of Our Nature. Why Violence has Declined.* New York: Penguin Books.

Rawls, John. (1971) 1999. *A Theory of Justice.* Oxford: Oxford University Press.

Scheler, Max. (1912) 1954. *The Nature of Sympathy.* Hamden: Archon Books.

Scheler, Max. (1915) 1961. *Ressentiment.* New York: The Free Press of Glencoe.

Scheler, Max. 1987. *Person and Self-Value: Three Essays.* Dordrecht: Martinus Nijhoff Publishers.

Schoeck, Helmut. 1969. *Envy: A Theory of Social Behaviour.* Indianapolis: Liberty Fund.

Sen, Amartya. 1982. *Choice, Welfare, and Measurement.* Cambridge, MA: Harvard University Press.

Sen. Amartya. 1990. 'Individual Freedom as a Social Commitment.' *New York Review of Books* 37: 49–54.

Sen, Amartya. 2006. *Identity and Violence: The Illusion of Destiny.* London: Penguin.

Sen, Amartya. 2009. *The Idea of Justice.* Cambridge, MA: The Belknap Press of Harvard University Press.

Simmel, Georg. (1907) 1986. *Schopenhauer and Nietzsche.* Amherst: The University of Massachusetts Press.

Simmel, Georg. (1908) 2016. 'Sur la Psychologie Sociale de l' Hostilité (On the Social Psychology of Hostility).' In *Nachträge, Dokumente, Gesamtbibliogrpahie Übersichten, Indices. Gesamtausgabe, Band* 24, edited by Otthein Rammstedt, 38–46. Berlin: Suhrkamp, 38–46.

Smith, Adam. (1759) 1984. *The Theory of Moral Sentiment.* Indianapolis: Liberty Fund.

Turner, Stephen. 2010. *Explaining the Normative.* Cambridge: Polity.

Wilkinson, Richard. 2005. *The Impact of Inequality: How to Make Sick Societies Healthier.* London: Routledge.

Wilkinson, Richard, and Kate Pickett. 2010. *The Spirit Level: Why Equality is Better for Everyone.* London: Penguin.

Part III

Institutions, modernity and fundamentalism

6 'Capable institutions'?

Rebuilding social ethics

The shift to 'capable' institutions

In the previous chapter I examined the role of emotions, the promises and challenges they pose in the configuration of a just social order. Nussbaum (2013) made a powerful case for political emotions. She shared with Rawls and to a lesser extent with Habermas the placement of (patriotic) feelings towards the construction and self-maintenance of a just social order. A backdrop of her argument was the basic psychological fact of reciprocity, which Nussbaum argued to be worthy and capable of being extended from family and the realm of intimacy to higher levels of system complexity, like civil society associations and the nation. Having thus addressed emotions, it is now time to prompt questions around the validity of the social order that most CA theorists consider to be driven by an aspiration to justice. My remarks thus far about social institutions seen from a CA perspective should not be taken to imply that Sen and Nussbaum are not attentive to the institutional preconditions for normatively upgraded agency their theories address. To insist on any such omission in CA is a gross misinterpretation. Even a cursory look at programmatic assertions (e.g. Sen 1999a, xii–xiii) is enough to refute any claim that imputes to CA an institutional myopia. Sen emphatically declares:

> Individuals live and operate in a world of institutions. Our opportunities and prospects depend crucially on what institutions exist and how they function. Not only do institutions contribute to our freedom, their roles can be sensibly evaluated in the light of their contributions to freedom. To see development as freedom provides a perspective in which institutional assessment can systematically occur.
>
> (1999a, 142)

Not only does this statement clear the ground from some alleged neglect of institutions, but also it buttresses their function with an ethical goal (freedom), which aligns Sen with a long tradition in social theory. Yet, it performs also another task. It renders institutions 'open' spaces for the realization of people's freedoms and concedes that this freedom is a standard by which institutions ought to be appraised. Sen, as we shall see later but also in Chapter 7 distances his project from 'institutional fundamentalism' (Sen 2009, 83, 267) but not from institutions as such. Attempts at an institutional amplification of CA have indeed been made (Evans 2002, 2004; Little 2010) but the sociological input in these approaches remains scant. One reason for this breach in the pursuit of the institutional trail is the risk of institutional maximalism (see, for example, Evans 2004).[1]

Evidently, since there is no absence of institutional support for capability flourishing, the points I shall be making have to do more with the fact that an institutional approach to justice, like the one advocated by Rawls ((1971) 1999), is unnecessarily rejected by Sen and Nussbaum. The dialogue between Sen, Nussbaum and Rawls is rich and extremely nuanced.[2] I shall not address it though because it is not directly relevant to what I propose here, given also a relative lack of 'sociological' reconstructions of Rawls. A search for institutional configurations that nourish capabilities is often vitiated *inter alia* by the programme's identification of a normative theory of institutions with John Rawls' project of a theory of justice, which includes a more robust version of societal institutions than Sen's (2009) own theory of justice. Yet one evident cost of rejecting the institutional framework proposed by Rawls, insofar as institutional flexibility is gained on the part of CA, could be that the CA theory of justice (Nussbaum 2006; Sen 2009) abandons all too easily the Hegelian traction of institutionally interlinked levels of justice and freedom. Even the scant scholarly volumes on CA that address issues of power and injustice (Deneulin, Nebel and Sagovsky 2006; Esquith and Gifford 2010) do not seem to consider the issue of a logic of justice, patterned in broad, yet binding, institutional frameworks. One exception is Sagovsky (2006) whose argument aims to recover the Rawlsian project of a just society. He suggests instructively that CA falls short of accounting for 'social capabilities' (76–77), although he conceptualizes these social capabilities as symbolic resources (e.g. traditions) rather than institutionalized spheres of sociality (i.e. intimacy and family, market, law, state). This notion of the 'just institutions' is something though that seems presupposed when, for example, Nussbaum writes that the structure of nations that promote citizens' capabilities must include:

> legislature, courts, administration and at least some administrative agencies, laws defining the institution of the family and allocating privileges to its members, the system of taxation and welfare, the overall structure of the economic system, the criminal justice system, etc.
>
> (2004, 15)

It may not be accidental that such a robust statement occurs in the context of an Olof Palme lecture. Yet the institutional layout here recalls the institutional embeddedness of right. It is in this respect mainly that sociological theory can contribute to the already available in the CA intimations of this proposal's feasibility.[3]

Defending institutions does not prevent Sen from emphatically rejecting 'transcendental institutionalism' In his last major book on justice, Sen (2009) begins with an almost militant bracketing of a project that aims at arriving at correct institutions. For him, major exponents of this approach include Thomas Hobbes, John Locke, Jean-Jacques Rousseau, Immanuel Kant and John Rawls. In the antipodes of this paradigm, Sen launches the 'realization-focused comparison' approach. Here, instead of confining itself in a search for a perfect set of institutional arrangements that promote justice, the goal is considerably more modest. It only aims to address the distinction between justice and injustice, comparatively, and always with an eye to feasible chances for implementing frameworks of justice. Representatives of the latter model are, among others, Adam Smith, John Stuart Mill, Jeremy Bentham, Karl Marx, in spite the major differences among them. Sen clearly regards himself as a scholar working in this second model. What is intriguing in this listing is that, once more, Hegel is omitted. Sen (2009, 137) observes with temerity that Rawls mentions Adam Smith only on five occasions and on rather secondary matters. The same acrid observation can be made against Sen' total neglect of Hegel. This is doubly odd, given Hegel's attempt to complete a philosophical theory of justice across both strands that Sen typifies. Hegel's *Sittlichkeit* articulates a complex society (associated with modernity) and provides logically connected institutional frameworks, each fulfilling a distinct yet interdependent 'role' in cementing justice. At the same time Hegel's system contains some of the most remarkable tools for an approach to justice that primes realism, pragmatic shifts in evaluative relevancies and practical feasibility. It could even be asserted that a bundle of key principles in CA are launched from standpoints within the Hegelian system and its subsequent sociological manifestations.

Legitimate scepticism regarding the underestimation of social structures and institutions by CA arises at the point where an agent's capabilities are obstructed by unjust social structures or, conversely, if social structures inscribe and prescribe in terms of actual functionings the flourishing of human capabilities. In other words, a theory of *Sittlichkeit* (or 'organic solidarity') must be reconstructable so that the individualism of CA can be buttressed as moral individualism.[4] This shift would also rectify the limitation of configuring capabilities abstractly in terms of 'capacity'-conflicts, where 'social capacities for some will bring incapacities for others' (Jackson 2005, 114). This Weberian type of conflict that appears to be beyond reconciliation raises rightly, for Jackson, the imperative to abstract towards layers of capabilities. It is a step that I think CA should take. How are we to conceive then social institutions from a CA perspective? Clearly institutions do not exhibit the perceived immediacy of the individual self in terms of the latter's physical constitution, vocal gestures and the practical impact on the world that defines a person's lived experience. If, as it has been argued so far, individuals as moral persons are to be seen as capable social selves *pace* CA, isn't it odd to inaugurate a discussion about 'capable institutions'? Such a step, a critic can claim, extrapolates physical constitution, action-patterns, thought processes and a moral orientation from individuals (who are, ultimately, the only real bearers of capabilities) to fictional entities that are held to impact people's lives; yet their alleged 'reality' is sustained by collective practices, which, in their turn, presuppose some significant degree of coordination among individual members.

To mitigate the tension between the self and the institution, George Herbert Mead takes seriously the analogy between the institution and the self. He holds that 'without social institutions of some sort, without the organized social attitudes and activities by which institutions are constituted, there can be no fully mature individual selves or personalities at all' (Mead 1934, 262). For Mead, the individual, when placed within the complex web of interaction with others, embodies and performs in roles the institutional matrix to which she happens to orient her action-plans and trajectory of practical attitudes. I also draw inspiration for the 'capable institutions' thesis from Mary Douglas (1986) and her 'thinking institution' thesis. As systems of logical (and moral) classification, institutions set the coordinates for actors' capabilities; however, they need not be morally impervious or culturally sealed. This was a theme that was undertaken by Habermas (1974) when he recognized that societies developed a social identity based on projective world-images and institutional structures. This approach is instructive in that it provides a basic framework for dealing in a CA perspective with social institutions. Although the latter's salience for human flourishing is consistently recognized by CA, other CA positions betray an ambivalence on the status of the 'social'. For example, Nussbaum seems to adopt a 'social constructionist' approach. She claims that:

> For the social constructionist, change that does not include structural, institutional, and legal change is likely to be ineffective and short-lived. Social and institutional meanings have no agency and reality on their own, in my view, apart from their role in judgments and actions of individuals.
>
> (Nussbaum 1999, 265)

Nussbaum's reading of 'social constructionism' raises a number of questions. Initially it ought to be contextualized. It thus occurs as part of Nussbaum's arguments about the social constructions of emotions in a discussion driven by strong normative claims against women's subordination and diverse forms, crass and subtle, of exclusion. Nussbaum also accepts that constructionism does not imply suspension of biological hooks upon which human bodies and gender identities rely upon. In her reading, social constructionism is tantamount to a pragmatic pronouncement against reified hierarches and social structures. She seems to recognize an institutional level akin to Giddens' idea of a long *durée*. The span of time that is projected for any claims to social change to be effective requires patterns of institutionalization vaster in scope, and deeper in terms of entanglement in agents' everyday-lives, than mere individual meanings. Goffman, for example, whose work, as we saw in the previous chapter, serves as an inspiration for Nussbaum, does not make the mistake of succumbing into the social constructionist universe of negotiated meanings that would abort the very conditions of social construction itself. He recognizes some structural features that are off-stage and thus envelop the front-stage/back-stage distinction behind performance in everyday life. Thus, the social constructionist view, as Nussbaum portrays it, does not seem to endorse versions of a social universe that incessantly constructs nature and logic outside some 'givens'. It is not I think a theory of collective meaning-formation that absconds with the material and ideal constraints that envelop the very process of meaning construction. At the same time, Nussbaum rejects a reified notion of institutions apart from agents. What Nussbaum may intimate here is that institutions have validity as real entities only through the act of agents' consciousness that represents them as something that exists outside their consciousness. She also may mean that it is agents, in their practical engagement with experience, their negotiated meanings and intersubjective communication, who sustain those aspects of reality we typically understand as 'institutional'.

The lack of a Durkheimian approach to the social surfaces in Nussbaum's formulation of the problem, although this lack of the social is never total. The individuals her liberalism defends are not of course cut off from institutions. As individuals with claims (and rights) to human flourishing, who organize and manage their physical, cognitive and emotional repertoires at different degrees of abstraction from the collective entities, these same agents understand their coordinated outcomes as institutions. Hypothetically, even the most individualist oriented functioning that negates social conventions and prefers a Crusoeque life in isolation from others is still, in her functioning as an isolated being, an institutionally determined being (i.e. she *has to* reject institutions). Nussbaum's conception of the social, therefore, is not breaking completely from a Durkheimian approach. What is actually missing from her account is a systematic sociological twist of CA that incorporates her reading of constructionism with the normative account of sociality along the lines of a normatively robust (Durkheimian) version of constructionism. In this light then, Nussbaum cannot but affirm the 'social':

> The role of society goes very deep, in shaping matters that our tradition has tended to define as outside society, as 'private' and 'natural'. This can feel like a source of constraint, as we come to see to what extent we are artifacts, even in our apparently most internal and intimate lives. On the other hand, and this is what I want to emphasize, it can also feel like a source of freedom, because we can see that many ways of experiencing the body, the emotions, and the care of children that might have seemed given and inevitable are actually made by us and can therefore be otherwise.
>
> (1999, 274)

Although Nussbaum's quote can also be read ethnomethodologically about the social construction of gender, its deeper implications allow a Durkheimian route, which can align Society's authority with the freedom of the will that liberal societies cherish for their citizens. Thus, what separates this assertion from a debilitating relativism is some consensus on the 'sacrality' of the body, which Durkheim affirmed under conditions of organic solidarity, and Nussbaum posits as a core value in her CCL. To superimpose shifting social definitions on our biological constitution makes change and constancy mutually supportive. This idea is expressed characteristically both by Nussbaum (1999, 346) and Durkheim ((1897) 1970, 325n. 20) when the latter grants that human freedom and physical law-like regularities which constrain us biologically, can, as they do, operate without contradiction.

As we saw in Chapter 1, Nussbaum struggles to overcome the dualism structure-agency. The pragmatic liberalism she defends has abolished the social as the part of the distinction that actors make when they themselves invoke 'society' and treat it as a realm that is not merely distinct from them and thus constraining to their wills, but also as one that is morally superior. The claims Nussbaum makes in favour of human flourishing project, render as *claims*, their realization in a practical coordination of forces that forever escapes full visibility on the part of the agent. To *project* means to place a portion of the consequences of individual action (even if the latter is carried out at the maximum and humanly possible ethics of responsibility) to the realm of society in a dual sense: First, in the sense of the 'thing-in-itself', namely the totality that all action must posit, by virtue of the fact that agents select an evaluative space for description, explanation and action, without full knowledge of the factors of the situation or the consequences of their action; second, in the sense of the collective entity that will validate this project and thus legitimize it. This latter expectation is granted by Nussbaum (1999, 265) when she adduces institutional change and treats it as chronologically prior to changes in individual mind-sets. Agents are thus not externally related to Society. They do though, analytically and normatively, see themselves as being capable of retaining their particular claims to their life chances at some degree of relative autonomy from their inevitable embededdness in the social forces exerted by institutional life. (I shall not reiterate the physiognomy of institutions that Nussbaum herself accepts when she discusses the ethical function of memorials and the 'reality' of institutions in the countless classifications that coordinate a person's horizon of possibilities in everyday life.) The attribution of reification to institutional reality was persuasively rebutted by Durkheim. Indeed, institutions do not exist outside the judgments of individuals, yet institutions are judgments themselves, because they shape through roles patterns of human action and evaluate these according to collectively forged symbolic classifications.

In the context of an updated projection of social ethics we need to recall that certain moral prerequisites constitute foundational desiderata for a robust democratic polity. We have seen and defended at the start Marcuse's request for an a priori claim about a life that is worth living; we have also provided support for this judgment from philosophical anthropology; we also saw that life figures as the first capability in Nussbaum's CCL; we also considered the role that Nussbaum assigns to emotions as non-material pillars to institutional matrices of justice. Offering a slightly different version of her CCL she stresses that among the core values of a just social order is the '*moral salience of national sovereignty*' (Nussbaum 2013, 121 [original emphasis]). Other values of 'human development', 'treating persons as ends in themselves', 'human equality and dignity', equality in 'civil and political liberties', 'due process', 'prevention of violence and fraud', 'social and economic' entitlements (with 'significant redistribution' mechanisms), 'education and health' (118–124) function as objectifications (not reifications) of sympathy. We shall examine in the following sections the sociological reservoir that emerges from this patterned nexus of institutional goals. It is to be underscored though that Nussbaum configures this model along lines familiar to sociologists through the problem of agency and structure. As she emphasizes, '[a]gency and support are connected: it is on account of their capacity for activity and striving that human beings are entitled to support for their vulnerability' (120).[5]

Thus, the favourable placement of social institutions in CA is clear and unambiguous. If CA invites a theory of social institutions to discuss freedom through the concept and metrics of capability, then sociology's long-lasting and prescient contributions to a theory of normatively sound institutions seems, oddly enough, quite unfavourably treated by CA. If CA theorists neglect sociological theory altogether, sociologists are performing marginally better. They have offered scattered invitations to CA as part of a rather impressionistic normative agenda in the face of global problems and local deprivations that afflict many of our fellows. Yet, on the issue of institutional approach to the 'good society' it may be no accident that only 'Third Way' (Etzioni 2000; Giddens 2000, 87–88) social theory and communitarianism (Etzioni 1988) discerned in Sen's critique of utilitarianism the promise of a moral replenishment of the market (see the relevant sections in Chapter 2).

Probing into the problem of how individual capabilities intersect with institutions, I advance the claim that the institutional patterns developed by Talcott Parsons in the AGIL scheme anticipate the main institutional imperatives that Sen sees as central to a theory of development as freedom (a convergence between Parsons' analytically deduced functional prerequisites and Sen's, largely empirically derived, instrumental freedoms). This last step, however, would require a shift beyond Parsons to a sociological architectonic that enables us to reconstruct the normative core of CA according to the logic of institutional arrangements. Such an institutional logic is available today in the shape of Axel Honneth's sociological theory of justice (for a sociological yet different approach to the just social order, see Phillips, 1986). Before this happens though I need to address the problem of pluralism, which in the CA vision of a liberal democracy figures as the stumbling block against a project of historically binding just institutions.

CA, institutions and pluralism

The oft-repeated emphasis on pluralism among CA scholars is thematized in two broad strokes. First, as a core value of the liberal outlook that aims to ensure that persons choose plural lifestyles they have reason to value. This pluralism stems not only from our voluntarism but also from the second dimension, namely the diverse cultural formations and patterns that make human society a differentiated entity, one that replenishes itself through the multitude of identities its members hold. As we discussed in Chapter 1, CA builds its policy scope on this pragmatic basis. The appeal of CA on situatedness rather than on some a priori institutional or policy programme finds its justification in this acknowledgement of pluralism. Pluralism as a collective fact (i.e. diversity of cultural patterns) and as a personal condition as we hold a bundle of ascribed and achieved statuses, affiliations and loyalties seems to be a *terminus a quo*. It possesses the status of an ultimate beginning. To be sure, pluralism as a liberal goal is also addressed, particularly by Nussbaum, as a *terminus ad quem*; a goal that is, that CA aims to serve and one towards which human flourishing is directed. In this way of putting the problem, pluralism is both an irreducible aspect of reality and, as it turns out, a value. In both ways as it were it is by CA standards in jeopardy from processes and institutional practices that seek to homogenize reality. Yet, this understanding of institutions by the CA is sociologically undertheorized (for instance, it is decoupled from systems theory). Pluralism is thus inserted into CA as a value, free of presuppositions. The risk here is seeing pluralism as a form of positivism where the 'facts' of this pluralism (i.e. the content of plural traditions, the prioritization for subjects of their plural affiliations) are taken to be ontological features of reality beyond reconstruction, unless this reconstruction stems from agents themselves and the shifting value-relevant descriptions they initiate.

There is however a third meta-level of justification for the two aforementioned defences of pluralism. This, as we have already discussed in previous chapters, relies on the epistemological assumption of incompleteness of orderings. Sen writes:

> The capability perspective is inescapably pluralist. First, there are different functionings, some more important than others. Second, there is the issue of what weight to attach to substantive freedom (the capability set) vis-à-vis the actual achievement (the chosen functioning vector). Finally, since it is not claimed that the capability perspective exhausts all relevant concerns for evaluative purposes (we might, for example, attach importance to rules and procedures and not just to freedoms and outcomes), there is the underlying issue of how much weight should be placed on the capabilities, compared with any other relevant consideration.
>
> (1999a, 76–77)[6]

CA's emphasis on pluralism appears as a corrective to the grand (even grandiose) proposals of transcendental theories of justice that seek to deduce a complete ordering of areas of justice. These approaches are held to advocate a vision of a 'perfectly just society'. The insistence on 'identifying perfectly just societal arrangements' (Sen 2006, 216) is counteracted by an alternative approach that compares these arrangements between societies and within a society and judges these to be 'more just' or 'less just'. This comparative approach is not necessarily tethered to a sort of transcendental theory of justice. What Sen finds wanting in Rawls' neglect of the 'impartial spectator' is summarized as follows: a) comparative assessment across societies and cultures; b) account of actors' social interactions beyond institutional norms and roles; c) accommodating incompleteness in assessment without jettisoning the ethical commitment of tackling social problems related to social injustice; and d) inclusive allowance of people's capability for voice outside the given social contract and the trappings of local parochialism (Sen, 2009, 70). Even if the transcendental approach to justice is seen as a sort of normatively laden heuristic device at distance from actual manifestations of justice or injustice in actual social settings, this does not necessarily imply that the comparative approach has to make do only by reference and approximations or deviations from that ideal sphere of justice. With plenty of irony Sen writes:

> To be sure, members of any polity can contemplate how a gigantic and totally comprehensive reorganization may be brought about, moving us *at one go* to the ideal of a fully just society. A no-nonsense transcendental theory can serve, in this sense, as something like the 'grand revolutionary's complete handbook'. But that handbook would not be much invoked in the debates on justice in which we are constantly engaged, which focus on how to reduce the manifold injustices that characterize the world.
>
> (2006, 221 [original emphasis])

Assuming that Sen has the Rawlsian model in mind when he disparages the ideal of a just society, both as a starting point and as an end-point on the problem of justice (Sen 2009, 105), one qualification would need to be added which I think is crucial: Rawls' 'just society' is not the sole model of a theory of just societal arrangements.

There are alternative models of sociological transcendentalism that make use of both a deduction of principles of justice and an inductive support from the historical evolution of societies. Hegel's theory of justice is one such example. Durkheim and Parsons proceeded similarly. Honneth's (2014) recent turn of Critical Theory to a logic of social freedom forged in distinct yet interrelated spheres of togetherness reconstructs this kind of deductive–inductive sociological transcendentalism. It is inductive because, like Sen, it takes seriously the actualities of justice and injustice. In giving voice to the historical dimension, none of these models of justice forfeit some connection to transcendentalism if by transcendentalism we understand the conditions that render justice possible. Those sociohistorical conditions were sought to have been available (even if, as all these writers acknowledge, in mixed and often incomplete shapes in actuality) in modernity. I get the sense that Sen lends himself a disservice on this point because by adducing with emphasis the 'at one go' hastiness of ideals of perfect justice he constructs a straw man easy to demolish. A careful consideration of the 'social ethics' approach to justice would have cautioned Sen from erroneously assuming that sociological transcendentalism proposes that one can 'leap over Rhodes' and build a utopia of justice at one stroke. To adduce sociological transcendentalism here is not a trump card externally introduced. The very reference to 'just society' and societal arrangements that meet the model imply that somewhere in empirical life we can muster fragments of socially institutionalized justice. The 'handbook' that Sen attributes to the 'revolutionary' is already partially 'in print'. Its pages include the Scottish, French and German Enlightenment to Hegel's idealism, classical sociology and contemporary social science, which converge, in spite of whether bolder or lighter highlight has been placed on the idea of the real possibility of institutional spheres of human freedom. Such arrangements may not be perfect in their historical particularities. Still, they are certainly steered by a logic of universal justice, immanent to the interdependent nexus of such institutions. Hence, abstract right, moral conscience, family and intimate relations, markets and property ownership, and the state, constitute an institutional universe of the idea of justice. These are not elaborate 'paraphernalia' (236), as Sen claims, but rather conditions for justice patterned at different degrees of 'completeness' or 'incompleteness' in history. The tension between a Hegelian approach to how progress towards justice that charts institutional formats of completeness and one that operates with a problem-solving idea of progress towards no goal whatsoever is evident here, if one, like Sen, takes the road towards incompleteness rather than the road towards an alternative view. Such a view would perceive incompleteness – due to our inevitable perspectivism – not necessarily through the lens of a *hiatus irrationalis* but rather by recourse to a perspective of justice sought from *within* the complete ordering of just institutions. Moreover, one cannot be sure either about the accuracy of the statement that the 'handbook' is not invoked when agents make efforts to combat injustice in actual settings. At least the claim's cogency does not seem entirely convincing. It would be really odd, and not at all complimentary – not to mention dispiriting – for human agency, if all attempts to capture not only the concept of a just society but also its historically actualized parameters did not visualize (and realize) the broadened overlapping consensus that Sen's theory indicates as a progressive problem shift made by CA to the problem of justice. For one thing, this would be bad news for the so-called flexibility of pragmatism and all promulgated ethics without ontology, since the flexibility invoked yields rather rigid denunciations of what this very flexibility, in taking into account diverse contexts, is designed to accomplish anyway, namely to bring resolutions to local injustices closer to one another.

Sen musters here various examples about common sense appreciation of relative weights or worth of something. For instance, he writes that knowing that 'Mount Everest is the tallest mountain in the world' does not prove particularly helpful in 'comparing the heights of, say, Kanchenjunga and Mont Blanc' (222). Indeed, if one wanted to make a comparison, particularly for practical purposes, say for climbing, considering the relative dangers of negative slopes, no reference to the most challenging negative slope in any mountain would really be necessary. Yet, actors all too often react to qualities and the worth of something by recourse to a perfect metric or standard. They do invoke a perfect notion of worth whether this is aesthetic, moral, juridical, utilitarian or of other kind. When I see Kanchenjunga I exclaim: 'A tall mountain', 'a beautiful mountain', 'a dangerous mountain'. The immediate perception of the object is marked by an intuition of its worth (or unworth if it's an ugly mountain). If I leave the movie theatre in ecstasy having seen Satyajit Ray's *Pather Panchali* and I exclaim that this is 'a masterpiece', I intuit its value not comparatively but in itself by reference to some absolute criterion of artistic perfection no matter how elusive this may be. I would then, maybe in trying to account for my judgment, provide immanent reasons for its validity and if the conversation would move this way I would engage in comparisons with the subsequent films of the *Apu Trilogy*, other films from India, or with paradigmatic Italian neo-realist masterpieces. Indeed, in all such occasions, it would not be very helpful to invoke aesthetic perfection. Sen is thus right to stress that such 'transcendental' criteria are of no (direct I would add) relevance when we compare societies or communities with one another. Indeed it would be very impractical (not to mention the manifold contestations by the parties involved in defining 'justice') to take recourse to this absolute measure. But this bracketing of 'justice' or any other cardinal moral value is also to be taken with caution. Although it cannot be invoked as a sufficient condition, its heuristic and transcendental status as a necessary condition in dealing with making unjust situations more just is important and necessary.[7]

The difference I note is that Sen's repulsion of transcendentalism is a move not outside transcendentalism but within it. It is an internal to justice demarcation of the relative merits and demerits of societal arrangements that if assessed in terms of how much justice they provide to citizens, somewhere in the process they presuppose or even 'bump' on an ultimate valuation: justice. So even if my remarks about Kanchenjunga pertain to its qualities, in all cases they recall the transcendental validity of 'tallness', 'beauty' and 'danger'. All the 'instrumental freedoms' proposed by Sen (1999a, xii–xiii, 38–40) as essential ingredients in advancing 'constitutive freedoms' are, in fact, part of the handbook's key chapters. The certainty with which Sen asserts that the 'world in which we live is not only unjust, it is, arguably, extraordinary unjust' (2006, 237) is complemented by a significant and not merely possible, as Sen contends, 'convergence of values' (234). It is part of the handbook's wisdom that incompleteness can be endemic to the project of justice, including viable attempts at rectification like public reasoning and the impartial spectator. The metrics that the community of scientists develop and the possibility of a universal 'we' from which we can scrutinize particular successes and failures of justice in various societal arrangements do not lose sight of the immanent (and sociohistorically transcendental)[8] conditions of possibility for intersubjective frameworks of (more or less) justice. With this issue in mind, Sen's concept of human freedom stops short of taking human freedom in its positive dimension (as opposed to freedom from interference) to imply human self-realization in a 'rational community' (see, for example, Prendergast 2005, 1160–1163). In other words, the limitation here appears to be one that ties Sen's notion of freedom to the moment of the Kantian

Willkür (the capacity for choice) rather than the freedom of the self in the life of the community. Interestingly enough, Stiglitz, Sen and Fitoussi (2009, 178–186) address quality of life implementation in the context of institutional patterns close to a conception of a *Sittlichkeit* – though it is not invoked by name. Additionally, the elimination of the so-called transcendental theory of just institutions makes Sen's project vulnerable to the binary logic his pragmatism and impartial spectator heuristics seek to overcome. In accommodating the role of social choice in a framework of reasoning about justice, Sen (2009, 106–111) makes room for the items of the 'comparative' (versus the 'transcendental') approach, the 'plurality of competing principles', the possibility of 're-examination', 'partial resolutions', 'diversity of interpretations and inputs', 'emphasis on precise articulation and reasoning' and 'role of public reasoning' in social choice. The epistemological grammar employed here makes, to be sure, for a powerful corrective to the transcendental approach. Yet, as an epistemological distinction, this move on Sen's part eliminates the 'other' in relation to which it posits its epistemological standpoint as a viable and 'better' alternative. In opting for one side of the implicit binary logic (i.e. comparative/relational approach to justice versus a transcendental approach), Sen retreats, eventually, from exploring the fusion of horizons between the two approaches. Support of the values of partiality, public sphere, pluralism, critical reexamination and so on is not a free-floating 'decision' of the research programme's protagonists. Rather, such values are couched on the very core of principles of justice that permeated modernity's institutional levels of justice, levels that incorporate the very principles adduced (even to the point of supporting the fiction of a pluralism, free of any conditions of possibility).

In short, CA has shown an understandable but mostly tactical reservation towards a substantive theory of 'capable institutions' as I'd like to call them. Yet as long as it insists on the project of a 'good society', the institutions that 'should', as is often claimed (Nussbaum 2011, 18), secure and develop human capabilities, CA cannot sever altogether the logical step that demands a vision of the (regulative or actual) idea of a 'good society'. When Nussbaum (90–91), for example, insists that neither Rawls nor her claim that the basic political principles both defend in their respective versions of justice must 'already be present in society' but, rather, that it 'is not unreasonable to suppose that society could arrive at that consensus', the argument's Kantian turn limits the CCL to the function of a regulative ideal of reason. 'We', CA scholars seem to say, 'treat institutions *as if* they could be coordinated by the CCL but we recede from identifying in empirical societies institutional arrangements stamped by the normative "logic" of capabilities'. Yet, at the same time CA theorists are adamant, rightly so in my judgment, in pointing out that the CCL should not be seen as an isolated normative benchmark for institutional aspirations in a society that likes to call itself just, but rather as a 'total set' (Nussbaum 2011, 92) of realizable aspirations. Moreover, capabilities are seen as a 'network' where each capability is part of a relational entity. This extremely important insight about the networked logic of capabilities resumes the theme of some sort of 'structural logic' in CA, which would enable us to work out patterns of capability accomplishment that are enduring, consensual and normatively binding. For if CA theorists hold that this possibility is not yet within the programme's reach, then we must scrutinize the justification for this decision and whether it strengthens or weakens CA's normative and policy core. Such institutional modesty though should be retained on realistic and feasibility grounds. For one thing, as Nussbaum correctly points out, people are not always either able or willing to change. It is the core principle of CA that structural demands as well as capability benchmarks must not appear taxing for the community in question.[9]

From the moment CA asks for deeper connections between capability deprivation (eschewing the significant but imperfect indicator of income) and other factors that affect the real impact income can have on its recipients, the transition to thinking about capable institutions makes room for the 'social aspect' that CA wishes to bring into sharper focus in economics, development policy and rational-choice theory. Sen's call for 'individualism as a social commitment' (1990) is an important thrust of his entire project. He even uses the phrase 'social ethics' which treats individual freedom both 'as a central value in any appraisal of society' and 'as an integral product of social arrangements' (1990, 49). Sen's claim is maximalistic and modernist through and through even if he recedes from both qualifications. It is maximalist – in the normative sense – because it implies that institutional arrangements have as their goal individual freedom along with its concomitant capabilities and conditions for leading a flourishing life. It is also modernist because it sees the goal of individual freedom to be derivative of a collective value. Although a welcoming gesture towards social frameworks that nourish the capable self, what precisely this 'social commitment' means is answered in an incomplete fashion. Because it has inscribed within its normative thrust robust, but certainly not mechanically foreclosed, quality of life indicators, CA aims to ground normativity in the considerable strengths of those societies that score better in terms of diminishing social inequality.[10] Hence, it bumps on the problem of institutional frameworks that secure most of the capabilities needed for a contemporary and defensible quality of life. This, for example, was Durkheim's core value of moral individualism in the social ethics of organic solidarity. This normative shift entails, however, the problem of the conditions under which this social commitment to individualism consolidates in modernity. Of course, the issue of modernity itself raises problems of social and cultural diversity. Sen introduces the historical factor in his scheme, operating, against his intentions to be sure, as a barrier to an institutionally binding normativity in the fashion of social ethics (*Sittlichkeit*).[11]

Rethinking social ethics: CA and Parsons

Let us consider this remark on CA by Richard Sennett:

> Failure to enable complexity is a sweeping theme in the work of the philosophers Amartya Sen and Martha Nussbaum. Their 'capabilities theory'

> argues that our emotional and cognitive capacities are erratically realized in modern society; human beings are capable of doing more than schools, workplaces, civil organizations and political regimes allow for. Sen and Nussbaum's views have been an inspiration for me [...]: people's capacities for cooperation are far greater and more complex than institutions allow them to be.
>
> (Sennett 2012, 29)

To be sure, Sennett has a point when he addresses the 'indeterminacy' of capability and its drive towards cooperation. However, in this chapter, I opt for the reverse line of argumentation, maintaining that the enrichment of the cooperative aspects of agency via capabilities remains an incomplete task, if capabilities become severed from 'capable' institutions. The 'capability of institutions' thesis is not as odd as it first seems. Numerous sociologists wrestled with the problem of founding and justifying institutional social arrangements. For many in the discipline these arrangements were assessed predominantly in terms of functional capacities. Others elaborated theories of social institutions with a view to impute ethical value on the functions that are generated and fulfilled for social integration. Normative questions arose also from the conflict in society's differentiated systems that stems from power relations and class, race and gender hierarchies. Emancipatory and conservative (for an overview, see Strasser 1976) schools of sociological thought developed with a view to identify, conceptually and historically, the contours of the good and just society. Thus, a recurring motif centred around the issue of those parts of society being held to be normatively just, in so far as their form of interrelationship entails freedom, reciprocity and communicative transparency, all essential requirements beyond administrative efficiency and functional coordination of other social spheres under their influence. Tied to this quest was the problem of disorder risks which beyond its Hobbesian heritage bequeathed to sociology a dual analytical scheme that hoped to locate causes and elements of disintegration at two distinct yet interrelated levels of social reality: system integration ('the orderly or conflictual' relationships between parts of the social system) and social integration ('the orderly or conflictual' relationships between actors) (Lockwood 1964, 245). It is beyond the scope of this chapter to address the potential and the limitations of Lockwood's almost canonical model. I shall use it heuristically in order to connect Sen's and Nussbaum's ideas to questions of sociological relevance. I thus hope to show that the focus lain on actors' experiences (their capability empowerment or capability deprivation) enables CA to claim that its categories are those that actors tend to make sense of their own experience, particularly when they assess their successful reproduction of routine orders of action and meaning on the basis of what *they* claim are capable of choosing and doing. It is actors' own experiences that are held to take the narrative of capability to explain social life, whether capability empowerment or impairment is attributed to social integration or to system properties (as for instance in the exploitation generated by capital's social relations of production). While system properties are acknowledged by CA, what remains absent in this account is the notion of configuring collectively validated action-patterns which actors themselves judge to be enabling or constraining of their capabilities to choose alternative functioning combinations.

Notions of capabilities and functionings are important because they cut across system and social integration narratives. Actors are held to possess physical, cognitive, emotional and practical capabilities that they test and develop under conditions of social interaction. Systems are also held to be driven by 'capacities' (organizational, material, technical, informational) to function and thus to steer 'human capital' in institutional reproductions of social order, ideally in line with actors' freedom and capability to choose if the lifestyles they have reason to value can be pursued in the social roles which form the self and social identity. The closest CA comes to considering the mutuality of system and social integration is the idea of 'individual freedom as social commitment' (Sen 1990, 1999a). I have just referred to 'human capital' having in mind an interesting distinction made by Sen. He writes:

> it can be said that the literature on human capital tends to concentrate on the agency of human beings in augmenting production possibilities. The perspective on human capability focuses, on the other hand, on the ability – the substantive freedom – of people to lead the lives they have reason to value and to enhance the choices they have.
>
> (Sen 1999a, 293)

What is salient here is the reproduction of system and social integration in CA. From the angle of system integration agents are problematized in the semantics of 'human capital'. Seen from the actual routine aspirations, Sen proposes the semantics of 'human capability'. For Sen, the two notions are interrelated but the distinction between the two is not invalid, provided that priorities are set. To argue that agents should be seen as 'productive' through the lens of system integration (i.e. economy) is to neglect the integration of economic and social aspects that Sen finds so attractive in Adam Smith. Thus:

> these [education, health care etc., SG] "social developments" must directly count as "development", since they help us to lead longer, freer and more fruitful lives, *in addition* to the role they have in promoting productivity or economic growth or individual incomes.
>
> (295 [original emphasis])

Sen's passage about Adam Smith recalls what was articulated in Chapters 2 and 4 and had to do with the Marxian vision of the 'social individual' whose fulfilled and multifaceted flourishing becomes a force of production! Sen therefore expects a problem shift to be initiated in CA that subsumes system integration properties to social integration, without inducing that 'human capital' is in itself 'alienated' or 'instrumental'; rather, it can – as often is the case – assume alienating features only in abstraction from 'human capabilities'. Thus, for Sen, the issue is not so much 'bad' system integration but, rather, the cutting loose of its interchanges with social integration. In Habermas' terms Sen sees the problem not simply in terms of 'colonization' but rather of the 'autonomy' not only of system but also of life-world. Evidently, actors cannot (nor want to) dispense with system properties (i.e. markets, instrumental rational action) that act as valuable and valued resources for the reproduction and pursuit of the lives they choose to value.

One route towards affirming such collective values recalls Parsons' emphasis on the 'fiduciary' aspects of AGIL. This aspect is recognized as a worthy goal by Sen (he refers to 'our fiduciary responsibility' (Sen 2009, 251)) but, again, without sketching the institutional contours for this trust and credibility to consolidate in societies. While it is emphatically asserted and empirically demonstrated by Sen that several institutions (economy, state, education, media) need to coordinate their action-plans in order to counter all kinds of appalling deprivations, what hampers the theoretical hard core of CA is its silence on what the 'logic' of these institutions can look like. The implication is that institutions are benchmarked pragmatically only, while no relation seems to be discerned or sought between their problem-solving success and the normative map of the institution the success of which is held to be conducive to the reduction and elimination of deprivation and inequality. As Parsons writes:

> Even if enforcement were effective, it would still be necessary to bring about an essential set of conditions concerned with qualifications for taking advantage of the opportunities offered. The newly included group must have the capacity to perform its role credibly. The mere statement that justice requires inclusion is not enough, because allegations of injustice must involve the capacity factor – namely, that the excluded group could make valuable contributions but is denied the opportunity to do so. Capacity must be asserted on the part of the excluded group, and, insofar as it is not yet present, the larger community must take steps to help develop it.
>
> (Parsons 1969, 262–263)

Passages like these reveal the conceptual subtlety of certain sociological concepts, in so far as they allocate individual or group capacities into institutionally differentiated patterns of roles-expectations. Thus, in Parsons, differentiation (as a system capacity) progresses to the extent that actors are capable of setting action-plans, uninhibited and without too much role strain.

In *Development as Freedom* (1999a) Sen sets the normative coordinates for a capability-based ethics. He makes a major distinction early on in the argument. He displays freedom's two aspects, namely the constitutive and the instrumental. This distinction in the book's architectonic is not limited to its analytical value. Rather, it denotes the covert logic of freedom's institutional presuppositions, which figure as moments of the agent's ascent to the ideal of freedom's constitutive essence. If we rely a bit on Hegel's institutional justification of freedom's actuality then Sen's constitutive freedom may as well be posited as the idea of freedom. Reading carefully the instrumental aspects of freedom one cannot fail to notice that these resemble distinct spheres of right. They are all set up in such fashion as to be able to fulfil an ethical goal. What I find even more remarkable is the morphology of the partial, as Sen admits, set of instrumental freedoms. The instrumental dimension does not have here a Weberian resonance but rather it reads more in line with normative functionalist approaches. If we take into consideration the acme of normative functionalism in Talcott Parsons' AGIL system of functional imperatives, this axiomatic scheme seems to resurface in Sen's template of instrumental freedoms. Clearly, this affinity belies Sen's intentions, who, to my knowledge, never mentions Parsons. Let us consider this parallel more closely.

Sen presents five areas of instrumental freedoms. Instrumental freedoms are defined as the '*principal means* of development' whereas the '*primary end*' refers to the constitutive role of freedom (1999a, 36). The latter is intrinsically connected to human flourishing and a person's capability to live an 'enriching human life' (36). Coupled to this, the instrumental function of freedom refers to different sets of entitlements and opportunities that can contribute to expanding human freedom. These are (38–40):

- Political freedoms: Broadly understood, they include civil rights and various democratic entitlements.
- Economic facilities: Access to markets, freedom to access the conditions of exchange, economic entitlements and distributional considerations fall under this provision.
- Social opportunities: These include arrangements about health and education.
- Transparency guarantees: Of cardinal significance here is the role of trust and openness in various social interactions including economic ones.
- Protective security: This is a social safety net that includes anything from unemployment benefits to famine relief.

If we continue the pattern-analogies that we introduced in Chapter 1 then we can conjecture that Parsons' axiomatic modalities of the social system prove quite resilient for any pragmatic undertaking that seeks to single out institutional helpers to individual freedom.

As displayed in Figure 6.1, the empirically driven instrumental freedoms that Sen configures as the normative benchmark for institutions across cultures, bears striking resemblance to a paradigm likely to qualify as a version of the 'institutional fundamentalism' he is at pains to avoid. The issue is not so much here a one-to-one correspondence in a 'one-size-fits-all' scheme. Rather, the drawn parallels aim to rerecruit the functional rigour of Parsons in a pragmatic undertaking like the one that feeds CA. It is evident that Sen regards these instrumental freedoms both as 'functions', conducive to the widening and deepening of constitutive freedom, and as intrinsically valuable social patterns. Yet all five qualify as

Figure 6.1 Amartya Sen's instrumental freedoms configured after Parsons' functional imperatives.

	Talcott Parsons (AGIL)	*Amartya Sen (Instrumental Freedoms)*	
L	Latent-Pattern Maintenance	Transparency Guarantees	**L**
I	Societal Integration	Social Opportunities, Protective Securities	**I**
G	Goal-Attainment	Political Freedoms	**G**
A	Adaptation	Economic Facilities	**A**

institutional processes with a view to make a society stronger in terms of the adaptive and quality of life capacities of its members. To be sure, one can debate the status of the categories and the demarcations between them. As Sen also recognizes, and is also the crux of sociology's quest for knowledge about institutions, mediations among all compartments are subject to change. Now this change, as Hegel, Durkheim, Parsons and Honneth – albeit in different ways – suggest, in spite of time–space lapses, tends to be undergirded in societies through collective activities and processes that bear on elementary conditions for social reproduction and societal evolution. This social evolution culminated in modernity. Modern society's institutional configurations were invested with sufficient ethical content to justify not only modernization processes of convergence but also universal discourses of human rights and justice. At the other end, criticism of their views stressed the historicist dimension of sociology and played up non-linear narratives that typically reconstruct comparative tracks between culturally unique societies. Notions of normative integration were taken to task by diverse and formidable critics (e.g. Weber, Foucault, Luhmann, Baudrillard, Deleuze) from different vantage points. Others opt for a discourse that relativizes any genealogical primacy of modernity's special sociocultural status, pointing not only, as Sen does (1999c), to the multiple threads across cultures that nourished global ideals like democracy, but questioning the normativity of modernity given its colonial presuppositions and its own internally erupted potential for catastrophes, emblemized in 'Auschwitz'. I shall take up some of these criticisms in Chapter 7. For the moment, I shall stick to the so-called 'privileged' status of modernity as an inclusive and universal institutional possibility for justice.

In a manner that is both programmatic and strikingly close to the theoretical aspirations sought by Parsons, Sen regards *Development as Freedom* as a work that:

> outlines the need for an integrated analysis of economic, social and political activities, involving a variety of institutions and many interactive agencies. It concentrates particularly on the roles and interconnections between certain crucial instrumental freedoms, including *economic opportunities, political freedoms, social facilities, transparency guarantees*, and *protective security*. Societal arrangements, involving many institutions (the state, the market, the legal system, political parties, the media, public interest groups and public discussion forums, among others) are investigated in terms of

> their contribution to enhancing and guaranteeing the substantive freedoms of individuals, seen as active agents of change, rather than as passive recipients of dispensed benefits.
>
> (Sen, 1999a, xii–xiii [original emphasis])

Elsewhere, Sen (2004) makes a strong case for highlighting the presence and crucial influence of cultural factors in a society's economy, an influence that is largely sidestepped or missed by the economics orthodoxy today. This qualifies as an insertion of cultural values (L) into economy (A). He also concedes (Sen 2009, 77–78) that Rawls sketches only basic templates for institutional principles of justice, leaving open the breadth of their interdependence with actual social interactions. Parsons' institutionalized individualism sets the parameters for conceptualizing the capability of action in normative terms and in conjunction with some common value-system. Once more, Parsons tells us that:

> changes in the *society* in a desirable direction must be those which contribute to the generalized achievement or performance *potential* of the system as a whole and of its units taken distributively. If we use the term *capacity* to refer to all the equalities of a unit which bear on its potential performance, and the term *opportunity* to refer to the situational factors which facilitate or impede his or its effective performance, then we can say that performance potential in the system is a direct function of the level of the capacity of units and of the level of opportunity open to them. Anything then which contributes to raise the level of capacity of important units, or to improve the level of opportunities open to them, will tend to be positively valued.
>
> (Parsons 1991, 53–54 [original emphasis])

What is clear from this passage is the emerging picture of a 'sociological transcendental idealism' (Lechner 1991, 183) that renders normative institutions in modernity a historical a priori for conceptualizing action sociologically. I do not regard this as a limitation of Parsons' theory, in the similar sense in which the 'scientific stage' is not a limitation for Comte, 'organic solidarity' for Durkheim or *Sittlichkeit* for Hegel.[12] Rather, it seems that Parsons discloses the implicit commitment to some notion of normative institutions upon which capabilities are incumbent.

The challenge of Luhmann's systems theory

The osmosis between CA and normative functionalism that I advanced would in all likelihood be unpalatable to a posthumanist systems theory. As I see it posthumanist systems theory as it was developed by Luhmann would consider two major problems:

1 First, it would treat CA as a new moral codification of society. As society's proposed self-description (assuming that CA would gain ascendancy and

universal appeal), CA must rely on a functional distinction. It must demarcate between what promotes capabilities from what inhibits them. This distinction is no other than 'capability/incapability' or 'capability/capability deprivation'. From Luhmann's perspective this moralization of policy that bears on other social systems (economy, polity, religion, law etc.) in order to be functionally effective as a systemic (and systematic) programme must differentiate itself internally. This means that for every prime distinction, which functions as a meaning-generating codification of the programme, CA would need to apply this distinction to itself. Hence, on the side of capability a new distinction would need to surface (between 'capability/capability deprivation') in order for 'capability' to acquire the requisite functional flexibility that will enable its proponents to establish relevancies to other social systems. (For Luhmann, these relevancies form structural couplings between social systems.) Thus, if, for example, the capability to control one's material environment is conceded, such capability would soon need to differentiate internally between further 'capability/capability deprivation distinctions' (like those between labour/capital, worker trade unionism/unionized work, proletarian/immigrant worker and so on.) If these examples pertain mostly to stratification exclusions, Luhmann's procedure would aim at the functional differentiation of society. Thus, inclusion in one social system would require exclusion. The capability to serve life is on a par – in systemic terms – with the (military) capability to annihilate life. Mobilizing such arguments Luhmann ((1997) 2013, 281) would want to expose the paradox of CA and reveal the latter's categorial 'foul play': a category (i.e. capability) can yield mutually exclusive outcomes, but as a category it is *decided* that, for normative purposes, the distinction between the capability to serve life and the capability to destroy life, will be further differentiated from the side of the 'capability to serve life'. The 'foul play' in this case would concern the moralization of this condition, namely that we are capable to demonstrate (from the perspective of life-affirming social theory and policy) that the distinction is moral, whereas for Luhmann the distinction would be existential and evolutionary in terms of the functional differentiation of the moral system. So the putative wedge in CA on Luhmann's part would question the moral dimension of the arch-distinction between 'capability/capability deprivation'. Rather than being moral, it is evolutionary and functional. In other words, the neutrality modicum of CA would have somehow to be suspended if this chief distinction is to be able to be drawn at all. Talking about 'capabilities' qualifies as a moral distinction and as such it already presupposes a (evolutionary and functionally differentiated) decision on the relevant evaluative space. Sen, I take it, would not necessarily see this as fatal tension in CA. As long as the latter carves an evaluative space on reality, this methodological decision stands or falls with the normative and descriptive force of the distinction. Luhmann would not disagree. He would though raise the objection that CA is another discourse of inclusion. As such it seeks to counter social exclusion by redrawing its master code of functional differentiation (i.e. capability/capability deprivation). CA would maybe resort to the pragmatic and flexible code of capabilities, which tackles the inclusion/exclusion problem on the micro-environments of different situations, social interactions, local and regional milieux and is loosely coupled to CA's more ambitious entanglement with the UN or with globalization. But although this 'milieu-specific', as Luhmann would say (291), rescuing operation is a formidable way of retorting, it would still, I think, fail to satisfy Luhmann's scepticism. Is capability empowerment in one area (e.g. control over a person's material environment) excluding capability empowerment in another (e.g. capacity to enjoy the natural habitat)? CA could maybe still retort that regardless of the logic of functional differentiation of social systems (which by default 'exclude' in order to 'include'), it seeks capability empowerment deontologically as it treats human beings as ends in themselves and pragmatically as it avoids inflating its moral requirements precisely because it is conscious of the overlapping 'conflicts' in a logic of complex system differentiation. But this would violate the consequentialist flexibility of CA. And, consequentialism in its turn would require coordination issues, which as Luhmann would suggest are impossible (in exclusion-free terms) under global conditions of functional differentiation.

2 Second, a systems theory adversary would consider Nussbaum's proposal for the irreducible status of the CCL as a reduction of complexity. In other words, instead of establishing relations between capabilities, these, on the one hand, are placed together in the same normative cluster, while on the other hand the internal relations among them are 'explained away', being treated as 'residual' categories that surface only on the level of comparisons and policy-making in actual social settings. The latter is not a negligible accomplishment for CA because, as we have discussed, it enables governments, NGOs and communities to act without recourse to some master-set of institutional coordinates. Real problems are addressed effectively and real people as well as communities witness significant gains in their freedoms. Nussbaum's 'irreducibility' (seen as a reduction of complexity and thus as a barrier to establishing stronger linkages, or even priorities, among capabilities) thesis contradicts her recourse to grappling with 'complexity', which she raises against models that invoke 'complexity' to avoid measuring with wider, but no less essential, facets of people's capabilities. She writes that the 'right response to the complexity is to work harder at identifying and measuring the pertinent factors' (Nussbaum 2011, 61). Luhmann would not welcome such a response. The very categories employed to curb complexity are utilized from the bygone era of stratificatory differentiation, which assumes that 'soon enough' complexity will be curbed. Complexity can assume ideological masking and can often work as an unjustified barrier to problem-solving policies. What is often a theoretical, methodological and normative limitation of a research programme is imputed to reality's complexity. In this spirit Sen also champions informational broadening and

> transpositional scrutiny. Yet, the objection to Nussbaum cannot be so easily overcome. First, because 'complexity' is built into CA and thus at least as far as her version is concerned complexity always comes to an (artificial for Luhmann) halt (i.e. the CCL). For our account here, this would suffice as a natural law buffer against absurd and deleterious reductions of the human to the non-human or against the determinist fascination with the reduction of the rich bundle of our capacities to our genes. But for Luhmann, this would be an irrelevant halt because communication in society takes place over and above the human, taking thus the form of communication between systems. Here Luhmann transfers the problem of communication into meta-communicative processes as far as markets, political parties, activist groups, religious leaders and systems communicate with each other, where the premium is placed not on what is shared in communication but on what is excluded from this sharing. This happens, because, in alignment with the logic of the *hiatus irrationalis*, 'exclusion' is the condition of possibility for 'inclusion', the latter, of course, being a paradoxical concept as it has, eventually, to include 'inclusion' in the process of its own reproduction (what for Luhmann would constitute the pretensions of the Habermasian ideal of undistorted communication). If we stretch this to CA and visualize the utmost broadening of information, then, the logic of Sen's project is carried to its full consequences. But such haughty project of integration to which Luhmann needs always to recall in order to undermine processes and policies of inclusion is deemed by Sen's epistemology and policy proposals to be not immediately relevant. The critical question Sen might pose, for example, is if the demographically unobserved 'missing women' in India (Sen 2009, 167) and other parts of the world constitute a condition for functional differentiation. On normative grounds he would surely oppose it. He does recognize though (Sen 1992b, 2003) the unfortunate loose coupling of gender bias in religion and demographic exigencies as a factor of complexity that leads to the increase of 'missing women' rather than to the anticipated decrease of this regrettable phenomenon.

For critics of this benign model of evolutionary normative differentiation, modernity as a system develops in a direction of functional differentiation that leaves actors with little option of changing the institutional pattern. Claus Offe, for example, contends that 'the more options we open up for ourselves, the less available as an option is the institutional framework itself with the help of which we disclose them' (1987, 9). This is a mild version of the TINA logic that is currently in circulation. To translate this into CA-language, the more people gain capabilities the less capable they will become to 'see' the risks involved in greater and more complex interdependence between society's subsystems. This will happen because capable agents will become autonomous generators of system complexity and self-steering capacities in thoroughly unpredictable ways. The cost of these capability-enhancements for all ('if *everyone* stands on their tip toes *no one* can see better') (9 [original emphasis]) is that with greater autonomy come increases in contingency. Offe reformulates here Luhmann's version of the *hiatus irrationalis*: Systems cannot function unless they draw on distinctions. This logic of distinctions presupposes that in every step an 'us' versus 'them' demarcation will be made. Offe is not as outspoken – normatively speaking – as Luhmann, yet for him any 'broadening' (Offe 1992, 89) of a normative agenda on the part of social integration (e.g. labour) would bear uncertainty and risk, concomitant outcomes of which increase in complexity. It would thus be forced to exhaust its strategic resources due to its spatial, temporal and systemic extension. To avoid the consequence of inflated (and hence unrealizable) normative commitments, subsystems would need to differentiate internally and establish internal criteria for 'distinction' (thus of 'exclusion'). That move *has* to be made because if a system (already differentiated from its 'environment', namely 'other systems') does not make it and instead opts for claims to full functional transparency (i.e. elimination of contingency) it will be rendered dysfunctional.

In different terms, this is the problem of 'solvency' addressed by Parsons. At a given moment the system has always to appear 'insolvent' in terms of fulfilling simultaneously all its obligations. Offe's critique of the logic of integration that 'traditional' accounts of modernity's institutions rely upon is premised on placing the problem of societal reproduction at the level of a system's steering capacities in the face of reality's contingency. At the same time the periodical 'zero-option' to opt out from a collectively sanctioned behavioural pattern (having an 'education', an 'income', a 'family') tends to lead either to curtailments in actor's responsible action (as they would prefer to 'co-opt' instead of 'opting-out' from the 'system', something which would put them at personal risk) or to an ideological repackaging of the utopia of every-option, and hence of zero-options (i.e. the example of everyone 'seeing', everyone drafting money from their accounts and so on). To address the 'utopia of zero-options' Offe pursues a track that seems to me to be in line with some of Sen's tractions. Given problems of contingency and impossibilities for full transparency (what appears also in Sen's critique of perfect ordering of preferences) the possibility to consider is not a move towards greater interdependence but, rather, to more system independence. The semantics of 'loose couplings', 'devolution', 'auto-centred development', 'self-reliance' (1987, 21) – with pragmatism as its ally on the level of social integration – opens up the possibility of 'capabilities' to qualify as the normative equivalent of the sequences that couple systems to actors' goal-schemes, routines and freedoms.

Because subsystems can never be uncoupled from each other – even Luhmann concedes this – the problem is transferred to what these loose couplings can mean. In essence, we return to the logic of mediations between social subsystems and if these mediations can be made 'loose' in a normatively meaningful sense. Offe gets us close to this solution because mediations imply an 'exchange of marginal renunciation of enhancement of options for a gain in steering capacity (or, more precisely, for a marginal saving of steering problems caused by unforeseen later consequences and results for action)' (1987, 22).

This solution rescues romantic values of humility and 'smallness' (values of moderation or 'ethics of responsibility') by transposing them to system-steering problems. It thus avoids Luhmann's posthumanism – at least its radical consequences, which are tantamount to exclusionary logics – and the perils of value-fundamentalism (see the next chapter). As Offe suggests, shortening the sequences of causal chains of effects, implies that problems relating to 'externalities' across subsystems can become more manageable. So if for example individuals desire 'zero-options' in the domain of earned incomes, systemic provisions should be available to mitigate for such deviant cases. Such individuals therefore, 'should not be punished with severe loss of income, but rather should be able to claim a "basic income"' (22). (This connects to public policies on UBI and to the gradual as well income-independent – as in sabbatical leaves – provisions Offe makes elsewhere on the feasibility of UBI (Offe 2001).) Such systemic adaptations are reflexive and capable of absorbing the effects of externalities. Offe is reluctant to take recourse to 'traditional' normative weapons like 'natural law' or 'moral individualism'. Rather, he advances a functional rationale that introduces into a system's reflexive capacities additional requirements for self-limitation coupled to the greater self-referential autonomy of units. The outcome is a vision of rescuing modernity's complexity by reducing the impact or system risks and dangers, giving thus greater allowance to tolerable levels of 'zero-options'. Sen's partial orderings are not far from this solution as Sen is also unhappy with system and social integration, which when inflated prime organizational efficiency and moral purity respectively as functional and normative societal operations. Where the difference with Offe lies is that Sen does not repel the invocation of the 'ultimate resource' or 'ultimate value' of a free actor upon whom the entire system depends for its own productivity. He sees, like Offe, the perils of overused and haughty normative commitments, yet does not abandon the agent's capability to steer action-patterns on the basis of choices he can freely make. In essence, however, Offe and Sen share the same conviction that some discharge of rigid interdependencies is both functionally and normatively feasible (as well as necessary).[13] They also share the idea that internal system differentiation implies greater independence (autonomy, freedom) for actors who are thus brought to maximize their own self-referential capacities; thus, actors are brought to a position where, equipped with greater capabilities, they are now able to minimize the externality risks that go with greater interdependence.

The upshot here is that given the reality of system complexity, Sen's work provides a promising revision of a theory of justice. The handful of sociologists who detect in Sen's theory of justice something of a potential merit for sociology are attracted to the idea of incompleteness that suffuses Sen's programme. Promoting justice and combating injustice does not require a complete theory of justice as its condition of validity. Sen outlines this with force and clarity in his *The Idea of Justice* (2009). With this argument in mind Bauman (2017), for example, welcomes Sen's paradigm shift. Bauman writes that: '"Just society" is a society permanently sensitive and vigilant to all cases of injustice and undertaking to take action to rectify them without waiting for the search of the universal model of justice to be completed' (2017, 22). Thus, the motif that Sen's work introduces is 'complexity' and openness of 'critical examination' (2009, 83). The first is a bulwark against de-differentiated reductions of the problem of justice to a single causal factor (e.g. class structure in capitalism), while the second is held to safeguard explanation from a lapse into moral dogmatism, if the recommended institutional arrangements are regarded as being 'best'.

Axel Honneth and the sociological theory of justice

Axel Honneth must be credited with a forceful sociological renewal of Hegel's political philosophy. He is also to be credited with the opportunity he gives to sociologists to reclaim a theory of justice and thus to become key players in the relevant discussions with political philosophy. Moreover, the theory of institutional spheres of freedom that he suggests should also be seen as a qualified response to the challenges posed by posthumanist systems theory like the one launched by Luhmann.

To my knowledge it is Paul Ricoeur's reconstruction of a fundamental groundwork of capabilities that paves the way to a theory of recognition with its institutional manifestation in Honneth's later work on *Freedom's Right* (2014). Ricoeur (2006) anticipates the trail I have tried to pursue in sociological connections to CA because he likens the discourse of capabilities to philosophical anthropology (2006, 17). He considers that some basic species capabilities must be underscored before one enters the project of reconstruction. Because these take me into a different landscape, I will not analyse them now in any detail. What matters most is that beyond the 'capacity to speak', the 'capacity to act' (which I explored in Chapter 3) and the 'capacity to tell', and thus construct a narrative identity (18–19), Ricoeur's focus on normative coordinates of these anthropologically foundational features of human sociality bears on the topic of recognition. An essential moment here is Ricoeur's contention that the prime modality of self-recognition relies on the capability to confidently assert that 'I strongly believe that I can' (21 [original emphasis removed]). For Ricoeur then the challenge for a theory of intersubjective recognition is to engage the capability of self-recognition (condensed in the three capacities) to a claim to 'some sort of need to be recognized and thus developing a right to accomplishment, fulfillment and flourishing' (22). From that moment onward the reconstruction must follow the Hegelian trajectory, which leads the will to successive stages of sublation before an intersubjective landscape of mutual recognition begins to become (as a logical configuration) engraved on patterns of social interaction. To recover its critical standpoint and retain its relational gain of freedom, the will must recognize the world of determinations as its own freedom. It must feel at home in this world, which is a world of intersubjective relations.[14] These social relations constitute the moments of being oneself in the other and encapsulate the arduous process of sublating the negativity that is implies in any encounter with the other.

Because Honneth's latest work (2014) on freedom and social institutions constitutes the most recent and elaborate reconstruction of *Sittlichkeit*, I need to highlight its main theses. This shall enable us to judge the level of abstraction in terms of the social reach of CA on the institutional spheres that promote human flourishing. The sociological recovery of Hegelian normativity in sociology developed by Honneth (1995) identifies three major shapes of recognition: self-confidence, self-esteem and self-respect. Regarding self-confidence, Honneth resorts to findings and shapes of intersubjective recognition from Hegel's ideas about love as a reconciliation of unity with difference, to research in developmental moral psychology. Mead's interactionism is also a powerful trope in Honneth's exposition. Self-respect addresses the legal and normative fortification of the self in the form of rights and stems from T.H. Marshall's division between political, civil and social rights. Human dignity appears here to encapsulate the normative anchorage of the agent's attainment of self-respect; last, self-esteem encompasses the formation of collective sympathy and solidarity in the public sphere. Honneth's proposed moral grammar in the struggle for recognition weaves the normative social fabric that binds individuals into a morally cohesive framework of interaction with the three normative claims constituting an irreducible ground towards the goal of cooperative human sociality. Once this happens, Honneth takes this drive to recognition (which clearly involves struggles with the 'other' based on the logic of will's intersubjective formation as shown previously) to the highest level of system complexity, namely the modern spheres of freedom. This enables him to tackle forms of disrespect *within* institutional frameworks of intersubjective claims to recognition and justice. Thus, threatened components of the human personality are located within a sphere of recognition. For example, abuse and rape (Honneth 1995, 129) would threaten a person's physical integrity (i.e. most of the capability deprivations in the bodily components of the CCL), social exclusion and denial of rights abuse a person's social integrity (hence capabilities like affiliation, inability to control one's economic and political environment would be located in this normative space), and insult or denigration, which for Honneth violate a person's self-esteem and her dignity (as we saw in Chapter 5, this pertains to Nussbaum's sustained critique of stigmatization and its corollaries relates to this problem).

Honneth's recent work extends this normative pursuit but this time, and more ambitiously, it emulates the logico-historical exposition of freedom in Hegel's political philosophy. Hegel's transition (as a form of dialectical enrichment of normativity) from abstract right to morality and to the culmination of *Sittlichkeit* (ethical life) is effected through a renovated theory of justice tailored now as a sociological project. To accomplish this feat, which gives voice to sociology on the discourse of justice unduly monopolized in political philosophy, Honneth incorporates the Parsonsian element of cultural integration fulfilled by the function of universal values, upon which notions of just social institutions relies in the context of are renovated Critical Theory (see Gangas 2017). Justice under social freedom – the equivalent exposition to Hegel's 'ethical life' – requires sociological knowledge that reworks the mediations between the spheres of personal relationships (friendship, intimacy, family life), the market economy and the sphere of public will-formation. (We can recall momentarily the MM model under the rubric of which I discussed Sen's project of 'ethics and economics', the middle configuration in Honneth's exposition of social freedom relies on the moral economism of thinkers like Hegel and Durkheim, among others.) Areas of alienation and domination (and hence of capability deprivations) are now problematized in their institutional specificity, taking into consideration an institutional sphere's coupling to other subsystems (institutions) of society. Under the canopy of the social totality's multiple and interlocking spheres of justice, Honneth (2014) is able to identify risks like legalism (114), character personalities that exaggerate and caricature moral integrity (115) and, of course, the fundamentalist de-differentiation (Luhmann) of morality by recourse to terrorism (118). The lack of 'discursive mechanisms' (217) in the field of consumption, the gradual decline of workers' 'community-building' efforts (232) as a by-product of the welfare-state, in conjunction with a de-regulated market (245) are theorized by Honneth in the context of the historical deficits that block the logic of a just coordination of the market economy. It is as if the normative principles and promises (196) of the market economy suffocate under distorted historical manifestations of it.

But even in the realm of the democratic will-formation, Honneth recedes from an uncritical celebration of the public sphere. He retains the relevance of the 'culture industry' thesis to account for oligopolistic and manipulative distortions of media (298), or for the democratic decline of interactive networks (303) in the information society. Sen, for example, gives importance to the role of media in ways that conform to a logic of institutional arrangements under the aegis of justice. Referring to 'an unrestrained and healthy media', Sen (2009, 335–336) considers their upgraded functions to be marked by: a) the 'direct contribution' free speech and the press can have on quality of life; b) the dissemination of knowledge (crucial also for Sen's epistemology of informational broadening); c) the 'protective role' media can play to enhance the capability for voice, particularly, for people who are disadvantaged; and d) the 'formation of values' that depends crucially on open and unrestrained communication as well as on the reasoned argumentation aired in the media. For Sen (2009, 337) then 'a well-functioning media' is an essential component for promoting 'public reasoning' and, consequently, through this latter role can turn to a major factor in 'the pursuit of justice'. One could hardly detect a more normatively committed belief in the 'just society' and the 'just institutions' that is at odds with Sen's association (and repulsion) of the ideal of a just society after Rawls' transcendental theory of justice. The crux of the matter here is that for any coupling of a theory of justice to actual social settings 'we must assume that our norms and values have absorbed enough rationality to be regarded as a social context whose moral guidelines we must generally consider to be beyond doubt' (Honneth 2010, 41).

If the reconstruction proposed sounds too sociological and institutionally laden outside the pragmatic versatility of CA, we need to recall that this revision of social ethics is no longer a 'double' integration ('system integration' vs.

'social integration') moving in diametrically opposed normative and functional trajectories but one that expands the value-formation process across the institutional board: 'The formation of values and the emergence and evolution of social ethics are also part of the process of development that needs attention, along with the working of markets and other institutions' (Sen 1999a, 297). In this fashion, the nation-state operates under the overarching project – partially realized – of universal values and formal frameworks of collective action held to be binding by all relevant participants.[15]

Deliberative democracy and CA

The normative shift to deliberative democracy has expectedly taken the front stage in extended debates on the implementation of CA. Deepening democracy in the way CA scholars suggest is a central track for the project of freedom. Sen and Nussbaum devote, as we have shown, extensive justifications that offer convincing and fruitful pathways for enhancing democracy without trapping it, as a universal value, into some monolithic institutional matrix.

Studies of CA (Bonvin and Laruffa 2018; Bonvin, Laruffa and Rosenstein 2018) support and explicate this normative deepening of democracy, extending it often to similar ventures in sociology, like for example, to Appadurai's 'capacity to aspire'. They all underscore the merits of a CA-based model of deliberative democracy in contrast to Habermas' procedural emphasis on deliberative democracy. They also contend that the existence of injustice is the starting point in Sen's approach in the antipodes of Rawlsian and Habermasian formalism. It is rightly emphasized by these authors that Sen's constructive model of deliberative democracy reclaims the political processes in the production of knowledge and thus contains an important critical edge. Others (De Leonardis, Negrelli and Salais 2012) link CA with problems of labour policies in the EU, the displacements of neo-management and technocracy in both governance and the workplace, synchronizing thus different perspectives towards a progressive problem shift in CA, namely the 'capability for voice' (Bonvin and Farvaque 2006, 135–137). 'Capability for voice' deficits are thus perceived as an intensified shortage of democracy in marked contrast to core values both of the European heritage and of the global reach of a cosmopolitan convergence implies and promotes. In the context of EU-strengthening of public processes of deliberation with ventures like the European Social Dialogue (this takes place at levels that aim, among other things, to foster dialogue between employers, trade unions and workers but also expands on areas beyond labour issues), inspiration has been sought from CA (Salais and Villeneuve 2004) so that implementation mechanisms that complement national policies or legislation be launched, often in alignment with a vision for a social Europe (Delors 1992). A CA-based recalibration of public deliberation would enhance collective negotiation and bring with greater commitment and capabilities various actors (firms, trade unions, employees, local authorities) into spaces of dialogue patterned after the EU and CA values of deliberation on common goals and goods. Instead of restricting EU policies to macroeconomic agendas, a CA-driven overhauling of social dialogue would challenge the neo-liberal paradigm and would seek to institutionally empower labour so that social justice and effective market coordination and productivity reclaim paths of mutual realignment. This, as Salais and Villeneuve (2004, 17) persuasively argue, would initiate deliberation on the level of 'practical actors' whose daily knowledge of the processes of work and innovation are infused with the benefits of a pragmatic approach to outcomes. This shift to the 'life-world' bears directly on Habermas but it is set up not in the latter's mutually exclusive terms; rather, in unison with a vision of information broadening, the role of the firms or of governments is upgraded in helping to create – in alignment with core EU values about dialogue – this possibility.[16] A shared assumption in this drive towards a piecemeal and pragmatic deliberative democracy is that it protects itself against universally 'imposed' patterns of democracy while, at the same time, its acceptance of real and concrete situated claims of agents under duress disarms a lapse into idealism.[17]

Yet, even if the institutional turn deserves detailed articulation in CA the threat of institutional closure in terms of fundamentalism should be looked at along with the risk of moral fundamentalism for CA itself. The last chapter takes up this challenge.

Notes

1 For example, when Sen (2002) replies to criticisms (Evans 2002) about the limited opening of CA to the horizon of 'collective capabilities' he seems to endorse a nominal and even relativistic view of the 'collective'. The 'collective' figures as an entity little beyond the aggregate possibilities at hand when a society, for example, demonstrates its 'capability' to launch nuclear missiles. It is thus examined at a level of abstraction that, in line with Marx's similar objections to a reified concept of 'Society', invoked by Sen in this passage, reproduces the collective as an entity divested of the real individuals whose actions tend to make, unmake and remake all collective conventions and patterned coordinates of action.

2 Rawls' idea of 'primary goods' should be seen as a major input in CA. His idea of 'primary goods' is transformed to capabilities (Sen) and then to the CCL (Nussbaum). Yet, CA is set up by its advocates as a radical in its implications problem shift that departs significantly from Rawls. Beyond the unattractive to both Sen and Nussbaum's idea of a perfect theory of a just society, Sen objects to Rawls' idea of primary goods on the grounds that Rawls' idea of 'justice as fairness' encounters a marked normative deficit in 'a person's difficulties – naturally or socially generated – in converting 'primary goods' into actual freedoms to achieve' (Sen 1992a, 148). For the debate with Rawls see Sen (1992a, 143–150; 2009), as well as Rawls (1988). In numerous writings Nussbaum on her part distinguishes her position from Rawls (indicatively, see Nussbaum 2006). Sagovksy (2006) provides a lucid and instructive comparison between Sen and Rawls.

3 Sen, for example, adduces CA as a project about growth that is relevant to both poor and rich societies (1999a, 5–6). Automatically, this implies that some high-income countries are less just than others and less equipped to covert incomes to low social inequality indices (see Wilkinson and Pickett, 2010). This injunction presupposes a tacit recognition that some social structures operate with greater degrees of justice among societies at similar and comparable level of development like those one would

conventionally designate as 'high-income' societies. For Sen such disparities on freedoms and areas of justice afflict metrics for 'middle-income' and 'low-income' nations.

4 Jackson (2005), for example, in one of the scant articles on CA and social structures offers a useful typology. He distinguishes between 'structural', 'social' and 'individual' 'capacities to act'. The three modalities of the 'capacity to act' interact and relate under different situations and contexts. The reproduction of the enabling/constraining dualism of social action charts situations and possibilities where each of these modalities can be reproduced within each category. Thus, social structures can be seen as conducive to capability-enhancements when, for example, welfare-states remove tensions between family and career; they can though appear constraining in cases where – to name an extreme case – religious fundamentalism penetrates family environments. He points to the risks that follow when CA is seen as a sophisticated revision of models that visualize capability-enhancement strictly for the individual agent. As we have maintained, positioning capabilities in human agency cannot be severed from radical projects of emancipation. Jackson's reservations bear on a real rather than imagined deficit. Unwittingly, Jackson's emphasis on cultural normative renewal, in order for 'social incapacities' to 'begin to disappear' (120), keeps open the dialogue between CA and a sociological theory of fiduciary subsystems, like the one we intimated in Chapter 3 with regards to Parsons. In order for this cultural renewal to be seriously considered, theory must be able to emancipate itself from viewing its object (i.e. society) as vacant of worth and as enunciated only in culturally diverse and historically contingent manifestations.

5 One distinguished scholar whose work Nussbaum approvingly mentions is Charles Larmore. Although Larmore does not deal with modernity as an *object* invested with value, nonetheless, he clearly thinks that a project of contemporary morals must be framed in consideration with the modern vision of *Sittlichkeit*, which, as he rightly discerns, connects Hegel to the sociology of Durkheim and Parsons (Larmore 1996, 58n.18). He departs though from all those writers in his proposal that this shared form of life (i.e. modernity), which inscribes a humanist morality to our core – yet minimal – mapping of 'reasoned disagreement', is anything more than 'historically contingent'.

6 In commenting on this passage Salais (2004), for example, argues that the non-dogmatism of CA does not tell us which policy model should be adopted across, say, Europe. This is held to be reflected in CA's fruitfulness. He cites the three models of welfare-state as typified by Esping-Andersen (1990) and claims that CA 'would refuse normative priority' among these models (Salais 2004, 292). This can be granted to Salais and CA but the sociological question in the logic of 'capable institutions' does not tell us if the welfare-state is an irreducible component of a society oriented towards mitigating the dysfunctions of capitalism. The critical question therefore is if the three models adduced (and the pluralist potential of CA) constitute a second-order justification, or if CA can – or is intended to – extend its scope to the logic of (modernity's) institutions, which includes the welfare-state. Along similar lines Salais offers a groundwork for supplanting Esping-Andersen's three-model cluster of welfare-states with a fourth one that considers work as an agency function and therefore as a positive value. Informed by CA this fourth 'possible world', as he puts it gives

> priority in reform to equality of capability and encourages effective access to basic functionings that constitute a "good" life and a "good" job. By enhancing the values of inclusion, participation, autonomy and effective freedom, it also fosters the transformation of work. This could offer a positive compromise between flexibility and security.
>
> (Salais 2004, 295)

The idea of the welfare-state is methodologically developed and defended in Holmwood (2000) with its locus firmly rooted in the Hegel–Durkheim institutional normativism, before extended to subsequent thinkers (T.H. Marshall, Polanyi, A. Myrdal).

7 As we may recall from Chapter 1, Nussbaum pointed to the practical significance of 'abstract values'. In fact, it was subjugated women who, under circumstances of adversity, invoked 'abstract values' as a means to aspire to a better life. This invocation of abstract and objectively valid values and realistic comparisons need not be seen as a mutually exclusive exercise. Yet, as was evident from the deprived women's own invocations, perfect or absolute values prove surprisingly recalcitrant and quite necessary, even in our secular, postmetaphysical, age.

8 The idea of just institutions is powerfully argued for by Richard Dien Winfield (1988). Although Winfield relies heavily on Hegel criticizing also Rawls and transcendental models of justice, he nonetheless presupposes them in the 'non-foundational' validity of the Hegelian model he endorses. Hegel, we may be reminded from previous discussions in this book, sublated and did not completely eliminate a transcendental justification to freedom and justice.

9 As Sabina Alkire (2010, 198–199) writes: 'A comparative approach to justice functions by undertaking pairwise comparison and ranking of alternative societal arrangements in terms of justice (whether some arrangement is 'less just' or 'more just' than another)'. Others raise similar concerns and bring the institutional broadening of CA closer to sociology. For example, Stewart and Déneulin (2002, 68) write that 'flourishing individuals generally need and depend on functional families, cooperative and high-trust societies, and social contexts which contribute to the development of individuals who choose "valuable" capabilities'.

10 Wilkinson and Pickett (2010) tackle the problem of inequality in terms similar to what CA claims to accomplish. These authors document the institutional prerequisites, as well as the value-sets across the richest societies in the world and come up with similar to CA conclusions, regarding the entanglement of recognition and material capabilities as indices of social integration based on equality. Sen (1999b, 30–31) shows the importance of international comparisons of functionings. In spite of the variation invoked, he selects to list as examples for (rich) countries the 'ability to entertain friends, be close to people one would like to see, take part in the life of the community' to 'live a life without being ashamed of one's clothing' to enjoy 'literary, cultural and intellectual pursuits', 'vacationing and travelling'. These aspects of a 'good life' indicate not only that Sen is not at all distant from a CCL but also that inevitably the patterns of sociality revealed in those well-being functionings approximate, despite the admittedly existing variation among nations, a model of institutional spheres of 'we' not too distant from what Wilkinson and Pickett's (2010) findings tell us, or from the (historical) pattern of a social organization where these functionings are both nourished, secured and valued.

11 Sympathetic critics of Sen (Stewart and Déneulin 2002) address the limitation of neglecting institutions in terms of how some contribute to enhancing capabilities, while others clearly systematically obstruct them. They argue that issues of power and inbuilt inequalities (for example in the context of corporate global conglomerates and their role in national agendas and international relations) are virtually silenced by Sen. This is partially true for Sen as he is evidently sensitized on how institutional frameworks and organizations can sustain capability-diminishing effects. What Sen's theory lacks is a reconstruction of the institutional spheres the substantive moral logic of which can reflect the vision of a capable social self. On the one hand his critics point to structures of 'living together' (Stewart and Déneulin 2002, 66) as a project that can broaden Sen's corrective on utilitarian conceptions of human well-being. The idea however of structures of living together risks being locked by the authors into nominalism as they interpret 'togetherness' also as an aggregate arrangement of people whose interaction and social relations can also be the possible under 'structures

of oppression' (70 n.4). Oppressive structures can indeed constrain people into some sort of 'togetherness', yet the question remains if togetherness is infused by the reciprocal communicative freedom that any institutional shape of togetherness is, by default, premised upon. Because degrees of oppression suffuse most societies, the imperative of penetrating into the ethical moments of 'togetherness' is all the more pressing so that we may be in a position to distinguish between the durable illusion of 'togetherness' from a togetherness where the social members in question forge it under conditions of public reasoning, mutuality and intersubjectively anchored freedom. Yet the authors fail to consider a logic of institutions that would deserve to be called ethical to the extent that freedom is intersubjectively anchored and cultivated in structural configurations that have some purchase in history, instead of being either deductively legitimated or tentatively and pragmatically tested. But the claim that the 'nature of society in which a person lives is therefore an essential component of his or her QOL [Quality of life, SG]' (67) is diagnostically correct about the broadening possibilities of CA in the direction of a *Sittlichkeit.* For practical illustrations of structures of living together reconstructed from a CA perspective, see Déneulin (2006). In this direction a scholar invoked positively by Sen, Drucilla Cornell (2004), musters Hegel's institutional priming of agents' freedom (81–82), via Balibar, preferring Sen's vision of institutional supports in terms of a Kantian regulative ideal (83–84). Although I am very sympathetic to this 'as-if' injunction this argument omits the point (elided also by Cornell) that the lax institutions Sen cherishes are already Hegelian and remarkably close to Parsons' functional prerequisites.

12 Oddly enough a hint on the convergence between CA and Hegel comes from a critic of Nussbaum's notion of the state. For Menon (2002, 157), of course, any Hegelian intimations of Nussbaum's picture of the state in its 'rational' aspects would make her programme even more culturally monolithic.

13 A pertinent and, I think, better response particularly against Offe is the realization by Hauke Brunkhorst that, paradoxically, the functional differentiation diagnosed by Offe (and Luhmann) is only dimly perceived. The global world is encountered instead as a homogenized and homogenizing entity that diminishes functional self-making within it and across the local zones that are colonized by system properties (neo-liberalism, austerity politics, parliamentary 'Caesarism', fundamentalist defences of local functional differentiation). Thus, as a sort of immanent critique on Luhmann, the 'dysfunctional difference between inclusion and exclusion, and between over-integration and under-integration' (Brunkhorst 2005, 125) requires representing democratically those who are left out as an (at least) functional condition for functional differentiation itself against homogenizing tendencies and TINA logics. In this sense, Sen's capability empowerment promises the functional differentiation envisaged here by making the 'units' (human beings) of any subsystem freer and more capable so that differentiation can turn against de-differentiations of sorts – traditional (Islamic fundamentalism) and modern (market efficiency).

14 I use intersubjectivity here in a double sense: Certainly, in the meaning attached to it by phenomenological sociology on the irreducible level of the common experience and understandings of two or more agents. As John Heritage explains this was the task and accomplishment of Alfred Schütz. Important here is the move of idealization of mutually coordinated standpoints and congruence of relevances assumed (Heritage 1984, 54–61) on the part of both agents. Actors communicate as if they could interchange their standpoints. I retain this use but following Williams (1997) I extend it to Hegel's request for intersubjectively valid institutions, which do not merely secure a common world in the 'here and now' as Schütz contends (Schütz in Heritage 1984, 58) but takes into account that for any rational self the 'here and now' is everyone's 'here and now' set up as a universal property of human communication and mutual recognition. Because phenomenological and interactionist approaches in sociology often make recourse to mundane and tacit trust, they omit that the mundane reality of

a common 'we' is now, in the era of global systems, transferred to institutional trust. On trust as a mechanism of reducing complexity and applied to social systems, see Luhmann (1979, 24–31, 71–77). Here, the function of 'as-if' (and I contend that this applies also to Hegel's complex mediations of freedom in modernity) takes the shape of self-reference, namely 'trust in trust' (66–70).

15 This is a challenge that CA will soon have to face. Can we not possibly reconstruct in terms of capabilities, the valued choices and freedoms that citizens of developed and developing nations enjoy, in terms of well-being values (Inglehart 1997), or greater equality indicators (Wilkinson and Pickett 2010) for the nation-state? Can such a reconstruction serve as world-paradigm in which all communities are committed and bound to engage in deliberative decision-making and policy implementation? This type of thought-experiment is conducted by Meyer, Boli, Thomas and Ramirez (1997). They persuasively demonstrate the shaping of a world-frame where democratic citizenship, socioeconomic development and rationalized justice (148) by recourse to which all collective participants (even as the thought-experiment goes of a newly found isolated island) would have to adopt. Thus, in their capacity as nation-states societies would need to broaden their local and culturally particular institutional patterns. This injunction that we saw in Sen, the authors promote when they argue that the culture of the world society 'stimulates copying among all nation-states' (163). Thus, they advance the idea of a universal value-convergence (i.e. world-culture) as a non-hierarchical 'sacred canopy' (163) and one that is driven by consensus on human rights and issues of justice as a condition for struggles to be waged, voiced and won. Interestingly enough, they evoke this world of moral, differentiated and plural consensus, 'a world of Durkheimian and Simmelian integration' (175).

16 For the relevance of CA in the Habermasian model and the qualified accommodation of CA in the model of deliberative democracy, see Bohman (1997). As Habermas (2012, 121) points out with respect to the crisis of the EU, capable institutions constitute the urgent task of solidifying democratic societies and regulating politically the perilous financial speculation that deprives millions of European citizens of major capabilities. This problem separates Habermas from Bohman's defence of a capabilities-based model of deliberative democracies. For Habermas (1992, 325–327) systemic asymmetries deprive citizens from access to information.

17 For example, Bonvin and Laruffa write:

> Sen insists that democracy in the real world is concerned with real and concrete citizens, thus avoiding the pitfalls of overly idealistic conceptions of deliberative democracy. This calls for the inclusion of all relevant positional objectivities as well as for the development of the capacity to aspire, which in turn implies that due attention is paid to conversion processes and how they combine individual agency and social structures.
>
> (2018, 229–230)

For all their calls for a sober and sufficiently tied to reality model of democracy, the authors compress Sen's model into an overly idealistic pattern, like the one they aim to avoid. Inclusion of 'all relevant positional objectivities' begs the question of relevance. To be sure, the agents in question include also those who happen to obstruct their capacity fulfilment or freedom opportunities since all belong to the context at hand. If 'all' relevant positional objectivities are expected to be mustered, the ensuing democratically ascertained collective consensus that is hoped to emerge must ensure that its collective agreement has no spill-over effects to neighbouring communities. If this is so, then the problem of relevance can smuggle into the context of deliberation, what Sen himself tries to avoid: namely, an unrealistically broadened model that has to be invoked each and every time a problem of relevance for people's lives emerges as a practical and urgent call for freedom and dignity.

References

Alkire, Sabina. 2010. 'Development: A Misconceived Theory Can Kill.' In *Amartya Sen. Contemporary Philosophy in Focus*, edited by Christopher Morris, 191–220. Cambridge: Cambridge University Press.

Bauman, Zygmunt. 2017. *A Chronicle of Crisis 2011–2016.* London: Social Europe Edition.

Bohman, James. 1997. 'Deliberative Democracy and Effective Social Freedom: Capabilities, Resources, and Opportunities.' In *Deliberative Democracy: Essays on Reason and Politics*, edited by James Bohman and William Rehg, 321–348. Cambridge, MA: The MIT Press.

Bonvin, Jean-Michel, and Nicolas Farvaque. 2006. 'Promoting Capability for Work: The Role of Local Actors.' In *Transforming Unjust Structures: The Capability Approach*, edited by Séverine Déneulin, Mathias Nebel, and Nicholas Sagovsky, 121–142. Dordrecht: Springer.

Bonvin, Jean-Michel, and Francesco Laruffa. 2018. 'Deliberative Democracy in the Real World, the Contribution of the Capability Approach.' *International Review of Sociology* 28 (2): 216–233.

Bonvin, Jean-Michel, Francesco Laruffa, and Emilie Rosenstein. 2018. 'Towards a Critical Sociology of Democracy: The Potential of the Capability Approach.' *Critical Sociology* 44 (6): 953–968.

Brunkhorst, Hauke. 2005. *Solidarity: From Civic Friendship to a Global Legal Community.* Cambridge, MA: The MIT Press.

Cornell, Drucilla. 2004. *Defending Ideals: War, Democracy, and Political Struggles.* London: Routledge.

De Leonardis, Ota, Serafino Negrelli, and Robert Salais, eds. 2012. *Democracy and Capabilities for Voice: Welfare, Work and Public Deliberation in Europe*. Brussels: P.I.E. Peter Lang.

Delors, Jacques. 1992. *Our Europe: The Community and National Development*. London: Verso.

Déneulin, Séverine. 2006. *The Capability Approach and the Praxis of Development.* Basingstoke: Palgrave Macmillan.

Déneulin, Séverine, Mathias Nebel, and Nicholas Sagovsky, eds. 2006. *Transforming Unjust Structures: The Capability Approach.* Dordrecht: Springer.

Douglas, Mary. 1986. *How Institutions Think.* Syracuse, New York: Syracuse University Press.

Durkheim, Émile. (1897) 1970. *Suicide: A Study in Sociology*. London: Routledge and Kegan Paul.

Esping-Andersen, Gøsta. 1990. *The Three Worlds of Welfare Capitalism.* Princeton: Princeton University Press.

Esquith, Stephen, and Fred Gifford, eds. 2010. *Capabilities, Power, and Institutions: Toward a More Critical Development Ethics*. University Park: The Pennsylvania State University Press.

Etzioni, Amitai. 1988. *The Moral Dimension: Toward a New Economics*. New York: The Free Press.

Etzioni, Amitai. 2000. *The Third Way to a Good Society*. London: Demos.

Evans, Peter. 2002. 'Collective Capabilities, Culture, and Amartya Sen's *Development as Freedom*.' *Studies in Comparative International Development* 37 (2): 54–60.

Evans, Peter. 2004. 'Development as Institutional Change: The Pitfalls of Monocropping and the Potentials of Deliberation.' *Studies in Comparative International Development* 38 (4): 30–52.

Gangas, Spiros. 2017. 'Recognition, Social Systems and Critical Theory.' In *The Palgrave Handbook of Critical Theory*, edited by Michael Thompson, 547–565. New York: Palgrave Macmillan.

Giddens, Anthony. 2000. *The Third Way and its Critics*. Cambridge: Polity Press.

Habermas, Jürgen. 1974. 'On Social Identity.' *Telos* 19: 91–103.

Habermas, Jürgen. 1992. *Between Facts and Norms: Contributions to a Discourse Theory of Law and Democracy*. Cambridge, MA: The MIT Press.

Habermas, Jürgen. 2012. *The Crisis of the European Union: A Response*. Cambridge: Polity.

Heritage, John. 1984. *Garfinkel and Ethnomethodology*. Cambridge: Polity.

Holmwood, John. 2000. 'Three Pillars of Welfare State Theory: T.H. Marshall, Karl Polanyi and Alva Myrdal in Defence of the National Welfare State.' *European Journal of Social Theory* 3 (1): 23–50.

Honneth, Axel. 1995. *The Struggle for Recognition: The Moral Grammar of Social Conflicts*. Cambridge: MA: The MIT Press.

Honneth, Axel. 2010. *The Pathologies of Individual Freedom: Hegel's Social Theory*. Princeton: Princeton University Press.

Honneth, Axel. 2014. *Freedom's Right. The Social Foundations of Democratic Life*. Cambridge: Polity.

Inglehart, Ronald. 1997. *Modernization and Postmodernization*. Princeton: Princeton University Press.

Jackson, William. 2005. 'Capabilities, Culture and Social Structure.' *Review of Social Economy* 63 (1): 101–124.

Larmore, Charles. 1996. *The Morals of Modernity*. Cambridge: Cambridge University Press.

Lechner, Frank. 1991. 'Parsons and Modernity: An Interpretation.' In *Talcott Parsons: Theorist of Modernity*, edited by Roland Robertson and Bryan Turner, 166–186. London: Sage.

Little, Daniel. 2010. 'Institutions, Inequality, and Well-Being: Distributive Determinants of Capabilities Realization.' In *Capabilities, Power, and Institutions: Toward a More Critical Development Ethics*, edited by Stephen Esquith and Fred Gifford, 40–57. University Park: The Pennsylvania State University Press.

Lockwood, David. 1964. 'Social Integration and System Integration.' In *Explorations in Social Change*, edited by George Zollschan and Walter Hirsh, 244–257. Boston: Houghton Mifflin.

Luhmann, Niklas. 1979. *Trust and Power*. Chichester: John Wiley & Sons.

Luhmann, Niklas. (1997) 2013. *Theory of Society. Volume Two*. Stanford: Stanford University Press.

Mead, George Herbert. 1934. *Mind, Self and Society*. Chicago: The University of Chicago Press.

Menon, Nivedita. 2002. 'Universalism without Foundations?' *Economy and Society* 31 (1): 152–169.

Meyer, John, John Boli, George Thomas, and Francisco Ramirez. 1997. 'World Society and the Nation-State.' *American Journal of Sociology* 103 (1): 144–181.

Nussbaum, Martha. 1999. *Sex and Social Justice*. New York: Oxford University Press.

Nussbaum, Martha. 2004. 'Beyond the Social Contract: Capabilities and Global Justice.' *Oxford Development Studies* 32 (1): 3–18.

Nussbaum, Martha. 2006. *Frontiers of Justice: Disability, Nationality, Species Membership*. Cambridge, MA: The Belknap Press of Harvard University Press.

Nussbaum, Martha. 2011. *Creating Capabilities. The Human Development Approach.* Cambridge, MA: The Belknap Press of Harvard University Press.

Nussbaum, Martha. 2013. *Political Emotions: Why Love Matters for Justice*. Cambridge, MA: The Belknap Press of Harvard University Press.

Offe, Claus. 1987. 'The Utopia of the Zero-Option: Modernity and Modernization as Normative Political Criteria.' *Praxis International* 7 (1): 1–24.

Offe, Claus. 1992. 'Bindings, Shackles, Brakes: On Self-Limitation Strategies.' In *Cultural-Political Interventions in the Unfinished Project of Enlightenment*, edited by Axel Honneth, Thomas McCarthy, Claus Offe, and Albrecht Wellmer, 63–94. Cambridge, MA: The MIT Press.

Offe, Claus. 2001. 'Pathways from Here.' In *What's Wrong with a Free Lunch?* Edited by Joshua Cohen and Joel Rogers, 111–118. Boston: Beacon Press.

Parsons, Talcott. 1969. *Politics and Social Structure*. New York: The Free Press.

Parsons, Talcott. 1991. 'A Tentative Outline of American Values.' In *Talcott Parsons: Theorist of Modernity*, edited by Roland Robertson and Bryan S. Turner, 37–65. London: Sage.

Phillips, Derek. 1986. *Toward a Just Social Order.* Princeton: Princeton University Press.

Prendergast, Rénee. 2005. 'The Concept of Freedom and its Relation to Economic Development-a Critical Appreciation of the Work of Amartya Sen.' *Cambridge Journal of Economics* 29 (6): 1145–1170.

Rawls, John. 1988. 'The Priority of Right and Ideas of the Good.' *Philosophy and Public Affairs* 17 (4): 251–276.

Rawls, John. (1971) 1999. *A Theory of Justice. Revised Edition*. Oxford: Oxford University Press.

Ricoeur, Paul. 2006. 'Capabilities and Rights.' *Transforming Unjust Structures: The Capability Approach*, edited by Séverine Déneulin, Mathias Nebel, and Nicholas Sagovsky, 17–26. Dordrecht: Springer.

Sagovsky, Nicholas. 2006. ''Capable Individuals' and Just Institutions.' In *Transforming Unjust Structures: The Capability Approach*, edited by Séverine Déneulin, Mathias Nebel, and Nicholas Sagovsky, 63–81. Dordrecht: Springer.

Salais, Robert. 2004. 'Incorporating the Capability Approach into Social and Employment Policies.' In *Europe and the Politics of Capabilities*, edited by Robert Salais and Robert Villeneuve, 283–300. Cambridge: Cambridge University Press.

Salais, Robert, and Robert Villeneuve. 2004. 'Introduction: Europe and the Politics of Capabilities.' In *Europe and the Politics of Capabilities*, edited by Robert Salais, and Robert Villeneuve, 1–18. Cambridge: Cambridge University Press.

Sen, Amartya. 1990. 'Individual Freedom as a Social Commitment.' *New York Review of Books* 37: 49–54.

Sen, Amartya. 1992a. *Inequality Reexamined.* Cambridge, MA: Harvard University Press.

Sen, Amartya. 1992b. 'Missing Women: Social Inequality Outweighs Women's Survival Advantage in Asia and North Africa.' *BMJ: British Medical Journal* 304 (6827): 587–588.

Sen, Amartya. 1999a. *Development as Freedom*. Oxford: Oxford University Press.

Sen, Amartya. 1999b. *Commodities and Capabilities.* Oxford: Oxford University Press.

Sen, Amartya. 1999c. 'Democracy as a Universal Value.' *Journal of Democracy* 10 (3): 3–17.

Sen, Amartya. 2002. 'Response to Commentaries.' *Studies in Comparative International Development* 37 (2): 78–86.

Sen, Amartya. 2003. 'Missing Women-Revisited: Reduction in Female Mortality Has Been Counterbalanced By Sex Selective Abortions.' *BMJ: British Medical Journal* 327 (7427): 1297–1298.

Sen, Amartya. 2004. 'How Does Culture Matter?' In *Culture and Public Action*, edited by Vijayendra Rao and Michael Walton, 37–58. Stanford: Stanford University Press.

Sen, Amartya. 2006. 'What Do We Want from Theory of Justice?' *The Journal of Philosophy* 103 (5): 215–238.

Sen, Amartya. 2009. *The Idea of Justice*. Cambridge, MA: The Belknap Press of Harvard University Press.

Sennett, Richard. 2012. *Together: The Rituals, Pleasures and Politics of Cooperation.* New Haven: Yale University Press.

Stewart, Frances, and Séverine Déneulin. 2002. 'Amartya Sen's Contribution to Development Thinking.' *Studies in Comparative International Development* 37 (2): 61–72.

Stiglitz, Jospeh, Amartya Sen, and Jean-Paul Fitoussi. 2009. *Report by the Commission on the Measurement of Economic Performance and Social Progress*. Accessed 11 October 2018. http://ec.europa.eu/eurostat/documents/118025/118123/Fitoussi+Commission+report.

Strasser, Hermann. 1976. *The Normative Structure of Sociology: Conservative and Emancipatory Themes in Social Thought*. London: Routledge and Kegan Paul.

Wilkinson, Richard, and Kate Pickett. 2010. *The Spirit Level: Why Equality is Better for Everyone*. London: Penguin.

Williams, Robert. 1997. *Hegel's Ethics of Recognition*. Berkeley: University of California Press.

Winfield, Richard Dien. 1988. *Reason and Justice*. Albany: State University of New York Press.

7 The crisis of capability?

Value-fundamentalism and solitarist identity

Introduction: decline – again?

Hegel once wrote that to him 'who looks upon the world rationally, the world in its turn presents a rational aspect' ([1830–1831] 1956, 11). The burgeoning sense of crisis that I noted at the beginning of this book has taken cataclysmic proportions, making Hegel's rational commitment look like a furtive pun on contemporary global turbulence. There is an intense feeling that the accumulation of social problems, social sufferings and capability deprivations of sorts have entered a zone of untrammeled entropy. Suddenly, Spengler's pessimistic *Kulturkritik* has been upgraded (e.g. Bauman and Donskis 2013) with diagnostic resonance about the technical and plebeian Occident in irrevocable cultural decline. While one needs to be weary of the explanatory validity of such apocalyptic imagery, one should not bypass the fact that the *Sittlichkeit* we defended in the previous chapter is often relegated to a bygone project of social integration. A new sociological toolkit of 'liquidity', 'risk', 'simulacra', 'systems', 'communicative action', 'network society' and 'scapes' depict symptoms of society that urge for new categories that enable sociology to enter with greater confidence the domain of the growing global interdependencies and contingencies, no longer absorbed by nation-states in a postindustrial and globalized era. Associated mostly with the captivating frame of a multicentred, liquid, risk-susceptible/reflexive, systemically contingent and globally networked postsocial society, these concepts exacerbate, unwittingly most of the times, a sense of normative helplessness.[1] From various corners of the discipline the voice of alarm has been transformed to one of despair or, at best, to a stoic scepticism and modest expectations about correctives.

CA has not escaped the charge of succumbing to postmodernist romanticism as an 'occasion' for human choice and as a neo-liberal spectre in the shape of an 'open signifier' (Walby 2012, 114).[2] Given its formation as a flexible yet normatively committed programme, to the point even of reclaiming 'essentialism', is CA 'capable' of escaping from the fate of a normative simulacrum? And, moreover, as Luhmann complains (2013a, 337–338), isn't sociology's semantics of despair that has transformed it into a 'science of crisis', a symptom of 'its own theoretical crisis'? The purpose of my book was to show that aggravated social problems and inequalities are not conceded if we shift to categories which do not play up the semantics of despair that Luhmann appositely diagnoses as a problem of the discipline. Yet, despair takes real shape in contemporary societies and CA addresses it through a fecund categorial shift. It is time that we address this shift in light of the problem of fundamentalism.

Cultural identity and cultural illusions: how CA responds

Essential to positing the problem of value-fundamentalism in critical and normative terms is the question of how CA fares with systems theory given the latter's absorption of agency into the complex sequence and operations of global networks and social systems. What is adumbrated here is a posthuman environment, stripped from the moral capability of responsibility and hence of agency in the normatively enhanced sense used by CA. Called to rebuild its institutional arsenal but abstaining from identifying what capacity-fulfilment and capability-enhancements can mean as overarching values, CA concedes the necessary project of coordination between value-systems that can supplant a new moral vision under conditions of globalization. This is a the Janus-faced implication of network societies and the incuperbale gaps that are created between civil society and those segments of society that (re)claim their identities in fundamentalist articulations of what Manuel Castells terms a 'self-centered view of the world' (2010, 421n2).

In Chapter 5 we addressed how Sen (2006, 2008b, 2011) hopes to undermine the illusions, as he calls them, of reducing the complex web of affiliations that enable persons to hold multiple identities into a single, all-inclusive and all-pervasive status. Sen draws from a rich pool of sources (literature, history, religion, politics) to debunk the illusion (the latter though sufficiently real in its flammable and violent consequences for people and communities) of a constantly prevailing identity that obscures all others. Indeed, he challenges 'the presumption of the unique relevance of singular classification' (Sen 2006, 11). That people for a period in their lives prime this or that identity can be quite restrictive but Sen argues that even more problematic is a situation where a specific identity seems to be 'uniquely relevant'. In order to relativize, therefore, this granite view of cultural integration, Sen brings diversity back in the cultural identity that claims purity. Diversity and dissent, partial identification with the mainstream culture attest to a far more fragmentary cultural universe. Another tactical move is intercultural interaction. Here, the channels of communication and mutual borrowings between cultures provide serious empirical and historical evidence against the monolithic identity that inflates and inflames people's invocations of it. To mitigate the drama of violence and suffering, the roots of which overtly, or less so, take recourse to a solidary (and solitary) identity at the expense, exclusion, and all too often extermination, of others, Sen advocates identity pluralism for the agent, the community or even an entire 'civilization'; that is, a pluralism that yields overlapping interests, aims and values. This happens as a realistic alternative in spite of his own sympathies to 'grand universalism' (Sen 2002, 39–40).

Despite references to a 'common' or 'shared humanity', Sen seems reluctant to delve further on the commonness of our humanity, at least in a systematic justification, besides mustering eloquent literary sources to that end. For example, on one of the few occasions where Sen (2004) cites sociology he takes issue with Weber's thesis on the Protestant Ethic. He argues that historical evidence shows that Catholic countries, Japan and other East Asian economies grew faster than Protestant Europe. Thus the initial overarching category (i.e. Protestantism) entailed a series of modifications against potential refutation by empirical evidence. Gradually, thus, it had to abandon its culturally unique validity (i.e. that Protestantism was the privileged ethic that in conjunction with the universal tendency for money-making led to capitalism). Sen's point is useful if Weber was launching indeed a dialectical argument. But Weber was arguing from a different epistemological standpoint, namely that of a genetic condition of a world-historical phenomenon like capitalism. In fact, Weber's argument has more to do with the universal surplus of rationalization that emerged in Protestant Europe, a facet of which was capitalism and how its pattern became appropriated in conjunction with other cultural values (Confucian, Buddhist, etc.). If thus pushed towards the technological side of rationalization, the cultural determinism that Sen considers counterfactual is not altogether obliterated, given the West's technological supremacy in modernity. If technology is part of a culture's material components then one is forced to reconsider the validity of Sen's tendency to cultural commingling as a forceful argument against cultural determinism. In fact, cultural commingling is premised 'in the last instance' on some implicit acceptance of cultural supremacy at a given historical epoch, which either through military means makes itself imposed on other peoples and civilizations or, alternatively, is taken on board as an immanent need of a culture to borrow various achievements from other cultures. Getting rid of the supremacy of a culture merely transfers the issue of supremacy to a smaller and, for Sen, more manageable, scale. Shouldn't what is worthy of being imitated or borrowed (ranging from classical music to McDonaldization) necessarily rely on intuitions or judgments about a real or alleged supremacy of worth among the members of a culture that initiates the activity of borrowing? Sen's move is to start from the asymmetric – due to an odious past of colonization, dependency, neo-colonialism and cultural imperialism – initiation of what a society retains or emulates from other vantage points of 'superiority'. He then moves to strengthening public reasoning and capabilities for substantive political participation. As he writes:

> There is no particular 'compulsion' either to preserve departing life styles, or alternatively, to adopt the newest fashion from abroad, but there is a need for people to be able to take part in these social decisions. This gives further reason for attaching importance to such elementary capabilities as reading and writing (through basic education), being well informed and well briefed

> (through a free media), and having realistic chances of participating freely (through elections, referendums and the general use of civil rights). There are institutional demands for cultural democracy.
>
> (Sen 2004, 56)

But this ingenious normative move does not obliterate cultural supremacy. It merely transfers it to the collective authority of a society governed by those principles of democratic freedom that CA calls for. The argument thus is one about how one evaluates 'cultural supremacy' instead of hyperdifferentiating an allegedly supreme culture in order to decentre its authority. If the issue of whether there is a 'right' or 'wrong' culture is justifiably taken to task by Sen, given people's tendency 'to celebrating or lamenting the rigidly delineated cultural boxes in which the people of the world are firmly classified by muscular taxonomists' (38), the benefits of democratic mutual learning from each other sustains essentially the division rather than eliminates it. While it may rightly and judiciously subvert the overarching classification that one may see both as ethically suspect and historically refutable, the argument that surfaces in favour of democracy is one that tells us that the ground for any cultural feature to be seen as worthy or not cannot be predetermined but only reached after we engage in democratically processed public debate. The coordinating mechanism for this to happen must be raised to the status of an overarching value the content of which should be 'the need for participatory decision making on the kind of society people want to live in, based on open discussion, with adequate opportunity for the expression of minority positions' (53).

Sen's argument is informed by the realization that power mechanisms at work can transform imperceptible differences into rigid classificatory cells and it is this context when sociology gets mentioned when Sen (2006, 27) invokes Pierre Bourdieu's relevant work on society's 'pressure' to draw boundaries in strictly functionalist justifications. The undue outcome of this pressure can have many sources and it is certainly among Sen's claims that capability deprivations, dispossession and systemic deficits at the national and global level blur our vision to relax such cultural rigidity. With dialectical skill, Sen (2001, 2006) undermines the semantics of 'West – anti-West', 'pro-globalization – anti-globalization' standpoints without forfeiting the reality-tests that such relativization entails.[3] In short, condensing reality's complexity into such binary schemes not only carves an extremely rigid space for tactics, policy and people's empowerment but for the sides that 'communicate' via such coded blinders the alarming tension is that each side replicates the other. In effect, the replication of classificatory dualisms is operating not merely as an external shield against each side's ploys but rather within the very category that is held to be 'pure'. Thus, the 'colonized mind' in its fixation with the West may reproduce both 'admiration and disaffection' (Sen 2006, 85). If the West, as Sen is tirelessly emphasizing, is held to be responsible for an enormous amount of suffering, humiliation and dependency legacies, it is actually its monolithic view of the 'Other' that takes effect more egregiously in the postcolonial constellation. As he claims:

> to lead a life in which resentment against an imposed inferiority from past history comes to dominate one's priorities today cannot but be unfair to oneself. It can also vastly deflect attention from other objectives that those emerging from past colonies have reason to value and pursue in the contemporary world.
>
> (89)

Raised to a person's sole source of esteem (regardless the socially produced resentments) reactive and militant anti-Western positions empower, in the last analysis, the construction of the hierarchical 'West' as they play straight into deeply rooted prejudices; unintentionally, they help to trigger further types of racist and discriminatory motives (see, for example, Law 2009, 139–142).

Such a release would have been spurious had it simply involved a shift of perspectives towards mutuality from the vantage point of the categories themselves. Configuring the hyper-differentiation of the 'West–anti-West' code in order to relativize the rigidity of each category from inside, as it were, as well as between them in the overlapping areas that are obliterated when this dualism is at work, enables Sen to hint at the relaxation of similar classifications on each side. Because the dualism is powered, envisioning one side as the victim, opposed to the aggressor, opens the sluices for further duplications of it. The previously held 'aggressor' (e.g. the 'West'), appeased by recourse to universal values that were designed to foster a broadening of civilizational scope, can regress to a position of fundamental classification and thus redouble the logic of 'getting even' (e.g. the rise of neo-nationalism in Europe against previously cherished multiculturalism). Having thus recognized, since the end of colonialism, millions of those whom it had dispossessed, the standpoint of the 'West' is 'getting even' with those who are held now, as a result of flows and migration, to 'dispossess' European or the North American citizens. Regress into neo-nationalist fundamentalism thrives on this dialectics of seeing the 'West' as a victim of hitherto legitimated policies of inclusion. These value-shifts within the 'West' recoil whatever accomplishment the 'West's' self-acknowledgement of a history of deep colonial aggression had yielded. Analogously, the standpoint of the 'victim' (the 'anti-West' perspective), precisely because of its still asymmetrical interdependence with the 'West', can regress to the status of a 'master' against those weaker groups that happen to be latecomers in the sharing of power; holders of precarious rights take now the role of the 'victim'. This type of false-consciousness in the colonized mind bears for Sen on combinations of cultural fixities, which place agents into a single status of having to act exclusively within the dual framework of inter-civilizational clashes. As Sen puts it:

> the dialectics of the colonized mind can impose a heavy penalty on the lives and freedoms of people who are reactively obsessed with the West. It can wreak havoc on lives in other countries as well, when the reaction takes the violent form of seeking confrontation, including what is seen as retribution.
>
> (2006, 92–93)

Such neatly carved-out niches of cultural 'otherness' take the shape of positional fundamentalism.

Sen (2006, Ch.6) provides numerous examples (a telling one is Japan) of initiated broadenings within a culture that insert into its core values a cosmopolitan vision based on the idea that cultural intersection lies at the core of human functionings. He also reminds his readers of the efforts, since millennia, to understand and appreciate different cultures in the 'immense richness of the multiple identities that human beings have' (Sen 2008b, 6). Because cultures are neither the single most important aspect of people's identities, nor free of internal pluralism themselves, their very heterogeneity implies rejection of the idea that culturally shared ways of life are static or fixed in time (as evidently they change in history). In fact, as Sen argues, an important attribute of human capabilities is the type of balance that people can accomplish between the freedom to prioritize or rearrange cultural attributes and the freedom to conserve culture. Corresponding to Sen's broader methodology, even the causal linkage between poverty (an admittedly grand theme of Sen's work) and violence is being relaxed in order to make room for far more complex causation between the two variables. Accepting that economic inequality can indeed be correlated to violence and social indignation, Sen (2008b; 2011) requires from the social scientist to couple the explanation of violence to a broadening of causes (e.g. traumatic histories of national identities, different communal prioritization of identities, multicultural softening of racial and ethnic rigidities) in order for economic deprivations to emerge as a critical factor that fuels partitionism and sectarian violence.

What is fundamentalism? A sociological explanation

Sen (2006) addresses the problem of the clash of civilizations and finds it both wanting in terms of its explanatory binary code and odious in its escalation of violence. Curbing this binary logic requires a paradigm shift to a comparative broadening of cultural identities and perspectives. This is possible, for Sen, only because cultures are marked by internal heterogeneity and by communicative exchanges with other societies. But CA, as we have seen, faces difficulties when questions arise as to the institutional matrix of functional and normative prerequisites that enhance the freedom aspect of development. It also faces the challenge of prioritizing institutions. Leaving this to historical contingency and cultural diversity is tactically reasonable, and maybe required given how 'logics' of institutions have backfired historically, yet if CA cannot afford, like any other normative theory, to expand into the institutional settings, the content of which nurtures capability empowerment, then it opens itself to risks of getting trapped into an inflationary moral spiral. (By this we mean, as we shall explain shortly, an overestimation of its normative potential based on an overdraft of trust.) The threat of value-fundamentalism can be initially conceived in terms of reducing system complexity, whether we address the system of human personality, the social or the cultural system. Among our plural identities a single identity is severed and then elevated to becoming the chief social catalyst for action and for elated feelings of self-esteem.

Fundamentalism as a sociological category can be traced to the thought of Talcott Parsons. In the systematic exposition of the functional imperatives (AGIL) Parsons provides a complex theory of mediations and interchanges that keep the operation of each subsystem in check. This, as we have already discussed, is for Parsons not only a functional requirement but also a normative one. The normative realm in Parsons entails three levels. An obvious one stems from the function of latent-pattern maintenance, the subsystem equipped with value diffusion. This is a formal function in Parsons' scheme but the 'normative' is without difficulty being extrapolated from the diffusion of moral sentiments across society. It is thus similar to Durkheim's affective values. On a second level the 'normative' is enhanced when Parsons' evolutionism considers the liberal democratic order as the culmination of the AGIL interface. Thus, modernity's differentiation along the lines of an upgraded and collectively sanctioned moral individualism is held to provide the cybernetically justified possibility of a relatively frictionless societal evolution: Frictionless in the sense of being in a position to hold in check anomic tendencies not because people have necessarily accomplished moral excellence but mainly because of the high degree of intra-system interdependence and the flow of reciprocal interchanges between the various subsystems. This brings us close to the third level of normativity in Parsons, which has to do with the architectonic of AGIL. In line with evolutionary theories but also in striking similarity to Hegel and in direct dialogue with Durkheim's configuration of organic solidarity, Parsons' theory of (modern) society is governed by a principle of moderation, one that strives to hold the balance between subsystems intact or, at least, at a sufficiently functional degree of system self-regeneration, so that excessive demands and functional operations by each subsystem be curbed and minimized. Even his last and incomplete work on American society is marked by a constant search to moderate extremism (Parsons 2007, 35–52).

This third meta-level of normativity brings us to the heart of fundamentalism as a sociological category. For each of the subsystems Parsons identifies a code of communication and boundary drawing. Thus, adaptation (A) operates by recourse to money, goal-attainment (G) mobilizes power, societal integration (I) depends crucially on influence and latent-pattern maintenance (L) relies on the diffusion of value-commitments. Having deduced the functional code of each system Parsons proceeds by elaborating his theory of excessive (de)formations of the social. This happens when each subsystem shows inflationary and deflationary tendencies. For Parsons (1969) inflation represents, roughly, the system's overconfidence of its capacity to steer appropriate functions. Inflationary tendencies, particularly in the subsystem (L), which is our focus here, tend to idealize a value system. Over commitment of values is marked by a growing gap in the system's capacity to routinize values and to implement them via the appropriate functional channels of diffusion to the rest of the social system. In contrast, deflationary tendencies appear when system capacities tend to intensify the semantics of their validity; unable to sustain legitimacy they thus draw on moral absolutism or even on force and coercion. In a characteristic passage Parsons writes:

> However, the focus on fundamentalism may not be on religion in the analytical sense, but on tenets about the organization of society or 'personal' morality, the other most important contemporary focus. From this point of view, the sharp ideological dispute between socialist and capitalist commitments constitutes a 'deflationary' movement within the development of Western society and its commitment system. Each side claims the absolute moral legitimacy of its own commitments, thereby justifying, in the extreme case, 'war', if only of the 'cold' variety, against the other. Fortunately, from my point of view (but then I am neither a committed capitalist nor a committed socialist), we have been experiencing a certain loosening of these fundamentalist rigidies, and new degrees of freedom are now beginning to appear.
>
> (1969, 465)

While Parsons may not have estimated correctly the tendencies American society would take as is evident with the proliferation of subcultural fundamentalism or system fundamentalism (e.g. the National Rifle Association) in the US, the openings of freedom that promise the relaxation of moral rigidity seem today to be in serious jeopardy.[4] Burning bridges of shared value-orientations with other subsystems (Parsons 1951, 292–294) or with other heterogeneous components of a nonetheless integrated subsystem is among the key dysfunctions of fundamentalist tendencies. Frank Lechner summarizes the Parsonsian usage of the 'fundamentalist syndrome' as follows: 'Fundamentalism is interpreted as the effort to 'deflate' media, especially value-commitments, by imposing tight restrictions on degrees of freedom in value-implementation. Value absolutism is the common feature of all such deflation' (1990, 93). It was also Parsons' hope that as humanity progressed such national and race tensions would be eased if not eliminated. His moderate fusion of liberal and social democratic ideals aligns the overall political orientation (Nielsen 1991) to the construction of categories.

We need not repeat the sociological justification that values are central to notions of social integration and solidarity that we discussed in the previous chapter (e.g. '*Sittlichkeit*', 'organic solidarity', AGIL, theory of recognition). Sceptical critiques in favour of value-incommensurability (Weber, Luhmann) resort to value-fundamentalism, as a system risk, equating it with a normatively binding value-integration that effaces historical contingency or subsystem autonomy. Max Weber's 'value-wars' that we encountered in Chapter 1 are marked precisely by the escalation of deflationary tendencies in the incommensurable sphere of values (economic, political, legal, aesthetic etc.). In the moral domain such fundamentalisms confiscate a value (e.g. human rights) as the normative content for which they appear as the sole representatives and claimants. In terms of a differentiated social system (i.e. modernity) fundamentalism takes a markedly anti-modernist turn towards de-differentiation.

If we leave aside for a moment our normative cluster of sociologists and we explore some typical – and conservative models – of axiology, we bump onto approaches to the value-problem that take distance from value-decisionism and value-incommensurability. For instance, philosopher Nicolai Hartmann points to the inevitable risk of value-tyranny where 'every value […] has the tendency to set itself up as the sole tyrant of the whole human ethos, and indeed at the expense of other values, even of such as are not inherently opposed to it' (1932, 423). Hartmann seems to argue that tyranny is the inverse of synthesis. The latter is identified as the law of '*συμπλοκή*' [*symploke*], namely 'interwoveness', 'reciprocal conditionality' (392) rather than 'conflict'. Radical conflict or clash between values is apposite to the notion of '*απεμπλοκή*' (*apemploke*). We need to underline the source of potential confusion here because the Greek terms contain also the opposite meaning to the one Hartmann discusses. Thus '*symploke*' conveys rules of engagement and conflict while '*apemploke*' signals the termination of such rules of engagement. Sociologically, this binary code translates as 'differentiation' and 'de-differentiation' respectively in the sense Hartmann uses these concepts.

Carl Schmitt, for his part, built on both Weber and Hartmann. In a short essay titled *Tyranny of Values* Schmitt ((1979) 1996) conceptualizes the 'tyranny of values' in the shape of a 'valorization of value'. For Schmitt, value-standpoints always disvalue. They are thus turned into an arena of conflict because the 'valuation pressure of a value' turns a value into its opposite. (Hence, the derogatory recourse to the opponent's 'value-blindness'.) Thus, conflicts between the valuator, the devaluator, the reevaluator and the implementer are held to be 'inevitable'. This inevitability stems from the inherent 'ambivalence of values', as subjectively driven valuations, with an 'immanent aggressiveness' at their point of practical enactment (brought about by real people and bearing on real people.) We can thus safely assume that 'value-fundamentalism' bears also on 'disvalue', on the 'valorization of value' and on 'aggressiveness' due to its practical perspectivism and subjective decisionism.[5]

Luhmann, for his part, built his entire and extremely nuanced sceptical attack on normative sociology with this value-problem in mind. He had to mount a critique of Parsons and question the primacy of (L) as a cybernetically privileged standpoint that diffuses moral commitments to every corner of the social system. Value-universalism is a formal code of reducing system complexity (thus of de-differentiating society.) Values are mere 'viewpoints' rather than 'fixed stars' representing ultimate concerns. They resemble 'balloons kept on hand to be inflated when called for, especially on festive occasions' (Luhmann (1997) 2012, 204). Luhmann's biting irony intends to hit two birds with one stone: First the normative inflation of values, like, for example in a Kantian or Durkhemian ethics, and second, the pragmatic illusion that values can be simply compressed to actions without some sort of reference to an ultimate realm. With the reference to 'festive occasions' Luhmann must have in mind Durkheim's collective effervescence. For Luhmann, the Parsonsian code of 'inflation/deflation' is just another modality for sociological descriptions and under no circumstances an empirical reality of subsystems, as is clearly indicated by phenomena of 'stagflation' (230–232). The bottom line for both Luhmann and Schmitt is that for the dual code 'value-disvalue' to be crossed, as always is the case when pragmatic implementation takes the lead, some 'cheating' (222) is being involved, simply because the chief conceptual distinction cannot be thematized consistently by recourse to its extremes (value-disvalue) without generating paradoxes. This is where the avoidance of paradox may call for inflationary and deflationary rectifications (occlusions) that, for Luhmann too, lead to violence. He even names morality 'polemogenous' and ascribes to it 'war-generating traits' (presumably immoral) (244). Thus, Luhmann, like CA, bumps on the same problem of a 'fundamentalist guise' (323) of particularist solidarities that intensify the 'us' and 'them' code in various contexts but now with a conspicuously different (non)normative orientation of descriptive rather than prescriptive semantics. This issue raises the question if CA is itself open to the risk of moral excess and thus to the fundamentalism that Luhmann imputes to the deflationary shift in every moral system of communication. Even if no normative excess can be attached to the question of how democracy is being founded – a meta-code for CA, particularly Sen's version of it, an unmoved mover, so to speak – Luhmann's critique elicits those questions about a theory's appropriation of its own blind spots.

Indeed, many twenty-first century social problems have been formulated in terms of 'value-fundamentalism'. Examples include: Islamic fundamentalism, free-market (neo-liberal) fundamentalism, ethno-nationalist/white-supremacy fundamentalism and left-wing fundamentalism. If such narratives of de-complexification are swelling then sociology's task must be to locate the institutional junctures where values (e.g. economic, political, moral) tend to claim an 'absolute' status, which leads them to 'devalue' other values and, hence, to de-differentiate society. Viewed in terms of systems theory (Luhmann) value-fundamentalism can be curbed in two ways: First, via claims to each system's 'binary-coded' autonomy (autopoiesis vs allopoiesis); second, via the structural-coupling of each system with other systems. However, Luhmann's system-driven value-pluralism (we recall that it lacks an overarching 'L'-imperative) excludes the possibility of a 'normal' functioning of functional systems (a principle that aligns Marx with Durkheim), simply because he makes exclusion the cardinal factor in the very possibility of drawing system boundaries. Yet contra Luhmann, and as Brunkhorst (2005) suggests, too much exclusion renders large population segments functionless and thus risks 'de-differentiating' society in the inverse direction Luhmann anticipates (his fear is that de-differentiation as 'de-complexification' stems from 'too much' integration).

Parsons' sociological concept of value-fundamentalism operationalizes what earlier and also subsequent critiques of value-integration view as a reductionist inevitability of normative projects of modernity. In Parsons, an ideal-typical use of 'value-fundamentalism' enables sociologists to test it in empirical cases in terms of deviations from modernization according to binary-coded system processes: 'internal vs. external' modernization, 'gradual vs. sudden', 'early vs. late', 'deep vs. superficial'. Evidently, as Lechner (1990, 106) suggests, a historical contingency on the right hand side of each pair (i.e. external – sudden – late – superficial) of concepts is likely to generate fundamentalist responses. Since Lechner's excellent book chapter remains the most systematic reconstruction of Parsons' concept of fundamentalism it is worth probing into some problems that stem from his approach. Parsons' limitations (via Lechner) open a field of rethinking value-fundamentalism in terms of its normative content: a) the moral constitution of modern institutions (Durkheim); b) the claims to societal 'revitalization'. Lechner's analysis moves from the reality of globalization to the need of nation-states to combine global interdependence with particularist identities. As the problem of legitimation is primarily coordinated in the (G) (politics/state) and (L) (religion) subcomponents of a social system, fundamentalism is likely to emerge as a corrective to what is perceived as a corrosive and threatening impact of a globalization that homogenizes particularist notions of social order. The reactive response to this threat of delegitmation is fundamentalism. This explanation would suggest, in Lechner's view, that 'in the face of global developments "relativizing" societal coherence and identity, more or less absolutist fundamentalist revitalization efforts aimed at reestablishing coherence, conflating different spheres of life, and "closing" the society are to be expected' (1990, 113–114). In this sense, as a differentiated system's response to globalization by regress to de-differentiation, fundamentalism is for Lechner a 'modern phenomenon' and one that belongs to the very design of modernity as a system's deflationary reclaiming of its orderly social fabric (i.e. its value-commitments.) Hence, tensions in the shared cultural core of a society allow, in Lechner's view, to advance the terminological shift from 'revision'/'reform' to 'revitalization'. The latter is held to suffuse society if ultimate valuations are subjected to the tensions wrought by intense differentiation processes.

Yet a number of problems arise in Lechner's formidable but also formal analysis. First, 'modernization' lacks precise normative content and thus we have no indication if the normative content of value-commitments in this or that society is likely to generate mild or severe fundamentalisms. Second, the process of 'revitalization' is couched on an indeterminate notion of vital forces that replenish the social system that often offer a legitimating cover for predatory interests: What precisely are the vital streams of society, indications of which Chapters 3 and 4 of this book analysed?

If, as Lechner argues, fundamentalism is not a tradition-driven reaction but a system reaction of modernity's differentiation process, then one would need to ask if the 'modernity' of value-fundamentalism bears on modern society's system properties or if a content-based vision of a 'good society' is defensible in system-differentiated terms at odds with fundamentalist closure/monopoly of such vision. This problem bears precisely on the 'revitalization' function of value-fundamentalism. Lechner resorts to the function of 'revitalization' as a problem of a contemporary and complex notion of 'order'. Lechner (following, unwittingly perhaps, Weber and Luhmann) rightly accepts the inevitable 'activism', 'decisionism' and 'tragedy' of modernity because 'generalized values cannot be "realized" '; thus, the surging 'deficit' of the non-implementable residue of values justifies in Lechner's view value-fundamentalism's 'modernity'. Yet, on this occasion, Lechner is silent on the content and scope of modern society's mechanism (value-fundamentalism) that steers its capacities for self-revitalization. In effect, the 'residue' of non-implementative value-content of generalized values is taken to be more 'solid' than the 'implementable' value content that cements social order. In other words, if conflict is expected and is even desirable in modernity due to value-dissensus on the level of 'unrealizability' (objective or perceived) of mutually exclusive value-orientations, then one presumably should ask if this conflict extends also to coercion and violence. If the latter is precluded due to the consensus-based binding aspect of generalized values, then value-fundamentalism has to concede a specific set of means (violence) in its effort to de-differentiate society and reclaim a legitimate social order. Thus, some prioritization of the degrees and the nature of value-generalizability in modern society needs to be ascertained. Such a move of modernity's normative recovery would reduce, I think, the paradox of shifting modernity's source of self-regeneration to the realm of violent collective effervescence, which was precisely what modernity sought to rectify by recourse to the legitimacy and legality of its values based upon Durkheim's moral individualism (i.e. the socially embedded human dignity in organic solidarity).[6] Thus, the vital streams called upon by fundamentalism have to conform to the hard core of what revitalization is all about (namely, augmenting 'life'). If not, as this appears to be the consequence of Lechner's nuanced analysis, then these streams are restricted to a heuristic and formal function in, at worst, a de-differentiation of values by recourse to a sort of 'magmatic' (Castoriadis) value regeneration; at best, on Lechner's account, vital streams would have a constructive role to play in enriching value-commitments by making them sensitive to the specific (binding) value, which to the fundamentalist's self-perception is under threat. The problem here is that neither of these options can – based on a constitutionally founded democratic morality – generate unilateral withdrawals (aiming at reclaiming validity) among nation-states; yet value-fundamentalism is the proof that institutional/structural deficits do nourish such unilateral redefinitions of the 'system' (facticity).

If this argument is plausible, then Nicolai Hartmann's notion of '*symploke*' (engagement) of values is indeed apposite. It enables us to reinterpret value-fundamentalism as '*apemploke*' (disengagement) from the wider networking of values and the implementative flexibility that a differentiated global society requires. While Hartmann's Platonism may sound odd in the context of a polyvalent twenty-first century modernity, its contemporary resonance can be evinced in the opportunities provided by rethinking values as a network rather than as a lexical ordering or an a priori hierarchy. This reciprocal conditionality – the law of '*symploke*' – needs to be reclaimed to counter not only the logical contradiction of a partial value that presents itself as a 'system', because it claims for itself the whole and thus distorts it in fundamentalist fashion; but, moreover, to halt the multitude of suffering that the balkanization of identity-politics is implicated with as a twisted response to the 'tyranny of values'.

There are other issues that call for scrutiny in Lechner's powerful analysis of fundamentalism. These include, for instance, the question of where material interests lie in the process of globalization. As social inequality is on the rise nearly everywhere, are fundamentalist responses galvanized by such widening inequality gaps? In Chapters 2 and 4 we scrutinized this problem. It is now time to reflect on implications for CA.

Sen's comparative broadening and the sociological problem of parallax or of blind spot

The appeal of Sen's proposal for comparative broadening is fruitful and prescient. Evidently it is tuned to a cosmopolitan ethic. Its epistemological justification is a version of methodological cosmopolitanism (Beck 2012) as it hopes to instantiate units of analysis that eschew restriction to national, cultural or regional homogeneities. Epistemologically though, the standpoint of comparative broadening is vulnerable to the sceptical wedge of Luhmann's systems theory and to the problem of observation that intense system differentiation produces for modernity. It is interesting to note that Chapter 3 of Sen's *Identity and Violence: The Illusion of Destiny* (2006) titled 'Civilizational Confinement' relies heavily on observation metaphors. Section headings include: 'Singular Visions and the Appearance of Depth', 'On Seeing India as a Hindu Civilization' and 'Botched Abstractions and Foggy History'. Sen's not accidental recourse to such terms that denote seeing and its distortions raise meta-theoretical questions that run deep into sociology. Beyond the discourse on communicative action and deliberative democracy what is at stake here is the problem of observation itself as thematized by Luhmann's systems theory. For Luhmann the problem of observation is held to be locked into what we identified in Chapter 1 as the epistemological challenge of *hiatus irrationalis*. That is, I observe to the extent that I do not observe and the residual gap in what I exclude from observation is the condition of possibility for my (indeed any) observation. The broadening that Sen advocates rests on this problem of observation for the agent and the sociologist alike. Luhmann tells us that everytime I make an observation I am immersed in my standpoint and regardless of claims to broadness I do not see how I do not see in the process of seeing. If this limitation can be rectified what is required is a shift to a second-order observation (I 'see' how I see); yet for Luhmann this is a provisional termination of the blind spot of seeing because I still do not see how I see myself seeing. Thus, a third-order perspective is required and so on *ad infinitum*. Everytime a shift in the level of observation is required what essentially happens is a transference of the blind spot when we (as observers) initiate a new distinction so that the push-back step on observation can be effected. The comfort of a disinterested observation provided by a 'free-floating' intellectual as it is known since Karl Mannheim is itself maintained only at the cost of ad hoc modifications so that the code of observation is merely transposed to another distinction, rather than seeing itself as part of what it observes (and thus locating the condition of possibility of observation in the observed object itself). When Sen, for example, tries to debunk the myth of a single and homogenous culture that can be immediately observed as an unambiguous entity, by underscoring its immanent cultural heterogeneity and intercultural communication, he blocks the possibility of an unassailable prime distinction, like those that lead to relativism, cultural supremacies or clashes between civilizations. Luhmann (2013b, 114–119) addresses these dilemmas continuously in order to expose the self-referential character of sociology. Moreover, he hopes to push observation in the direction of its own condition of possibility, which, for Luhmann, is no other than a functionally differentiated global society. This, for him, shatters the problem of culture in terms of broadening that Sen's cosmopolitan outlook sees as a corrective to fundamentalist myopia. In effect, the entire argument in *Identity and Violence* reverberates this difficulty. What Sen seems to imply is that when we construct categories of cultural confinement or singular classification, essentially we don't see that we don't see when we claim to fully see, as in the case of unambiguous and 'pure' classifications of cultural identity. When this happens we hope to be able to subsume an entire, and for Sen an extremely diverse culture, to a single, overarching feature allegedly shared by all its members. This haughty attempt at observation blinds us to the fact that, as an all-encompassing observation, it omits a host of other features, identities or aspects of one's identity blocked from view through the logic of civilizational confinement.

To counteract this limitation Sen encourages the moves we noted. Intracultural diversity and intercultural interaction soften the alleged rigidity and can educate the standpoint of observation to focus on pluralism and difference rather than aiming to squeeze the latter into some empirically mustered or logically deduced conceptual legitimation of this or that identity. In effect, comparative broadening can be theorized as a pragmatic transference (and decentering) of any prime distinction that governs our viewpoint about a singular identity. The permeation of functional systems with the problem of the circulation of the blind spot is rapidly becoming a recurring ingredient of contemporary sociological currency.[7] This problem of parallax cannot be avoided in Sen's proposal for a broadening of perspectives. Let us recoup this discussion via Žižek's problem of parallax. As he puts it:

> The standard definition of parallax is: the apparent displacement of an object (the shift of its position against a background), caused by a change in observational position that provides a new line of sight. The philosophical twist to be added, of course, is that the observed difference is not simply 'subjective', due to the fact that the same object which exists 'out there' is seen from two different stances, or points of view. It is rather that, as Hegel would have put it, subject and object are inherently 'mediated' so that an

> 'epistemological' shift in the subject's point of view always reflects an 'ontological' shift in the object itself.
>
> (2006, 17)[8]

In Luhmann's sociology this phenomenon is equivalent to the 'blind spot' that all distinctions do not immediately see, although they 'know' that such 'blind spot' operates in all observations behind the observer's back, as it were. In other words, following the Kantian way – that Žižek proposes – of solving the problem of the antinomies of parallax concepts, agency and structure can only be 'transcended' regulatively, i.e. by an act of metaphysical grounding in an 'as if' cognitive leap, which functions as a transcendental condition for sociological experience. It is this blind spot that resurfaces once distinctions are being redrawn as part of sociological observations of its own code in making sense of reality. This recalcitrant X (see, for instance, Elster 1989) is not to be seen as a defect in the categories themselves but rather as the inbuilt zone of indeterminacy that operates as a condition of possibility of the very freedom to determine myself as a rational and free agent able to draw distinctions in my acts of choice.

I can think of no better illustration of a sociological case of this parallax than Durkheim's encrypted Kantianism. Durkheim incites us to this thought-experiment:

> Imagine a society of saints, a perfect cloister of exemplary individuals. Crimes, properly so called, will there be unknown; but faults which appear venial to the layman will create there the same scandal that the ordinary offense does in ordinary consciousness. If, then, this society has the power to judge and punish, it will define these acts as criminal and will treat them as such. For the same reason, the perfect and upright man judges his smallest failings with a severity that the majority reserve for acts more truly in the nature of an offense. Formerly, acts of violence against persons were more frequent than they are today, because respect for individual dignity was less strong. As this has increased, these crimes have become more rare; and also, many acts violating this sentiment have been introduced into the penal law which were not included there in primitive times (calumny, insults, slander, fraud, etc.)
>
> (Durkheim (1895) 1966, 68–69)

The aspired elimination of all deviance is tantamount to the attempts by haughty projects of social reconstruction. This, as Durkheim asserts, creates a semblance of eliminating the parallax as it would adopt God's observational omnipower that governs a society of saints. It would resurface as another distinction beyond the normal and the pathological, the universal and the particular, the sacred and the profane. 'But a uniformity so universal and absolute', he explains:

> [it] is utterly impossible; for the immediate physical milieu in which each one of us is placed, the hereditary antecedents, and the social influences

> vary from one individual to the next, and consequently diversify consciousness. It is impossible for all to be alike, if only because each one has his own organism and that these organisms occupy different areas in space. That is why, even among the lower peoples (*sic*), where individual originality is very little developed, it nevertheless does exist.
>
> (69)

Durkheim describes here a concession of human freedom and the flaws brought about by our agency under the pretensions of a mechanical regulation of the individual will (if by 'mechanical' we understand the concept of a 'perfect' coordination of all constituent elements in a system).[9] Mechanical solidarity, which as this passage denotes, operates on such pretensions to a perfect, frictionless, coordination of dualities, particularly those of freedom and necessity, individual and society. Yet, even in its rudimentary shapes it contains 'difference' (i.e. individuality) and, therefore, parallax. Once the force of indeterminacy, which flows from the moral inscription of individuality in organic solidarity (modernity) and the division of social labour is unleashed (with the spectre of anomie looming if and when 'difference' is unchecked) then organic solidarity risks overloading itself with morality and thus reproducing the parallax at the point when it aspires for the highest of syntheses. As we saw in Chapter 5, even when cherishing organic solidarity's free and spontaneous synthesis Durkheim is conscious of the risk of morality's excesses. For our purposes Durkheim's invocation of 'physical milieu' in the extract we cited above is important at it is central Sen's argument in *Identity and Violence.*

Values, globalization and *Ausgleich*

Beck captures astutely the problem that systems theory poses for ethics today. He writes:

> corresponding to the highly differentiated division of labor, there is a general complicity, and the complicity is matched by a general lack of responsibility. Everyone is cause *and* effect, and thus *non*-cause. The causes dribble away into a general amalgam of agents and conditions, reactions and counter-reactions, which brings social certainty and popularity to the concept of system.
>
> ((1986) 1992, 33)

Beck's apt image of 'chains of causality and cycles of damage' (32) depicts the spill-over effect of risks in a chain of causal links, the activation of which requires the bracketing of responsibility by agents, groups and organizations. How can the 'nodes' of this chain of causality be fortified with responsibility so that the externalities are no longer passed on to the next node? If CA can be of help here it must address how such hazards can be averted by implicating power-holders too. This issue of 'coordination' crops up in Drèze and Sen

(1989) when they address the problem of public action against hunger. Alkire (2006) adds a web of players who can induce power-holders to act against severe and urgent deprivations. Quoting Drèze and Sen, Alkire (52) stresses democratic practice based on 'facilities' (functional democratic institutions), 'involvement' (informed public engagement) and 'equity' (fair distribution of power) to be catalysts for public action. Yet, like Beck, Drèze and Sen address these foundations in the context of threats to democracy and grave dysfunctions stemming from vested interests and major inequalities. The logic of the proposal for countering complexity combines both the urgency of action (as a moral – and perhaps functional – imperative) (Drèze and Sen 1989, 257–258) and the capability to operate from within complexity, launching public action from whatever node is available. Thus, any requirement for completeness will be suspended and prevented from usurping public action of its power to act upon aggravated situations like hunger. If the Kantian trail is followed then the 'nodes' could be seen as new causes capable of generating a new sequence in the technocratic teleology that treats them as mere 'effects' of the allegedly fully determined causal sequence. Sen's injunctions (2009, 402–407) for global justice converge, I think, with Beck, both on the 'interdependence of interests' and on 'non-parochialism' as requirements for justice. Interdependence under conditions of global interconnectedness figures as a possibility beyond the exigencies and risks that are posed from systemic complexity and network entanglements. A moral convergence is required which makes sympathy the fitting emotion for the osmosis among local battlegrounds against injustice, a process of value-formation and not just a functional response to threats.[10]

The pragmatic influence is once more evident here. As we have pointed out earlier it can contribute greatly towards a principled approach to reality in the face of the latter's inbuilt contingency. It thus has the advantage that it turns contingency on its head and instead of eliciting a politics of despair (Weber) or decisionism (Schmitt, Huntington)[11] it invokes public reasoning as the highest tribunal in this collective problem-solving endeavour. Yet pragmatism itself is not immune to the problems of the 'blind spot' and to his credit Sen (1984, 307) perceives this as a limitation of pragmatism's nearly fetishistic devotion to the art of making a selection in reality, in order to be able to obtain a perspective on reality. Yet Sen (2008a) visualizes the community – and nationalism, in particular – as a circumstantial problem: under some sociocultural situations nationalism can be virtuous (as was the case with Indian nationalism versus British colonialism), while in others it can trigger and inflame divisions, conflicts and hostilities (the First World War figures for Sen as a palpable case since European nations proved unable to abstract towards their cultural and religious common identity and let themselves carried into the typhoon of nationalist hatred), What seems implicit but undeveloped in Sen's problematization of nationalism is that it can function as a source of moral cohesion in the face of partitionism. It can align identities that operate within the nation but each by itself is less broad in scope to monopolize collective sentiments. In 'reading' the collective into their own particularism, holders of these identities can be 'educated' to see behind the veil of partitionism and abstract towards the common identity of their fellows. Conversely, for Sen, nationalism is particularly insidious if it elides the cosmopolitan vision and seeks to act as the single determining factor in international affairs.

There is of course the set of objections that imputes value-fundamentalist tendencies to the entire project of CA and Nussbaum's CCL in particular. Many of these objections raise nuanced points of concern. These address CA – implementation issues in a global world distraught by growing inequalities across the developed-developing zones of global interdependence, political extremism, unstable markets, even anti-humanist utopias that openly promulgate the end of human life – thus, pilloring Marcuse's a priori of a life that is and can be made worth living (for anti-humanist fundamentalism, see Geoghegan 2013). Charges of value-imperialism (Menon 2002) against CA have been effectively tackled by Nussbaum (2011, 101–112) and Sen (2006). In fact, sometimes it is odd that such critiques are mounted against CA given, for example, arguments and evidence provided about democracy's genealogical dissemination in history and its global roots and reach (e.g. Sen 2003). Western or not, values stand or fall with respect to the opportunities they generate to all members in a society so that any notion of 'we' can be collectively voiced and forged. A sufficiently broad 'we' must be cosmopolitan in scope yet universal in the set of values that would trigger agents in local contexts to flourish and become themselves generators as well as recipients of the collective borrowing of ideas upon which any cosmopolitan vision must be necessarily couched. CA contains the inbuilt safety valves that protect it from relativism and undifferentiated universalism. In this sense Sen's defence of universal values is apposite: 'I would argue that universal consent is not required for something to be a universal value. Rather, the claim of a universal value is that people anywhere may have reason to see it as valuable' (Sen 1999b, 12).

The semantics of a global politics resume – against postmodern sceptics – a binary coding enhanced by contingent urgencies and emergencies. 'Kant or Schmitt' (Habermas 2006), Hegel or Schmitt codified as 'cooperate or bust' (Beck 2012), recurs as social theory's acute dilemma that continues to alert us about de-differentations based on solitarist illusion. In this binary semantics the recalcitrance of human rights in the vocabulary used by nearly all partners in global dialogue, except rogue states, points to at least one space of normativity that in spite of implementation procrastinations retains unconditional anthropological validity. As Nussbaum (2002, 138) says, a language of rights *qua* capabilities articulates the ground from which 'normative conclusions' can be drawn that requires no conflict with other goals and aspirations people may have. Instead, it can be seen in the form of a CCL as 'urgent items that should be secured to people no matter what else we pursue' (143). It is this vision of a 'human ethical life' that develops capabilities to transcend 'local and partisan interests and striving towards conceptions of flourishing, of justice, and of citizenship' (Nussbaum 1994, 217) beyond identity characteristics of age, gender, race, ethnicity and sexual orientation that, in its partial entanglement with historical reality and social forms of human solidarity, keeps open the validity of abstract values.[12] Like Beck's call for an urgent politics of cooperation, Nussbaum underscores too the functional parameters of risk in terms of planetary survival (1990, 207). This linkage of capabilities with risk and disadvantage are thematized in the context of 'paralysis of will' in the face of perceived or real uncertainties (see Wolff and De-Shalit 2007, 69). Beck's shift of sociological theory to the problem of risk recaptures the technological angst of the postwar era but this time it puts into better use reactionary motifs about crisis and human existence. We could paraphrase Hans Jonas' 'heuristics of fear' (1984, 26–27) and follow him in attaching the formation of common value coordinates to humanity's fear about what is at stake and in danger. Sen (1986), for his part, takes a more sanguine approach to risk. As expected, he accommodates the right to personal risk as part of the capability to choose a lifestyle an agent has reason to value, yet drawing on the consequentialist view of ethics, he requires that regulation of risk-inducing behaviours must cofactor a number of potential hazards that may stem from such risk behaviour. Faithful to the relaxation of binary logics, Sen would be reluctant to embrace a draconian sanctioning of risk-taking behaviours (his example is unbelted driving) on a number of grounds. His agency-driven perspective though undermines the cogency of a lifestyle defence of unbelted driving on the grounds that it would constitute some sort of heroic conception of individual lifestyle that would derive its chief merit from the trivial practice of not wearing seat belts (165). Thus, both sanctions and lifestyle are accommodated but both are simultaneously repelled as extreme articulations of social well-being and individual well-being respectively. This is why beyond macrosociological matters the problem of reconceptualizing the human being along the lines of CA and the listings that emerge to meet normative concerns must focus on the problem of loss of what humans cherish and freely regard as worthy of pursuit and support. This planetary coordination though cannot be activated behind the backs of agents in different settings and cultural milieux. On the problem of methodological cosmopolitanism, Beck, for example, renders system differentiation à la Luhmann a social problem that is not discarded (i.e. totally negated) but only subsumed (sublated) under the problem of '*functional coordination*, cross-thinking, harmonization, synthesis' (Beck 1997, 27 [original emphasis]) in line with the methodologically '*positive* [...] progressive problem shift for assessing complex research programmes [...]' (39 [original emphasis]). In the Fitoussi Report, for example, Stiglitz, Sen and Fitoussi visualize environmental risks as providing opportunities for convergence: 'In our view, such a formulation of the sustainability issue has the potential to provide the common language necessary for constructive debates between people from very different perspectives' (2009, 73).

Long before Beck, it was Max Scheler who revised his ecumenism with a secular vision of *Ausgleich* (balancing-out) that sought to correct positional illusions across all identities (the inclusion of animal species makes it an intriguing predecessor to the CCL) by recourse to what pragmatist and postcolonial critiques also seem to endorse, namely a convergence among cultural actors that makes explicit what has also been either implicit and accepted only regionally due to power asymmetries, or was implemented unilaterally because of these asymmetries: the borrowing and cross-fertilization of ideas. In effect, Sen's argument in *Identity and Violence* boils down as far as its cosmopolitan outlook is concerned to a vision of such 'balancing-out'. Whereas for Scheler that process of 'convergence' was still 'dictated' from the vantage point of an all-encompassing Person as the highest 'We-formation' of planetary solidarity, and thus resonated a conciliatory compensation governed by a theological justification, a CA vision of 'balancing-out' relies for its inspiration in the broadening of horizons and choices 'civilizations' have taught to each other. Against a belligerent and resentful version of this 'balancing-out', as if one should 'get even' with the West, what Sen envisions is a parallel shift, one that engulfs the mutuality of diverse cultural contributions to a shared world of freedom. Sen is also sensitive to the fact that the 'as-if' invocation (which I connected to its normative uses prescribed by the Kantian architectonic) can itself assume reified forms. In chiding Dick Cheney's '1 per cent doctrine' when this was invoked as sufficient reason (that is, the 1 per cent chance of Iraqi capability to develop weapons of mass destruction), Sen (2009, 368–369) rightly exposes the arbitrary twisting of the Kantian heuristic to a simulacrum of normativity. In such distorted use any informational broadening was terminated by recourse to the 'decisionist' use of 'as-if'. Fundamentalism thus can thrive paradoxically through a cunning travesty of the very Kantian imperative. Now, instead of acting as if my action is to become a universal law, the 'as-if' modality relegates the Kantian 'thing-in-itself' into a positivist deferral of the certainty of confirmation at the moment when falsification tests are suspended merely by recourse to the belief that the outcomes would be the same as if severe tests at falsification (which could include the informational broadening in question) were indeed being carried out. Analogous is Sen's caution to the distorted short-circuit use of 'as-if' as a symptom of 'institutional fundamentalism' (here against Ronald Dworkin) when markets operate 'as-if' such 'auctions', based solely on individual decision about personal characteristics, had taken place with no consideration either for relational goods (i.e. the environment) or of the deliberative presuppositions on matters about justice (see Sen 2009, 264–268). In fact, CA as a development programme is both a new anthropological grammar and a 'portal' through which the past can be reconstructed with a view to 'rewriting' it under the precepts of human freedom. Thus Sen does not hide the scope of CA when he writes that 'development in terms of substantive freedoms' [...] is not essentially different from the history of overcoming these unfreedoms' (Sen 1999a, 33). This assertion strikes me as a philosophy of history: A philosophy of history that remains unarticulated, to be sure, but yet present though throughout the ethical thrust of CA.[13]

The vision of this cosmopolitan and universally mobilized coordination envisioned in Scheler's *Ausgleich* was considered by Carl Schmitt as a neutralization vanishing point of all existential struggles, tantamount to the sublation of the political 'friend–enemy' distinction. Because, however, technology remains locked in facticity it can never reenchant the world and nourish it with meaning. It can though dilute all political concepts and accelerate the double-talk that makes ‘humanity’ a buzzword that can be invoked when a nation sees itself as its guardian, in order to (theologically) demonize and morally incapacitate the dissenter (who, by definition, is also part of humanity). Schmitt’s pertinence for contemporary politics need not be taken up further. It suffices though to underscore its resonant scope because the logical impossibility of a world-state that would annul fundamentalisms and animosities among nation-states is a task that is premised on something largely fictitious for Schmitt: namely, the unproblematic, non-dual human nature. If we take a close look at this implication we shall discern Schmitt’s connection of the world-state to a commercial network of producers/consumers that would be entirely free of conflict. Oddly enough the polarity invoked here is that the associated producers/consumers would oscillate between ‘ethics’ and ‘economics’ (Schmitt (1932) 2007, 57)! This polarity that Sen is also wishing to transcend is deemed by Schmitt as being premised either on the technical solution of economic problems or on the ethical adjustment of free human beings in a world community. For him, both visions contradict the problematic, open-ended human nature and thus both give insufficient attention to the friend–enemy groupings that will resurface in any such historically real and geographically circumscribed constellation of mutually annulled animosity (as a problem of de-differentiating the ‘political’). The relevance of Schmitt here extends beyond Sen’s (2006) critique of Huntington. Schmitt is a far more formidable adversary than Huntington, and CA, since it extends to global ethics, must meet the challenge of existential decisionism. It would seem that, by Schmitt’s standards, the very flexibility of CA to provide realistic and accessible ‘climbing grips’ for virtually any conflict and situation when agents are struggling for fulfilment within their anthropologically motile and problematic nature, is essentially a utopian undertaking: It accepts the problematic human nature (hence the capability to aspire) but at the same time it does not seem to visualize a state of reconciliation. Schmitt’s pejorative remarks that accuse defenders of ethical-humanism of ‘confiscating’ the concept of humanity are merely the logical radicalization of Weber’s preceding repulsions of human rights seen for him as ‘extreme rationalist fanaticism’ (Weber (1922) 1978, 6). In other words, as Nussbaum (2013) claims, it is precisely on account of a perspective of ‘anthropodenial’ (the denial of base, profane and flawed aspects in human beings) that negative emotions gain the upper hand. Projected disgust to an enemy stems precisely from this sort of blindness. Defending universal principles of justice and equality is not necessarily incompatible with an acceptance of our fragile and precarious nature. Rather, it is premised on a double negation: the negation of negating our Hobbesian, so to speak, proclivities, embracing a realistic philosophical anthropology, outside the extremities of ‘anthropodenial’. As we saw, it was Luhmann’s turn to denigrate humanism as an appeasement of conflicts and inequalities under the moral pretensions of an inclusive concept of integration, although Luhmann (2006) is far more empathetic towards the plights of those ‘excluded’ by the binary logic of functional differentiation. If the palliative potential of CA can survive the tests posed by Schmitt's Hobbesian existentialism, it should consider becoming more conscious of its own metaphysical presuppositions. To develop a theory that aims to enter a multidimensional reality across the local, the national, the regional and the global (these are Sen's geographical designations that carry of course a geopolitical sign), aspiring to cut across, in moral and policy terms, people's plural identities, seems, inevitably, to be anchored in metaphysics, the latter though nowhere openly articulated by CA scholars. Given such Schmitt-driven reservations, the jargon of capabilities is, too, like most narratives, vulnerable to inflationary and deflationary tendencies. It can, in other words, become 'ideological'.[14]

Is CA under this risk? Is capability empowerment likely to become a new normative 'theology', even if assumed that a theology has redemptive and palliative functions? Is Nussbaum's CCL echoing the approach's recourse to a solid base, a deflationary tendency maybe in order to protect CA and Sen's more flexible version from inflationary tendencies? Isn't Sen's model for an unspecified idea of capability open to the risk of inflationary tendencies as it hopes to include all sorts of potential cases under its rubric without being able to honor its value-commitment? Isn't Nussbaum's counter-proposal subject to the eagerness – necessity maybe – to identify its scope as close as possible to the capabilities that constitute the approach's hard core and thus to deflate the merits of CA, simply through its sustained recall of a minimally binding CCL? What I think we are reminded of here is the risk of CA 'fundamentalism'. This could be one of the reasons why Sen wished to render capability vague and Nussbaum qualified her CCL with a modicum of vagueness. In fact both Sen and Nussbaum ensure that the moral programme they advance should not be conflated with value-fundamentalism, 'value-imperialism' (Nussbaum 2011, 101) or 'benevolent colonialism' (Nussbaum 2000c, 132–133). Although not fully developed either in the direction of a newly refurbished moral anthropology or along the tracks of a communitarian-liberal synthesis (Hegel, Durkheim), CA does provide a template for 'compensating' past sufferings that postcolonial theory as well as utopian Marxism seek to legislate on behalf of those who perished in history's slaughterhouse.[15] Nussbaum's work on emotions (2013) with her perceptive analyses on memorials comes closer than anyone, on this matter, within CA. The CCL opens avenues of retrospective 'capability empowerment' *as if* it would have been possible for people who perished to bear the fruits of a fullfilled life.

We thus reach a last and crucial turning point. Nussbaum has insisted that her CCL is a list that is minimal and thus open to revision. Yet the design of this list stemmed from her dissatisfaction with Sen's intentionally indeterminate notion of 'capability'. Having discussed CA and its hard core of a CCL we may pause and reflect if Nussbaum's pragmatic openness justifies the designation of the CCL as minimal. If we observe closely the capability-fulfilment of life (as worth living and free of undue risks), the capabilities of bodily integrity and bodily health, play, emotions, practical reason, relationship to other species, and control over political and economic environments, the picture that emerges is not in the least minimal. In fact, it is as maximal as it can be. The injunction to see it as open so that it is flexible enough to stand the test of deliberation, cultural pluralism and historical contingency masks the epistemological justification of it as a regulative idea of the basic human capacities and potential. As a regulative ideal it guides our practices, theoretical models and efforts at our own self-understanding in universal terms, providing a foundation for our place in social and natural reality as rational and free beings. This is why I insisted in underscoring the anthropological and natural law subtext of the CCL. Beyond Marx, whose thought is admitted as a source in the CCL, the latter fits also the ideal of the 'All-Man' that Schelerian philosophical anthropology correctly anticipated even if contemporary sociologists still treat it with undue neglect. For what is the CCL, other than the 'free self-moulding' of human capacities, this time though as communal and cultural capabilities that Scheler's 'mutual adaptation' (*Ausgleich*) detects as an actual historical tendency? Scheler's ecumenical calling is evocative:

> Mutual adaptation in almost all characteristics and specific features (physical, psychical, intellectual-spiritual) which belong to human groups as such, but at the same time a tremendous *increase* of all individual and relatively-individual (national, for instance) variations, will be part of the process. Again and further, mutual adaptation of *race* tensions; mutual adaptation of the *mentalities* and the ways of regarding onself, the world and God in all the great cultures; mutual adaptation between the special capacities of the *male* and *female* principles in Man; mutual adaptation between comparatively *primitive* and *hypercivilized* mentality; relatively mutual adaptation between *Youth* and *Age* in the sense of adequate evaluation of each other's spiritual attitudes; mutual adaptation between *class*-logics, class conditions and the rights of the upper and lower classes; mutual adaptation between *national* diversities and the contributions which the separate nations can bring to our civilization and our common culture; and finally, mutual adaptation between the one-sided *ideas* of Man as we have, in a few typical examples, become acquainted with them.
>
> (Scheler 1928, 106–107 [original emphasis])

Behind the veil of anthropological metaphysics in Scheler's cosmopolitan *Ausgleich* we can discern a pragmatic vision of piecemeal mutual coordination of the many identities that give human species and human history its many-coloured richness. Even if argued that mutual adaptation presupposes reified categories and is thus externally conditioned, Scheler's idealization of convergence accommodates the congealed structure of solitary identities as the result of a historical process of disvaluing other equivocal value-standpoints. Thus, the recovery of the full development of cultural or other identity-capacities (e.g. 'Female', 'Male') is forced to retain a feature of 'external' adaptation, precisely because of the negativity with which identities have been mediated. This accounts for the theological ring of 'compensation' (*Ausgleich*), which inevitably, since it deals with historically shaped identities, stretches also to prehistory.

Sen's comparative broadening is perfectly compatible with this vision of intercultural communication and intracultural inclusiveness. It would configure a first-order observation from the standpoint of each cultural niche, category or group but, then as a second-order observation (one that, contra Luhmann, sublates all distinctions as mere distinctions of exclusionary intent), it would crown a revalidation of a cunning of reason that shapes a common wealth and ownership in the 'All-Man' that Scheler's phenomenological deduction of human capabilities assigns to the irrevocable planetary trend of *Ausgleich.* In the last instance, the matter resides whether a theory turns essentially to a 'misconceived theory' that 'can kill' (Sen 1999a, 209) or whether, like CA, in a well-conceived theory that can empower, emancipate, save and coordinate. After all, the breadth of global interconnectedness leaves little doubt about the grounds of our shared identities and far-reaching quests for social justice. As Sen puts it: 'Even our shared frustrations and shared thoughts on global helplessness can unite rather than divide. There are few non-neighbours left in the world today' (2009, 173).

Notes

1 Eschatological discourses, other than those that reconsider Spengler (Bauman and Donskis 2013) address the collapse of value-hierarchies in a world of disjunctive realms (i.e. social systems). Such perceptions of a surging relativism proliferate in the context of profligate system differentiation. A sense of interdependence (along with its concomitant synecdoche of solidarity) is wanting in the surging vitalist neo-tribalism and the mutually hostile (or indifferent) diverse allegiances among groups, subcultures and counter-cultures that Maffesoli (1996, 15) aptly identifies as the 'law of the milieu'. The principle of differentiation according to incompatible milieux was thematized systematically by Max Scheler. It is surely not coincidental that the solitary advocate of a hierarchy of values as opposed to a Weberian war among values proposes the 'sublation' of the giveness of these milieux. Scheler accomplishes this resolution in two moves: a) he ascribes to each milieu a content, which acts like 'a firm wall' (Scheler (1916) 1973, 144). Its giveness implies the possibility of relating to it through different modes of intentionality. Thus, for example, a natural habitat is a given milieu, 'available' to be perceived or become an object of phenomenological 'intention' from the value-modality of aesthetics, religion, utilitarian interest, technological appropriation; b) Scheler subsumes the diverse cognizance of milieux – even the competitive struggle among perspectives – to a common meta-milieu, so to speak, that is 'common to the units of life in this struggle'. Rather than this struggle being governed by a logic of 'adaptation', Scheler wants to suggest that 'struggle' leads to the need to transcend one's mileu and summon a 'relational' bond to life-units belonging to other milieux. This comparative broadening – a standing theme of CA – will have, as a result, that

> the units of life in question, to the degree that they develop and extend their milieu, will make this struggle redundant or will reduce it; and they will be able to live side by side in the whole of the universe with its abundantly rich table (283).

But when 'man has fallen in love with his milieu' (287) then, as a consequence, broadening capacities atrophy (adaptation without extension beyond the milieu, as Scheler writes) and identity fundamentalisms intensify. We shall recapture the thread of Scheler's relevance at the end of this chapter, connecting CA's overlapping consensus to the project of *Ausgleich.* For a normative reading of Scheler's ethics of convergence and its affinity to Durkheim's organic solidarity, see Gangas (2011).

2 By this stage of the argument it must be clear why the centrepiece of Walby's accusations against CA has been rebutted. As we have seen, staunch critics of the neo-liberal empire, like Hard and Negri, read Sen as unambiguously incompatible to neo-liberal simulations of normativity. Chapter 4 also dispels this intimation on Walby's part. Yet, Walby (2009) rightly discerns the importance of the complexity dimension in systems theory but misconstrues this complexity when it turns capabilities to their opposite, namely the capability 'to choose inequality as a way to obtain a difference' (9).

3 Now the epistemological issue that confronts us here is whether one is persuaded by a Hegelian or a Luhmannesque reading of Sen's operation, which takes place over and above, as it were, binary pairs. For example, if the latter standpoint is taken (i.e. Luhmann), then the limitations of a strictly 'pro-globalization–anti-globalization' controversy (let's call these theses G+ and G– respectively) are launched from a non-dualistic standpoint that regards these mutually exclusive standpoints to be limiting of one's evaluative space on an important event like globalization. Seen in Luhmann's terms, one may argue that Sen opts here for reentry. His non-binary observation is taken from a standpoint, which could initially be seen as G+o (i.e. acceptance of the complexity and historical irreversibility of globalization (o), yet also of globalization's benefits (+)). However, it could be configured as standpoint Go (namely, a neutral standpoint that observes G+ and G– from the standpoint of value-neutrality and thus scrutinizes their merits in terms of the fruitfulness as selection of evaluative spaces.) The neutrality in question here would correspond to a merely descriptive function of sociology on globalization. Yet, Sen's standpoint carries a prescriptive load too. Sen (2001) is at pains to highlight the benefits of globalization (its great challenges too) and thus – if read in Hegelian lenses – the standpoint G+o would represent a sublation of the mutually exclusive (G+ and G-) perspectives, but now from the standpoint of a normative privilege that would assign to the object 'globalization' (Go) an axiologically positive value (e.g. universal broadening, human rights, economic interdependence, global solidarities among others), capable of incorporating the negations that any project of creating unity with difference is destined to confront. On Sen's part this would require a philosophy of history, which his reflections presuppose – as, for example, in his defence of democracy as a universal value – but, regrettably, are obscured by the strongly pragmatist approach he adheres too, particularly at those points when pragmatism brackets – although it presupposes it – the 'democratic', 'public' and 'problem-solving' capacity of science, as part of the universally actualized values – and thus contents – of a philosophy of history. Yet, for Luhmann the 'Hegelian' move on Sen's part would be compatible with system theory reentry processes and duplications of those distinctions (selection processes) that make observation possible (again, the *hiatus irrationalis* problem). This time though such a move would be akin to 'foul play' in normative terms, namely as a pro-globalization (G+o) critique of 'pro-globalization' (G+) and 'anti-globalization' (G-). This resolution must lie with something like a Hegelian mode of grounding self-observation on the object itself and its movement towards (collective) consciousness (Spirit) in history. In such fashion G+ and G– would appear as standpoints at different levels of abstraction rather than as standpoints drawn from informationally limited selections of evaluative spaces in reality. Precisely because Sen always raises the issue of informational broadening, he is closer I think to Hegel than to Luhmann. Sen's position though – due to his pragmatism – occludes this line of interpretation. Thus the question: 'Is the distinction between pro-globalization and anti-globalization a pro-globalization or an anti-globalization one?' remains unanswered. Luhmann, to his credit, recognizes Hegel's logic as the 'never surpassed attempt' (1991, 92) of a system to observe itself through and beyond all distinctions.

4 As there is currently no shortage of political extremism and of personalist moral supremacy – rightly perceived by Žižek (1999) as a no longer 'dysfunctional' *Id*-Evil – the problem of fundamentalist polarizations deserves reexamination. We lack the competence to delve into the Lacanian subject in Žižek's critique of Id-Evil (contemporary emanations of which range from Breivik to the 'Blue Whale'). Yet, even unwittingly, Žižek 'has' Parsons in mind when he inverts the stakes. Critically suspect of the refined and apologetic logic on inclusion diffused by the postpolitical, as he calls it, society, Žižek believes that what

> such tolerant procedure precludes is the gesture of *politicization* proper: although the difficulties of being an African-American unemployed lesbian mother are adequately catalogued right down to its most specific features, the concerned subject none the less somehow 'feels' that there is something 'wrong' and 'frustrating' in this very effort to mete out justice to her specific predicament – what she is deprived of is the possibility of 'metaphoric' elevation of her specific 'wrong' to a stand-in for the universal 'wrong'.
>
> (Žižek 1999, 203–204 [original emphasis])

Formally, at least, Žižek's charge seems to capture a real risk in CA.

5 If CA is close to resolving this contradiction, what indeed is at stake, is this controversy over fundamentalism. Nussbaum (2013) has come close to easing the tension of the tragic clash of values. This is also a rare occasion in CA when Hegel gets a mention. In commenting on Sophocles' tragedy *Antigone* and the seemingly irreconcilable clash between Creon's concern of the stability of the city and Antigone's right to bury her kin, Nussbaum cites Hegel approvingly and follows the solution he proposes, namely to rearrange our 'practices: to 'remove the tragedy' (2013, 271). In other words, Hegel's point is that values appear as incommensurable and thus open the field for tragic value-wars when each valuator fails to acknowledge the other valuator's standpoint in the shared reality they both occupy. This condition of mutual value-blindness can of course be extended to Schmitt's aggressive dualism between the valuator and the dis-valuator. If, as Nussbaum writes after Hegel, this tension between value-spheres appears to be beyond reconciliation, this may happen because our categories have not been reconstructed or our practices redeployed so that 'a harmonious fostering of two apparently opposed values can be achieved' (270). This pragmatic reading of Hegel is I think correct but, again, only partially correct as far as the insistence of CA goes in pursuing the rearranged categories Hegel proposes in his systematic (and systemic, as far as the institutional levels of freedom are concerned in modern society) justification of an ontology of freedom. In this sense, if CA is to avoid a lapsus in this infinite process of transference (i.e. boundary-drawing distinctions under a pluralist veneer) it needs to recover something of the pure deontology that informs it but its practitioners have to install with greater confidence into the moral core of their theories. It is disappointing though that Nussbaum's brief sojourn to Hegel (Nussbaum 2000b, 2000c, 127–128) ends only with her approval of the solutions he offers to the problem of seemingly irreconcilable value-conflicts and does not extend to *Sittlichkeit* and the avenues it opens up for CA. But she asks the correct Hegelian question:

> Asking [the tragic question, S.G.] in the Hegelian way requires [...] a systematic critical scrutiny of habit and tradition, in search of a reasonable *Aufhebung* of the contending values. And this scrutiny requires of us nothing less than a comprehensive account of justice and central human goods.
>
> (2000b, 1017)

This reading of Hegel is an improvement compared to her earlier articulations. What is often difficult to disentangle is what Nussbaum attributes to Hegel in terms of Hegel's own 'correct' reading of *Antigone* and Nussbaum's own reading of the consequences of Hegel's *incorrect* reading by the standards of Nussbaum's commitment to liberalism. Thus, Nussbaum conjures the Hegelian system in terms of a higher-order conflict rather than a reconciliation. She writes:

> For we must choose, it seems, between active harmonizing or ordering and open responsiveness, between being the makers of a consistent conflict-free world of value and being receptive to the rich plurality of values that exist in the world of nature and history. Every human forming of a scheme of value seems to involve a balancing of these two values, which have been explorted throughout the play.
>
> (Nussbaum (1986) 2001, 78)

That Hegel sublated the tragic conflict and the schism of Greek *Sittlichkeit* in the Roman legality, which is by no means a conflict-free zone, as we follow Hegel's dialectical exposition, is something largely bracketed in Nussbaum's commentary on Hegel. Nussbaum has a point about the necessity of conflict in a plural universe of values but Hegel is not the advocate of perfect harmonization. Rather, this conflict is now enveloped in the modern *Sittlichkeit* although it bedevils the level of international relations. Hence the need for Kant's regulative ideal of perpetual peace and the community of learners in the domain of Absolute Knowledge (see also Chapter 1 of my book).

6 Explaining this thesis of modernity's validity against tradition (particularism) and postmodernism (arbitrary decision to prime this or that perspective, including its own), Winfield writes:

> It is the universality of modernity, enshrined in institutions of freedom, that allows the modern to represent not just a particular moment in history, inevitably overtaken by the postmodern of a later date, but a uniquely valid form of civilization, valid in the special sense of not falling prey to the problems of legitimacy that afflict any practices that claim authority on the basis of privileged foundations.
>
> (2001, 92)

In pursuing this strong normative claim, Winfield does not shy away from the history of dispossession and plunder that colonial modernization inflicted upon premodern communities. In fact, he argues that modern freedom's lack of foundation is essentially vindicated by these counter-cases as they all seem to demonstrate, under the guise of 'fundamentalist' recourse to cultural particularism, the unfree (particularistic or arbitrary) claims to authentic and non-foundational freedom of rational institutions. If I read Winfield's 'Hegel' correctly, the march of reason in world history (i.e. the global potential of modernity) rests on a cultural osmosis for its validity rather than on some sort of linear and cumulative cultural evolutionism. Rather, freedom's march resembles

> a transmigration of soul, where the development of freedom leaps from one nation to another, albeit within the general orbit of the West, before a modernity arises that can spread its wings beyond a particular people and make itself a global civilization (95).

I get the sense that Winfield, although correct in stressing the non-authoritative, non-particularistic features and overarching logic of immanent justification of modern freedom (this thesis aligns with Sen's idea of democracy as a universal value), treats the problem in similar form as Weber's argument for the Occident's superiority in its rational mastering of reality. As another major Hegel commentator writes, this time against Fukuyama's Hobbesian defence of market liberalism:

> [in the Hegelian world] of the absolute religion – which as to become a philosophical ideal of universal fraternity in order to be absolute – a plurality of ideologies

> and cultures will continue to flourish, because the achievement of religious 'absoluteness' involves the sublation of 'superiority' and 'authority'.
>
> (Harris 1996, 232)

Of course, the symmetrical style in Winfield's explanation guards itself against regress to some cultural foundationalism because it maintains that even 'modern' developed states are, as history has bitterly proved, open to 'foundational' colonizations of modernity's freedom (e.g. Nazism) just as postcolonial states may embrace traditional and fundamentalist negations of modernity.

7 Thus, within observation the qualification used as to the situational positionality of the observer (the 'observed by' trope that Luhmann speaks of) must be premised on the portion of reality that resurfaces as a residual category every time the observer draws a distinction. It is thus not at all irrelevant that Luhmann conceives this problem in Kantian terms as 'the transcendental condition of seeing' (2013b, 114), which, I think, is a reformulation of Lask's *hiatus irrationalis*. Sen circumvents the problem in the pragmatic and democratically animated politics of deliberation. The solution though that is primed by Sen and Nussbaum is that democratic environments cultivate the informational broadening with regards to sciences, arts, humanities, social sciences and thus enhance the possibility of sublating, so to speak, the incommensurability of perspectives (Luhmann's 'observed by' clause). If piecemeal broadening from each vantage point is securely found and inscribed in the deliberative scope of the capacity to imagine oneself through the eyes of others, then the diverse perspectives – diverse in terms of the situational particularity of their genesis in history and culture – are likely to meet on the way in what shall emerge as an 'overlapping consensus'. This overlapping consensus though is itself a blind spot as it excludes everything that remains outside the periphery of the dawning consensus. Now, looked at horizontally, as it were, the perspectives that prove recalcitrant to an overlapping consensus may take the character of the absolute otherness as the condition of possibility for being able to engage in observation and to see the world on the basis of a practical distinction. In an ingenious section Karatani (2003, 47–53) shows that even the Socratic ideal of dialogues (which, for example, Nussbaum promotes) is trapped in the 'mirror' of reflection. In this sense whatever resists to fit in the dialogue between cultures or among 'others' is nothing mystical, but simply the realization that just as we can never observe our face (by analogy our own culture except via the reflection provided by other cultures) except by reflection in an image (photographic or other), so we can never entirely step outside our position of observation. Rather than leading to relativism this realization opens the road to universality *qua* the otherness of the observer who observes but cannot see himself observing except by reflection on how others observe him observing. Thus, the other serves as a 'transcendental condition' for conceiving universality. In this fashion Sen's comparative broadening takes the status of a regulative idea of reason, impossible though to prove theoretically and accomplish in full in reality. Laterally, however, the same problem is given a different twist in the Hegelian approach to observation. Now, the observer is no other than the community of observers (cultures). This community of 'we', which realizes that alterity appears as a thing-in-itself only because the mediation by negativity (a positional standpoint's attempt to observe, albeit particularistically, universality), does not duplicate itself in the particular vantage point from which the subject (or the culture in question) observes the world. Thus, membership in the world ceases to be a factor of observation for the observing entity. I merely observe 'everything else'. In such a way I omit that I am also determined by this 'everything else' to which I also belong not merely because I relate to this 'everything else' but also because I am incorporated in it since I constitute part of 'everything else' for all other 'I's or other particular standpoints. Yet, even Luhmann (2013b, 118) is forced to admit that observation is premised on a living observer and

that life, as a biological system preempted of normative orientation, is a condition for observation to occur. It is important that Luhmann acknowledges this a priori but as we already know from his posthumanist exposition, it lags behind a richer conception of life as an a priori as Marcuse has theorized it.

8 Žižek (2006) extrapolates from Karatani the possibilities opened by Kant's remark:

> I formerly used to regard the human understanding in general merely from the point of view of my own understanding. Now I put myself in the position of someone else's reason, which is independent of myself and external to me, and regard my judgments, along with their most secret causes, from the point of view of other people. The comparison of the two observations yields, it is true, pronounced parallaxes, but it is also the only method for preventing optical deception, and the only means of placing the concepts in the true positions which they occupy relatively to the cognitive faculty of human nature.
>
> (Kant (1766) 1992, 336)

9 Žižek (2006, 22) brilliantly shows in the context of his own reconstruction of Hegel and Marx – not Durkheim! – this connection, by drawing our attention to a remarkable passage from Kant's *Critique of Practical Reason*. Kant discusses the prospect of accessing the 'thing-in-itself' in terms that may have inspired Durkheim's own accommodation of the parallax. Thus Kant thinks that seeing '*God and eternity in their awful majesty*' would instil law externally to Reason because the latter would not 'gather strength to resist the inclinations by a lively representation of the dignity of the law'. In this case of absolute grasp of the Ideal, 'human conduct would thus be changed into mere mechanism in which, as in a puppet show, everything would *gesticulate* well but there would be *no life* in the figures' (Kant (1788) 1997, 122 [original emphasis]). For a sharp analysis of this Kantian dimension and how it can decentre via its accommodation of the parallax the utilitarian homo economicus, see Žižek (2006).

10 Such was, for instance, the wave of solidarity against Islamic State of Iraq and Syria (ISIS) attacks in various metropolitan regions. This resurgence of spontaneous solidarity that operated simultaneously on the level of system integration (cross-country collaboration of surveillance technology and political decision-making) and social integration (the ground solidarity among afflicted and non-afflicted citizens, the symbolic digital national 'flag-wavering' across social media user profiles, the resilience of routine against the regime of fear) had one additional dimension to showcase. This time, unlike the 9/11 immediate aftermath, it was relatively free of the 'resentment' syndrome that, rightly pointed out by Žižek, befouled even the so-called humanist Left (for an example of this critique against the Left, see Žižek 2012, 64–68). This syndrome of resentment, following Donald Trump's election in US presidency, that poisons both conservatives and radicals, even members of the intellectual elite, is noted by Nussbaum (2018, 159), but is mistakenly, I think, codified as envy. Actually, it is a form of resentment.

11 When fundamentalism returns with a growing force and frequency as an inter-system and intrasystem multiplication, then it can no longer be seen as merely an exception. Rather, it figures as an immanent system reaction when a system claims total self-transparency and positivity of operation. Baudrillard's iconoclastic writings may not offer a social palliative but they alarmingly capture the problem of the virtually accomplished 'forgetfulness' of values. The paradoxology of integration is captured by Baudrillard in terms of a negative *Ausgleich*:

> Reason would doubtless dictate that [...] a peaceful use be found for nuclear power, that all debts be paid off, that speculative capital be reinvested in social wealth, and that the whole information become part of knowledge. But this is no doubt a dangerous utopia.
>
> (Baudrillard (2004) 2014, 149)

Such unthinkable but idealistically postulated 'balancing-out' acts would transform the world into a revolutionary lab. As Baudrillard suggests it is safer if the Enlightenment ideal of inclusion and integration is replaced by this 'ersatz transcendence' (149) that generates 'fundamentalism' as a means to sustain its 'negative integration' This approach is close to the Schmittian 'tyranny of values' and as long as CA or any other normative theory cannot account for the systemic eruption of neo-fundamentalism, Baudrillard's scandalous and provocative broodings will remain topical.

12 The premium placed on broadening and universality could block from view the historical entanglement between societies. In sociology, John Holmwood (2007) has powerfully argued against a polarity 'universal-provincial'. Critically reconstructing Mills' sociological imagination, public sociology and pragmatic epistemology, Holmwood argues for a 'connected history' of societies no longer tied to the ideal-typical conceptions of modernity that omit colonialism. Part of Holmwood's request is that within a sociology of interconnections '[n]ot only will 'private troubles' be different in different locations, but these different locations will provide alternative perspectives on the nature of social structures, their mechanisms and their trends of development' (85), has to do with a pragmatic – beyond a normative one – commitment to problem shifts that stem from reconceptualizations of hitherto available categories, themselves unsettled from reality's difference. Seen in this light, CA would easily fit the reconstructed 'sociological imagination' that Holmwood envisions as a new template for social science. But as I have argued earlier in the book, the very idea of connectedness reshuffles the evaluation space from which an observer looks at societies, yet still within a 'universal' totality, within which connections are made possible. One can still see connections – as Sen also does – in terms of incomplete causal sequences, rather then hoping to discern causal connections in their full unfolding and operation. Because the latter is not humanly possible, although it has to be seen as regulatively binding, the request for metaphysics, as Kant had shown, is still apposite. While pragmatic connections can be extremely helpful as problem shifts open to experience, the 'totality' that should emerge from whatever public issues, private troubles in a triptych between biography, social structure and history that Mills suggests, does not seem to exclude the possibility that the same triptych can be sought for the single totality of global society. One of course can argue for complexity in order to counter 'universality' or 'totality', either due to different provinces of experience which engage with 'established categories' in different interpretive schemes, or due to the sheer problem shifts that a democratic and public discourse entails, as it 'connects' bottom-up different social histories and actors' experiences. Yet, given the global nature of risks, different experiences cease to be merely 'different'. While connected histories (or sociologies) can serve greatly to show why such risks accumulate when monophonic accounts of universality take hold of media, economic systems and political discourses, the reinterpretation of cultural connections must be conducted, for Holmwood, as 'engagement with those with different perspectives and locations and in the creation of dialogues across perspectives and locations' (85). The meta-value though of a dialogic connectedness has somehow to be universal and bind those who still seek to cut loose from dialogic engagement either because of fundamentalism of sorts.

13 This reminds us of Hegel's injunction to read the daily papers. This episode enables Buck-Morrs to muster evidence and, in the context of her judicious, heretical, but splintering in its consequences, linkage of Hegel and the Haitian slave revolution, argue that the 'master–slave' dialectic, in all likelihood, had the Haitian Revolution as its paradigmatic springboard. For Buck-Morrs coherent roles for masters ('Whites') and slaves ('Blacks') involved their own inversions. In this sense a determinate negation of universal history rotates the negation in the multiple spaces where human capabilities and freedoms are crushed and resurrected by the sheer ontological – in the last resort – capability to walk upright as Bloch reminds us. Buck-Morrs

accommodates this possibility of rescuing a universal history of freedom along a Haitized Hegel and a Hegelianized Haiti:

> If we understand the experience of historical rupture as a moment of clarity, temporary by definition, we will not be in danger of losing the world-historical contribution of the Saint-Domingue slaves, the idea of an end to relations of slavery that went far beyond existing European Enlightenment thought—and is, indeed, far from realized under today's conditions of a global economy, where sex-slavery is rampant and the bonded labor of immigrants is employed by all of the so-called civilizations, and where the myth of 'free labor' that Marx called wage-slavery is the reality for millions of members of the working class. Radical anti slavery is a human invention that belongs to no one, because it belongs to everyone. Such ideas are the residues of events, rather than the possession of a particular collective, and even if they fail, they can never be forgotten.
>
> (Buck-Morrs 2009, 147–148)

One can muster reservations against Buck-Morrs' own 'universality' of negativity if the 'West' can only be radically decentralized so that its discourses abscond their own historicity in fear of the new captivity of master-hierarchies. The latter are themselves dialectical illusions as long – as Sen sharply points out – they *have to* be denigrated and their accomplishments diminished. As illusions, they block broadening and mutual learning but so do solitary negations of the West's and modernity's accomplishments.

14 I do not have in mind so much Marxian critiques of CA but rather those launched from sympathetic critics. Thus, Nelson (2008) for example, thinks that the coherence of CA can only be purchased at the cost of constructing an inherently 'sectarian' list of capabilities. This happens because moral autonomy is incompatible with economic redistribution. This, for Nelson, applies to the entire theory of justice that extends from Rawls to Sen and then to Nussbaum. It would seem to require a 'bird's-eye view' from which each group or person would consider to choose the lifestyle that they value. Nelson's nuanced critique correctly addresses the tensions between the Kantian principle of autonomy and the human 'embeddedness' aspects of the difference principle and its implicit sociality. We have addressed responses in Chapter 2 with Marxian Liberalism, which persuasively I think combines the two. One could add that the 'disinterested' prerequisite of 'neutrality' would stand for an upgraded CA role geared to society's own reproduction, which as a Marxian claim, is tangent on human perfectibility in history. Globalization today no longer renders plausible the recall of merely local criteria that would damage the CCL. The risk of CCL 'paternalism' is taken into account by both by Nussbaum (2000a) and CA defenders (Déneulin 2002). Nussbaum reads 'paternalism' as a collective constraint on what people can do (like a democratic constitution or the Bill of Rights). She (Nussbaum 2000a, 51–59) qualifies paternalism by reference to acts that treat human beings 'as an end' that 'allows people plenty of liberty to pursue their own conceptions of value, within limits set by the protection of the equal worth of the liberties of others' (55). Wisely and effectively Nussbaum understands paternalism (I would choose transcendentalism, which is also more in line with her Kantian orientation) in terms of what needs to be commonly agreed and enforced, if needed, to guarantee the real possibility of people actualizing their freely chosen functionings. Modified in this way, so-called paternalism is nothing other than 'non-indifference to the suffering of people lacking the conditions for living dignified human lives' or, affirmatively put, it stands for 'respect for people in their choices for living a worthy life' (Déneulin 2002, 516–517). Similar objections and attempts at 'rescuing' the CCL from its value-paternalism are voiced by Kögler (2005).

15 While work on postcolonialism prefers to side with a pragmatic approach that establishes connections among local 'histories' under a 'universalism-free' shift in value-relevancies (e.g. Bhambra, 2007), other critics of Eurocentrism rescue the 'universal intent' of Enlightenment and with it a moderate and incomplete 'universality of reason' (Buck-Morrs 2009). On her part Benhabib (1995) sides in significant ways with CA and argues along the lines of a universalism that is no longer tied to the need to refer to some ontological essence but, on the contrary, to one where the idea of identities, as Sen and Nussbaum have suggested, redefines constantly the 'us' and 'them' boundaries, duplicating each standpoint within the other. Under this rubric then confronting the West's colonial past is a project anchored in both 'us' and 'them'. This happens as it cuts across those among 'us' who reject both colonial history as well as precolonial dispossession of minorities within what became later the dispossessed continents of Africa, South America, Asia and Oceania and among 'them' as it seeks to 'balance-out' the disconnectedness of a hitherto colonial and Eurocentric 'universality' with claims to broader conceptions of inclusion: historiographical, disciplinary and normative. As I have argued though this is a convergence that has to engage in its own acts of determinate negations across the still extant – and intensifying, regrettably – global differentials of power. Thus, on the 'us' side the determinate negation is colonial history, while on the 'them' side it is the history of countless 'internal' dispossessions, coupled to the widespread recognition that the moral geography of rights and democracy, is still one that makes Europe and North America, as well as Japan, South Korea, Australia and New Zealand, the bedrocks of what a life without extreme suffering and deprivations can look like. If this is the case, as data and reports suggest – beyond daily news reporting – from the World Value Survey, the World Bank, The Organisation for Economic Co-operation and Development (OECD), the United Nations, NGOs, the Red Cross and the Red Crescent among other organizations, then some sort of *Sittlichkeit* appropriate to the spheres of modern freedom is still discernible as a partially actualized project that survives both its own contradictory trends at de-differentiation and the criticism that comes from deconstructive trends and from tradition-ridden fundamentalisms. Sen's and Nussbaum's own entanglement with the history of India does not lead them to giving up sobriety as to modernity's normative accomplishments. In this sense, value-relevant tiltings of problems become relevant under the aegis of the democratic community of 'we', if value-relevancies are to disqualify regression to prenormative concepts of scientific explanation and human flourishing, a project that entails 'negotiated standards of relationships within and between communities' (Bhambra 2007, 148). Thus, although value-relevancies can surely shift in making civic morality irrelevant, one would have to wonder if this is a shift in value-relevancies that is acceptable. Some sort of non-negotiable valid value needs to be in place, shared or shareable, if negotiation is to be carried out without coercive, adversarial and patronizing communication. The free-floating pragmatic effect of self-rectification of categories is meaningful only if the 'freedom' to rectify and reconstruct is 'founded'. (This was Hegel's motif of 'true infinity', to which, however, we cannot enter at this point.)

References

Alkire, Sabina. 2006. 'Structural Injustice and Democratic Practice'. In *Transforming Unjust Structures: The Capability Approach*, edited by Séverine Déneulin, Mathias Nebel, and Nicholas Sagovsky, 47–61. Dordrecht: Springer.

Baudrillard, Jean. (2004) 2014. *Screened Out*. London: Verso.

Bauman, Zygmunt, and Leonidas Donskis. 2013. *Moral Blindness: The Loss of Sensitivity in Liquid Modernity*. Cambridge: Polity.

Bhambra, Gurminder. 2007. *Rethinking Modernity: Postcolonialism and the Sociological Imagination.* Basingstoke: Palgrave Macmillan.

Beck, Ulrich. (1986) 1992. *Risk Society: Towards a New Modernity*. London: Sage.

Beck, Ulrich. 1997. *The Reinvention of Politics: Rethinking Modernity in the Global Social Order*. Cambridge: Polity Press.

Beck, Ulrich. 2012. *Twenty Observations on a World in Turmoil*. Cambridge: Polity.

Benhabib, Seyla. 1995. 'Cultural Complexity, Moral Interdependence, and the Global Dialogical Community.' In *Women, Culture and Development: A Study of Human Capabilities*, edited by Martha Nussbaum and Jonathan Glover, 235–255. Oxford: Oxford University Press.

Brunkhorst, Hauke. 2005. *Solidarity: From Civic Friendship to a Global Legal Community*. Cambridge, MA: The MIT Press.

Buck-Morrs, Susan. 2009. *Hegel, Haiti and Universal History*. Pittsburgh: University of Pittsburgh Press.

Castells, Manuel. 2010. *The Information Age: Economy, Society, and Culture. Volume II: The Power of Identity*, 2nd edition. Chichester: Wiley-Blackwell.

Déneulin, Séverine. 2002. 'Perfectionism, Paternalism and Liberalism in Sen and Nussbaum's Capability Approach.' *Review of Political Economy* 14 (4): 497–517.

Drèze, Jean, and Amartya Sen. 1989. *Hunger and Public Action*. Oxford: Clarendon Press.

Durkheim, Émile. (1895) 1966. *The Rules of Sociological Method*. New York: The Free Press.

Elster, Jon. 1989. *The Cement of Society: A Study of Social Order.* Cambridge: Cambridge University Press.

Gangas, Spiros. 2011. 'Values, Knowledge and Solidarity: Novel Convergences between Émile Durkheim and Max Scheler.' *Human Studies* 34 (4): 353–371.

Geoghegan, Vincent. 2013. 'An Anti-Humanist Utopia?' In *The Privatization of Hope: Ernst Bloch and the Future of Utopia*, edited by Peter Thompson and Slavoj Žižek, 37–60. Durham: Duke University Press.

Habermas, Jürgen. 2006. *The Divided West*. Cambridge: Polity.

Harris, Henry. 1996. 'The End of History in Hegel.' In *The Hegel Myths and Legends*, edited by Jon Stewart, 223–236. Evanston: Northwestern University Press.

Hartmann, Nicolai. 1932. *Ethics. Volume II: Moral Values*. Atlantic Highlands: Humanities Press.

Hegel, Georg W.F. (1830–1831) 1956. *The Philosophy of History*. New York: Dover Publications.

Holmwood, John. 2007. '"Only Connect": The Challenge of Globalisation for the Social Sciences.' *21st Century Sociology* 2 (1): 79–93.

Jonas, Hans. 1984. *The Imperative of Responsibility: In Search of an Ethics for the Technological Age*. Chicago: The University of Chicago Press.

Kant, Immanuel. (1766) 1992. 'Dreams of a Spirit-Seer Elucidated by Dreams of Metaphysics.' In *The Cambridge Edition of the Works of Immanuel Kant: Theoretical Philosophy 1755–1770*, edited by David Walford, 301–359. Cambridge: Cambridge University Press.

Kant, Immanuel. (1788) 1997. *Critique of Practical Reason*. Cambridge: Cambridge University Press.

Karatani, Kojin. 2003. *Transcritique: On Kant and Marx*. Cambridge, MA: The MIT Press.

Kögler, Hans-Herbert. 2005. 'Constructing a Cosmopolitan Public Sphere: Hermeneutic Capabilities and Universal Values.' *European Journal of Social Theory* 8 (3): 297–320.

Law, Ian. 2009. *Racism and Ethnicity: Global Debates, Dilemmas, Directions.* London: Routledge.

Lechner, Frank. 1990. 'Fundamentalism and Sociocultural Revitalization: On the Logic of Dedifferentiation.' In *Differentiation Theory and Social Change: Comparative and Historical Perspectives*, edited by Jeffrey Alexander and Paul Colomy, 88–118. New York: Columbia University Press.

Luhmann, Niklas. 1991. 'Paradigm Lost: On the Ethical Reflection of Morality.' *Thesis Eleven* 29 (1): 82–94.

Luhmann, Niklas. 2006. 'Beyond Barbarism'. In *Luhmann Explained: From Souls to Systems*, by Hans-Georg Moeller, 261–272. Chicago: Open Court.

Luhmann, Niklas. (1997) 2012. *Theory of Society. Volume One.* Stanford: Stanford University Press.

Luhmann, Niklas. (1997) 2013a. *Theory of Society. Volume Two.* Stanford: Stanford University Press.

Luhmann, Niklas. 2013b. *Introduction to Systems Theory.* Cambridge: Polity.

Maffesoli, Michel. 1996. *The Time of the Tribes: The Decline of Individualism in Mass Society.* London: Sage.

Menon, Nivedita. 2002. 'Universalism without Foundations?' *Economy and Society* 31 (1): 152–169.

Nelson, Eric. 2008. 'From Primary Goods to Capabilities: Distributive Justice and the Problem of Neutrality.' *Political Theory* 36 (1): 93–122.

Nielsen, Jens Kaalhauge. 1991. 'The Political Orientation of Talcott Parsons: The Second World War and its Aftermath.' In *Talcott Parsons: Theorist of Modernity*, edited by Roland Robertson and Bryan Turner, 217–233. London: Sage.

Nussbaum, Martha. 1990. 'Aristotelian Social Democracy.' In *Liberalism and the Good*, edited by Bruce Douglass, Gerald Mara, and Henry Richardson, 203–252. New York: Routledge.

Nussbaum, Martha. 1994. 'Valuing Values: A Case for Reasoned Commitment.' *Yale Journal of Law and Humanities* 6: 197–217.

Nussbaum, Martha. 2000a. *Women and Human Development: The Capabilities Approach.* Cambridge: Cambridge University Press.

Nussbaum, Martha. 2000b. 'The Costs of Tragedy: Some Moral Limits of Cost-Benefit Analysis.' *Journal of Legal Studies* 29 (2): 1005–1036.

Nussbaum, Martha. 2000c. 'Aristotle, Politics, and Human Capabilities: A Response to Antony, Arneson, Charlesworth, and Mulgan.' *Ethics* 111 (1): 102–140.

Nussbaum, Martha. (1986) 2001. *The Fragility of Goodness: Luck and Ethics in Greek Tragedy and Philosophy.* Cambridge: Cambridge University Press.

Nussbaum, Martha. 2002. 'Capabilities and Human Rights.' In *Global Justice and Transnational Politics*, edited by Pablo De Greiff and Ciaran Cronin, 117–149. Cambridge, MA: The MIT Press.

Nussbaum, Martha. 2011. *Creating Capabilities.* Cambridge, MA: The Belknap Press of Harvard University Press.

Nussbaum, Martha. 2013. *Political Emotions. Why Love Matters for Justice.* Cambridge, MA: The Belknap Press of Harvard University Press.

Nussbaum, Martha. 2018. *The Monarchy of Fear: A Philosopher Looks at Our Political Crisis.* Oxford: Oxford University Press.

Parsons, Talcott. 1951. *The Social System.* New York: The Free Press of Glencoe.

Parsons, Talcott. 1969. *Politics and Social Structure.* New York: The Free Press.

Parsons, Talcott. 2007. *American Society: A Theory of the Societal Community.* Boulder: Paradigm Publishers.

Scheler, Max. 1928. 'The Future of Man.' *Monthly Criterion* 7: 100–119.

Scheler, Max. (1916) 1973. *Formalism in Ethics and Non-Formal Ethics of Values.* Evanston: Northwestern University Press.

Schmitt, Carl. (1979) 1996. *The Tyranny of Values.* Washington: Plutarch Press.

Schmitt, Carl. (1932) 2007. *The Concept of the Political. Expanded Edition.* Chicago and London: The University of Chicago Press.

Sen, Amartya. 1984. *Resources, Values and Development.* Cambridge, MA: Harvard University Press.

Sen, Amartya. 1986. 'The Right to Take Personal Risks.' In *Values at Risk*, edited by Douglas MacLean, 155–169. Savage: Rowman and Littlefield.

Sen, Amartya. 1999a. *Development as Freedom.* Oxford: Oxford University Press.

Sen, Amartya. 1999b. Democracy as a Universal Value. *Journal of Democracy* 10 (3): 3–17.

Sen, Amartya. 2001. 'Ten Theses on Globalization.' *New Perspectives Quarterly* 18 (4): 9–15.

Sen, Amartya. 2002. 'Justice Across Borders.' In *Global Justice and Transnational Politics*. Cambridge, edited by Pablo De Greiff and Ciaran Cronin, 37–51. Cambridge, MA: The MIT Press.

Sen, Amartya. 2003. 'Democracy and its Global Roots.' *The New Republic* 229 (14): 28–35.

Sen, Amartya. 2004. 'How Does Culture Matter?' In *Culture and Public Action*, edited by Vijayendra Rao and Michael Walton, 37–58. Stanford: Stanford University Press.

Sen, Amartya. 2006. *Identity and Violence. The Illusion of Destiny*. London: Penguin.

Sen, Amartya. 2008a. 'Is Nationalism a Boon or a Curse?' *Economic and Political Weekly* 43 (7): 16–22.

Sen, Amartya. 2008b. 'Violence, Identity and Poverty.' *Journal of Peace Research*, 45 (1): 5–15.

Sen, Amartya. 2009. *The Idea of Justice*. Cambridge, MA: The Belknap Press of Harvard University Press.

Sen, Amartya. 2011. 'Violence and Civil Society'. In *Peace and Democratic Society*, edited by Amartya Sen, 1–25. Cambridge: Open Book Publishers/Commonwealth Secretariat.

Stiglitz, Jospeh, Amartya Sen, and Jean-Paul Fitoussi. 2009. *Report by the Commission on the Measurement of Economic Performance and Social Progress*. Accessed 11 October 2018. http://ec.europa.eu/eurostat/documents/118025/118123/Fitoussi+Commission+report.

Walby, Sylvia. 2009. *Globalization and Inequalities: Complexity and Contested Modernities*. London: Sage.

Walby, Sylvia. 2012. 'Sen and the Measurement of Justice and Capabilities: A Problem in Theory and Practice.' *Theory, Culture and Society* 29 (1): 99–118.

Weber, Max. (1922) 1978. *Economy and Society.* Berkeley: University of California Press.

Winfield, Richard Dien. 2001. 'Postcolonialism and Right.' In *Beyond Liberalism and Communitarianism: Studies in Hegel's Philosophy of Right*, edited by Robert Williams, 91–109. Albany: State University of New York Press.

Wolff, Jonathan, and Avner De-Shalit. 2007. *Disadvantage*. Oxford: Oxford University Press.

Žižek, Slavoj. 1999. *The Ticklish Subject: The Absent Centre of Political Ontology*. London: Verso.

Žižek, Slavoj. 2006. *The Parallax View*. Cambridge, MA: The MIT Press.

Žižek, Slavoj. 2012. *Welcome to the Desert of the Real: Five Essays on September 11 and Related Dates*. London: Verso.

Epilogue

Throughout this book I have adopted a normative conception of the social. Taking into account the 'crisis' rhetoric since the Great Recession and the ensuing discussions on economic and political challenges, I sought to identify a promising framework for sociological theory's normative broadening. I suggested that CA constitutes a major accomplishment in the ongoing debate about justice, freedom and development. It figures as a rigorous normative model suited to replenish sociology's dialogue with economics and theories of justice. Thus, the theoretical rigour, empirical fruitfulness and policy relevance of CA generates a valuable dashboard for improving human life.

It is my contention that sociological theory's prolific range of explanatory categories and normative commitments invite, rather urgently, a dialogue with CA with visible benefits to sociological theory. This happens because CA equips scholars and policy makers with a normatively robust model of agency, moral elements of which sociology failed to thematize appropriately, in spite of the richness of its perspectives. Conversely, I maintained that CA remained, for too long perhaps, locked in the disciplinary silos of economics and moral philosophy – understandable up to a point, given the scholarly background of its major protagonists – and thus deprived itself from sociological insights that would have enabled it to expand without risking an epistemological concession of its core principles.

Behind its emphasis on what people have reason to value, CA makes human priorities an ongoing test (hence its affinity to pragmatism) but evidently a non-negotiable test (hence the normatively binding function of CCL). I have argued that the binding axiological core of CA is understandably flexible but also unjustifiably too 'unmetaphysical'. The problems detected in pragmatism and pluralism jettison, eventually, the very focus of CA. The spirited defence of human dignity in CA is theorized as a *terminus ad quem* (the goal of the pragmatically open capability deliberation) and less so as a *terminus a quo* (the ultimate point of reference in an ontology of *life*). To avoid a lapse to metaphysics or to an ahistorical philosophical anthropology CA opts for making the former its programmatic position supplemented at the other end by a curtailed (but not altogether absent) eagerness to delve into the ontological foundation of human freedom (i.e. the kind of natural law utopia, which Daniel Bell brilliantly affirmed with a nod to CA.)

If the CCL is to be seen as a binding template of a flourishing human life the critical question is this: What are thus the conditions of possibility of a good life based on the CCL? I argued that to introduce this epistemological requirement does not aim at flanking CA. Rather, it points to some latent hierarchy of capabilities that CA tacitly presupposes but retreats from coming full circle in terms of drawing the sociological parameters of CCL. For CA scholars this requires addressing the historicity of the very concepts they put to use. I do not simply refer here to the heritage from Aristotle or Marx, but rather to the historical conditions of possibility that render CA a voice of reason. I insist that the idea of an 'overlapping consensus' as the only viable answer to moral dogmatism and relativism possesses a noticeable metaphysical anchoring. I do not regard this invocation of metaphysics as a desperate retro gesture to some transcendent foundation. Rather, foundationalism's hostile critics lapse into metaphysical assumptions either by ascribing to hybridity an ontological, non-reductive, facticity (thus opting for *ersatz* dialectics in jettisoning mediations) or by extolling some non-reducible particularity; or, even, by xeroxing identities in an *ad infinitum* spiral of hyper-differentiation. Generous critics of normative foundationalism also need to consider metaphysics. Pragmatism, as we have shown, has to concede that the freedom of openness to provisional problem-solving and its democratic broadening constitute values beyond negotiation. Thus, pragmatist fascism or pragmatist fundamentalism would in all likelihood be considered as a contradiction in terms. Even if seen as a successful test, it is freedom that allows pragmatism to step back and look at history through the lens of this 'modernist' accomplishment and to propose that democracy is what guarantees pragmatic, non-haughty, problem-solving towards a future coordination of historical contingency with the 'good'. Seen in this light, pragmatism can indeed offer invaluable services as a paradigm for normative action. Thus, this pragmatic turn can come into full circle only as a second-order problem shift that cannot succeed unless anchored in a logic of the good society and the institutions that support and replenish it.

Thus, the overlapping consensus I propose can be reconstructed on three levels:

1 Initially, the level that CA is mostly concerned with, namely the coordination of the multiple identities of the self (Chapters 3, 4 and 5). This, as I suggested, requires recalibrating an ontology of humanness. Informed by various traditions of social theory (Marx, Scheler, natural law, Mead's social self, agency theories), I intimated that CA provides a coherent, normatively bonding and secular template of our shared humanness (i.e. the CCL). Such a conception should be sufficiently supple and open to revision. It may also be empirically sound to accommodate partial implementations of CCL, given the multitude of contingent contexts and conditions that are marked by servitude, alienation and coercion in overt or covert forms. The value of this list, however, gives us a thick (yet, normatively binding) template to consider issues of justice and freedom and to work harder to come up with solutions.

2 Then, an appropriate level of reconstruction would concern a society's mode of coordinating its differentiated subsystems. This is the dialectical logic of the 'good' and 'capable' institutions that binds Hegel, Durkheim, Parsons and Honneth to a single project of institutional normativism (Chapters 2 and 6). Although underdeveloped in CA, it was shown that the project of 'capable institutions', which foster human freedom, can draw from non-authoritative configurations of institutional spheres of togetherness that modernity has suffused with sufficient normative rationality. This institutional turn coincides with Nussbaum's version of CA that upholds the value of national identity in a renovated shape of patriotism. This patriotism is furnished with strong emotional contents and is in no way another claim to a purity of identity. Rather, it is built on a pluralist foundation, one that makes ample room for dissent (with the qualifications that follow from accommodating dissent, both constitutionally but also in mundane shapes of social life).

3 Finally, I focused on the level of international – and global – coordination of particular cultural identities under an overlapping template of universal values (Chapter 1). This project animates, for example, Beck's methodological cosmopolitanism and Scheler's *Ausgleich.* Even if the nation retains its command over people's loyalties as a sacred collective representation of the 'we' aspect of the self, under globalization, virtually unimaginable to undo, interdependence among nations extends beyond functional communicative and market networks to a dimension of citizenship with cosmopolitan badge. Sen and Nussbaum address this possibility in terms of a mobile and self-propelling process of comparative broadening. In Chapter 7 though, I argued that value-fundamentalisms constitute a hugely regressive early twenty-first century option. A CA perspective would thus need to address nation-states and smaller communities, since struggles for freedom reopen traumas from colonial histories and ethnic insurgencies. If, following Nussbaum, the moral core of human love and care is to be located in the early stages of mutual trust that accompany our infancy and the relations to our caregivers, then one may wonder why this sphere of morality is severed from the wider areas of morality that CA explores: the market (Sen), civil society (Nussbaum), culture (Sen, Nussbaum) and cosmopolitan globalization. It seems that all versions of CA and its pragmatist epigones bracket what they all presuppose in their justified defence of a liberal and deliberative process of an ethical elevation of a social life infused by sufferings and unacceptable deprivations. What I have undertaken to argue here is that what they all presuppose is a theory that likens all these stages of ethical relations in a shape of an institutional, albeit open social totality.

This pitfall is not solely one that CA reproduces in what is otherwise a noble normative programme. Sociologists too succumbed all too easily to the temptation to denigrate totality and, while wisely avoiding relativism, they adopted 'middle-range' positions like relationism, pragmatism, 'connected histories' or epistemologies of hybridity. To be sure, these short-circuit solutions are important because they heighten our conceptual and empirical antennae to local sites and struggles, otherwise obfuscated by grand narratives of sorts. They also leave open conceptual reconstruction in light of contingent problems, not humanly possible to anticipate. Yet, such correctives to dogmatism and relativism operate under the aegis of a totality. For all these claims to 'continuity' function as surrogates to mediations that glue connected parts, even if some cannot be seen by us and our positional perspective in the grand totality of our concepts, our place in nature and society. Hegel, Marx, Durkheim, Parsons and Honneth held fast to the belief that such totality was discernible by rational beings prompted by the reconstructive (dialectical) power of reason. An essential facet of this reason is the freedom to lead a life a person has reason to value and, consequently, as a result of this freedom, to draw and redraw value-relevant problem areas. Thus, the problem is not totality as such but, rather, impoverished notions of it. If totality is held to be beyond our grasp and representation, a serious risk is announced for social theory (and how this can impact countless human lives for better or worse). Abolishing totality makes it, regrettably, available to totalitarian confiscations of it. Precisely because totalities cannot be abolished (would we be able to think, communicate and act outside the totality of human history and human experience?), retaining differentiated conceptions of them – as Hegel did – protect theory and practice from hasty and hubristic de-differentiations of their mediated fabrics. Conversely, but with equally debilitating outcomes, nihilist articulations of totality's nothingness and acclamations of the futility of human affairs, generate deeply unsettling claims to partisan validities given the alleged bankruptcy of totalities, ontologies and essences. Even if these extreme appropriations of totality into some sort of partial totality return under different guises, they are clearly defective as final verdicts on society and the human condition. They do though offer lessons for theories of justice and freedom. Looking instead at totality rationally, one sees *pace* Hegel that within its system (logic, nature, society), differentiation, contingency, non-authoritative norms, dissent and non-foundational thought have a valid place and function. What cannot though be excised from totality is the precondition of all the aforementioned elements; namely, the community of free agents who build together the categories that enable them to progress through cosmic contingency. Paraphrasing Kant, if the starry skies still captivate human imagination, the moral law within the human agent is now a shared global project and one with human capabilities as its value-relevant space and just societies as its institutional compass.

Index

Page numbers in *italics* denote figures.